URBANIZATION AND GOVERNANCE IN INDIA

A publication of the French Research Institutes in India and
South Asia Institute, New Delhi

SOUTH ASIA INSTITUTE, NEW DELHI BRANCH
HEIDELBERG UNIVERSITY
SOUTH ASIA STUDIES NO. XLII

South Asia Institute, University of Heidelberg was founded in 1962 as an interdisciplinary centre for research and teaching on South Asia. It is a central academic institute of Heidelberg University, Germany, whose role is to advance cross-cultural knowledge and understanding by combining the social sciences with the humanities. The institute has Branch Offices in Colombo, Kathmandu and New Delhi to support cultural exchange, coordinate research projects of the SAI and promote and strengthen academic partnerships with scholars and institutions from South Asia.

South Asia Institute, Im Neuenheimer Feld 330, 69120 Heidelberg, Germany
Tel.: +49-6221-548900/-8954, Fax: +49-6221-544998
E-Mail: info@sai.uni-heidelberg.de
website: http://www.sai.uni-heidelberg.de
New Delhi Branch, 3, Kasturba Gandhi Marg, New Delhi - 110 001
Tel.: +91-11-2332 60 01, Fax: + 91-11-2371 66 84
E-Mail: saidelhi@del2.vsnl.net.in
website: http://delhi.sai.uni-heidelberg.de

Centre de Sciences Humaines (Centre for Social Sciences and Humanities): Created in New Delhi in 1989, the CSH is part of the network of research centres of the French Ministry of Foreign Affairs. The Centre's research work is primarily oriented towards the study of issues concerning the contemporary dynamics of development in India and South Asia. The activities of the Centre are focused on four main themes, namely: Economic transition and sustainable development, political dynamics, institutional set-up and social transformations, regional dynamics in South Asia and international relations and urban dynamics.

Centre de Sciences Humaines, 2, Aurangzeb Road, New Delhi 110011, India
Tel: (91) 11 2301 62 59, Fax: (91) 11 2301 84 80
E-mail: public@csh-delhi.com
Website: http://www.csh-delhi.com

Institut Français de Pondichéry (French Institute of Pondicherry): Created in 1955, the IFP is a multidisciplinary research and advanced educational institute. Major research works are focusing on Sanskrit and Tamil Languages and literatures—in close collaboration with the Ecole Française d'Extrême-Orient—ecosystems, biodiversity and sustainability, dynamics of population and socio-economic development.

Institut Français de Pondichéry, 11 Saint Louis Street, PB 33, Pondicherry 605001
Tel: (91) 413 2334 168/2334 170, Fax: (91) 413 2339 534
E-mail: ifpdir@ifpindia.org
Website: http://www.ifpindia.org

Urbanization and Governance in India

edited by

EVELIN HUST
MICHAEL MANN

MANOHAR

CENTRE DE SCIENCES HUMAINES

SOUTH ASIA INSTITUTE
2005

First published 2005

ISBN 81-7304-609-3

Published by
Ajay Kumar Jain for
Manohar Publishers & Distributors
4753/23 Ansari Road, Daryaganj
New Delhi 110 002

Printed at
Lordson Publishers Pvt Ltd
Delhi 110 007

Distributed in South Asia by
FOUNDATION BOOKS
4381/4, Ansari Road
Daryaganj, New Delhi 110 002
and its branches at Mumbai, Hyderabad,
Bangalore, Chennai, Kolkata

Contents

INTRODUCTION

PROBLEMS OF URBANIZATION AND URBAN GOVERNANCE IN INDIA

EVELIN HUST

According to the United Nations (2001: 5) the year 2007 will mark a watershed in the history of human settlement when for the first time the number of urban dwellers will equal those of the rural ones. The report on *World Urbanization Prospects: The 2001 Revision* furthermore states that all the population growth expected at the world level between 2000 and 2030 will be concentrated in urban areas. This population increase will be mainly absorbed by the urban areas of the less developed regions, where growth will also be particularly rapid – averaging 2.4 per cent per year during the years mentioned.

This fast increase of urban population puts a heavy strain on the cities' infrastructures causing deficiencies in the supply of housing, electricity and water supply, sewerage systems, health, education, and public transport. And many cities are hardly able to provide sufficient services (in terms of quantity as well as quality) to the already present city dwellers and the gap between the haves and have-nots is widening day by day. Yet, also the cities in the North struggle hard to become sustainable in economic, political, social and ecological terms (Hall and Pfeiffer 2000). In this respect, problems of urbanization and urban governance are not a predicament for the 'developing' world only, but are also a deep concern for the industrialised nations. In this context, urban areas and how they are governed has become an important concern for policy makers and social scientists around the globe. However, major interest is geared towards the urban areas of the South, because they pose especially threatening scenarios of deterioration of human quality of life and environmental degradation.

FEATURES OF URBANIZATION IN INDIA

India is rather notorious for its urban problems: Kolkata (Calcutta) and the plight of her urban poor, well publicised in the West through the life and work of Mother Theresa or Dominique Lapierre's fairly romanticised 'City of Joy' (1991), has become the epitome for the urban nightmare; Dharavi-slum of Mumbai (Bombay) has the distinction of being the largest in Asia; Delhi has the infamous reputation of being one of the most polluted cities in the world; and the former much lesser known Surat has entered the public consciousness as the city where a supposedly extinct disease of the middle ages – the plague – had raised its head again in the year 1994.

Yet, India is also one of the least urbanized countries in the world. Her urban population comprised only 27.8 per cent in 2001 and the higher projected growth rates for urban areas have not materialized.[1] One reason for the low rate of urbanization in India lies in her history. The process of rapid urbanization is essentially a modern phenomenon, linked to the advent of industrialization and later sustained through the development of the tertiary sector. Though the rise of urban civilizations dates back to 3000 B.C., only a very small percentage of the world population lived in cities up to the early nineteenth century. Industrialization, coupled with advances in agricultural productivity, led to unprecedented growth in economic productivity. For the first time economies could sustain an ever growing population not engaged in agriculture, which is a precondition for urbanization at a larger scale. However, especially in the politically and economically dependent colonies both processes took place on a very different scale and followed a different pattern than in the West. In India, the establishment of large industries was concentrated in a few pockets, like the textile mills in Bombay or the jute mills in Calcutta. Other cities, like Kanpur, Lakhnau or Allahabad specialised more in small scale industries, like the leather industry or the manufacturing of pig bristles (see, e.g. Bellwinkel in this volume).

---

[1] According to the internet-edition of the Census 2001, 27.78 per cent of Indians live in urban agglomerations (GoI 2001). This is around 2 per cent more than the 25.7 per cent recorded for 1991 but more than 5 per cent less than the projection of 33.1 per cent made in 1991 (GoI 1991). With respect to the estimation one can say that the Indian experts were more "optimistic" concerning the growth of urban population than the UN study (1995) who stipulated a rise to 28.6 per cent, which is still nearly 1 per cent higher than what was actually achieved.

Not many industries were established, and India remained largely a producer of raw materials with the majority of its workforce engaged in agriculture. As a consequence, India started the twentieth century under-industrialised and with less than 11 per cent of her population residing in urban areas. India's urban areas started growing at an increasing pace especially after Independence in 1947, although the high urban growth rates reported in the census period 1941-1951 of 3.5 per cent have been largely attributed to problems of non-standardization of the concept of 'urban centres' (Kundu 2003: 3080).

What, then, makes a place 'urban' in India? The Indian definition of urban areas and towns is, first of all, in terms of their political organization, namely the form of local self-government: all places with a municipality, corporation, cantonment board, or notified area committee are considered towns no matter their other characteristics. Further criteria in force are in respect to demographic features (population > 5000), employment patterns (male population engaged in non-agricultural activities > 75 per cent), and settlement patterns (density of population >400 persons per km^2). Unless the political condition is met, all the other three criteria have to be fulfilled in order for an area to be considered urban (Visaria 1997: 266).

Though the thus defined urban areas are still growing in terms of population, the annual exponential urban population growth rates have dropped considerably from the highest rate ever recorded for India of 3.8 per cent in the 1971-1981 census period to 3.1 per cent in the 1981-1991 period to 2.7 per cent in the 1991-2001 period (GOI 2001).[2] Considering this, there is neither much truth in the popular imagination of an 'exploding' growth of Indian cities nor in the scenario of a massive population shift from rural to urban areas (Kundu 2001 and 2003).[3]

Nevertheless, although urban growth has slowed down in India in relative terms, the increase of urban population in absolute terms (composed out of natural population growth and migration) puts formidable challenges to the cities' administrations. Furthermore, the urban growth taking place is neither uniformly distributed across India nor between different types of cities. There are some high growth centres and the main trend appears to be the metropolization of India's

2 The latest growth rate of 2.7, however, is still 27 per cent higher than the global average of 2.11 annual exponential growth rate (UNCHS 2001:14).

3 In fact, Papola argues that *net* rural-urban migration has slowed down over the decades because of a significant increase of urban-rural migration (Papola 1997: 316).

cities. In 2001 India had 35 urban agglomerations with a million plus population including 27 cities (GoI 2001). Surat, incidentally, was registering the fastest growth of all urban areas in the 1991-2001 census period with a whopping 85 per cent making it the ninth largest city in India (HUDCO/UNCHS 2001: 15,16). India will also add 3 to the already 6 urban agglomerations with more than 5 million inhabitants in 2015 (UN 2001: 94). Obviously the smaller cities are growing too but they have even less problem solving capacities than the big cities, which can attract more investment as well as qualified manpower (Singh 1994).[4]

The major dilemma with this growth pattern is that the distribution of population in different class size of settlements has become distorted over the years. Urban areas are growing in population and mature from one class of settlement to the next.[5] The problem is regarding the fact that mainly the population of already existing urban centres is growing while the process of a graduation of large villages into towns is hardly taking place – they often lack sufficient growth of industrial and tertiary sector activities (Kundu 2001 and 2003). The rates of urbanization also show a high spatial inequality ranging from only 9.79 per cent in Himachal Pradesh to 49.77 per cent in Goa[6] in 2001 (GoI 2001) which creates imbalances on the national scale.

Considering all these factors, one can hardly view the pattern of Indian urbanization as promising. Hence, one has to maintain that although the growth rates of India's urban agglomerations have slowed down and India is far from being sufficiently urbanized, the absolute increase of urban population – by natural growth as well as by migration – is still impressive. Combined with the unbalanced pattern of urbanization this puts a heavy strain on urban infrastructure and environment.

Apart from the undeniable problems created by urbanization affecting a large number of people in India, and the attention-demanding advent of the 'urban age', urban areas and their governance attract a growing

---

4 Visaria (1997: 270) refutes the impression held by many that India's larger cities are growing faster than the smaller towns, as being a problem of non-adjustment of changes in the number of towns by the census authorities', yet Kundu (2003: 3082) argues that growth is indeed concentrated more in the larger cities and argues that the urban structure in India is becoming more and more top-heavy.

5 The Census Authorities define urban settlements in different class sizes, ranging from Class IV that have a population of less than 5000 (but apparently have a municipal form of local government) to Cities of Class I with a population of 100,000 and more.

6 Excluding the obviously highly urbanized Union Territories of Delhi, Chandigarh and Pondicherry that are city states.

interest also for other reasons. The increasing importance of cities is mainly due to two global processes, namely the triumphant progress of the ideologies as well as practices of economic liberalization and political democratization that picked up momentum especially after the collapse of the Soviet Union. The embracing of a liberal economic model which led to an opening up of the Indian domestic market in 1991 served to enhance the importance of Indian cities. Cities have a greater capacity to attract and absorb foreign investments than the country side, and they also start competing at the global level for Direct Foreign Investment (DFI). Furthermore, the embracing of a more liberal economic model has led to new possibilities in the management of the city itself, e.g. through private service providers. The city of Bangalore – Asia's Silicon Valley – in the State of Karnataka can be taken as a symbol for the massive change that was introduced by liberalizing the Indian economy. Joël Ruet's chapter in this volume takes up this case and provides interesting insights into a fruitful public-private partnership as exemplified by the Bangalore Agenda Task Force (BATF).

The second process of democratization is unfolding at the same time. Though India has been a democracy since Independence in 1947 (barring the interlude of the Emergency in 1975-77), there is still a large scope for the deepening as well as widening of her democracy in terms of enhancing the participation of marginalised social groups in formal politics, as well as in terms of a devolution of powers to lower levels of the political system. Especially the inclusion of women into local governance was deemed important. The major milestone for India in this respect was the passing of the 73rd and 74th Amendments to the Indian Constitution in 1992 that made the institutions of local government mandatory in rural and municipal constituencies respectively. One of the bold features of both Amendments was the introduction of a 33 per cent quota for women and also proportional quotas for socially marginalised groups, like the Scheduled Castes (SCs) and Scheduled Tribes (STs). An open question today is in how far the introduction of new social groups does really change the governance of a village or a municipality. There has been already considerable research at the level of the rural Panchayati Raj Institutions while the effect of women's inclusion in the municipalities has attracted much less research so far.[7] In this respect it is fortunate to have Tawa Lama-Rewal's contribution on the impact of the elected women representatives in the Delhi Municipal Corporation.

---

7 Concerning studies on women in rural local government see, e.g. Hust 2004.

Apart from a wider representation and participation, the decentralization initiatives in India have also devolved additional functions to the municipalities, like poverty alleviation, town planning, or environment, and also laid a special focus on fiscal decentralization, though the process is far from being satisfactorily.[8] In that respect the duties of the municipalities were enlarged which demands even greater problem solving capacities. Furthermore, the ideology of democratization as well as liberalization promotes civil society as an important actor and in its form as NGOs, CBOs or SHGs it has become salient in the cities' governance.

URBAN GOVERNANCE

What, then, do we mean by urban governance? The prominence and the dominant understanding of the concept of governance are linked to the global paradigm shift towards economic liberalization and political democratization as well.

The etymological root of the terms 'governance', 'government', 'governor' or 'government' lies in the Latin verb 'gubernare', which means basically the steering of a ship. However, it also stands for the art of governing a state. Whereas the term gained prominence in the development debate and increasingly also beyond, it was hardly used anymore in daily speech and became regarded as an 'archaic' word. In modern dictionaries we find under 'governance' often no entry but the link to 'government', or 'governance' is even given as the more adequate modern expression for the outdated term 'government' (Shihata 1990: 36).

However, there is a difference between 'government' and 'governance', though they are often used interchangeably, which has led to various confusion about the concrete meaning of governance. 'Government' usually refers to the sum of state institutions and laws, and can be described as "the complex of political institutions, laws, and customs through which the function of governing is carried out in a specific political unit" (Webster's 2002). At the centre of attention is the government as state authority acting in a formal and legally defined framework. 'Governance', on the other hand, has a wider focus. Apart from denoting what is done by a government, it means the "manner in

---

8 For a short overview of the various initiatives in respect to urban governance related reforms see HUDCO/UNCHS 2001: 84-101.

which power is exercised in the management of a country's economic and social resources for development" (World Bank 1992: 3).[9] Thus, it refers to informal means of the execution of power as well as to decision-making processes taking place outside of state institutions by business corporations or civil society.[10]

The concept of governance, especially the normative extension 'good governance', was mainly popularized in the field of development economics from the beginning of the 1990s. It invariably carries the imprint of international donor agencies, although one can now encounter the term also in more 'general' social-science research, and it has become expanded beyond the focus on Third-World Countries. The term features in titles for publications on nation states, on corporate governance, IT governance, global governance, urban governance and so on and so forth.

As one can already see here, governance occurs at various levels and is employed for a limited economic sector as well as for the whole globe. For this reason, there can not be one definition of the concept, but rather several ones. Since this volume deals with urban India, definitions of the international donor agencies are among the most influential and dominant definitions. Their importance does not only lie in their power to define what governance is supposed to mean, but even more in the concrete policies that get promoted and implemented under their banner. For the purpose of our discussion we take the definition of UN HABITAT as point of departure.

As argued above, 'governance' does not specify the locus of the decision-making process. In a treatise on principles of "Good Urban Governance" UN HABITAT states:

> Governance as a concept recognizes that power exists inside and outside the formal authority and institutions of government. Many definitions of governance include three principal groups of actors: government, the private sector and civil society. Second, governance emphasizes 'process'. It recognizes that decisions are made based on complex relationships between many actors with different priorities. It is a reconciliation of these competing priorities that is at the heart of the concept of governance.[11]

---

9 The World Bank refers to Webster's New Universal Unabridged Dictionary (London: Dorset & Barber, 1979).

10 Some include also the media, like Plumptre/Graham (2000).

11 http://www.unhabitat.org/campaigns/governance/principles.asp, 19.12.2002.

In the same paper the following definition of governance appears:

> Urban governance is the sum of the many ways individuals and institutions, public and private, plan and manage the common affairs of the city. It is a continuing process through which conflicting or diverse interests may be accommodated and cooperative action can be taken. It includes formal institutions as well as informal arrangements and the social capital of citizens.

Such a view on governance became acceptable at a time when the paradigms of liberalization and democratization/decentralization became nearly globally accepted, and when the private sector and civil society groups acquired a new prominence. Understood in this way, the art of 'good urban governance' is about devising strategies through which the various actors or stakeholders come together to solve problems of urbanization, each taking on those issues for which they are well equipped and thus contributing in a constructive way to the governance of a city. The background is the belief that the state alone can not solve the tremendous problems ushered in by rapid growth of the urban population. It follows the liberal paradigm that the state should withdraw from activities it is ill equipped to perform, like the provision of goods and services, and leave these, e.g. to private service suppliers. Furthermore, problems should be identified and solved at the local level and through participation of the various stakeholders, which led to the devolution of power and finances to lower level political institutions, like the local governments, and to promote the participation of the civil society.

The above definition first of all acknowledges that it is not the government agencies alone but the corporate sector as well as the citizens that are engaged in governing the city, which is just stating a matter of fact. It nevertheless also includes a policy content in the sense that the analytical focus needs to be expanded to include in principle a myriad of actors or stakeholders. Nonetheless, although the definition states the obvious, namely that conflicting or diverse interests exist, it somehow suggests that 'good governance' solves them in a more or less harmonious way. But this is not easily accomplished and might be even impossible considering the multitude and heterogeneity of the stakeholders' interests. It appears that the definition misses out one major variable – namely power.

Although the UN HABITAT recognizes "that power exists inside and outside formal authority and institutions of government" it does not seem to really analyse it and remains conspicuously silent on power *differentials*. The actors contributing to the governance of a city are equipped with very different resources (economic, social and political) which impinge tremendously on the part they actually play in the decision-making process. The pertinent question then seems to be who is going to establish priority of one interest over the other as well as the legitimacy of interests, especially if new actors are introduced, like companies or NGOs, who are not necessarily representative.[12]

If we look for example at the role civil society groups play in city governance one has to very carefully scrutinise who is speaking for whom. CBOs or NGOs are often limited in their outlook, and some sections of society are more likely to participate, since they have more resources for collective action than others. The art is to differentiate between various aspects of civil society and whose agenda they promote. A good example is provided by Zérah in this volume who relates a positive practice of NGO involvement in the case of toilets provided in Mumbai's slums by SPARC, an NGO that has a long term pro poor rather than a project oriented approach. However, other NGOs promote more middle class agendas, which argue for the removal of slums in order to create more parks and public space for leisure activities. The question here is not to reprimand the middle class aspirations for clean and green areas or for other vital environmental concerns. It is more to alert the reader that there are a host of conflicting interests that are not easily reconciled, a fact which sometimes seems to be glossed over in the demands for 'good' governance.

Civil society participation as well as decentralization is an accepted policy recommendation in order to identify these diverse interests at the local level. Although the importance of participation has been endorsed by the development agencies as well as by national political actors already for some time, it often appears that aid agents as well as city administrators or NGO-members still fail to appreciate the full dimension of this policy. Should one consider, e.g. having a TV-set as really less important

---

12 This is also part of Neera Chandhoke's (2003) criticism on the concept and practice of the 'governance' agenda. She argues that the concept of governance has led to a scenario where the state has become pluralized, and shares power now with lower level governments, a variety of quasi public and private organizations, or civil society networks. She asks how to democratize bodies that are out of reach of representation, which is basically a question about the legitimacy of those non-elected actors.

to a poor family than having a water filter installed?[13] Is it just lack of knowledge on the part of the poor concerning the benefits of clean drinking water that informs their choice, or is entertainment as well as access to information, the feeling of being part of a larger, even global community less significant than having clean drinking water? In the larger city context, is it more desirable to get rid of obnoxious industries, or is it more important to keep a significant employment base for the cities' blue colour labour force within accessible distance? Is it more important to have a neat and green neighbourhood park, or to have conveniently located space for low cost housing or even a slum? This is not to say that one is faced always with either-or decisions – one goal of good governance should definitely be to accommodate diverging interests. However, this is obviously not possible in all cases and the outcome will very much depend on the power of those promoting certain interests.

Whether the voice of the poor is actually heard depends also very much on how they are viewed. Marginal people are often merely seen (as well as treated) as powerless and dependent on benevolent acts. This attitude usually leads to a paternalistic treatment of the poor as recipients of information or services that are 'good for them'. Yet, we have to understand that the poor are agents in their own right and more often than not they take their fate in their own hands, creating settlements for themselves – however precarious – when the responsible agencies fail to deliver; self-organizing their communities in the view of scant government penetration (see the contribution by Martin Fuchs on Dharavi); develop strategies of economic survival and dignity in the case of economic slowdown and social discrimination (see Maren Bellwinkel's chapter on the Dalits in Kanpur); acquire space for illegal use in order to get affordable housing (as discussed by Véronique Dupont for the case of unauthorised colonies); or struggle for getting into an urban lifestyle and occupation, when the state puts them behind a *lal dora* and leaves them to fend for themselves (as discussed by Mehra in the case of urban villages in Delhi). In this respect, various contributions to this volume focus on the individual strategies of marginal people or communities to bridge the gap created by the mal-performance of cities' administration, as well as on their capacity as agents that are not merely responsive to city failures, but also active in developing their own agendas.

---

13 See the cut-out from the New York Times provided in World Bank 2003: 19, where the presence of a TV and the lack of a water filter are mainly understood as a lack of knowledge of what is 'good' for the poor.

Thus, the contributions show that the agency of the poor, which appears from the planners point of view as a nightmare and which undeniably often leads to suboptimal solutions, is nevertheless a major contribution to how a city is governed and shaped: spatially, economically, socially, culturally and politically. This is not to deny that various strategies of the poor are indeed a nuisance for other city dwellers (like pigs on garbage heaps in posh localities), the stress, however, lies on a reassessment to acknowledge that the poor are *citizens* who contribute in many ways positively to city governance, like in respect to creation of shelter, self-organization (as well as self policing) of communities, economic survival, or creation of immaterial resources like dignity and a vision of a good life. In addition, many richer citizens who often complain about the 'filthy and ignorant villagers' flooding 'their' city fail to acknowledge that the slum dwellers as well as squatters are a very important economic factor, either through their services in the domestic sector or through the production of goods at competitive prices. Yet, if they are not accepted as full fledged citizens, their interests are not treated as legitimate ones.

Furthermore, what is not always recognized because the major problem of urbanization is mostly understood as being caused by the explosion of the cities' poor population, is that especially members of the richer classes are responsible for flouting rules of 'good' urban governance, be it major power theft by companies, that turns illegal tapping by slum dwellers into 'peanuts', or encroachment of public land by the rich, like the infamous farm houses of Delhi (Soni 2000). And it seems that efforts to promote better governance more often than not put the major brunt on the poor like, e.g. through their resettlement to the urban fringes without prospects of income generation or disregard for their social and cultural aspirations and needs.

This does not mean that slums, which put their inhabitants in precarious life situations and economic degradation, or pigs on garbage heaps bred there by Mafiosi elements, should be regarded inherently as something 'good' or 'desirable'. Yet, in the absence of other support for the communities' physical as well as psychological survival they have to be treated as legitimate. What we wish to show is basically that if the complex nature of city life and processes of urbanization in its political, economic, social and cultural dimensions are neglected, city governance will fall short of something which one could label as 'good'.

We obviously do not claim to provide definite policies to solve all these dilemmas, we just plead for a fresh look on 'good' urban governance that puts the issue of power differentials and the treatment of all city dwellers as citizens with agency at the heart of the agenda. Who will make the value judgements as well as the prioritization of one goal over the other appears to be the critical lacunae of the 'good governance' agenda as exposed by donor agencies as well as national governments. It effectively means that a major ingredient of good governance would need to engage itself with analysing and devising forms of negotiation and coordination of interest while taking care of power differentials, and work out strategies to balance them. And this will be necessary at all levels.

Yet, in order not to obscure and overstretch the concept, one needs to distinguish between different forms and different levels of governance. By different forms we mean the distinction between self governance, social governance and state governance, by different levels the sites like at the community level, the local level, the sectoral level, the national or even the global level. Though we should distinguish these forms and levels for the sake of analysis, the major challenge lies in understanding the interplay of these various modes of governance and how they create or obstruct certain outcomes. There is still an immense lack of knowledge of how things really work in a city. Yet, looking at problems of urbanization and urban governance from a multidisciplinary point of view should contribute to broadening our understanding on some of the crucial issues.

This volume starts off with four articles that sketch some of the major determinants of the framework of urbanization and urban governance in India today. Apart from being significant contributions in their own right they serve to set the canvas for the other chapters in terms of background information as well as conceptualization. This part is followed by another set of four articles that look at two sectors each, namely the provision of water and sanitation on the one hand, and garbage disposal on the other, analysed from two different points of view in order to highlight the complexities of the issues at stake. The last part of the book is devoted to four case-studies on housing in Delhi. It starts with a historical perspective on slum clearance programmes and the re-settlement of partition refugees, followed by the description of the anomaly of 'urban villages', and concludes with a chapter giving a contemporary assessment of the problems of unauthorised settlements.

All chapters are informed by the authors' specific view on urban problems and urban governance. Yet, and this is the rationale of editing the volume, the chapters do all contribute to our understanding of urban governance in various ways and reading them together serves to widen our horizon on this extremely complex issue. For this purpose the introductory essay here confines itself to spell out the chapter's contribution to a differentiated understanding of urban problems and urban governance, leaving out themes of the chapters that are contributions to other questions pertinent to the author's scientific interest.

THE FRAMEWORK OF URBAN GOVERNANCE IN INDIA TODAY

Urban environment and the sustainability of cities has become a very important policy arena especially since the *Local Agenda 21* and the *Rio Declaration on Environment and Development* were adopted at the United Nations Conference on Environment and Development in Rio de Janeiro in 1992 and reaffirmed at the World Summit on Sustainable Development in Johannesburg in 2002. Thus, it is appropriate to start the volume with a chapter that addresses this question.

The contribution by Bhaskar and Shiraz Vira gives a macro-view on three areas of environmental problems of Indian cities, namely solid waste, water and air, out of which the first two areas will be scrutinized in greater detail by the four case studies in Part 2. This chapter furthermore serves as an introduction into the official policy framework of urban governance. The authors spell out important trends in India's urbanization and then lead the reader through India's urban policies as formulated in successive five year plans. It becomes obvious that urban policy, though being officially a state subject, has for the greater part since India's independence been steered and organised by the central state. This is why the analysis of the biases of the central state is quite important in order to understand governance at the municipal level. This fact is most clearly highlighted in the historical chapters by Ravinder Kaur and Michael Mann on Delhi, but surfaces time and again in other contributions to this volume as well.

The next two chapters are concerned with the impact of two global trends: Liberalization and decentralization-cum-democratization. Ruet's contribution deals with the economic aspects especially of metropolitan cities and urban planning. He proposes four areas necessary to urban planning, namely the organization of a techno-economic optimum, the dealing with the demographic dynamics, the organization of the city space in terms of densification and extension, and the choices to be made with respect to the economic and spatial segmentation of cities. To a large extent, urban planning on this scale becomes the prerogative of state institutions and is likely to remain there. Yet, Indian metropolitan cities have often failed in the management of these issues, partly due to coordination problems or an unrealistic centrally planned approach. He argues that the social complexity of Indian metropolitan cities requires complementary sources of information, decision-making, and implementation and hence calls for diversifying the sources of governance. In this respect liberalization of the economy has opened up opportunities for public-private partnerships that could help to strengthen the capacities of the state institutions, on the one hand, and take over some responsibilities, on the other. The example of the Bangalore Agenda Task Force serves to illustrate the positive though limited possibilities of this approach.

Chapter 3 by Stephanie Tawa Lama-Rewal looks at a specific aspect of the decentralization agenda in India that was introduced by the 74th Constitutional Amendment. It was mentioned before that one aspect of the agenda of good governance is the deepening and widening of democratic governance through securing the participation of hitherto politically marginalized groups. Women are one social group that has been recognised as important for participating in political decision making, especially at the local level. For instance, in 1996 Bhoutros Bhoutros Ghali stressed the importance of women's inclusion into especially urban governance in the preface to the *UN World Population Report* (Bernstein 1996). One rationale behind promoting women councillors is the belief that they will take up women issues that have so far been neglected by male dominated legislatures. Tawa Lama-Rewal discusses the conception of women which led to propose that their inclusion into the municipalities will change the nature of work done there. Taking the case of women councillors in Delhi she scrutinizes whether these expectations have been fulfilled. The author comes to the rather sobering conclusion that the impact of the newly elected women in the Municipal Corporation of Delhi is so far very limited. It seems due to various constraints faced by the female new comers, like resources or the patriarchal environment. Yet, since women councillors are not necessarily feminists, most of them do not really wish to make a difference. Apparently, the presence of women in urban local bodies does not automatically lead to a gender perspective in urban governance.

The last contribution to Part 1 of this volume by Martin Fuchs leaves the 'governance discourse' as formulated by the International Donor Agencies and informed by the processes of liberalization and democratization. He introduces the concept of 'governmentality' coined by Foucault and contributes to this volume's framework of urban governance in a decisive way. Fuchs' site of investigation is the largest slum of Asia – Mumbai's Dharavi. In a rather provocative title he presents this slum as an achievement, which by others is seen as the greatest abomination. Fuchs focuses on the quest of the slum dwellers for a new niche in society and turns to the people who actually make Dharavi into a place. He looks at the multitude of strategies employed by marginal groups to negotiate their differences as well as their integration into mainstream society.

One of Fuchs' major contributions to the way this volume defines governance is the focus on the slum dwellers' agency, and what he calls their social (self-) governance. Dharavi is a locality where state penetration is so low that its agencies are in fact unable to govern. It is the social (self-) governance of communities and networks which presents the main mode of governance in Dharavi. Yet, the form of self governance of communities or networks is also found beyond the confines of Dharavi and makes its own contributions to urban governance that should not be neglected in our analysis. In addition, urbanization is not only addressed through the demand a growing population makes on infrastructure, like housing or service delivery, but focuses on the social transformations that take place in an urban setting, a topic that is also taken up by the contributions of Weiz, Bellwinkel and Mehra to this volume.

These four background papers portray different forms as well as different levels of urban governance that have to be distinguished analytically and even more so when it comes to policy recommendations. The view on governance called for with the combination of various approaches in this volume could be characterised as paying attention to institutions (and institution building), on the one hand, and arguing for strong focus on the agency of individuals as well as communities and what really makes them 'tick', on the other. So far the discourse on governance as propagated by the major donor agencies mainly deals with 'getting the institutions right'. This is without doubt an important step towards better city governance, and is discussed by various authors in this book. Yet, it seems that a crucial point is missed out, which could be called 'social' governance as well as attention paid to social aspirations that go far beyond efficient service delivery. The point is that urban governance needs to take these aspirations into account and though the state might not actively promote them it should at least take care not to undermine these self governing capacities especially of the poor. In the chapter of Fuchs we can see that the inhabitants of Dharavi strive for social dignity, for a meaning in life, for the recognition of their differences as well as their inclusion into mainstream society. These 'social' needs are not mutually exclusive of e.g. getting services to poor people. As Appadurai succinctly put it, having a private toilet to shit in is one important step to gaining dignity (Appadurai 2002).

Institutional and Cultural Aspects of Governing a City's Infrastructure

Differing aspects of urbanization and diverse modalities of urban governance are exemplified in Part 2 of the volume which analyses two specific sectors, namely, water, sanitation and garbage disposal. The authors pursue varied approaches to deal with the sectors, where the first could be broadly called the 'institutional or technical' approach with a policy orientation, and the second is the 'social or cultural' approach that is primarily descriptive and analytic.

Marie-Hélène Zérah, drawing on rich empirical material from intermediary and large Indian cities, looks at the recent transformations of the water and sewage sector involving private operators and the civil society. She delineates how strategies by civil society as well as the business sector–ranging from storing water or installing illegal booster pumps to providing bottled water and water tankers – are basically the response to public sector deficiencies. Yet, the problem is that these strategies are very costly, either in terms of money or opportunity costs, leading to inequitable distribution, and that they are in many cases not environmentally sustainable, like the indiscriminate pumping of ground water. She comes to the conclusion that the liberalization process so far has not had a major impact on this sector because its specificities require a strong public involvement for ensuring equity as well as sustainability. It follows that for a better governance of this sector the reform of the public sector is unavoidable, since private providers and civil society groups are not necessarily equipped to guarantee this. Reform needs to take place at the macro level regarding the institutional environment and the respective role of the three levels of government as well as at the micro level for the internal functioning of the municipal departments and boards.

Zérah's 'institutional' approach is juxtaposed with a contribution on water infrastructure in a place that is yet to become a city. Bettina Weiz lucidly shows that the introduction of a water supply system in an urbanizing setting is not merely a 'technical' process. The water infrastructure is shaped by a social discourse on privileges, distribution of assets, rights to access to service or the hopes for future possibilities. An urbanizing locality in northern Tamil Nadu serves to show how the development of an urban municipal water supply also introduces new spatial identifications, social affiliations, and new ways to appropriate resources. It describes how notions of purity and pollution contribute to completely different infrastructural arrangements in semi-urban contexts. In this respect, this contribution makes the reader aware that those who govern the sector of water supply need not only to understand the technical aspects but have to be sensitive to the social, cultural and political setting as well.

The second pair of articles deals with the problems of solid waste management. Michael Köberlein discusses the widespread problems of Municipal Solid Waste Management. So far, solid waste disposal is mainly in the hand of the municipalities, which are, however, not very well endowed in terms of personnel, expertise, equipment, or finances. The approach by the municipalities is mainly technical and clearly does not address the complexity of the issues at stake. Furthermore, vested interests, like organised sweeper communities, can obstruct reforms. There are many stakeholders involved, playing different roles and pursuing diverse objectives and approaches, which is why sector governance needs to be able to deal with complexities. Köberlein also scrutinizes the various civic engagements and community based activities and discusses their potentials as well as limitations. He comes to the conclusion that they alone can only be part of the solution and that the municipal agencies will remain the biggest stakeholders. He advocates that the main role of the municipalities should be that of a supervisory body and implementer, to coordinate contractual arrangements and to subsequently monitor them.

The chapter by Maren Bellwinkel takes a rather different approach to the problems of solid waste disposal. She presents us the narrative of pigs and power in Kanpur weaving together the tale of the industrial decay of the 'Manchester of the East' and the rise of Dalit assertiveness, symbolically evident in pigs on garbage heaps. Kanpur's 'sanitary' governance is thus informed by Dalit politics as well as Hindutva ideology, by global economic forces, and by shifts of symbolic meanings. The pig symbolises Dalit culture as well as anti-Muslim sentiments, and in the changing political coalitions Dalit Mafiosi that let their pigs loose in posh localities are tolerated by Hindutva forces. Bellwinkel thus alerts us that pigs might signify more than just a problem for sanitation or insufficient garbage disposal strategies. If the wider meaning of pigs on garbage heaps is not understood, initiatives of cleaning up the city might fail miserably, as the description of the futile efforts of the young and energetic development agent Anna cited in this chapter reveal. So, in order to solve problems of garbage disposal in Indian cities, one might have to look more closely at the political equations and cultural as well as social movements that deal with immaterial rather than only material goals.

These four chapters serve to illustrate that looking at specific urban problems from differing perspective broadens our understanding about the complexity of the issues involved. It is acknowledged that the institutional approach can help to formulate important policy recommendations. And it is significant that the 'institutionalists' in this volume come to similar conclusions although they deal with different sectors. Ruet, Zérah and Köberlein converge on the point that the strengthening of government institutions is important in order to achieve equitable distribution of services as well as environmental sustainability. Only representative state institutions have the legitimacy to set the rules of the game, and they should be strengthened for acting as moderator, facilitator and coordinator of the undeniably necessary and important inputs by civil society and private corporations. In some cases the state might also need to remain the chief provider of a specific service.

Yet, such institutional arrangements work in cultural and social settings that are quite diverse even in the same country, and the generating of knowledge on political, social, and cultural determinants is important in order not to miss out crucial factors that impinge on governance. If, as the two examples show, the social and cultural meanings of pigs or water are not properly understood, chances are high that the outcomes of a policy might be rather different from what was originally envisaged. Furthermore, the 'culturalists' show that immaterial aspirations like dignity, notions of purity, or religious identity are not only important in their own right and a decisive part of the social governance of a city, they also impact strongly on the rather prosaic activities like service delivery. All articles thus maintain that there are many stakeholders involved in a sector's governance who might follow completely different rationales.

To illustrate the variety of forces that shape the governance of creating habitat for a city's population, Part 3 of this volume presents four case-studies on the creation and distribution of housing in Delhi, and especially the role the central state played in this respect from colonial times till today.

In Time and Space: Urban Settlements and the State

That history plays an important role in determining governance arrangements has been accepted by development agents (see e.g. World Bank 2003: 15). Nevertheless, policy makers as well as development agents quite often take an a-historical approach, and merely analyse the situation we find today without taking much cognizance of how the present state of affairs came about. Yet, to understand the antecedents of certain practices is often crucial if one wishes to change them.

In this respect it is interesting to analyse the governance of one sector in one place diachronically, in this case the sector of housing and settlement in Delhi. The capital, being the home to the most powerful politicians, has a rather special governance set-up with a plethora of state and quasi-state institutions that are all engaged in city governance.[14] Generally speaking, the central state plays a very crucial role for urban politics in India, as exposed by Vira and Vira in this volume. However, Delhi, being the capital, is even more marked by the influence of the central state in its urban politics and governance and it seems that even full statehood for Delhi won't change this completely. Therefore, Delhi is rather unique in the Indian setting. Nonetheless, being the major city in North India, Delhi has tremendous weight which goes far beyond its political boundaries, affecting the hinterland in a major degree which justifies the special focus.

The planning of urban space is a vital function that mainly rests with state institutions, and is unlikely to become delegated to private actors, as also argued by Ruet in this volume. This is why in order to understand the governance of this sector, one has to take into account the capacity as well as the bias of the state, which is predominantly responsible for the outcomes. It serves to highlight that urban governance can not be treated in isolation from political developments at the higher levels, since

---

14 For an overview of the various state and para-statal agencies as well as municipalities governing Delhi refer to Pinto 2000.

they influence in general, and as argued above, for the case of Delhi in an even more immediate way, governance at the local level.[15]

The last part of this volume starts with the chapter by Ravinder Kaur on the resettlement of partition refugees. She argues that for present day Delhi, partition was one of the most defining moments. In the span of only a decade Delhi had to cope with unprecedented population growth when its inhabitants nearly doubled. This was to a large part due to partition refugees especially from the Punjab, since less Muslims emigrated to Pakistan than Sikhs and Hindus came to Delhi. Kaur chastises the romantic view on pre-partition Delhi which puts the onus of urban decay primarily on the influx of the 'uncouth' Punjabi. She argues that the chaos of unorganised housing and flouting of building rules that is blamed mainly on the refugees was the responsibility of the state. In fact, the Ministry of Relief and Rehabilitation along with the Town Planning Department exposed a strong class bias while "planning" the settlements: "The state was creating a new citizenship through its permanent rehabilitation schemes where one's place in the new hierarchy was largely decided by one's social status in the pre-partition order." Kaur juxtaposes the experiences of settlers in the Purana Quila refugee camp with the autobiographical notes of a judge from Lahore. Whereas the former were at the mercy of the new state they hardly knew, the gentleman of the ICS, through his networks and intimate knowledge of political developments managed to re-establish his life in Delhi without much loss. The old class structure was reduplicated by the nascent state, and the fallback on old networks by the well equipped citizens paved the way for the nowadays ever present corruption in allotment of urban space.

The chapter by Michael Mann takes up the issue of town planning and resistance against it. He not only exposes the class bias of the State in urban planning, but also the communal one, especially in the implementation of slum clearance schemes. He proposes that urban space is intrinsically contested and that historically a major role of town planning became to organise, police and discipline the poor, while the larger chunk of resources is spent on the urban middle classes and the rich. Like Kaur, Mann also argues for a remarkable continuity of urban policies from the British colonialists to the Indian nationalists, who both viewed the urban poor as objects to be 'uplifted and civilized'. Yet, in

---

15 In her inspiring case study on the 'Welcome Colony', Tarlo (2000) shows how the politics of the nation state can be traced in the settlement pattern of the resettlement colony 'Welcome' in Delhi.

spite of portraying the slum dwellers as hapless victims he focuses on their agency in resisting the state policies though scrutinizing various incidences of public action against eviction or resettlement. In this respect he saves the poor from being mere objects in town planning initiatives and sees them as agents in their own right. Only if town planners start to understand that the poor cannot be pushed to the fringes without a fight, they might start to design settlement policies that are sensible, sustainable, and sensitive to the needs of the people.

Whereas the first two chapters expose the overtly biased and thus flawed state intervention in Delhi's urban planning, the chapter by Ajay Mehra takes a different view when analysing the fate of three villages that became part of Delhi between the 1950s and 1980s. In the case of 'urban villages', it is rather the non-action of the state that led to detrimental outcomes for the population concerned. 'Urban villages' were created since the growth of Delhi took place mainly through spatial expansion rather than densification, overrunning villages and encapsulating them in an urban framework. Instead of developing an economic, political, and social policy helping the villagers to move from a rural to an urban lifestyle, these settlements were put behind the *lal dora* (a demarcation that excludes them from urban policies) and, in effect, were basically left to their own devices. The villages lost their agricultural land to the city, and the inhabitants lost their basis of livelihood. The majority being agricultural labourers, one could not expect them to switch to an urban occupation in the course of few years. Even though compensation was paid for the acquisition of land (however, in the initial phases neither sufficiently nor speedily enough), neither the rehabilitation of village economy nor the economic and occupational rehabilitation of villagers was planned. The whole process was flawed in the sense that it was not participatory. Although villagers learned to cope with the situation, especially in the villages that were urbanized at a later stage, the fact that they were excluded from the decision-making process led to unnecessary delays and painful readjustment for the new citizens concerned.

The last chapter by Véronique Dupont leads us to the contemporary situation of contested city space, exemplified by unauthorised colonies. Such settlements provide shelter to around one fourth of Delhi's low to medium income population today, despite regularization policies implemented in the 1960s and 1970s. Dupont argues that this is mainly due to the failure of the public and private formal land and housing delivery systems, which are unable to respond to the needs of large sections of the urban population. Hence, the government as well as planners should acknowledge the dual role of unauthorised colonies in the making of a city. These are, on the one hand, their direct contribution to land development and production of affordable housing, and, on the other hand, the provision of an important rental sector for the working classes. Although unauthorised colonies appear to be a planner's nightmare, they might very well constitute the most appropriate response for the large section of low income urban population. In that respect the role of town planners and urban governments should be more in assisting the production of a city than in regulating it by often rigid, unrealistic, and inadequate rules. It seems that one needs to accept the limits of urban planning in the given socio-economic scenario, though unauthorised colonies definitely pose several problems, not at least from an environmental point of view.

The four case studies on urban housing in Delhi show that the regulation of space in a city is essentially contested. Even though Delhi has in principle a lot of space at its disposal, affordable and sufficient housing – a basic human right – is still a dream for most. Looking at the history of urban settlements in Delhi in the last seventy years one can detect the continuity of a policy that is anti-poor right from colonial times till today. Furthermore, part of the blame for the 'illegal' use of space – by refugees and their descendents, by slum dwellers, by villagers who use their land commercially in a purely residential area, or by other low income groups looking for affordable housing in unauthorised colonies – has to be levelled against the state. In principle, the state institutions are doubly responsible. First, since they are unable or unwilling to fulfil their duty of providing affordable housing, people, and especially the poor, have to use 'illegal' strategies to fulfil their basic needs. In this respect one has to acknowledge the efforts of the poor as a positive contribution to urban governance, since they fill the gap of non-provision of housing. The second way in which state institutions are responsible is that in many cases it is only because of corruption and negligence by municipal authorities that the illegal use of space, by the rich as well as by the poor, is made possible.

Conclusion

Urban governance is one policy area that is becoming more challenging day by day. The problems created by rapid urbanization dazzle practitioners, scientists and the city dwellers themselves because of their complexity as well as severity. We hope that with this volume we can contribute some important aspects to the debate on 'good' urban governance, especially the need for, and value of, looking at the issues from a multidisciplinary point of view. Our knowledge on urban dynamics in their complexity is still extremely limited, often exactly because of a myopic disciplinary focus. Policy makers in particular need to understand that urbanization goes far beyond the growth of urban population; it involves changes in life-style, economic challenges and opportunities, political re-figurations and so on.

Up to now the discourse on urban governance led by the international donor agency mainly focuses on 'getting institutions right'. The call for institutional reform is often coupled with a rather indiscriminate preference for market solutions and private citizen participation. This is not to deny that these inputs are important and that the state institutions are often ill equipped and mired by corruption, thus failing to fulfil their basic duty. It appears that in many cases the dismal performance of state institutions is at the core of the problem, but that the difficulties might not be solved by just switching to other actors. There is still a lack of proof that the private sector is always better equipped to fulfil the requirements of urban governance, especially when it comes to sustainable and equitable service delivery in a social setting that is marked by great spatial and social inequalities. In fact, most authors in this volume who take an institutional point of view rather call for a reform of the state institutions as a major factor for bettering urban governance. Hence, one can say that the state will always be at the heart of urban governance although with a Janus-faced quality – the state institutions are not only part of the problem but also part of the solution.

Another difficulty with the donor agencies' discourse on urban governance is that the city dwellers are chiefly conceptualised as *population* in a statistical dimension, as a number to be housed, educated, or connected to water and sewage systems. This is not to discount the need to do exactly this, and especially service delivery to the poor is an important and challenging policy arena that has been taken up by the World Bank recently. Yet, in order to achieve something that could be labelled 'good' governance, *people* as acting human beings with their visions of a good life need to be put at the heart of the agenda. And it is especially the recognition of the poor as full-fledged citizens that is important, since the richer sections of society have enough resources to put their interests forward. In this respect, as argued before, one important ingredient of 'good' urban governance needs to be the understanding of power and the commitment to balance power differentials. Instead of merely stating the fact that conflicting interests exist and proposing that they should be amiably solved by 'good governance', one will have to seriously deal with the issue of power, like the power to define policies, the power to implement them, but also the power to defy them.

REFERENCES

Alexander. K.C., *The process of development of societies*, New Delhi, London: Sage Publications, Thousand Oaks 1994.

Appadurai, Arjun, Deep democracy: Urban governmentality and the horizon of politics. in *Public Culture* 14 (1) (2002), pp. 21-47.

Bernstein, Stan, *Weltbevölkerungsbericht 1996. Welt im Wandel: Bevölkerung, Entwicklung und die Zukunft der Stadt*, Bonn: UNO-Verlag 1996.

Chandhoke, N., 'Governance and the Pluralisation of the State. Implications for Democratic Citizenship', in *Economic and Political Weekly*, July 12, 2003 (internet edition without pagination).

Dupont, Veronique, Tarlo, Emma and Vidal, Denis, eds., *Delhi. Urban space and human destinies*, Delhi: Manohar, 2000.

GoI (Government of India), *Census of India 2001. Rural - Urban distribution of population - India and states/Union territories: 2001*, at: http://www.censusindia.net/results/rudist.html.

GoI (Government of India), *Census of India 1991, Series 1, Paper 2 of 1991, Provisional Population Totals: Rural Urban Distribution.*

Hall, Peter and Pfeiffer, Ulrich, *Urban Future 21. A Global Agenda for Twenty-First Century Cites*, London and New York: E & FN Spon, 2000.

Heggade, O.D., *Urban development in India. Problems, policies and programmes*, New Delhi: Mohit Publications, 1998.

HUDCO (Housing and Urban Development Corporation) and UNCHS (United Nations Centre for Human Settlements - HABITAT), *The State of Indian Cities 2001*, New Delhi, 2001

Hust, Evelin, *Women's political representation and empowerment in India. A million Indiras now?*, Delhi: Manohar, 2004

Jones, Gavin W. and Pravin Visaria, 'Urbanization of the Third World Giants', in idem, eds., *Urbanization in large developing countries. China, Indonesia, Brazil and India*, Oxford: Clarendon Press, 1997, pp. 1-23.

Kundu, Amitabh, 'Urban development, infrastructure financing and emerging systems of governance. in India: A perspective', in *Management of Social Transformation – MOST*, Discussion Paper No. 48, April 3, 2001, 4 (15).(internet edition without pagination).

Kundu, Amitabh, 'Urbanisation and Urban Governance. Search for a Perspective beyond Neo-Liberalism', in *Economic and Political Weekly*, July 19, 2003, pp. 3079-87.

Papola, T.S., 'Extent and implications of rural-urban migration in India', in Jones, G.W. and Pravin Visaria, eds., *Urbanization in large developing countries. China, Indonesia, Brazil and India*, Oxford: Clarendon Press, 1997, pp. 315-20.

Pinto, M., *Metropolitan City Governance in India*, New Delhi: Sage Publications, 2000.

Plumptre, Tim and Graham, John, *Governance in the new millennium: Challenges for Canada,* Ottawa, Canada: Institute on Governance, 2000, (to be found at: www.iog.ca).

Ramachandran, R., *Urbanization and urban systems in India*, Delhi et al.: Oxford University Press, 1989.

Rudolph, Lloyd and Hoeber Rudolph, Susanne, *The modernity of tradition. Political development in India*, Chicago: University of Chicago Press, 1984.

Shihata, Ibrahim F., *Issues of "governance" in borrowing members: The extent of their relevance under the Bank's articles of agreement. Memorandum of the Vice President and General Counsel*, December 21, 1990, Washington: World Bank, 1990; mimeo.

Singh, S., *Development planning and policies. Medium and small towns in India*, New Delhi: Anmol Publications, 1994.

Soni, A., 'Urban Conquest of Outer Delhi: Beneficiaries, Intermediaries and Victims. The Case of the Mehrauli Countryside' in Dupont, V., E. Tarlo and D. Vidal, eds., *Delhi. Urban Space and Human Destinies*, Delhi: Manohar, 2000, pp. 75-94.

Tarlo, Emma, 'Welcome to history: Resettlement colony in the making', in Dupont, V., E. Tarlo and D. Vidal, eds., *Delhi. Urban Space and Human Destinies*, Delhi: Manohar, 2000, pp. 51-74.

United Nations, *World Urbanization Prospects:* New York: UN Population Division, 1995.

United Nations, *World Urbanization Prospects: The 2001 Revision*, New York: UN Population Division, 2001.

UNCHS (United Nations Centre for Human Settlements - HABITAT), *The state of the world's cities 2001*, Nairobi: UNCHS 2001.

UN-Habitat (United Nations Human Settlement Programme), *Principles of Good Urban Governance*, at http://www.unhabitat.org/campaigns/governance/principles.asp.

Visaria, Pravin, 'Urbanization in India: An overview', in Jones, Gavin J. and Pravin Visaria, eds., *Urbanization in large developing countries. China, Indonesia, Brazil and India*, Oxford: Clarendon Press, 1997, pp. 266-88.

Webster's Third New International Dictionary of the English Language, 2002.

World Bank, *Governance and development*, Washington: World Bank, 1992.

World Bank, *World Development Report 2004*, Washington, 2003.

The Framework:

Environment, Decentralization, Liberalization and Governmentality

1

GOVERNING INDIA'S URBAN ENVIRONMENT: PROBLEMS, POLICIES AND POLITICS

BHASKAR VIRA AND SHIRAZ VIRA

INTRODUCTION

India's towns and cities are important centres of production, employment and income generation, and are estimated to contribute about 60 per cent of the country's GDP (UNCHS and HUDCO 2001). At present, about 28 per cent of India's population resides in its urban spaces, with a growing proportion of these urban residents located in large towns and cities. The role and significance of the urban sector has made it a dynamic engine of growth for the Indian economy. However, the process of urbanization has essentially been haphazard and unplanned, and has been associated with a significant deterioration in the quality of life for a very large proportion of the country's urban population. This chapter reviews the urbanization process in India, specifically focusing on the impact of this urban expansion on environmental quality, and issues of governance that arise in this context.

URBAN GROWTH

A distinctive feature of urbanization in India is the increasing concentration of the urban population in relatively large cities. What is noticeable in the Indian context is that the weight of different size classes of cities in the total urban population has shifted in favour of these large cities. While the share of settlements with over 100,000 population (Class I cities) in the total urban population was just 26 per cent in 1901, by

1991, this had risen to 65.2 per cent (see Table 1). This suggests a significant change in the pattern of habitation in the country.[1]

Table 1: Percentage Distribution of Urban Population by Size Class Settlements

Census Year	over 100,000	50,000 to 100,000	20,000 to 50,000	10,000 to 20,000	5,000 to 10000	under 5000
1901	26.0	11.3	15.6	20.8	20.1	6.1
1971	57.2	10.9	16.0	10.9	4.5	0.4
1981	60.4	11.6	14.3	9.5	3.6	0.5
1991	65.2	10.9	13.2	7.8	2.6	0.3

Source: CPCB (1997)

Another noticeable trend is that the number of metropolises (cities with over 1 million population) and their share in urban population has risen dramatically in recent decades.[2] In 1971, the number of cities in this category was 9, and their share in urban population 25.5 per cent. By 2001, the number had increased to 35 and the population share to a little over 37 per cent (see Table 2). These 35 million plus cities together contained about 108 million people. So, although the pace of urbanization in the country as a whole is slowing down,[3] cities are becoming more metropolitan in character.

---

1 It is not necessarily the case that large cities have grown faster than small towns. Due to the size of the bigger cities, the proportion of urban population living in Class I cities (100,000 and above) continues to form a larger proportion of the total population. As cities grow, they graduate into the category of Class I cities, while none drop out. Although Class I cities have grown faster than smaller towns, the differences in growth rates are not very large in general (Venkateswarlu 1998).

2 Cities in India are classified into different sizes according to population. Class II cities are defined by a population of 50,000-99,999; Class I by a population of 100,000 or above; Metro cities have a population of 1 million or above, while Mega-cities have a population of 5 million or above. The concept of urban agglomeration is used by the Census. The urban agglomeration forms a 'continuos urban spread' and normally consists of a town and its adjoining urban outgrowths if any (Visaria 1997).

3 The annual rate of growth of urban population during 1991-2001 was 2.71per cent, down from the 1981-91 rate of 3.11per cent, which in turn was slightly less than in the previous decade, 1971-81 (3.79 per cent).

Table 2: Metrocities Share in Urban Population

Census Year	Number of Urban Agglomerations/ Cities	Population (millions)	Metro pop as a % of Total population	Metro pop as a % of Urban population
1901	1	1.51	0.63	5.84
1911	2	2.76	1.10	10.65
1921	2	3.13	1.25	11.14
1931	2	3.41	1.22	10.18
1941	2	5.31	1.67	12.02
1951	5	11.75	3.25	18.81
1961	7	18.10	4.12	22.93
1971	9	27.83	5.08	25.51
1981	12	42.12	6.16	26.41
1991	23	70.16	8.37	32.54
2001	35	107.88	10.50	37.81

Sources: Misra and Misra (1998); Registrar General (2001)

India currently has six urban agglomerations with population in excess of 5 million, called mega-cities (Greater Mumbai, Kolkata, Delhi, Chennai, Bangalore and Hyderabad). It is important to recognize that the million plus cities are located in different geographic zones (see Figure 1), have very different histories, and have very specific characteristics, functions, economic structures and relations to their hinterland. Thus, although some of the problems faced by these cities may be similar, because of their size, the specific details are likely to vary, as is the nature of responses to these challenges.

Figure 1: Million plus cities in India

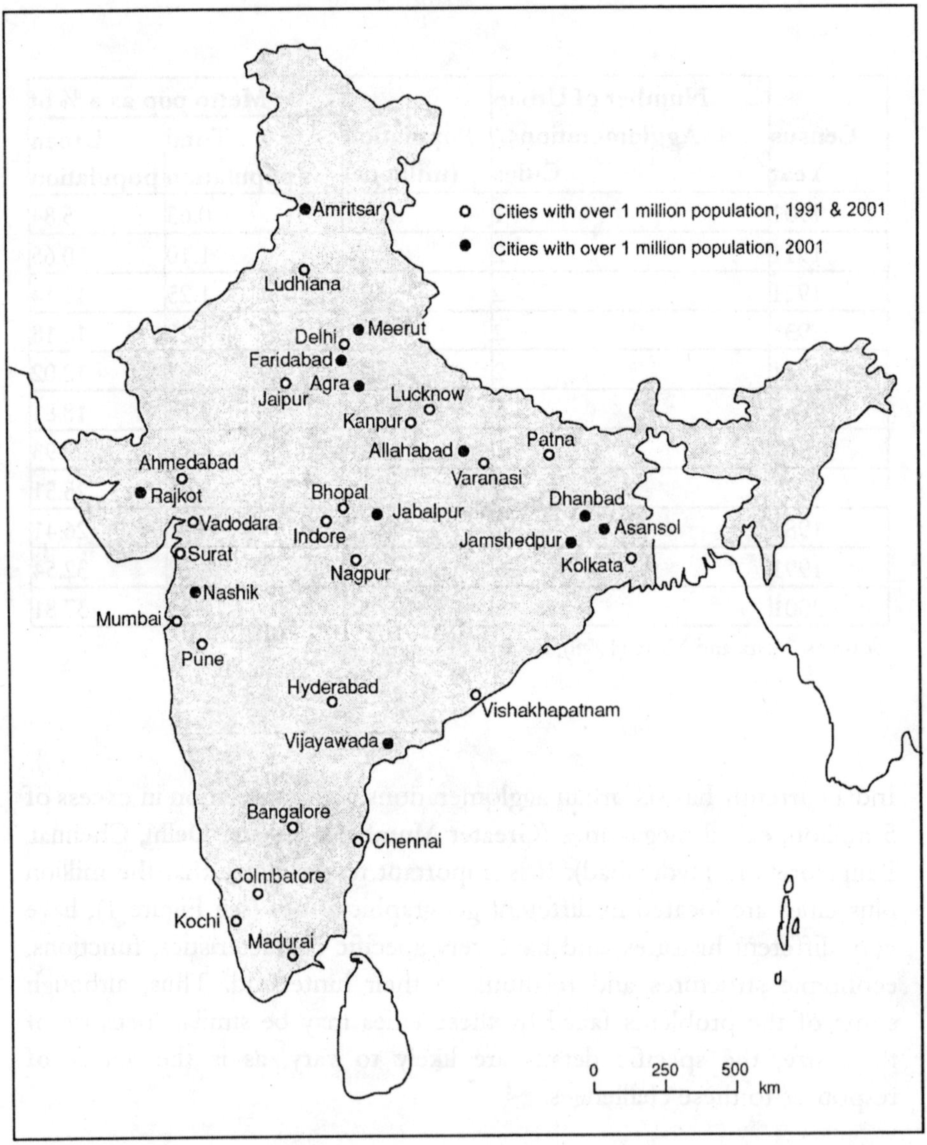

URBAN POLICY IN INDIA – A REVIEW

> A realistic assessment of urban policy in India since Independence needs to recognise the fact that much of what has been written on paper has remained ineffectual in practice or has not affected a large part of the Urban Environment, this is especially true with reference to small towns and non-metropolitan areas. These have grown on their own and in their own way.
> (Shaw 1996)

Though successive Five Year Plans have stressed the significance of balanced economic growth and massive investments have been made in the core sectors like industry, agriculture, irrigation, power and transport, and urbanization, which is the logical outcome of these investments, has been ignored. No comprehensive effort has been made to link economic and social development efforts with the growth of urban areas through a well-developed policy frame (Gnaneshwar 1995).

According to the Indian Constitution, urban policy and planning are state subjects. Without constitutional amendment, the central government does not have the power to pass legislation on urbanization and urban planning. It can issue directives, provide advisory services, set up model legislation and fund programmes, which the states can follow if they choose. On the other hand, in spite of being empowered to do so, very few state governments have taken the initiative for policy making in this area, and much of what exists as policy has come from the central government. Thus, the central government's allocation of resources to the urban sector and statements on urban policy as expressed in the National Five Year Plans assume considerable importance. Table 3 reports the share of allocation to the urban sector in successive Five Year Plans, which has been steady at slightly over 2 per cent of the overall plan allocation since the mid-1970s.

Table 3: The urban sector in the five year plans

Plan	Total Outlay	Housing & Urban Development	% share
First Plan (1951-56)	20688	488	2.1
Second Plan (1956-61)	48000	1200	2.5
Third Plan (1961-66)	85765	1276	1.5

Annual Plan(1966-69)	66254	733	1.1
Fourth Plan (1969-74)	157788	2702	1.7
Fifth Plan (1974-79)	394262	11500	2.9
Annual Plan (1977-80)	121765	3688	3.0
Sixth Plan (1980-85)	975000	24884	2.6
Seventh Plan (1985-90)	1800000	42295	2.3
Annual Plan (1990-92)	1338350	3001	2.2
Eighth Plan (1992-97)	4341000	105000	2.4
Ninth Plan (1997-2002)	8592000	NA*	NA*
Tenth Plan (2002-7)	12943250	297190	2.3

Sources: MUA (2002a); GOI (2003); Figures in Rs. Million

The sectoral allocation for the urban sector in the Ninth Plan is unavailable, since allocations were made under broader categories (Housing and Urban Development were part of the allocation to Social Services). *Actual* expenditure on Housing and Urban Development during the Ninth Plan as a proportion of the overall plan expenditure was 4.2 per cent (MEA 2002).

India's First (1951) and Second (1956-61) Plans were rather low key about the urban sector. The need for planned development of urban areas was recognized but the emphasis was on housing problems, partly due to the refugee problem confronting India after partition. It was agreed however that urban growth had been haphazard. It was by the Third Five Year Plan (1961-66) that government for the first time formulated an urban planning and land policy. There was an emphasis on procurement and control and development of land by public authorities to enable 'planned urbanization' in the country. The Five Year Plan also highlighted the need for town planning, and provided master plans for the planning of cities. Almost all the states have introduced town-planning legislation with varying scope (GOI 1961: 689).

Evident in the Third Plan was the Government's interest in directing the entire process of urban growth, from the actual take-over of land, to its involvement in the development and sale of this land, to its continued control through the granting of lease-hold (and not ownership) rights over developed plots. Large-scale public acquisition of land had started in Delhi in the 1950s well before the Third Plan period. In other cites the process began with the Third Plan. The need for public intervention in the urban land market was made explicit towards the end of the Third

Plan period in a report published by the Urban Land Policy Committee appointed by the Government of India (Ministry of Health). It was justified on the grounds of the need to "achieve an optimal social use of land" to control land prices, and to ensure a widening base of land ownership (GOI 1961: 690). With regard to public management of urban land and rationalization of land use in individual cities, the Third Plan can be regarded as critical for urban policy making in the country.

The Fourth Plan (1969-74) period saw the establishment of Housing and Urban Development Corporation (HUDCO) to provide funds for housing and urban development projects to metropolitan authorities, state housing boards and other institutions. Most of the funds were for larger industrial cities to house the working class. Several large urban projects were started (development of new state capitals, for example, Chandigarh and Bhopal). There was also an emphasis on improving urban legislation (GOI 1969; Shaw 1996).

The Fifth Plan (1974-79) provided a more detailed statement on urban problems. The objectives of the urbanization policy as stated in the plan were:

- to augment civic services in cites and towns
- to tackle the problems of metropolitan cities in a more comprehensive and regional perspective
- to promote the development of small towns and new urban centres including industrial towns
- to assist the metropolitan development projects having national significance

A number of measures were also suggested to control land prices, including differential taxes on land based on its use, higher taxes on vacant lands to discourage speculation, tax on change of land-use and enhanced stamp duty on transfer of lands (GOI 1974).

The Urban Land (Ceiling and Regulation) Act 1976 was enacted to promote equitable distribution of urban land and also to discourage land speculation in large urban centres. A ceiling on private land holdings was proposed and excess lands were to be surrendered to the governments for taking up developmental activities. This act failed to yield the desired results due to a number of legal and procedural loopholes, and was repealed in 1999.

The Sixth Plan (1980-1985) laid emphasis on decentralization observing that a national urbanization policy should involve "specific consideration of regional problems and greater investment must be given towards the development of small, medium and intermediate towns" (GOI *Sixth Five Year Plan*, quoted in Gnaneshwar 1995). These small and medium level towns were visualised as growth and service centres having the potential to attract migrants from the rural area and thereby reducing migration to the larger cities and contributing to a more balanced urban development. A centrally sponsored scheme called Integrated Development of Small and Medium Towns (IDSMT) was launched to facilitate growth in towns with less than 100,000 population. However, the scheme did not make much progress during the Sixth Plan "due to lack of appreciation of its aims and objectives at the state and local levels, inadequate experience in project formulation process at the local levels and, more significantly, absence of institutional linkages at the operation levels" (GOI *Sixth Plan*, quoted in Shaw 1996).

The Seventh and Eighth Plans were both different from the earlier ones in some important ways. They continued to emphasise the need to divert investment into small and medium towns, but departed from the previous plans in view of the state's role in urban development. In the Seventh Plan, there was an emphasis on the need for greater devolution of funds (and hence power) to urban local bodies, for the revitalization of civic bodies and for greater 'community participation'(GOI 1985: 297). It was noted that was a need for more "private initiative and investment in urban development" because "the delivery of basic public services to everyone is simply not feasible without such an approach" (GOI 1985: 298). It also stressed that government funds were limited given the poverty in the rural areas and, therefore, that it was necessary for urban local bodies themselves to mobilize additional resources. This was also a period of increased donor interest and involvement in the urban sector, which generated additional resources (Seventh Plan quoted in Shaw 1996).

During the Seventh Plan, the first serious attempts were made to grant constitutional status to urban local bodies as a precursor to their revitalization. On August 7, 1989, a Bill was introduced in the Lok Sabha to strengthen urban municipal bodies. It was not passed by the Rajya Sabha when presented in 1989, largely due to the misgivings of state governments, which saw it as a means of central/union interference in their areas of jurisdiction. After some modifications the Bill was reintroduced for ratification as the 74th Act 1992. It came into force in March 1993. The philosophy behind the Act envisages urban areas as units of democratic self-governance, accountable to the local population, but the states have been slow to adopt the Act and give effective powers to urban local authorities (Gnaneshwar 1995; Shaw 1996).

At the end of the Seventh Plan, a scheme aiming to provide more employment opportunities to the Urban Poor, the Nehru Rozgar Yojana (NRY) was launched in October 1989. This was carried on in the Eighth Plan. The Eighth Five Year Plan tried to converge related programmes i.e., IDSMT, the housing and development programmes of HUDCO, and the NRY. In the programmes of urban development, the emphasis was on employment generation, access to urban basic services for the deprived sections and promotion of small and medium town development (GOI 1992). Most of the programmes were an extension of the Seventh Plan but were revised in content, coverage, and funding pattern in accordance with the policy thrust provided in the Eighth Plan. The progress of these schemes is reported in Table 4.

Table 4: Central assistance released under IDSMT

Plan Period	No. of Towns	Central Assistance Released
VI Plan	235	635.7
VII Plan	145	801.2
1990-91	77	191.0
1991-92	60	134.4
VIII Plan	387	1078.0
IX Plan		
1997 – 98	16	260.2
1998 – 99	25	353.5
1999 – 2000	60	434.6
2000 – 2001	53	561.7
2000-2002 (up to 31.03.2002)	114	767.1

Source: MUA (2002b); (Rs. in million)

The Ninth Plan admits that "the lack of comprehensive urban planning in the past to promote regular upgrading and renewal has resulted in a backlog of development activities" (GOI 1997: 262). It stresses that civic amenities in the cities (especially in the mega and metro cities) have suffered due to lack of maintenance and have consequently outlived their operational efficiency. Upgradation and renovation of these has been made difficult due to high "population density and commercial activities at the locations where these assets are installed" (GOI 1997: 262). The Ninth Plan lays emphasis on the growing gap between demand and supply of basic services, and gives high priority to the development and upgradation of urban infrastructure services to meet the needs of the growing population. As compared to the earlier plans, there is greater stress on problems concerning certain environmental indicators such as water supply, sewerage and sanitation. The Ninth Plan also discusses the need for 'environmental sustainability' and improvement of the urban environment. Like the other plans however, it also highlights the need for development of housing for low income groups; alleviation of poverty and unemployment and development and upgradation of urban infrastructure services (GOI 1997)

The Tenth Plan stresses the need to bear in mind the Constitution (74th) Amendment Act in 1992 which was intended to "give a more focussed thrust to decentralization and the creation of a democratic governance structure with local responsibilities being assumed and managed at the local level" (GOI 2003: 611). The emphasis, like in the Seventh and Eighth Plan, was on giving more responsibilities to the urban local bodies (ULBs) as "institutions of self government" (GOI 2003: 611). The Tenth Plan acknowledges that the real challenge for sustained development in the urban sector is strengthening and developing of the ULBs. The ULBs it maintains require both functional as well as financial autonomy to be more effective. The Tenth Plan has reiterated the Ninth Plan's need for better maintenance of civic amenities.

There is also talk of introducing and promoting public-private partnerships for "improving efficiency and better service delivery" (GOI 2003: 620). It also focuses more strongly on urban poverty alleviation and slum improvement. It admits that implementation of programmes for the urban poor are ridden with problems. In this context it says "The problem of inadequate funding has been compounded by under-utilization of Central funds, diversion of funds released for specific programmes and infructuous expenditure" (GOI 2003: 627). With regard to slums, the Tenth Plan paints a dismal picture. It admits to minimal improvement in the condition of slums despite decades of programmes for the environmental improvement and upgradation of slums. The Draft National Slum policy drawn up in 1999 has been the subject of controversy and debate and the Tenth Plan stresses the need for a comprehensive National Policy on Slums.

Decentralization, integrated development, poverty alleviation, and people's participation appear as recurring themes in planning documents over the last two decades. While on paper, there have been suggestions for the better management of urban growth and various schemes like IDSMT have been initiated, in practice their implementation has been ad hoc, half hearted and insufficient relative to demand. The roles of central and state governments have not been clarified and there exists much confusion in this respect. As a result, the central government has adopted an advisory style while the state governments have shifted the burden on the centre, with high expectations in terms of resources.

A lack of adequate urban development and growth has led to innumerable urban problems such as increasing slums, lack of shelter, rising unemployment, crushing pressure on basic civic infrastructure and services, increasing crime and insecurity and environmental pollution. *Bastis* or *jhuggi-jhompris*, in particular, are the most pronounced indicators of urban poverty. In the metrocities, the percentage of such settlements ranges from 8.5 per cent in Bhopal to 63.5 per cent in Patna. In general, the percentage of population resident in these settlements increases with the size of cities: it was 17.5 per cent in the case of towns with less than 100,000 population, 21.5 per cent in the case of cities with 100,000 to 1 million and 33.5 per cent in the case of million plus cities (Nath 1989: 256).

Since the 1990s, policies of liberalization and privatization have been pursued vigorously in India. In view of the exorbitant costs of urban infrastructure development and decreasing public sector performance, innovative policies such as cost recovery, privatization of services like solid-waste disposal, sanitation, and public transport have been advocated. However, privatization poses complex problems such as ensuring accountability and equity, and coordination of various sectors. For many services, there is no guarantee that the problems of the public sector undertakings will disappear with a change in ownership.[4]

Urban Environmental Quality – Some Trends

Despite the important economic role of cities, rapid population growth is degrading the urban environment and placing strains on natural

---

4 The recent experience with the privatisation of the Delhi Vidyut (Electricity) Board may be a case in point, although it is probably too early to judge the long term effects of this policy change that was implemented earlier in 2002.

resources, thus undermining sustainable and equitable development. The most critical environmental concerns in India's cities include problems relating to water supply, sanitation, drainage, solid waste management and transport, and pollution from urban wastes and emissions. This chapter focuses on three specific issues in its discussion of 'the urban environment' – solid waste, water, and air.[5] This section summarises current trends in these environmental quality indicators, based primarily on official data sources.

Solid Waste

With increasing urbanization and changing lifestyles, management of municipal solid waste has emerged as a major environmental issue in India. Municipal solid wastes are a heterogeneous mixture of paper, plastic, cloth, metal, glass, and organic matter generated from households, commercial establishments, and markets. On account of unregulated land use across many urban areas (such as commercial and small-scale manufacturing activity) and the presence of unauthorized industrial and health care activities (e.g. clinics or nursing homes) within residential areas, there is a possibility that hazardous wastes are also present in the municipal waste system (TERI 1998; Bhide and Shekdar 1999; Joardar 2000).

The total municipal solid waste generated by the 23 million plus cities (as per the 1991 census) was reported to be 30,058 tonnes per day (CPCB 2000a). The total solid waste generated by all 299 Class I cities was estimated at 48,134 tonnes per day (CPCB 2000b), while that produced by 345 Class II towns was estimated at 3,401 metric tonnes per day (CPCB 2000c). The average per capita generation of solid waste was 0.449 kg /day for the million plus cities, 0.376 kg/person/day for all Class I cities (100,000 population and above), and 0.152 kg/person/day for Class II towns (50,000-99,999). Out of the 113 Class II towns that responded, 56 towns fell under the category of less than 0.15 kg/capita/day generation of solid waste.[6]

---

5 We recognize, however, that the term 'environment' could potentially include a number of additional dimensions, such as the quality of social infrastructure, the availability of shelter and recreational space, the type of architectural form.

6 Out of 299 Class I cities, 210 cities responded to questionnaires sent out by CPCB, while only 113 Class II towns out of a total of 345 responded to these. For the non-respondents, total solid waste generation was estimated on the basis of average solid waste generation in each size class.

According to CPCB data, among the larger cities, Chennai generates the highest amount of waste per capita at 0.657 kg per day, while Kolkata generates 0.347 kg per day, well below the average for all metrocities. Kochi, which has the lowest population among the million plus cities (approximately 1 million) produces well above the average level of waste at 0.514 kg per capita per day, more than that generated in each of the three mega-cities, Mumbai, Kolkata and Delhi. Similarly, the per capita generation of solid waste in Class I cities ranged between 0.1 kg/day for Junagadh to 0.929 kg/day for Jalgaon. The per capita generation of solid waste in Class II towns ranged from 0.019 kg/day for Puliyangudi of Tamil Nadu to 0.747 kg/day for Virar of Maharashtra (CPCB 2000a).

What this suggests is that within each size class, there is considerable variation in the quantity of solid waste that is produced by Indian cities, and that it would be simplistic to conclude that per capita solid waste generation increases monotonically with city size. A recent survey on solid waste in all the major cities of India conducted by NIUA also confirms that there is considerable variation in levels of per capita solid waste generation within cities in urban India. Other studies conducted by the Operations Research Group in 1989, Central Pollution Control Board in 1997 indicate similar sorts of differences between different cities. The broader literature (for instance, van Beukering 1994; Bhide and Shekdar 1999; Rohilla and Bansal 1999; Joardar 2000) provides some interesting case studies, but does not allow us to compare differences in solid waste generation across cities and towns in a more general sense. Overall, these trends suggest that it is difficult to conclude that urban growth is automatically associated with higher levels of per capita waste generation.

Water Availability and Quality

Data from CPCB suggests that about 88 per cent of the population in Class I and Class II cities are covered by an organized source of water supply. Slightly over a quarter of the Class I cities and 14 per cent of Class II towns and cities report 100 per cent water supply coverage, while about one sixth of such towns and cities report less than 75 per cent coverage. In terms of levels of water supply, the average availability of water in metrocities is 214 litres per capita daily (lpcd), while that in all

Class I cities is 183 lpcd, and in Class II cities 103 lpcd (CPCB 1997; 2000d; 2000e).[7]

What is striking about water supply data within these size classes is the extent of variation between cities and towns. Among the metrocities, Delhi has a high water supply of 341 lpcd, while Madurai reports a very low supply of 74 lpcd. Similarly, supply levels in Class I and Class II cities vary from single figures to between three and four times the 'normal' figure, as defined by CPCB. A further problem with the aggregate CPCB data is that, since it provides only an overall supply figure, disparities in water distribution within each city are not clear. CPCB (2000d) cites an independent study on disparities done by the Operations Research Group in 1995, which indicates that per capita availability of water varies between 36 lpcd and 310 lpcd within the metrocities.[8] Despite the fact that water supply systems are designed for twenty four hours service at 150-200 lpcd, water is generally available for between one and six hours, with average per capita consumption between 80 and 100 lpcd (Venkateswarlu 1998). Within *jhuggi-jhompri* areas, water availability tends to average between 25 and 27 lpcd and is considerably below the desirable minimum level of 40 lpcd as fixed by the National Drinking Water Mission (EGCIP 1996).

Of the total wastewater generated by Class I cities, about 59 per cent comes from the million plus cities. Within the metrocities, the four largest, Mumbai, Kolkata, Delhi and Chennai, generate 58.5 per cent of the overall wastewater (CPCB 1997). The figures for installed treatment capacity suggest that a very large proportion of urban wastewater re-enters the hydrological system untreated and contributes to pollution. Out of an estimated total wastewater generation of 18,312 mld from Class I and Class II cities combined, as much as 14,213 mld (77.62 per cent) is untreated (CPCB 2000d; 2000e). Where wastewater treatment facilities exist, they do not function properly, and remain closed most of the time due to improper design and poor maintenance, together with a non-technical and unskilled approach. The Centre for Science and Environment's Second Citizen's Report claims that out of India's 3119

7 The CPCB classifies towns and cities into four different categories, depending on average levels of water availability – low for areas with less than 100 lpcd, normal for areas with supply between 100 and 200 lpcd, high for areas with supply between 200 and 300 lpcd, and very high for areas reporting more than 300 lpcd.

8 In the case of Delhi, which has a very high average of 341 lpcd, some areas get over 450 lpcd (New Delhi Municipal Corporation area, and Delhi Cantonment), while others get less than 35 lpcd (Mehrauli, Narela) (Buch 1993; Misra and Misra 1998).

towns and cities, only 209 have partial sewage and sewage treatment facilities and eight have full facilities (CSE 1985).

The CPCB data suggests that slightly over 25 per cent of Class I cities, and less than 5 per cent of Class II towns have either primary or secondary treatment facilities. Among the metrocities, Delhi stands out as having the highest treatment capacity, and has 5 treatment plants with a further 4 under construction.[9] Chennai also has 5 treatment plants, and the percentage of population served by sewage treatment is 93 per cent, which is very high compared to Mumbai where it is only 65 per cent (CPCB 1997). Among the other million plus cities, Pune has the highest treatment capacity (981 mld) and 85 per cent of the population is served by sewage treatment, while Jaipur has the lowest treatment capacity at 27 mld.

Air Quality

Indian cities are among the most polluted in the world, with concentrations of a number of air pollutants being well above recommended WHO levels. The major pollutants are sulphur dioxide, nitrogen oxides, carbon monoxide, hydrocarbons, photochemical oxidants, metals and other gases and vapours. According to analysts, the major sources of air pollution are industries, thermal power plants and motor vehicles (TERI, 1998). Trends indicate that transport in cities is a key factor, often responsible for 60 to 70 per cent of the local air pollution (CSE 1996; Parikh (ed.) 1999; HUDCO and UNCHS 2001). The other major sources of air pollution are industries (toxic gases) and thermal power plants (fly ash and sulphur dioxide). Air pollution in Indian towns and cities is responsible for serious health ailments. For instance, a widely cited World Bank study (Brandon and Homann 1995) estimated that 40,351 premature deaths per year across 36 Indian cities could be attributed to air pollution alone. Other recent studies referring to links between health and air pollution include a report by Cropper et al. (1997), Kandlikar and Ramachandran (2000) and Parikh (1999).[10]

---

9 While the installation of new facilities in Delhi has increased treatment capacity from 450 mld in 1977 to 1270 mld in 1997 it has not ben able to meet the demands created by the increased flow of wastewater, which rose from 960 mld in 1977 to 1900 mld in 1997.

10 Other recent studies referring to links between health and air pollution include a report by Cropper *et al* (1997), Kandlikar and Ramachandran (2000) and Parikh (ed.) (1999).

CPCB's (2000f) analysis of air quality trends over the nine-year period between 1990 and 1998 suggests that SPM levels remained consistently high in various cities over this period, while SO_2 and NO_2 levels were within permissible limits for most cities. However, there is also great variation, with average recorded levels of each of the three pollutants fluctuating considerably over this period in most cities. Trends are constant in some cities, worsening in some, while they are improving in others, and the data shows no overall pattern. SPM provides most cause for concern, and CPCB concludes that the data suggests that annual averages for both residential and industrial areas have probably "been frequently violated at most cities" (CPCB 2000f: 95).

A survey of smaller towns and cities by the Centre for Science and Environment found high air pollution levels in many (Kazimuddin et al. 1999: 30). Available case study evidence confirms this. For instance, a report released in January 1999 by the World Resources Institute of Washington, pointed out that Rajkot in Gujarat is the fifth most polluted city in the world with regard to air pollution (cited in *Down to Earth* 1999). A relatively small city, Dehra Dun (now the capital of Uttaranchal) registered the highest SPM level in the country in 1992, an extremely high 4,809 ug/cum. Agra is also highly polluted with annual average SPM levels exceeding the limits permissible even in industrial areas (TERI 1998). Similarly, Pondicherry, Kota, Gajraula, Shimla and Rohtak are a few other examples of smaller cities/towns which have regularly exceeded the SPM, SO_2, and NOx permissible limits.

Data on each of these air quality indicators separately does not necessarily provide a good indication of overall air quality in a city. Using CPCB data for 1993 and 1994, TERI (1998) constructed a single index, which provides an indication of the cumulative effect of the three pollutants on air quality in urban India. According to TERI's Air Quality Index, out of 62 cities for which data was available, 20 had 'dangerous' levels of pollution, while the situation was judged to be 'bad' in 14, 'poor' in 9, 'fair' in 12, and 'good' in 7.

Sustainable Development of Cities: Questions of Governance

Given the scale of urban environmental problems, there is a general policy consensus that there is a need for the 'sustainable development' of cities. However, there is relatively little literature on sustainable development and cities. Exceptions are Stren, White and Whitney (1992) as well as Hardoy et al. (1992).

> The sustainability component is the impact of each city (or rather producers and consumers located within the city) on environmental capital: local and global sinks, renewable resources and non-renewable resources. The development component (political, social, economic and cultural goals) is the performance of each city and its institutions in meeting its inhabitants' development needs, this also has an environmental component since the quality of home, work, neighbourhood and city environment and the extent to which inhabitants are protected from biological pathogens and chemical pollutants in the water, air, soil, food or other environmental hazards has a major influence on health and well-being of the population. (WHO 1992, quoted in Hardoy et al. 1992)

It is difficult, however, to consider 'urban policy and management' for sustainable development in these abstract terms. In most cities there are contradictions between sustainability and development. Many of the cities which can be judged positively by development criteria (where social, economic and political goals are met) have amongst the highest per capita draws on environmental capital (in terms of non-renewable resources, draw on watersheds, forests and agricultural systems, ecosystems waste absorption capacities and per capita emissions of green house gases). The least draw on environmental capital is often by those cities which perform worst in development terms.

National governments have the key role in linking local and global sustainability. Internationally, they have the responsibility for reaching agreements to limit each nation's claims on the world's environmental capital. Nationally, they are responsible for providing the framework to ensure local actions which can meet development goals without compromising local and global sustainability.

At the level of the city and municipal government Hardoy et al.(1992) identify four areas of policy focus:

1. Respond to citizens' demands for safe and healthy living and working environment which includes ensuring the availability of shelter and provision of basic infrastructure and services;

2. Penalize polluters (establish appropriate mechanisms and enforce them), provide incentives to encourage innovative ways to reduce pollution, encourage recycling, re-use and reclamation of both non-renewable and renewable resources and waste materials;
3. Manage urban growth to promote minimal use of environmental capital while meeting social and economic goals. For example provide for city generated wastes (especially toxic wastes and point source water pollution);
4. Identify and support the development of new economic activities, which enhance both the urban centre's economic base and its environment.

It falls upon Municipal Corporations to manage and provide various urban services and deal with local environmental problems faced by the city. In India, the municipal governments have become very weak, with their authority and functions progressively taken over by state governments and state-sponsored urban development agencies. Municipalities have become financially more dependent on transfers and grants from state and federal governments, which control important tax bases, since few taxes are devolved to local government. Property taxes, the municipalities' principal revenue source, have stagnated, not only because of inefficient assessment and collection procedures, but also because urban rent control froze property taxes at artificially low levels. Urban services have deteriorated as responsibilities for maintaining infrastructure planned and constructed by state agencies have outstripped the financial resources of municipalities (Repetto 1994).

In addition to the lack of financial resources, Municipal Corporations are unable to cope with all the development aspects of urban management. As a result, the task of managing urban areas has been assigned to a large number of agencies at the local, state and central levels. So, for example, there is the Water and Sewerage Board, Pollution Board, Electricity Board, State Public Works Department etc., but due to the lack of clearly laid down programmes and a common set of objectives for these agencies it is virtually impossible to coordinate activities (Sharma 1989). Some development bodies have assumed more responsibilities than originally envisaged and this too has created problems. The Delhi Development Authority (DDA), for example, was originally established for updating the 'master plan' for Delhi and overseeing its implementation. Over the years, however, it has assumed a variety of functions including construction of low and middle-income group housing and some purely municipal functions such as approval of building plans. The latter creates conflicts of jurisdiction and problems of coordination of activities with other agencies (Nath 1989: 256). In addition, civic management itself is a highly specialized task for which most administrators heading municipalities are not specially trained.

The main reason for the failure of urban planning can be seen in the weak revenue situation of the urban local bodies which have been revitalised by the 74th Amendment, but have immediately faced the painful experience of the 'resource crunch' of the 1990s. This weak tax income has been accentuated by political populism which has prevented urban local bodies from exploiting whatever revenue potential exists. At the local level, local authorities have inadequate budgets, large backlogs in providing basic infrastructure and a resource base that is not capable of generating the capital required to address the backlog. The 74th Amendment to the Constitution has transferred powers to local bodies to raise tax and non-tax revenues to enable them to exercise their responsibility of planning and development. However, analysts remain sceptical about the extent to which the constitutional amendment will be translated into any real improvement in the financial position of urban local bodies (Kundu 2000).

Given their limitations (especially financial), Municipal Corporations in India can contribute to but cannot be expected to take the lead in addressing broader issues such as reduction of green house gas emissions, or fuel efficiency among road users. This has to come from the national or state government which must provide the legislative, regulatory and fiscal framework within which the representative urban government can operate and meet its own regional sustainable development agenda – and contribute to national and international goals. In addition, there is a need to examine the scope for the adoption of incentive based measures such as ecological taxes and tradable permit schemes, which punish polluters and reward ecologically-sustainable activities through market mechanisms.

The Role of the Private Sector

A frequent justification in favour of privatization by its proponents is that the government is short of capital, and hence the private sector could take over some of the responsibilities of local government. In some senses, in a country like India, many of the poorer inhabitants already use the 'private' sector to obtain land for housing, rented accommodation and certain services. Private enterprises are often the main supplier of water through water vendors. But the high price and often poor quality water sold by the water vendors also suggests problems of 'privatization' (Nath 1989; Hardoy et al. 1992; Tovey 1998).

Privatization of land in India is also complicated. Squatters often occupy public land, to evict them is usually a politically sensitive issue as these communities are 'vote banks' and used politically. In the event of such land being privatised, the squatters would definitely be evicted. There are also suggestions that privatization could play a role in water supply, especially because people pay as they consume and often pay for the cost of connection (Hardoy et al. 1992). This scenario seems improbable in India as those most affected by water shortages are the poor and those living in *jhuggi-jhompris*, who do not have water connections within their homes. As with land, illegal use of water and electricity is tolerated by municipal authorities. However, if service provision was privatised, such illegal use would not be accepted. At the same time, private companies would be reluctant to make a big investment in poorer areas if they were uncertain of willingness to pay for the product by the customers.[11] The most positive role for privatization is with regard to garbage collection, with regulation by local government. This could be an attractive option for local governments which cannot obtain the necessary investment funds.

The Ministry of Urban Affairs and Employment in a recent press release (January 1999) says that private investment for provision of urban infrastructure cannot take place unless a proper legal and regulatory framework for such investment is created and developed which ensures full cost plus recovery of such investment. It advocates innovative reforms in municipal tax structure, and user charges, taking into account poor paying capacity of a sizeable section of the urban population. It also states that various modes of Private-Public-Partnership (PPP) are being experimented by different urban local bodies in the country (MUA 1999).[12]

---

11 This is probably largely an empirical matter, and there is insufficient conclusive evidence. For instance, Tovey (1998) reports on willingness to pay for water services from residents of urban slum clusters (*jhuggi-jhompri* colonies) in New Delhi.

12 According to the Ministry of Urban Affairs and Development, Municipal Bond, Tradable Development Rights, Urban Shelter and Infrastructure Fund, use of Land as a Resource are some of the new techniques being applied by the city authorities (MUA 1999). Details of these schemes are not provided, but would provide an interesting focus for further research.

Role of NGOs

Hardoy et al .(1992) see tremendous potential in the role of local NGOs in assisting with urban environmental problems. They advocate partnerships between local governments, local community organizations, and local NGOs. The Orangi Pilot Project with low-income households and community organizations in the largest unauthorised settlement in Karachi shows what can be achieved with minimal external funding and with most of the investments made by poor households themselves (Hasan 1990). There are also NGOs involved in the collection and disposal of garbage – either seeking to provide (or improve) services in low-income settlements which are not served through public provision, or seeking to provide a better livelihood for people making a living from garbage. For instance the Waste Wise project in Bangalore seeks to combine innovative waste separation and recycling programme (with composting of organic wastes and collection of recyclables) with income generation for street children (Furedy 1992).

There are suggestions of NGOs being involved in other ways. For example, funding could be provided by local governments to residents' organizations formed by the inhabitants of an area (e.g. a certain sum of money for site improvements). The residents have the flexibility of how to spend the money and can hire a local NGO for technical advice as well as for the supervizing of the loan. Organizations of this sort are already operating at some level in cities like Delhi where there are well-organized residents groups in some colonies.[13] However these organizations mainly consist of middle-class people whose basic needs are already taken care of. Schemes of this sort are urgently needed in the poorer areas of towns and cities if they are to impact significantly on the quality of the urban environment in the country.

Though there is no mention of financing of community-based groups, the Ministry has recently specified that the new urban poverty alleviation scheme, the Swarna Jayanti Shahari Rozgar Yojana (SJSRY), rests on the foundation of community empowerment. 'It relies on establishing and promoting community organizations and structures to provide a supporting and facilitating mechanism for local development. Community organizations like Neighbourhood Groups (NHGS), Neighbourhood Committees (NHCS), and Community Development Societies (CDS) are to be set up in cities and towns. The CDS, being a federation

13 These groups are being encouraged by the Delhi state government under its new 'Bhagedari' (partnership) scheme.

of different community based organizations, shall be the nodal agency for the programme. It is expected that they will lay emphasis on providing the entire gamut of social sector inputs to their areas including health, welfare and education, provision of community sanitation, through establishing convergence between schemes being implemented by different line departments within their jurisdiction" (MUA 1999: 2).

The role of NGOs in assisting in the management of urban environmental problems in India is crucial. If there is to be more community participation it would be virtually impossible without the mediation of credible NGOs. Sharma (1989) for example, points out that Municipal Corporations on their own (or rather people who are in charge) are actually not in a position to carry out technical tasks with community organizations. With the professional and educational background they have, they are simply not trained in this sphere. In India, there is also the problem of bureaucracy and widespread corruption in the context of urban governance. Decisions are often taken on partisan and political considerations as against on the merits of individual cases. Favours are shown to the residents of wards belonging to the councillors of the party commanding power in the municipal body at a particular time. Working in conjunction with responsible NGOs may help keep these problems in check, and provide for greater accountability.

Whatever the problems of the urban environment, there is a major stress on using local institutions for local problems. Hardoy et al. (1992) point out that outside agencies, whether national or international, often misunderstand the nature of the problem and range of options from which to choose the most appropriate solutions. There is an emphasis on channelling more funds directly to community based organizations (CBOs) and local NGOs with whom they choose to work. Often innovative local solutions which are cheaper and more appropriate may be ignored in favour of far more expensive but less effective solutions funded and supported by external aid and designed by foreign consultants. In addition, Hardoy et al. (1992) suggest that aid agencies can never stay in a city long enough to guarantee the maintenance and expansion of the new water or sanitation or garbage collection system they helped to fund.[14] Outside agencies may bring knowledge, expertise, capital and advice, but they cannot solve most environmental problems without effective local institutions. They also operate on a 'project by project'

14 This assertion needs to be tested empirically in the Indian context.

basis when what is needed is a long-term process within each city to strengthen the institutional capacity overseen by democratic governance.

Each city has its own unique set of environmental problems that, with limited resources, can only be addressed with knowledge of local resources, local constraints, and possibilities for innovative approaches that reduce capital requirements. Solutions need to be discussed locally and influenced by local citizens' own needs and priorities. Partnerships between municipal authorities, local NGOs and community organizations formed by low-income groups within particular neighbourhoods have often proved more cost-effective than conventional approaches (Gnaneshwar 1995).

In addition to NGOs assisting with urban environmental problems, there is a need for more citizen led action to press for changes in the urban environment. In Europe and North America, action on environmental problems has always been citizen led. Citizen groups and NGOs provided the lobby, which eventually produced changes in government policies. In India, there is a proliferation of citizens' groups pressing their demands for water, sanitation, healthcare and other services, but they have not had much effect on government policies. A number of these causes are finding that they have little support from middle class professionals (Hardoy et al. 1992). Shah (1997: 33) observes that "the middle class which at one time played a progressive role has become reactionary, anti-poor, and anti-state, a victim of consumerism." This is especially true of issues relating to service provision for the poor, who are increasingly being pushed to the fringes of middle-class urban consciousness, even though their services are frequently called upon in the informal sector such as waste disposal, wherever municipal provision is inadequate. The poor play a critical role in providing labour and services to the middle class, but their needs and entitlements often do not feature prominently in discussions about the urban environment in India.

Environmental Problems or Political and Economic Constraints?

Some authors (Nath 1989; Gnaneshwar 1995; Jain et al. 1995) as well as environmental institutions (such as CSE and TERI) who have written about urban environmental problems in India claim that it is probably misleading to refer to the most pressing environmental problems as 'environmental' since "they arise not from some particular shortage of an environmental resource (such as land or fresh water) but from economic or political factors which prevent poorer groups from obtaining them and organising to demand them". They point out, for example, that the severe shortage of water supplies for much of the Third World's urban population is a serious environmental problem but rarely is its cause environmental. In most cities, it is not a shortage of freshwater resources but governments' refusal to give a higher priority to water supply (and the competent organizational structure that supply, maintenance and expansion require). It is the same with land; most cities or metropolitan areas in the Third World have sufficient unused or under-utilized land sites within the current built-up area to accommodate most, if not all, the low-income households currently living in overcrowded conditions.

A country like India has weak institutions and infrastructure on which to base effective actions to address urban environmental problems. The institutional structure is especially weak at the local level; they have very inadequate capital budgets, large backlogs in providing basic infrastructure, and an economy that is not adequately capable of generating the capital to address the backlog. Added to this problem is the total lack of coordination between different agencies responsible for various urban tasks within a city. Sewerage, drainage and solid waste services (including street cleaning) are often the responsibility of different agencies, yet their design, implementation and management needs to be carefully coordinated. Drainage systems for example, cannot work in most Third World cities without solid waste management which keeps drains clean. Drainage networks need coordinated action at household, neighbourhood and city level – and beyond the city for those living 'downstream' of the city – yet rarely do their design and operation take account of this fact.

Urban environmental quality is linked with personal consumption choices, production technologies and methods, as well as the role of policy in directing incentives for such activities. Changes in the urban environment depend on strategies adopted by the government, changes in environmental legislation and the stricter enforcement of existing legislation, the demand for better living conditions by urban residents, as well as the ability of local authorities to perform their functions, including in partnership with other actors. If there is a desire for an improvement in environmental standards, and this is supported by the availability of real alternatives for consumers and producers, the evidence suggests that significant changes are possible. Examples that are widely cited include the transformation in Surat following the 1994 plague (see

Appendix), and the dramatic improvement in air quality in Delhi after the implementation of higher emission standards and the phasing out of leaded fuel, among others.

However, these experiences are relatively recent, and it is difficult to draw any firm conclusions from them about the future of urban environmental quality and governance. There are at least as many cases where attempts to improve environmental standards or to ensure greater compliance with existing laws have met with considerable resistance. In Delhi, the controversy about relocation of non-conforming industrial units from residential areas as well as the ongoing debate about the appropriate choice of fuel for public transport, are two examples. Here, a complex web of interests (consumers, businesses, workers, the judiciary, and various branches of the executive from the national government to municipalities) is involved, and this has made the process of political implementation of desirable changes very difficult.

Concluding Remarks

From an initial examination of urban environmental problems in India, it is clear that there is a need for mobilization of resources and energy at every level of governance to begin to tackle some of these serious issues. Urban policy over the years has been fairly positive in terms of what it envisages, but reality has been quite different. One of the problems has been the lack of coherence between the national and state governments. The area of urban development has received very little attention at the national level which has been further neglected by the state governments, whereas local authorities have been provided little real power to exercise their new constitutional role. Many state governments have relied on the creation of special purpose agencies that act as extensions of the state governmental arms and undermine the municipal governments in the development process.

Even though the state governments have the constitutional responsibility and can draw up policy statements on urbanization, hardly any state government has contemplated such a step. During the past forty years all the initiative for policy making and even the programmes for implementation in the area of urbanization have come from the central government. Often state governments have to be persuaded to take action through substantial grants from the centre. Fragmented and paradoxical policy pursuits have led to a mis-governance syndrome in the Indian urban system.

What is also lacking on the part of the government is more up-to-date research (as well as acknowledgement) of some of the most pressing environmental problems in cities and towns. Air and water pollution have reached dangerous levels in some areas with serious health implications especially for the urban poor. There needs to be a more committed effort on the part of the government to investigate these problems. So far there is not much evidence of the government taking the issues of pollution and municipal solid waste seriously as there is no mention of these in the Five-Year Plans (in terms of acknowledging that air and water pollution have severe health implications). Although the regulatory framework of the Environmental Protection Act of 1986 provides some legislative support, the nature of implementation leaves sufficient loopholes for most polluters to operate in violation of established norms. In addition, there are not enough partnerships between NGOs, citizen groups and governmental bodies to try and resolve urban environmental problems. There is no doubt that there is an immense need for such partnerships and that these partnerships do work given the will and commitment on the part of the government.

There is also a need for more systematic information with regard to urban environmental problems in smaller Indian towns and cities. Much of the data on urban environmental problems in India tends to focus on the big mega-cities like Delhi, Mumbai and Calcutta. This often gives the (false) impression that most of the problems as well as much of the urban population are in the huge mega-cites. Hardoy et al. (1992) point out that there are hundreds of cities in the south with between 250,000 and one million inhabitants and thousands under 250,000. The quality of data collection and monitoring is simply inadequate to provide any accurate information about the environmental state of these towns and cities. While anecdotal local-level information exists, it is usually insufficient to provide the basis for a co-ordinated and proportionate policy response.

Finally, it is important to reflect on India's burgeoning urban population as a determinant of urban environmental problems in cities and towns. Most Third World cities (including some of the largest) are not very densely populated (in terms of persons per square unit). In many areas within most cities densities are so low or settlement patterns so varied, that costs per household of providing infrastructure are much increased. Often it appears that the problems are more to do with the provision of infrastructure than congestion. It is usually in the absence of the institutional means to ensure that infrastructure services and pollution controls are provided, that a high concentration of population and industrial production greatly exacerbates environmental health problems. A preliminary assessment of the situation suggests urban environmental problems may have more to do with problems of finance and inadequate infrastructure and, in general, a lack of perspective and structures of governance for planned urban development in India, rather than simply with the pressures of growing urban populations.

Appendix: Surat: A Case Study in Institutional Reform

The outbreak of the pneumonic plague in Surat in south Gujarat in September-October 1994 was largely due to a decay in the urban health system and urban conditions in general. (The WHO confirmed the epidemic in Surat as plague but medical opinion is divided and debate has not resolved the diagnosis). It is well known however that the incidence of disease in Surat has always been very high with almost 3-4 epidemics every year. One of the main problems is the actual filth and dirt present in the city and the inadequate collection of garbage. The city also faces a shortage of drinking water. The Municipal Corporation supplies water to only 43 per cent of its total area and 71 per cent of its population (1.52 million under the 1991 census). The poor performance of the Municipal Corporation has failed to meet the needs of the city.

In the aftermath of the plague a new Municipal Commissioner, M.S. Rao was appointed to oversee the functioning of the Municipal Corporation and ensure a clean-up of the city. Rao involved local citizens, NGOs and private contractors in leading a cleaning campaign and a programme for the development of the city. Because of his involvement, the health surveillance system was strengthened and procedures for planning infrastructure facilities, particularly sewage and water.

Rao decentralized the Surat Municipal Corporation (SMC) by creating 6 zones (Under Section 88(2) of the BPMC Act the Commissioner may with the approval of the Standing Committee "empower any municipal officers to exercise, perform, or discharge any powers which are his." By using this provision of the Act, he can delegate all his financial and administrative powers. He therefore granted Municipal Officers more responsibility and accountability and encouraged on-the-spot decisions to be taken without his consent or tedious bureaucratic procedures. This led to a more efficient and responsive Municipal service.

Rao initiated a number of radical changes, in particular the demolition of unauthorized buildings. More than 78.5 thousand square metres area was acquired by demolishing fully or partly illegal or unauthorized construction in a year's time.

One of the main problems was that of garbage. Rao recruited private contractors for cleaning the eastern bank of the river Tapi. An additional 675 sweepers were recruited for cleaning the city, in particular sewage and septic tanks. Private agencies were employed from time to time for brushing, scraping and lifting the solid waste to the final disposal sites. 415 'nuisance spots' (garbage collection points) were specially attended to on a regular basis. The intensive drive for cleaning the streets in June-July 1995 resulted in an increase in solid waste from 400 metric tonnes per day in 1995 to 850 metric tonnes per day in 1996.

SMC also launched a Healthcare Operation and carried out regular inspection of shops and hotels for cleanliness. Within two years Rao and the SMC had cleaned up Surat and the city was unrecognisable. It was even considered the second cleanest city in India by INTACH, an NGO. This was a tremendous achievement on the part of the SMC under the leadership of Rao. He was able to survive pressures of vested interests – political, economic, even religious because of public support, personal commitment, priorities and style of functioning.

Source: Shah (1997)

REFERENCES

Bhide, A.D. and Shekdar, A.V., 'Solid Waste Management in Delhi', India. (mimeo) Nagpur: National Environmental Engineering Research Institute, 1999.

Brandon, C. and Homman, K., 'The cost of inaction: valuing the economy-wide cost of environmental degradation in India,' (mimeo) Tokyo,

United Nations University, Symposium on Global Sustainability (Proceedings), October 1995.

Buch, M..N., Environmental Consciousness and Urban Planning, New Delhi: Orient Longman, 1993.

Central Pollution Control Board, Management of Municipal Solid Waste, New Delhi, Central Pollution Control Board, Ministry of Environment and Forests, 1995.

Central Pollution Control Board, Status of Water Supply and Wastewater Generation, Collection, Treatment and Disposal in Metrocities (1994-1995), New Delhi, Central Pollution Control Board, Ministry of Environment and Forests, 1997.

Central Pollution Control Board, Status of Solid Waste in Metrocities, New Delhi, Central Pollution Control Board, Ministry of Environment and Forests, 2000a.

Central Pollution Control Board, Status of Solid Waste Generation, Collection Treatment and Disposal in Class I Cities, New Delhi, Central Pollution Control Board, Ministry of Environment and Forests, 2000b.

Central Pollution Control Board, Status of Solid Waste Generation, Collection, Treatment and Disposal in Class II Towns, New Delhi, Central Pollution Control Board, Ministry of Environment and Forests, 2000c.

Central Pollution Control Board, Status of Water Supply and Wastewater Generation, Collection, Treatment and Disposal in Class I Cities, New Delhi, Central Pollution Control Board, Ministry of Environment and Forests, 2000d.

Central Pollution Control Board, Status of Water and Wastewater Generation, Collection, Treatment and Disposal in Class II Towns, New Delhi, Central Pollution Control Board, Ministry of Environment and Forests, 2000e.

Central Pollution Control Board, Air Quality Status and Trends in India, New Delhi, Central Pollution Control Board, Ministry of Environment and Forests, 2000f.

Cropper, M. L. et al. The Health Benefits of Air Pollution Control in Delhi, in American Journal of Agricultural Economics, 79 (5), 1997, pp. 1625-1629.

CSE, 'Citizen's Second Report-State of India's Environment', New Delhi, Centre for Science and Environment, 1985.

CSE, 'Campaign on Urban Vehicular Pollution in Delhi'. (Press Releases on the world wide web at http://www.cseindia.org), 1996-1999.

CSE, 'Citizen's Fifth Report - Part I, National Overview', New Delhi, Centre for Science and Environment, 1999.

Dyson, T. and Visaria, P., 'Migration and Urbanisation: Retrospect and Prospects,' typescript, London School of Economics. Output for a research project funded by the Wellcome Trust (grant no. 053660) – 'The Future of India: Population, Environment and Human Development', 2002.

EGCIP, 'The India Infrastructure Report –Volume I, Expert Group on the Commercialisation of Infrastructure Projects', New Delhi, Ministry of Finance, Government of India, 1996.

Furedy, C., 'Garbage: exploring non-conventional options in Asian cities', in Environment and Urbanization, 4 (2), 1992, pp. 42-61.

Gnaneshwar, V., 'Urban Policies in India-Paradoxes and Predicaments', in Habitat International, 19 (3), 1995, pp. 293-316.

Government of India Third Five Year Plan. Government of India, Planning Commision, 1961.

Government of India Fourth Five Year Plan. Government of India, Planning Commission. 1969.

Government of India Fifth Five Year Plan. Government of India, Planning Commission, 1974

Government of India Sixth Five Year Plan. Government of India, Planning Commission, 1980.

Government of India Seventh Five Year Plan. Government of India, Planning Commission, 1985.

Government of India Eighth Five Year Plan. Government of India. Planning Commission, 1992.

Government of India Ninth Five Year Plan. Government of India, Planning Commission, 1997.

Government of India Tenth Five Year Plan. Government of India, Planning Commission, 2003.

Hardoy J. E., Mitlin, D., and Satterthwaite, D., Environmental Problems in Third World Cities, London: Earthscan, 1992.

Hasan, A., 'Community organizations and non-governmental organizations in the urban field in Pakistan', in Environment and Urbanization, 2 (1), 1990, pp. 74-86.

Jain, D.K., Satsangi, P.S., and Kothari, D.P., 'Urbanization and Energy Related Problems in Indian Cities', in Energy Sources, 16 (1), 1999, pp. 177-182.

Joardar, S. D., ' Urban Residential Solid Waste Management in India - Issues Related to Institutional Arrangements', in Public Works Management and Policy, 4 (4), 2000, pp. 319-31.

Kandlikar, M. and Ramachandran, G., 'The Causes and Consequences of Particulate Air Pollution in Urban India: A Synthesis of the Science', in Annual Review of Energy and Environment, 25, 2000, pp. 629-84.

Kazimuddin, A., Chettri, M., Jeevan, S.S., Joshi, S., Lianchawii, C., Mukhupadhyay, A., 'Polluted and Ignored', in *Down to . Earth*, 8 (11), October 31, 1999, pp. 30-42.

Kundu, A., 'Urban Development, Infrastructure, Financing and Emerging System of Governnance in India: A Perspective', MOST Discussion Paper No. 48, Paris, UNESCO, 2000.

MEA Economic Survey 2002, New Delhi, Ministry of Economic Affairs, Government of India, 2002.

MUA, Urban Scenario, New Delhi, Ministry of Urban Affairs, Government of India. (On the world wide web at http://urbanindia.nic.in/urbanindia/scene.htm), 1999.

MUA, Housing and Urban Policy in India, New Delhi, Ministry of Urban Affairs, Government of India (accessed on the world-wide web August 29, 2002: http://urbanindia.nic.in/mud-final-site/policies/index.htm), 2002a.

MUA, Integrated Development of Small and Medium Towns, New Delhi, Ministry of Urban Affairs, Government of India (accessed on the world-wide web August 29, 2002: http://urbanindia.nic.in/mud-final-site/programs/index.htm), 2002b.

Misra, R. P. and Misra, K., eds., Million Cities of India - Growth Dynamics, Internal Strucuture, Quality of Life and Planning Perspectives (Volumes 1 and 2), New Delhi: Sustainable Development Foundation, 1998.

Nath, V., 'Urbanization and Urban Development in India-Some Policy Issues', in International Journal of Urban and Regional Research, 13 (2), 1989, pp. 256-281.

Parikh, K. S., ed., India Development Report - 1999-2000, New Delhi: Oxford University Press, 1999.

Planning Commission Mid-Term Review of the Ninth Five Year Plan, 1997-2002, New Delhi, Government of India, Planning Commission. On-line at: http://planningcommission.nic.in/midbody.htm, 2000.

Ramachandran, R., Urbanization and Urban Systems in India, New Delhi: Oxford University Press, 1989.

Registrar General Urban Agglomerations/Cities Having Population of More than One Million in 2001, New Delhi, Government of India, Office of the Registrar General. On-line at:

http://www.censusindia.net/results/million_plus.html, 2001.

Repetto, R., The "Second India" Revisited: Population, Poverty and Environmental Stress over Two Decades. Washington: World Resources Institute, 1994.

Rohilla, S.K. and Bansal, S.P., 'Delhi's Solid Waste Disposal and Management – II', in S.K. Rohilla, Datta, P.S. and Bansal, S.P., Delhi's Water and Solid Waste Management - Emerging Scenario, New Delhi: Vigyan Prasar, 1998.

Shah, G., Public Health and Urban Development: The Plague in Surat, New Delhi: Sage Publications, 1997, pp. 16-209.

Sharma, S.K., 'State-Municipal Relationship: An Analysis of Collaboration and Control in India', in Nagarlok, XXI (4), 1989, pp. 20-29.

Shaw, A., 'Urban Policy in Post-Independent India- An Appraisal', in Economic and Political Weekly, 31 (4), 1996, pp. 224-228.

Stren, R.E, White, R. and Whitney, J., eds., Sustainable Cities: Urbanization and Environment in International Perspective. Westview, Colorado, 1992.

TERI, Looking Back to Think Ahead: GREEN India 2047, New Delhi: Tata Energy Research Institute, 1998.

Tovey, K.S., 'Institutional Responses to the Water Needs of JJ Colonies: A Case Study of R K Puram, New Delhi', Unpublished M.Phil. Dissertation, Department of Geography, University of Cambridge, 1998.

UNCHS/HUDCO, The State of Indian Cities 2001, New Delhi: United Nations Centre for Human Settlements and Housing and Urban Development Corporation, 2001.

van Beukering, P., 'An Economic Analysis of Different types of Formal and Informal Entrepreneurs, Recovering Urban Solid Waste in Bangalore', in Resources, Conservation and Recycling, 12 (3/4), 1994, pp. 230-251.

Venkateswarlu, U., Urbanisation in India: Problems and Prospects, New Delhi: New Age International, 1998.

2

PLANNING OF INDIAN MEGA-CITIES: ISSUES OF GOVERNANCE, THE PUBLIC SPHERE, AND A PINCH OF CIVIL SOCIETY

JOËL RUET

This chapter looks at cities mainly as specific forms of economic organizations, that is, as sites that supply economic goods and services which benefit from scale returns when similar services are produced for a larger number of consumers as well as from positive externalities, when the simultaneous presence of complementary sectors benefit each other. In this respect this chapter mainly focuses on the size effect of cities. In order to lay down the Indian context one can quote Jain (1990: 111), who pointed out that "in metropolitan cities, about 3 sq. m of space generates one job, while in agriculture, 3 ha of land resource is required per job." Furthermore, India's three biggest metropolises account for populations of 12 million inhabitants and more. They recorded a steep level of growth in the last decades and harbour great economic inequalities. Thus, the perspective on space is not only relevant with respect to the dialectic between spatial extension and densification of cities, but also with respect to the spatial social homogeneity in India's mega-cities. Finally, issues related to the modes of municipal governance will be addressed (governance is still to a great extent regarded as a sole public matter by officials in all of these cities) as well as the avail-able tools of urban planning.

It will be argued that the administrative set-up of a city matters for all these questions. Further, the chosen economic characterization allows understanding the inertia forces, themselves parameters of governance and planning. It allows us to address the question of how the state and its municipalities can utilize the emergence of a structured modern private sector for managing the metropolitan cities in India. Especially, we advocate that the experiment of the Bangalore Agenda Task Force

(BATF), delineated in the last part of this chapter, should be considered also for other metropolitan cities like Bombay or Delhi.

URBAN PROBLEMS: THE CITY AS SOCIO-TECHNO-ECONOMIC FABRIC

Cities provide housing as well as services to their population and economy, in a geographically restricted space. This is the rather limited definition of the function of a city that will be explored in the present chapter on the planning of mega-cities. We speak of mega-cities when the population crosses 10 million people.[1] With this respect, the urban agglomerations of Bombay, Calcutta and Delhi are mega-cities, all of them exceeding 12 million dwellers (11.9, 13.2, and 12.8. respectively).[2] The agglomerations of Madras (Chennai), Bangalore and Hyderabad are mega-cities in the making, accounting today for 6.4, 5.7, and 5.5. million inhabitants respectively and reporting high population growth (in the case of Bangalore a 38 per cent decadal growth rate).[3] As argued, this chapter adopts a mainly economical, physical and organizational perspective. It does not dwell on other possible approaches like, e.g. the 'sociological' absorption of the annual influx of new inhabitants, which can be as large 500,000 people in some cities, or on the adoption of urban culture by these new arrivals.

THE URBAN STRUCTURE AS THE TECHNICO-ECONOMIC OPTIMUM

In this very restricted sense the socio-economic function of cities is to supply network services such as water, electricity, sewerage, road works and transport, as well as social services like education, health, and even leisure activities. As argued above, the 'city form' is in principle better equipped in providing these services than the 'rural form', which is possible because of the economies of scale as well as the spatial density, which considerably reduces the cost for, e.g., laying water pipes. Bonnet

---

1 We prefer the term mega-city or metropolis to the notion of megalopolis sometimes employed in this context. Hancock and Hiernaux (2000) indicate that the concept of megalopolis applies when a sufficient geographical extension leads to the loss of a centre, or gives rise to a pluri-centralism. This is not the case with the mega-cities of India, which remain central to their agglomeration.

2 "Greater Bombay" has 11.9 million inhabitants, but for the entire agglomeration the population is estimated to be around 16.4 million.

3 For all the figures see Census of India (2001).

(2000), for example, recalls the importance of the size factor and the metropolization factor of cities for their productivity, while Rousseau (1991) measures the 'extra productivity' of cities.

By incorporating the effects of congestion on a more subjective 'quality of life', Bairoch (1977) suggests that there is an optimum size for cities. According to him, it would be 250,000 inhabitants. This limit can of course evolve from time to time and take into account ethnic and organizational developments. However, on the methodological plane, it is made up of hypotheses of economic valorisation of social conditions which, though pertinent, are outside the purview of this article. In the case of the cities of the 'South', Dorier-Apprill (2000) mentions the positive effects of cities for a given nation in terms of wealth creation and its distribution. In a scenario of limited resources in the context of 'third world' cities, mainly two economic questions arise.

First, in order to produce services in an efficient way the type of public organization at the municipal level is of particular importance. In fact, each function of the city can come either under the purview of the municipal services, or of autonomous organizations involved in the development and management of public services networks, or of inter-municipal or even supra-municipal organizations at the level of the entire urban agglomeration. According to the choice taken and the level of administrative coordination and decentralization, the efficiency of service production may vary to a large degree (Ruet, Saravanan, Zérah, 2002).

Second, the question of equitable distribution or redistribution of these services arises, or, in other terms, the question of the production of social equality (through reduction of poverty) becomes a central issue. Here, too, the organizational form of a given municipality is not neutral especially for the establishment of priorities, and should hence be carefully studied. This subject of organizational economics is the first issue that will be addressed below with a special focus on the question of autonomy of public agencies.

THE THIRD-WORLD CITY: REMAINDER OF RURAL MIGRATORY PRESSURE?

In Indian mega-cities, demographic and migratory factors play a prominent as well as dynamic role. Economic policies designed to tackle this demo-graphic development are of two kinds: those articulated in accordance to market mechanisms, which can be sustainable beyond state intervention and those that are solely based on direct public expenditures, which has long been the most favoured Indian development model. Any public policy that is not mediated by market mechanisms needs financial commitments by the public authorities that need not only to be re-conducted on a yearly basis but also have to grow proportionally with the population. The success of public services supplies thus depends on the public authorities' ability to first bridge the gap between the have and have-nots of a given population as well as keeping pace with the dynamics of population growth.

The same holds for programmes of poverty reduction.[4] We can briefly indicate that a large part of the immigrant population is poor and is initially consumers of public services at a higher level than the marginal wealth they are generating.[5] It is true that in a (by definition static) stabilised trend the economic function of the city is to utilise economies of scale which is the comparative advantage it has over rural economy.[6] This chapter retains this central hypothesis and does not subscribe to theories arguing for the 'pseudo-urbanization' of third-world cities (Choudhuri, 1999).[7] However, in a more dynamic (evolutionary) perspective, the poor sections of society are a particularly large share in the population growth. Thus, even though cities are from the national point of view the most efficient sites for providing services and infrastructures to the inhabitants of a country in the long run, the short-term ratio is initially reversed from the city's own perspective, when it first has to support the poor rural migrants. Evolving credible and sufficient

---

4 The population of Delhi has for example gone up from 8 to 13 million between 1991 and 2001. Even more spectacular, medium sized cities (around 500 000 inhabitants in 1991) of Vizakapatnam and Aurangabad have each respectively witnessed a decadal growth of 75 per cent and 87 per cent from 1981 to 1991 (NIUA, 1997: 13). If it is lower in relative terms in the mega-cities, yet in absolute terms the municipalities were overburdened to service this heavily growing population.

5 The city shall be developed at the long-run marginal cost, including infrastructures, for the new-comers. The new-comer produces in a short-term structure: the slum dweller earns just enough to reproduce his working-force. Only in the long run might he be able to improve his living and that of his family.

6 This capacity is obvious limited since there is a size and density beyond which the congestion costs become prohibitive if not counterbalanced by very high value activities. But such modelling is beyond the scope of the present article.

7 Choudhuri's thesis is that, given the importance of the migration for urban population growth, the high amount of new-comers is not manageable and, hence, migration does not lead to urban industrialization as was witnessed in western cities. Looking at the industrial history of cities like Madras, Bombay, or even Delhi, this thesis is debatable.

programmes to fight poverty and to rehabilitate the slums is thus one of the major issues in the management of big Indian cities. In terms of area, e.g. 45 per cent of Delhi is "sub-standard as far as establishment of minimum essential environment facilities is concerned" (Ali 1990: 15), which leads us to the next subchapter.

THE SPATIAL ORGANIZATION OF CITIES

Urban growth has also a purely geographical dimension: should one favour an extensive spatial growth or should one opt for the densification on a limited space? Concerning this fundamental question the mega-cities of India have followed quite different paths. Bombay has over a period of 100 years proceeded through cycles of extension-densification, but the agglo-eration has now reached its physical limits for further extension as well as densification on its peninsular space. Bombay is thus gearing towards a development through pure extension on the main land with the establishment of New Bombay and the administrative district of the city of Thane. Delhi, on the other hand, has developed mainly through geographical extension, especially after the inauguration of New Delhi in 1931. From 1957 onwards, the Delhi Development Authority (DDA) has been the guardian of this extension by adopting the principle of garden cities. Finally, Calcutta is administratively a bounded city and the Municipality of Calcutta administers in fact only 35 per cent of the total population of the agglomeration. It is, as a municipality, limited and surrounded.

Its centre and peripheral localities continue incessantly to receive a constant flow of migrants who weigh upon the infrastructures without any physical hope of organised housing. Therefore, it is technically the six neighbouring municipalities of the Calcutta Municipality which are actually growing. The Municipality of Calcutta saw its population multiplying by a factor of 3.5 from 1901 to 1981, as compared to a 6.5 factor for the other neighbouring municipalities. The weighted average gives a multiplication by six for the whole set (Chakraborty 1990: 7). As an agglomeration (and it is in this latter sense that we will speak about 'Calcutta', unless specified otherwise) it is extending geographically at a slow but steady pace.

On a regional scale the best synthetic indicator of this extension-densification phenomenon is the 'Index of Spread Effect'. It is defined as the ratio between the growth of cities in a 100 km hinterland around the reference city and the growth of the considered city itself. In 1981, this index was 2.76 for Delhi[8], but 6.52 and 6.66 respectively for Bombay and Calcutta (Chakraborty 1990: 9). Only one third of the population growth of Calcutta is explained by in-migrations, while two thirds arise from natural growth. This indicates an even stronger polarization around medium sized cities, and the relative attraction that Delhi presents, compared to the two other agglomerations. Thus, apart from providing service infrastructure, the city has also to regulate its geographical extension. It is this second function, the space-related one, which is really specific to 'urban planning' as a discipline. In fact, once the spatial choice is made, providing infrastructure is just technical and comes under technico-economic characters specific to each sector, whether that is located in an urban milieu or not. The central question of urban planning pertains therefore to the tools at the disposal of the administration for regulating space. This question is again linked to the territorial type of administration.

The Spatial and Economic Segmentation of Cities

The final question to be addressed in the first section is whether cities should be homogenous. This issue does not only refer to social factors and urban planning (geographical as well as physical), but has also implications for the efficiency of economic production. The question that arises here is whether, at the scale of Indian metropolitan cities, it is more beneficial to have evenly spread industrial and service areas or establish concentrated zones. The evenly spread presence of pockets of value creation ensures a distribution of infrastructures that confers unity to cities and enables the full achievement of economies of scale that is so pertinent to the urban organizational form. These pockets, when well distributed, can have a 'locomotive effect' on the local infrastructures. Such a set-up for the production and delivery of goods and services might optimise the flow of inputs and of the inner-city transport, thereby

8 A complementary index is the rate of densification of cities; in the case of Delhi, the area of the city is in fact growing faster than its population (with a 3.92 per cent of growth rate every 10 years for the population and 15.44 per cent for its area, according to Dupont, 2000: 230). At the same time, geographical extension comprises in part the creation of farm house areas, huge bungalows for the richest, while Old Delhi is getting extremely densified.

limiting congestion as well as energy costs by limiting the average transportation distances.

On the other hand, a minimal local density of units of value creation – of companies – can have positive effects of externalities and might lead to 'industrial districts'. Too much of dispersion should thus be avoided and a proactive functioning of municipal administration usually favours the implantation of such localised areas. In this context, the role of satellite-cities and the dialectic between centre and periphery with respect to industrial areas becomes the main issue. This is, once again, linked to the mode of organization of urban administration, in the sense that these dynamics of space interact with land prices, on which the administration in turn has leverage through acquisition policies. More specifically, it has a direct impact on the value of areas regularly supplied by public services, which is a rare resource in the context of third-world cities. The capability of the administration to control or direct these prices determines the effectiveness of its urban planning choices.

It is with the background of these four functional dimensions Indian mega-cities have to address (namely the organization of a techno-economic optimum, the dealing with the demographic dynamics, the organization of its space in terms of densification and extension, and the choices to be made with respect to the economic and spatial segmentation of cities), that we can now look at the administrative characterization of Indian mega-cities and their rising linkage to the private sphere. The impact of the latter will be analysed at length through the experience of the involvement of the civil society in Bangalore: the Bangalore Agenda Task Force (BATF).

Planning of Urban Services in India: Which Tools for Which Policies?

Delhi: An Exemplary City of the Problems of Urban India

The analysis of housing programmes and rehabilitation of slums gives a dynamic measurement of demography in Indian mega-cities. According to Ali (1990: 22) there were less than 13,000 families of 'squatters' in Delhi in 1951.[9] Only 22 years later, in 1973, this figure reached more than 98,000. The Master Plan of 1962, developed by the DDA, was the

---

[9] A regular approximate estimate is to account an average of five persons per family.

official document for planning the city and included the implementation of programmes aimed at reducing the number of squatters. Yet, these programmes were most of the times not really implemented, nor were preventive measures taken. Only during the Emergency from 1975-77 these policies were enforced, albeit at the cost of extreme violence. As a result, the number of squatter families stands at a reduced 20,000 in 1977. However, with the acceleration of demographic growth of the city these programmes became overburdened with the task and Delhi accounted for more than 113,000 families of squatters in 1983 (Ali 1990).[10] In terms of location, Ali (1990: 22) indicates that out of this total, 94,000 families are concentrated around the rehabilitation localities for former slum dwellers, and that from the survey he conducted, migrants declare that their geographical preferences are more directly influenced by the access to services than by proximity to jobs. Brutal force proved ineffective.

As argued before, the city finances these 'imported villages' in the short run. Given this framework, Delhi has since then changed its policy and proposes a way of rehabilitation that basically amounts to the displacement of slum populations to periphery which is sometimes not even serviced and has no housing. In this respect, one could argue that the city is conquering back its urban space for its 'legitimate' inhabitants and is hardly interested in integrating its new population that derives from both natural population growth as well as from the continuous migratory flow which totals together 473,000 new inhabitants per year during the last census period (1991-2001).

The housing policy that was promoted by the DDA within the legal framework of the "Slum Improvement and Clearance Act of 1956", is being substituted by a politics of eviction and erection of geographical barriers. The city state of Delhi is counting on the development of existing cities in the vicinity but also of more distant 'buffer' cities in order to stop the flow of migrants. This is done under the auspices of the National Capital Region Planning Board (created in 1985), that has greater territorial competence than the DDA. Yet, though the NCRPB's territorial skills are on a larger scale, integrated city planning is out of its purview and it focuses mainly on regional incentives to locate newly growing cities beyond the limits of present day Delhi. This is a dramatic change in perspective: Delhi is no longer trying to house people but rather tries to limit its expansion.

---

10 Out of which 53 per cent live on streets or even highways of the city, and 26 per cent occupy its parks.

This emergency policy sometimes takes a rather schizophrenic character when, e.g. the "Delhi 21" report (Government of Delhi 2001) recommended the development of the rich satellite city of Gurgaon at its periphery. Value added technology niches are situated in the State of Haryana. Thus, Delhi (the Municipalities as well as the State of Delhi) is depriving itself of a sure source of economic gain in favour of a neighbouring state. Furthermore, when the satellite city does not succeed in attracting sufficient industries, the costs for the metropolis turn out to be prohibitive. The development costs of New Bombay, for example, basically involving land development, rose to more than 42 billion rupees from 1970 to 1988. Yet, New Bombay has not succeeded until now in creating autonomous activities to a sufficient level such as limiting the daily commuting of its inhabitants to Bombay proper, or in creating an urban environment that is not subject to the pressure of illegal constructions. It is also not certain whether the relative slackening in the population growth of Greater Bombay has to be attributed more to New Bombay or to other peripheral cities like Thane. On the other hand, it is certain that since the population of New Bombay is mainly composed of middle classes, this new city –its socially secessionist aspect- has not substantially improved the situation of the poor in Bombay (Shaw 2001).

Municipal Management

Indian cities no longer supply services in either sufficient quantity or quality. For the national level, the National Institute of Urban Affairs (1997) states that only 82 per cent of the urban population has access to drinking water and those who have access might not get the quantity needed. Hardly 46 per cent has access to toilet and only 28 per cent are connected to a sewage network. Out of the around 300 urban centres which have a sewerage system, only 70 actually treat waste water and that too in only a limited manner. Finally, only 60 per cent of the garbage is collected by municipal services.[11]

With respect to the functional control of space one could argue that Indian urban planning has been a complete failure. If we take the case of Delhi, first deviations from the 1962 Master Plan in terms of illegal constructions were regularised by the state in 1969 and, again, in 1977. Despite these regularizations, illegal constructions are still increasing in

11 Further details on this for the four metropolises (Bombay, Calcutta, Delhi, Madras) is provided by Ruet, Saravanan and Zérah (2002).

many places. Jain (1990: 77) estimates that nearly 25 per cent of land comprising 45 per cent of the buildings does not conform to the Master Plan.

In the fight against poverty, a large number of the poor can neither save money to get their housing organised on their own nor can they pay a sufficient rent. A survey conducted by the National Institute of Urban Affairs (NIUA, 1988) shows that 50 per cent of the population in slums is living below poverty line (defined in India as the capacity to feed oneself on a certain set of eatables). It also shows that 80 per cent of the budget of the slum dwellers is only spent on food, transport, and clothing. Studies referring to the contrary of a saving capacity of this section of the population (Lall 1986, and 1990; Mehta and Mehta 1992) were considered controversial and subsequently invalidated (Kundu 1993). Ahmad (1982, quoted by Kundu, 1993: 34) already indicated that a survey carried out in Delhi found that 33 per cent of the individuals were "negative savers", and 25 per cent "non-savers".

Regarding efforts to control the price of land which is an essential dimension for the socially mixed development of cities and for the public pre-emption of areas of common interest, there has also been a complete failure. This problem arises less in the case of metropolises that are absolutely or relatively limited such as Bombay and Calcutta, but the failure is flagrant in the case of Delhi, although the city has vast stretches of land right in the middle of the Indo-Gangetic plain at its disposal. Soni (2000) gives details concerning the eviction of farmers from peripheral rural areas for the establishment of 'farm houses' which basically amounts to a "new colonialism of the urban rich". Hence, the peripheries of the cities are basically acquired by the same affluent classes that also occupy the high value centres of the cities, and these classes are not really interested in housing plans for other sections of society. The social contract is getting modified when the social segregation reaches larger geographical scales and the poor get scattered at the peripheries of the cities.[12]

With respect to means of municipal management one can ask, what institutional structures and tools do the cities have at their disposal? The management of a city so far is subjected to an extremely centralized public accounting system. This mode of organization can prove to be useful and efficient for the financing of new infrastructures. Yet, it seems

---

12 Soni (2000) describes the case of farm houses in South Delhi, while Auclair (1998) indicates the magnitude of real estate speculations in the urban and rural-urban areas of Madras.

to be highly inefficient for the maintenance and usage of infrastructure or services, which finally results in minimizing the possibilities of resource creation and thereby for further financing the setting up of a new infrastructure and services (Ruet 2001 and 2002). According to the relevant State Municipality Acts, a municipality is neither free to decide on its own to finance its infrastructures externally (e.g. by loans or contracts with the private sector), nor can it decide on the tariffs for its services and, thereby, increase its capacity to generate own resources. These prerogatives are left at the State level in the Indian political system.

A study by the Indian Institute of Public Administration (IIPA 1990) shows that, in order to overcome this administrative iron collar of annual budgets, municipalities engage in a perilous management which is rather obscure. In fact, for all cities have a population of more than 100,000 inhabitants, 80 per cent of the capital expenditures are deducted on the 'opening balance' and 'closing balance', which are normally meant to be simple capital adjustment accounts. The study reveals that at the end of the day, these accounts are made up from surpluses transferred from revenue account. Due to this fact, there is confusion between the creation of infra-structures on the one hand and their operation on the other; moreover, since the accounting balance remains highly positive at the end of the year, it means that municipalities stall their investments and hold them back.

In this way, 30 to 40 per cent of the budgets of cities lie dormant over the year. This is one of the reasons why the management of the network of public services is comparatively little more efficiently (or less inefficiently) carried out in structures that are autonomous of municipalities, such as sectarian 'Boards' or 'Development Authorities'.[13] Yet, in such a scenario two problems arise: in the case of technically specialized Boards the coordination with the other sectors reduces, thus creating potential problems for the coherence of planning. Moreover, in both the cases, a 'Board', just as a 'Development Authority', comes under the State Government, and not under the municipality.

In the present administrative set-up with hardly any administrative autonomy and a still weak decentralization of municipalities, any endeavour to seek technical, economic, and *in fine* social efficacy, leads to further dispossession of the municipalities. The opposite strategy,

---

13 The only notable exception is the city of Bombay. It manages its water supply within a municipal service. By fixing the price properly the supply is functioning reasonably well, even though technical efficacy is only average.

consisting of reinforcing and professionalizing the municipalities, faces political and bureaucratic resistance from the States. Big metropolises like Calcutta, find themselves today in the worst kind of scenario, with a combination of all above mentioned disadvantages. In Calcutta, investments are made by the Calcutta Municipal Development Authority (CMDA) and the management of the infrastructures is carried out by the various municipal corporations and municipalities. The municipalities and, in particular, the Corporation of the City of Calcutta itself, not only do not maintain these infrastructures but, moreover, they do not repay them to the CMDA, which, in turn, invests less and less. A part of the prerogatives of the CMDA, concerning small investments, was transferred in 1979 to municipalities (Datta 2000). However, they have to ask the CMDA for authorization and have hardly any encouragement to invest on their own initiative. This type of earlier centralization followed now by decentralization without any real coordination has only succeeded in creating more confusion and a mixture of these various types.

Metropolitan Management

The development and management of mega-cities goes even beyond their geographical and administrative frontiers. What are the organizational structures that would ensure urban planning at this level? Jain (1990: 10-11) shows that, apart from some isolated attempts that were not implemented rapidly enough in any case, like the Master Plan of Delhi in 1962, urban planning actually began in India only with the fourth Five Year Plan of 1969-74. First, this Five-Year plan proposes to "tackle the problem of metropolitan cities on a regional basis", secondly, to "promote development of smaller towns and new urban centres", thirdly, to "overhaul the organizational and financial set up of the local authorities for implementation of the urban development schemes", and finally, "to formulate an urban land policy" (Delhi Master Plan 1962: 10).

The last two aspects pertain to the organization of the city itself and could have been employed by the Government of India to set up a framework for decentralising the administrative management. In reality, confronted with the concern of the states not to give genuine powers to the cities, for example financial powers in terms of loans, these proposals remained dead letters. The Fourth Plan emphasises the first two aspects, and gives priority to the creation of metropolitan institutions, more directly under the control of state governments, without solving the issue of the autonomy of cities. Indian cities are not able to become autonomous and to impose a veritable mode of government at three levels (federal centre, states, and cities). In particular, on the financial level, according to Raj (1991), Indian cities cannot levy taxes and lack sufficiently elastic resources, as well as an efficient system of collecting these taxes. A figure which corroborates the absence of financial power of municipalities is that of per capita budget expenditure. Raj (1991) values the municipalities' budget at 10 rupees per inhabitant (around 0.2 Euro). The rest of public expenses are in fact concentrated within state administrations. Since the majority of MLAs is drawn from the more populated rural areas more money of the state budget is spent there.

Let us place India in a larger, Asian framework. Sivarama Krishnan and Green (1986) divide the case history of Asian metropolitan management into three stages: the first to do with sectoral projects, the second pertaining to multi-sectoral coordination (to which multi-municipal, or strictly metropolitan coordination should be added), and the last stage involving experiments, isolated, and non-existent in India, of 'metropolitan government'. Let us study the first two points in greater detail. The authors point out the technico-economic advantage of institutionalised specializing supply of services by autonomous organizations, and likewise pose the question with regard to intra-sectoral coordination (between authorities responsible for infrastructure and the municipalities that are operating them) as well as inter-sectoral coordination. The multi-sectoral answer that was developed all over Asia in the 1970's was that of establishing Development Authorities at the level of metropolises.

Thus, in Calcutta, Madras and Bombay, respectively, the CMDA in 1970, the MMDA in 1973, and the BMRDA in 1975 were created. These authorities have acquired tremendous technical and financial clout in the institutional interstice that has been left vacant by the deficient municipalities. They moved from an initial role of development authorities to the actual status of authorities endowed with administrative powers. These powers include planning, construction, financial control, coordination, and the supervision of infrastructures. The CMDA for example has absorbed the Calcutta Municipal Water Supply Authority, the Howrah[14] Improvement Trust, and several public works authorities. All this, however, has not led to any increase in their representation or

14 Twin municipality of Calcutta, on the other bank of the river.

political legitimacy within the city. With help of these Development Authorities the State Governments actually further encroach the space of legitimacy and little margins of actions that the cities could have, were they efficiently managed. In terms of the effective-ness of coordination, the conclusion of Sivarama Krishnan and Green is that in Asia in general the Development Authorities failed in filling the void between the development of infrastructure and the management thereof.

However, in the Indian context, one may, contrary to these authors, consider that, as long as the administrative functioning of municipalities remains blocked, the increasing role of these institutions is a pragmatic solution. In terms of political economy, Delhi's example, moreover, suggests that municipalities find an interest in the presence of these administrations, which are at lobbying quarters with the States, and develop neighbouring cities to serve as geographical buffers on the migratory paths from country-side to the city. Besides, in a fast growing demographic environment, one has to manage the new arrivals and give them a space in a uniform manner. In this context, a model of super-municipality ensuring geographical coordination is preferable to a model of governance based on a local government only, as it is promoted in certain 'urban laboratories', such as Johannesburg for example.

On the other hand, a reinforcement of administrative flexibility in the implementation of metropolitan master plans by municipalities is necessary. Let us take the example of the extension-densification dialectic. The urban master plans that are at present in force in Delhi, Madras, and partly in Bombay and Calcutta, incorporate strict rules of urban non-densification (size and height of buildings). At the same time, these rules are not followed where private development is concerned, and prove to be highly restrictive for the municipal administrations, whose hands are tied. What is of a more serious concern is the fact that the municipalities do not have the administrative leverage to modify these rules. This gives rise to a tendency to spatially extend cities at the expense of their densification. In reality, densification does take place, beyond the control of municipalities that finally have no say in the matter and are administratively incapable to regularize these types of situations. A great number of unofficial localities then find themselves in paradoxical administrative situations, sometimes for more than 30 years, where neither the municipality nor the administrations actually have the right, technically speaking, to furnish them with services.

If metropolitan areas can only create infrastructures and not develop an integrated management of network services, their reach is limited by this fact. Also their capacities to perform their second role of creating obstacles for rural immigrants by the establishment of city barriers do not seem sufficient in a long-term perspective. In fact, migration to mega-cities is taking place more and more from other urban areas in any case (cf. for Delhi, Dupont 2000: 236 who shows that 44 per cent of the migrants come from other cities). The last hurdle though not the least is the redistribution of financial resources. It is true that massive and rapid growth of urban population is a short-term expense for cities. However, they possess a stock of capital which enables them, proportionately, to create absolutely sufficient wealth in the long run. For example, Sivarama Krishnan and Green (1986) point out that during the fiscal year 1980-81 the total expenditure on infra-structure in the city of Bombay represented hardly 5 per cent equivalent of the added value of only the manufacturing sector. In reality, considerable redistributive transfers had taken place from urban areas towards rural areas. On the macro-economic level, the maintenance of a sufficient level of equipment and infrastructures in the urban areas ensures the permanence of a creation of added value in the cities, to sustain the redistributive transfers. By this fact, and given the current political economy of fiscal and budgetary transfers in the Indian Union, investments in the cities also benefit, indirectly, rural areas.

Therefore, on the metropolitan level, urban planning is not only limited to simple urban land policy, but must be based on the results of experiences on the effectiveness of the implementation of socio-economic programmes for the target populations. The planning and the administration of urban development must therefore be integrated and coordinated on the informational plane. This type of administration has to be carried out at two levels: one of them certainly is integrated, at the metropolitan level (planning), and the second at the ward level (where, in closer interaction with users, the local officers can handle the operation and maintenance of the infrastructure and services). Also, the cities of the metropolis must have administrative flexibility with respect to the definition, execution and adaptation of these plans and their own administrative practices. As far as the existing public services management is concerned, it does not require geographical de-concentration as much as a veritable administrative and financial decentralization. From this point of view, it is not so much a 're-engineering' of the size of municipalities which is important, but rather to empowering the local officers to-pilot at a decentralized level project-oriented funding as well as income generating schemes.

Private Sector and Municipal Management: The Experience of the Bangalore Agenda Task Force

If we now take stock of the examples dealt with in the previous section, we have a better idea of what is lacking in the governance of Indian metropolistan cities for addressing the four issues a city has to deal with, namely developing techno-economic production and exchange modes; doing so in a dynamic demographic context; and tackling the issues of space and socio-economic composition. In this respect, we have indeed seen that Indian metropolitan cities have partly failed in the sectoral management of these issues, either because of coordination problems or because of an unrealistic centrally planned approach. But they have also not been successful in the framework of metropolitan management because of an incomplete transfer of power to the metropolitan development authorities, but also and most likely because the social complexity of Indian metropolitan cities calls for other complementary sources of information, decision-making, and implementation: in short, it calls for more diversified sources of governance.

Both the recent literature as well as practical experiments around the world, explore public-private-partnerships. Under this terminology one usually discovers set-ups that are either tilted towards the public side or to the private side, and which most of the time hardly involve a partnership dimension. We will deal here with a positive exception, namely the Bangalore Agenda Task Force (BATF), calling it positive in the sense that it is a (rare) attempt to really build a (long term) partnership, instead of just being based on a mere contract. Let us see with the help of the unique example of Bangalore (which, though it may not be technically considered as a 'mega-city', already prepares itself to become one and envisions a steep growth in population, income, size and relevance) how this model can enhance the overall urban governance. That is, how it can more efficiently address the economic, demographic, space and scale aspects of a city as discussed above.

The BATF which was established in 2000 by a Karnataka Government Order is certainly one of the currently most comprehensive urban experiments attempted in India in terms of a public-private partnership. Its aim is to bring together the expression of 'citizen demands', of administration's needs and prospects, as well as of private offers. Let us describe its mandate and its achievements, and analyse the space it occupies within the above sketched characterization of Indian cities.

BATF: Mandate, Practices, and Achievements so far

The BATF mandate is to:

- Work with city stakeholders to achieve the vision of role model city by 2001.
- Identify measures to upgrade city infrastructure & systems.
- Secure greater involvement of citizens, corporates, and industry for enhancing the quality of life.
- Providing intellectual and professional skills to ensure sustainability.
- Create an efficient, effective and pro-active administrative framework (BATF 2002)

Its competence zone is the Greater Bangalore Metropolitan area, which covers 225 sq. km, a population of 5.7 million or of 6.8 million if one adds its seasonal or 'floating' population. Its terms of reference are to improve both the internal capacities and resource generation of Bangalore's administrations as well as to better coordinate them through technical committees. From this very broad definition of its scope, the first mission given by the Government of Karnataka to the BATF was to evolve a practical 'agenda'. This was achieved through agreements with the various administrative stakeholders. By early 2001, they jointly decided to promote a "citizen-centred approach", mainly based on identification and prioritization of citizen concerns established through public meetings. In addition, the BATF attempted several public-private partnership models and facilitated pilot projects.

The BATF is composed of: (i) a Chairman (the Managing Director of the private software company, Infosys), (ii) the Commissioner of BMP, acting as Member Secretary, (iii) Nominated Members, and (iv) representatives of "Civic Stakeholders" (the authorities and administrations in charge of Bangalore). The latter are: the Bangalore Mahanagara Palike (that is, the Municipal Corporation), the Bangalore Police, the Bangalore Development Authority (BDA), the Bangalore Metropolitan Transport Corporation, the Bangalore Water Supply and Sewerage Board, the Bangalore Telecom, and finally the Karnataka Power Transmission Corporation Ltd. As can be seen from this list most of the stakeholders either belong to the State Government's sphere or have to report to it through their Board. Beyond the chairman and the member secretary, one can find a senior consultant, two academics formerly involved in policy-making, three businessmen, the former President of the Karnataka Chamber of Commerce & Industry, the Principal Secretary to the Government of Karnataka, Urban Development, an architect, and the head of a large NGO.

The BATF actually tries to involve, through its members, various networks of the civil society: that is the corporate sector and in a limited way also the social sector. The presence of all major public authorities and boards again illustrates the decisive power of the State Government in urban matters. The legitimacy of the BATF is in that way both in-built from its inception as well as subjected to the discretionary power of the State. The model is definitely public-private in the sense that (i) the members come from both backgrounds, while (ii) the BATF derives its legitimacy from the public and its money from the private.

Keeping in view long-term projects (infrastructure and roads, water and waste management, and slum improvements), the BATF has actually started its work with legal and administrative reforms, and small-scale projects. The ultimate goal is the privatization of civic services, but the BATF has until now worked out only accountancy rules, tax collection improvement, and coordination measures between administrations, that is, from within the public sphere. The BATF describes its key achievements for the year 2000-01, as following:

- Improvement of municipal collection, transportation, disposal and processing of solid waste, by favouring door to door collection initiatives, in collaboration with NGOs (in 50 per cent of the city).
- Of important financial impact, a Self-Assessment Scheme (SAS) has been put in place for property tax collection. According to BATF (2002), 'the initiative involved rationalization of both assessment and collection of tax, as well as empowering the citizen to self-assess tax. BATF was responsible for conceptualising the communication strategy as well as delivery mechanisms and computerization of data'.
- In the field of public transportation, it has worked in association with the BMTC. On logistics, a bus traffic management plan has evolved (BMTC has hence brought down cancellations of its buses from 15 per cent to 4.1 per cent). The BATF has contributed in the design of bus route maps and timetables and in the designing of a Build, Operate and Transfer (BOT) model for bus shelters.

Other fields have been addressed too; for instance, on public sanitation, the BATF has conducted studies for the private provision of public toilets.

The BATF is also a part of a whole network of other sectoral initiatives. Although the BATF has not been directly involved in this as of now, the Bangalore Water Supply and Sewerage Board (BWSSB) has achieved substantial results on its own. They are especially visible in the replacement of defective water meters, and in the detection of illegal connections (respective figures: 10,000 for defective meters and 36,770 for illegal connections in 2001; BATF, 2002). It has undertaken public-private partner-ships for recycling, treatment and distribution of water. The BATF is involved in completing such technical or commercial measures, to put them in a larger framework. Indeed, BWSSB, along with the BATF, has initiated several programmes on grievance redressal, greater access for payments (opening hours, modes of payment), easy availability of new water connections and a Citizen's Charter. For all these, the BATF functions as an organiser of meetings and as a facilitator both in terms of coordination and of input provider. Indeed, the administrative structure of most of the public sector undertakings usually prevents them from hiring specialists for limited periods only, which they would require for specific projects, revision of procedures, or evolving of new schemes. Similarly, providing some specific equipment may take substantial amount of time in an administrative frame-work. When both are easily available within private companies that are stakeholders in the BATF, it serves as a provider of expertise as well.

If one examines its various projects, the BATF simultaneously follows a three-fold strategy. In the short run, it basically supports administrations by helping them to fund some new activities and generate internal resources. But, in a sense, it also takes over some of the attributes that should fall under those of the respective administrations it works with, but which have never been tackled by them (like provisions of maps, timetables). And finally, in many ways, it prepares their very downsizing in the long run, since it works towards the privatization of public services. The long-term object-tive is the outsourcing of many of the municipal activities. The initial strengthening of the municipal administration is thus only a transitory strategy.

STRUCTURAL IMPACT OF BATF

Beyond its role as a facilitator, the BATF also promotes structural changes within the administrative sphere, especially on its structural ability to address new or citizen-centred demands. Let us study the impact on the BMP (Bangalore Municipal Corporation), the key administration with which the BATF has worked so far.

It has been argued that geographical de-concentration, and to a greater extent decentralization, is needed in Indian administrations. In the Municipal Corporation, a zonal system of administration has been adopted in order to separate implementation and policy-making as well as in order to build-up responsibilities and accountability. This system has also been transmitted to other administrations, like in the neighbouring city of Chennai (Madras), it has been implemented by the Water Board.

But most important are the tax and accountancy reforms. For achieving long-term sustainability, the BATF has been able to reform the tax system. A lot of tax evasion used to take place due to corruption. Property tax was based on surface and used to be evaluated by the BMP agents. The Self-Assessment Scheme puts the responsibility of this evaluation on the tax-payers themselves. The BATF has evolved clear guidelines for this. Tax-payers bear the legal responsibility in case of misreporting and wrong declaration. Results of this scheme need to be further assessed, but a BATF member has declared in an interview that for the current year 2002-03 the improvement in tax assessment could be in the range of 40 per cent (source: interviews). Although tax collection is not the main revenue source for municipal expenditures, it certainly constitutes an important part of the budget for the Corporations on which they have the highest control. The tax reform is, therefore, definitely even if limited step towards the administrative and financial autonomy of the Municipal Corporation.

Structurally, the BATF is now introducing the Fund Based Accounting System (FBAS) to the BMP. Accountancy rules in public administrations in India generally do not follow double-entry rules, or simple rules on declaration of dues and receivables, write-off of pending receivables unlikely to be recovered, subsidies, and so on. Hence, the Corporations can not use their account statements as a basis for decision-making since they are a mere reporting system. The clarification of fund sources, designing of project-specific accounts, normalization of rules, however, can in turn become a major tool for the evaluation of projects' cost-efficiency or for transparency in public policies. Well used, it can even serve the purpose of supporting the cities' claims for further autonomy. Indeed, municipal corporations could demonstrate their ability to manage funds, while giving the guarantee that their expenses can be properly traced. The effects of the implementation of such a scheme will certainly not be neutral in the coming years and, given the generality of the scheme, should be relevant for all Indian cities.

TACKLING ALL THE ISSUES AND REPRESENTING THE URBAN POOR?

Can experiments like the BATF tackle all the problems and issues raised in the previous sections? Can such arrangements be of some help for the urban poor? The answer is certainly 'no' for the first question, and might only indirectly be 'yes' for the second one, depending on other elements. A set-up like the BATF is a useful tool but it certainly requires complementary measures.

Metropolitan decongestion or size-control will still require higher level institutions. Furthermore, a proper three-tier government system is still to be evolved, and an experiment like the BATF is, in this regard, only a facilitator between the State level and a debilitated Municipal level. The latter may use the BATF to evolve its powers, but it is a difficult path in a national context that remains largely unaffected. In this respect, political stakes are higher than any public-private partnership. Arrangements like the BATF contribute undoubtedly to the professionalization of bureaucrats and to an improvement in inter-sectoral coordination, but, beyond a point, they do not improve the political power of cities *vis-à-vis* the State, nor give them means sound enough in their demographic context.

As far as the poor are concerned, but also, more generally, as far as citizen representation is concerned, an initial survey, prior to the actual start of the BATF projects, had led to the identification of citizen concerns. However, surveys in India usually focus on the middle and upper classes. This bias might be balanced by involving NGOs but it will definitely not vanish. However, compared to the way public action is organized in India so far, which hardly takes citizen matters into consideration, this approach already constitutes a progress. For instance, the BATF has so far been quite inactive on slums. In interviews, slum improvement has been referred to as too problematic and involving too many stakeholders with political connections. Which is true in any case, but which shows the limits of any public-private partnership in policy-making at the city level. The real impact of experiments like BATF could be as follows: If successful on their agenda, the private sector (either the private corporate sphere or civil society) will gradually take over many responsibilities. In that perspective, public administrations could concentrate more on the remaining issues like land planning and equal access to services. However, the question that could not be addressed here for lack of space remains, will the administration be keen on integrating the immigrants?

CONCLUSION

Indian mega-cities seem to be damned with their demography. They focus on numbers. No sooner is any scheme implemented than people ask for it again. Under these circumstances, many give up. Municipalities call for private enterprise and initiative in a non-structured way, or hope that distant cities will take the burden, and lament on their limited financial capacities. By doing so, they neglect to propose 'marketable' schemes, that would be partly financed through its beneficiaries, or to address real administrative reform.

These are the symptoms of urban non-management in India. An experience such as the BATF in Bangalore has immense merits: to show what a public-private partnership can do, including in the administrative sphere itself, which should not be neglected but needs to be strengthened as a priority also for private sector engagement. It as well shows the limits of the experiment itself and the limits of the whole genre of private-public partnerships as such. In other words, it reasonably shows what is available and feasible from a well-structured public-private partnership. This experiment is young and will needs further studies in coming years, for it aims at inspiring other cities across India.

The reform of the municipal administration remains at the core of the problem of tackling urbanization. Articulating it with the civil society is part of the way ahead. Public-private partnerships remain tools; though they are not a panacea and should not be mistaken for such, they are quite sufficient to address some specific issues. These, interestingly, go beyond technical matters and can address structural effects. These might even in time inspire the politicians.

REFERENCES

Ahmad, A., *Saving Behaviour in a Metropolitan Economy*, New Delhi: Atlantic, 1982.

Ali, Sabir, *Slums within Slums*, New Delhi: Har-Anand Publications, 1990.

Auclair, Christine, *Ville à vendre: voie libérale et privatisation du secteur de l'habitat à Chennai*, Institut français de Pondichéry, 1998

Bairoch, Paul, *Taille des villes, conditions de vie et développement économique*, Paris: éditions de l'EHESS, 1977.

BATF 2002, at : www.blrforward.org

Bonnet, Jacques, 'Globalisation, Métropolisation. L'effet de la taille sur les activités des grandes villes du monde', in *Les très grandes villes du Monde*, sous la direction de Elisabeth Dorier-Apprill, Paris : Editions du Temps, 2000, pp. 49-76.

Chakraborty, Satyesh, 'The growth of Calcutta in the twentieth century', in Sukanta Chaudhuri et al., ed., *Calcutta: The living city*, vol. II, Delhi etc.: Oxford University Press, 1990, pp. 1-14.

Chatterjee, Mondip, 'Town planning in Calcutta: Past, present and future, in Sukanta Chaudhuri et al., eds., *Calcutta: The living city*, vol. II, Delhi etc.: Oxford University Press, 1990, pp. 133-47.

Choudhuri, Keshab, 'Facets of the third world urban problematic', in *Urban Management* (1999), pp. 25-39.

Datta, Prabhat, 'Urban governance in West Bengal: evolution of institutional instrumentalities', in *Urban Management* (2000), pp. 13-36.

Dorier-Apprill, Elisabeth, 'Problèmes et défis de la gestion urbaine dans les très grandes villes du Sud', in *Les très grandes villes du Monde*, dir. by E. Dorier-Apprill, Paris : Editions du Temps, 2000, pp. 83-104.

Dupont, Véronique, 'Spatial and demographic growth of Delhi since 1947 and the main migration flows', in *idem*, Emma Tarlo, Denis Vidal, eds., *Delhi: Urban Space and Human Destinies*, Delhi: Manohar, 2000, pp. 229-40.

Government of Delhi, *Delhi 21*, Delhi Urban Environment and Infrastructure Improvement Project, New Delhi 2001.

Hancock, Calire and Hiernaux, Daniel, 'Mexico: vers un aménagement à l'échelle métropolitaine', in *Gouverner les Métropoles*, sous la direction de Marcel Rousset-Deschamps, Villes en parallèle no. 30-31, Université de Paris X, Nanterre 2000, pp. 297-320.

IIPA: *Municipal Finance Management in India*, report directed by Abhijit Datta, Centre for Urban Studies, New Delhi 1990.

Jain, A. K., *The Making of a Metropolis*, New Delhi: National Book Organisation, 1990.

Kundu, Amitabh, *In the Name of the Urban Poor: access to basic amenities*, New Delhi: Sage Publications, 1993.

Lall, Vinay, 'Family budgets and savings of informal sector households', paper presented at the International Workshop on mobilisation of informal sector savings, 8-12 December, Society for Development Studies, New Delhi,1986.

Lall, Vinay, *Saving Mobilisation – Methods, Norms and Policies*, New Delhi: Society for Development Studies, 1990.

Mehta, Meera and Mehta, Dinesh, 'Privatisation of municipal services', in *Urban India*, 22 (1992).

NIUA, *Who the poor are? What they do? Where they live?*, New Delhi: National Institute for Urban Affairs, 1988.

NIUA, *Financing urban infrastructure in India*, Research study no. 59, xvi, New Delhi: National Institute for Urban Affairs, 1997.

Raj, Mulkh, *Municipal Finance: a city management issue*, Nagarlok, vol. XXIII, no. 4, New Delhi: National Institute of Urban Affairs, 1991.

Rousseau, Marie-Paule, *La productivité des grandes villes*, Collection Villes, Paris: Anthropos, Economica, 1991.

Ruet, Joël, Winners and losers of the SEB reform, Occasional Paper no. 1, New Delhi: Centre de Sciences Humaines, 2001.

Ruet, Joël, Saravanan, V.S, and Zérah, Marie-Hélène, *The water and sanitation scenario in Indian Metropolitan cities: Resources and Management in Delhi, Calcutta, Chennai, Mumbai*, Occasional Paper no. 5, New Delhi: Centre de Sciences Humaines, 2002.

Shaw, Annapurna, 'Satellite town development in Asia: the case of new Bombay, 27-50', in Issues in *Urban Development. A case of Navi Mumbai*, R.N Sharma and K. Sita, eds., Jaipur: Rawat Publishers, 2001.

Sivaram Krishnan, K.C. and Green, Leslie:, *Metropolitan Management: the Asian experience*, EDI series in Economic Development, publié pour le Economic Development Institute et la Banque Mondiale, Oxford University Press,1986.

Soni, Anita, 'Urban conquest of outer Delhi : beneficiaries, intermediaries, and victims', in V. Dupont, E. Tarlo and D. Vidal, eds., *Delhi: Urban Space and Human Destinies*, Delhi: Manohar, 2000, pp. 75-96.

3

WOMEN AND URBAN DEVELOPMENT: DO THEY MAKE A DIFFERENCE? A CASE STUDY OF THE MUNICIPAL CORPORATION OF DELHI

STEPHANIE TAWA LAMA-REWAL

One of the boldest features of the decentralization policy adopted by the Indian Parliament through the 73rd and 74th Constitutional Amendment Acts (CAAs), in 1992, is the provision that one third of seats in elected assemblies at the local level shall be reserved for women.[1] The decentralization policy indeed aims at further democratizing the Indian polity: the representation of local interests is favoured both by the constitutional status provided to local self-government institutions, who are invested with a new, more important role in the management of public life, and by the presence in these institutions of social categories hitherto largely excluded from the electoral process.

This policy embodies with some anticipation the current consensus about the importance of gender in governance, a consensus repeatedly expressed at the international level through United Nations Conferences such as that of Beijing in 1995, or Istanbul in 1996. It is now agreed that the sexual division of labour and the reproductive role socially ascribed to women result, in all societies, in the fact that women have specific needs and can make specific contributions regarding the management of public affairs. Indeed, in the fourth UN Conference on Women in Beijing, the unequal distribution of political power between sexes was identified as one of the twelve critical domains for the improvement of women's condition. Again, the Istanbul Declaration on Human Settle-

---

1 The two CAAs also provide reserved seats for Scheduled Castes and Scheduled Tribes in proportion of their respective demographic weight in a given constituency and make it possible for seats to be reserved for Other Backward Classes as well.

ments pledged to "promote decentralization through democratic local authorities [and to] enhance the role of women" (The Habitat Agenda). The most prevalent form taken by this concern about gender in governance is a larger presence of women in government. In the 1990s, an increasing number of countries in South America, Europe and Asia, have experimented with policies of quotas for women in the political field, through various modalities and at different levels of political life.

One can notice two general trends concerning this phenomenon. Firstly, despite the diversity of national contexts in terms of women's condition and political systems, the debate about the objectives of an increased political representation of women involves everywhere the same three arguments (Hernes 1982). One, the massive presence of women, who form half the population, in elected assemblies, is a must for democracies to be truly representative. Two, women possess specific talents, qualities and/or values (whether those be due to nature and/or to the socialization process), which constitute a potential resource for political life, a resource that must be tapped through women's increased participation in the decision-making process. Three, women have specific needs, concerns, and interests and these can be adequately addressed only if women are better represented in political assemblies.[2]

Secondly, local politics appear to be a privileged site for experiments with women's quotas, albeit not always for good reasons. The case for promoting women's participation in the management of local affairs often rests on a series of assumptions that reinforce gender stereotypes, such as the concrete nature of issues dealt with by local representatives, the part-time character of their job, and its closeness to social work. In the Indian case, one can only be struck by the contrast between the reaction to women's reservations at the local level and at the state and national level: while the former were simply not discussed in the course of the parliamentary debates surrounding the decentralization policy, the latter provoked a violent debate and seem very far from becoming a reality.[3] In retrospect, it appears that reservations for women at the local

---

2 The French debate on parity (i.e. the legal obligation for political parties to give 50 per cent of their tickets to women) is an exception here; given the strong republican-universalistic tradition of the French polity, the argument that women constitute an interest group was carefully avoided by the defenders of parity, who emphasized rather the gender justice argument.

3 The Women's Reservation Bill proposes to extend the reservation of one third of seats for women to the states' assemblies and to the Lok Sabha. The Bill was

level resulted (i) from a convergence of interests between Rajiv Gandhi, who wanted to reform the State and modernize political life, and the Indian women's movement, who had been advocating an increased presence of women in political life (notwithstanding disagreements as to the desirable means and sites thereof) since the mid-seventies; (ii) from a political context (the destruction of the Babri Masjid) that diverted attention from the 73rd and 74th Amendments when they were submitted to vote, in December 1992; and (iii) from a sheer lack of interest: the stakes of participation in local self-government were not considered as very important by Members of Parliament.

WHY SHOULD WOMEN MAKE A DIFFERENCE?

The decentralization policy is now entering the second phase of its implementation (most local bodies are in their second term), thus allowing for a first assessment. This chapter presents part of the findings of a survey conducted in 2001-03 about the specific impact of women's reservations in Indian mega cities;[4] I will focus here on the performance of women councillors in terms of urban development in the Municipal Corporation of Delhi. This implies addressing two out of the three universal arguments supporting women's quotas mentioned above: quotas as a way to change the style of politics (i.e. women as a resource), and quotas as a tool to change its content (i.e. women as an interest group). However, for the sake of feasibility, these two ideas are being reformulated here through a very open question: what does the newly massive presence of women change in the work done by urban local bodies? Such a question postulates that women as such *may* make a difference, but one must distinguish the three conceptions of women on which this idea can be based:

---

introduced in the Lok Sabha for the first time in 1996, but has been facing a violent opposition since then, so much so that it has not reached the discussion stage so far.

4 The objective of this research project, jointly conducted by the Indian Institute of Social Sciences and the French Centre de Sciences Humaines, is to assess the impact of the reservation for women of one third of seats in the municipal corporations of Delhi, Mumbai, Chennai and Kolkata. The project has a triple focus: a) the socio-political profile of women representatives, b) their performance as councillors; and c) their behaviour in the electoral process. The survey covers the first municipal term under the 74th CAA in Delhi and Chennai, and the 2nd term in Mumbai and Kolkata.

1. Women as newcomers in the political field. Such a concept is value neutral, but takes into account the fact that prior to the implementation of reservations, women constituted only a very small proportion of councillors (from 0 per cent in Calcutta in 1952 and 1965, to 9 per cent in Bombay in 1968 and 1978),[5] which logically implies that post-1993 most women councillors are elected for the first time ;

2. Women as persons are generally more concerned than men with issues such as health, education, slum improvement. This concept tends to essentialize women, insofar as it relies on a series of associations which assimilate women to mothers, i.e. people primarily concerned with the well-being of children.

3. Women as representatives of women's interests, in other words, women councillors as a women's lobby in urban local bodies. This concept implies that women as such share a number of interests, and that only women can represent, that is, defend, these interests. It goes much beyond conception 2 insofar as it postulates the existence of a group consciousness among women.

This third concept has in fact grounded the demand for women's political representation for a long time. Indeed the argument that women's presence in elected assemblies is needed for women's interests to be taken care of was expressed in India as early as in the 1930s, when Indian women were demanding universal franchise. Following the 1932 Round Table, an Indian Franchise Committee was formed and placed under the leadership of Lord Lothian. In charge of defining a new enlargement of franchise, this Committee submitted to a number of groups and individuals throughout British India a questionnaire about extending the right to vote to new social categories, such as workers, Depressed Classes and women. Kumudini Basu, who was then councillor in the Municipal Corporation of Calcutta, wrote to the Lothian Committee, in 1935:

---

5 Source: *Year Books* of both Corporations.

> In the whole world women's suffrage was looked for, was the object of a struggle, and was obtained for a precise principle and objective. It was observed after a long experience that many vital questions concerning the social, domestic and public welfare, affecting the home and women's sphere of activity, were completely neglected and often fought against by male legislators. It was then that women came in and got the franchise. Therefore I think that women candidates should depend first and foremost on women voters on whose behalf they contest… (Oriental and India Office Collection, British Library, Q/IDC/12).

This utilitarian argument, that women's presence in political institutions is needed for women's interests to be represented, is a perennial one. It was heard many times in the debate evoked in India by the introduction in Parliament, in 1996, of the Women's Reservation Bill that proposes to extend the principle of reserved seats for women to state assemblies and to Parliament as well. Thus, the political scientist Neera Chandhoke wrote,

> It is not as if women have not occupied seats in the legislatures; it is simply that they have not addressed the questions which pertain to the problems of women adequately, seriously or with sensitivity. Had they done so, we would not have had all these missing women or illiteracy or hunger or homelessness or violence both at home and at the work place. The demand behind the Women's Reservation Bill is that women representatives should address the specific problems of their constituency (*The Hindu*, 06/12/2000).

What, then, is the impact, if any, of the new, large presence of women in the Municipal Corporation of Delhi (MCD), in terms of urban development? I will try to answer this question by addressing in turn three sub-questions:

1. What are the issues that figure prominently on the agenda of women councillors, what are their priorities, what do they want to achieve in terms of urban development? This first point will focus on the attitudes and perceptions of women councillors.

2. What issues have women councillors raised in House meetings, in the course of these five years (1997-2002 in Delhi)?

3. What were the means available to women councillors to achieve their objectives? In other words, I will focus here on the resources and difficulties met by women representatives.

The data used to answer these questions are of three types: (i) a detailed questionnaire submitted to all women councillors (46, i.e. 100 per cent) and to a sample of men councillors (24, i.e. 27 per cent) of the MCD; (ii) two focus group discussions with women members of the MCD, with urban development as the main theme of discussion; and (iii) the proceedings of the House meetings of the MCD between 1997 and 2002. While the first two sources indicate what women councillors think, the third one tells us what issues they actually raise in the monthly meetings of the MCD, which are an important route for actions to be taken.

What are Women Councillors' Priorities?

Urban development is obviously a critical domain in India, given the increasing proportion of city dwellers among the population and the inability of existing urban infrastructures (roads, housing, water, electricity, sewerage and drainage) to meet the needs of this growing population. Urban local bodies are generally in charge of the maintenance of basic infrastructures and services (such as public health and primary education), but they conduct development work *per se* only in the case of 'slum development', which consists in relocating slum dwellers and/or improving *jhuggi-jhompris*, by providing them with basic civic amenities. Indeed, women councillors lament the misunderstanding of voters who often expect them to initiate development activities, whereas their role is merely one of supervising the maintenance of civic amenities and occasionally to lend support, in a personal capacity, to government programmes such as for instance immunization drives. Yet the very diversity of those infrastructures which need to be maintained means that choices must be made, priorities must be set. What, then, are women councillors' priorities?

All women councillors present their priorities as a given, spontaneously emerging in each ward. In posh colonies, they say, parking and roads can be major problems, while in poorer, more crowded areas schools, water and electric supply are the main concerns. When asked what were the four main problems they had to face in their ward, the answers of women councillors are actually very close to those of men: while women mention (in this order) water, sewerage, electric supply and schools as their major concerns, men mention sewerage, drainage, water, and electric supply.

When asked whether they have done anything concerning women's issues, women councillors answer unanimously that they don't want to discriminate between male and female voters' problems, that the problems they deal with concern both men and women. The range of answers to the question "What are the main problems faced by women in your ward?" is actually an impressive one, covering issues such as marital disputes, alcoholism, unemployment, illiteracy, lack of public toilets, of schools, of maternity homes, of health care centres, of parks, paucity of civic amenities (water, sewerage and drainage, solid waste disposal), improper distribution of widow pensions and maternity benefits, and police harassment. But when it comes to actions actually taken on behalf of women, female councillors only mention that they have occasionally helped women confronted with domestic violence by reporting the case to the police, or directing the victim to a women's organization. To the question whether they have ever joined forces with other women councillors, across party lines, on issues concerning women, they reply that they are loyal to their party only, and that such a situation simply cannot arise.

Two important notions emerge from the above series of statements. Firstly, women representatives always present their work as an answer to some external demand. When asked why they decided to contest elections, women cite first the party, then the fact that their ward became reserved for women, then the people's demand. On the same subject, men too mention the party first, but the second most frequent answer is their "desire to serve the people". Beyond clichés, these divergences reveal two things. One, the fact that some of the female councillors were actually candidates "by proxy": they campaigned on behalf of a male relative, often the sitting councillor, rendered ineligible by the newly reserved status of "his" ward. Two, women councillors, unlike men, avoid asserting any personal will. Personal will, one presumes, is likely to be perceived as personal ambition, a feature usually not valued in women. In other words, presenting themselves as devoted, self-effacing servants of the people and /or the party might help female councillors solving the role conflict they find themselves in, as women and councillors.

Secondly, this reluctance to assert any individual dimension to their work means that women councillors are most unlikely to express a gender consciousness. Moreover, their position on the question of women's issues shows that even though they are aware of the range of women's problems, when it comes to action they consider and concern themselves only with private problems (family disputes, domestic violence), and in a purely personal capacity. For women councillors, obviously, the personal is not political.

ISSUES RAISED BY WOMEN COUNCILLORS

The proceedings of the House meetings are an important source of information for two reasons. Firstly, to raise an issue in the House meeting is one of the routes open to councillors to advance their projects, even if this is not the only one. Secondly, the detailed, systematic record of these meetings (which are part of the Corporation's archive) offers a unique view of what are the issues discussed, who is most active on these issues, and how these two facts evolve over time. The basic assumption here is that (i) the nature of issues that women councillors raise, and (ii) the frequency with which women councillors participate in the meetings, are two indicators of their effectiveness as representatives of women at large.

House meetings take place once a month, theoretically with the presence of all councillors; a quorum is there to ensure that even though many councillors are usually absent, the decisions taken reflect the will of the majority. Most of these meetings are actually devoted to "official business", that is, the agenda pre-set by the Commissioner who is the executive authority of the Corporation. Thus a number of administrative decisions, recommended by the relevant municipal committee, but really taken by the Commissioner, are then formally approved by the House. The practice specific to Delhi is that a pair of councillors (from the ruling party) usually presents together the agenda, and in about half the meetings this pair is composed of one man and one woman councillor (in one case only it was composed of two women councillors).

I will focus here on issues pertaining to the 'non-official business', since they reflect the individual concerns of councillors (even though most often issues are raised by a group of councillors, usually from the same party).

Table 1. The object and frequency of women and men councillors' interventions in House meetings from 1997 to 2002

Issues Raised	**Women 1997-98**	**Men 1997-98**	**Women 1999**	**Men 1999**
1	Budget	Budget	Budget	Budget
2	Personnel management	Personnel management	Personnel management	Personnel management
3	Public health	Taxes and revenue	Water and sanitation	Functioning of MCD
4	Water and sanitation	Functioning of MCD	Public health	Public health
Total number of interventions	65	333	98	341
Issues Raised	**Women 2000**	**Men 2000**	**Women 2001-02**	**Men 2001-2**
1	Budget	Budget	Budget	Budget
2	Unauthorized colonies	Unauthorized colonies	Functioning of MCD	Functioning of MCD
3	Functioning of MCD	Personnel management	Personnel management	Personnel management
4	Stray animals	Water and sanitation	Gardens	Public health
Total number of interventions	188	359	238	1011

Source: Archives of the Municipal Corporation of Delhi

Table 1 shows that the most important issue discussed in House meetings is the budget of the Corporation. Indeed, budget discussions take up the whole time of two meetings each year. The second most frequently raised issue is the same for men and women councillors: it is personnel management (that is, questions relating to the appointment, pay scale, disciplinary action, transfer etc.) of the thousands of employees of the MCD (here one sees that the MCD functions more like an administration than like a legislative assembly). Then come questions relating to unauthorized colonies, and lastly those concerning what I call the 'functioning' of the MCD (its rules and regulations, its relations with the state and the Centre etc.) As far as issues of the last two ranks are concerned, one can notice that public health and water and sanitation are themes of interest to both male and female councillors. The only difference is that taxes and revenues of the MCD are an important issue for men only, while stray animals and gardens are an important issue for women only.

As far as the frequency of councillors' interventions is concerned, Table 1 shows a dramatic (roughly threefold) increase in the number of both men and women's interventions over the years, which tends to validate the statement (see below) that councillors need time to learn how to use the means available to them to advance their projects – House meetings being one of them. Moreover, if one takes the total number of interventions over five years, it appears that men councillors intervene 3.5 times more often than women councillors, which is roughly proportional to the numerical importance of both groups in the MCD.

Now, a more detailed analysis of the issues raised shows that women councillors never raise issues that might be construed as especially interesting to women, such as the construction and management of maternity homes and child welfare centres, or the setting up of an agreement with a women's organization for crèches to be established within primary schools; these issues are invariably raised by male councillors only. Thus it appears that women councillors' place in debates concerning non-official business is proportional to their numbers, even though they do need a few years to use this one opportunity to forward their concerns; and that they intervene mostly on the same issues as men, but never on issues which might be thought of as women's issues.

Several reasons come to mind to explain such an observation. Firstly, as women councillors themselves put it, "in the House only the party matters". Thus the fact that the issues most frequently raised are often the same for women and men councillors might be due to the observance of party discipline on these issues. Secondly, women councillors do not consider themselves as the representatives of women; they thus avoid intervening on women's issues, which they consider sectarian, even though some of them do not hesitate to intervene on issues concerning specifically the scheduled castes; which shows that gender as a political category is not as legitimate as caste in today's India's polity (Tawa Lama-Rewal 2001).

DIFFICULTIES AND RESOURCES OF WOMEN COUNCILLORS

The first and foremost handicap mentioned by all women councillors is the lack of those competences which are necessary to fulfil their functions. This handicap stems, firstly, from the fact that 98 per cent of women representatives were elected for the first time in 1997, as against 71 per cent of men (this high figure is explained by the fact that the MCD was actually revived in 1997, after having been superseded for eight years). Newcomers, both men and women, obviously lack in experience. But this initial handicap is compounded by several factors:

- the absence of any handover by the previous councillor, lamented by women elected in 2002 ;
- the absence of information on what it is possible to do (for instance, the availability and conditions of urban development programmes);
- The absence of any coordination with State agencies supposed to collaborate with the Corporation, such as the Delhi Development Authority etc.;
- The absence of any training offered by the Corporation or by any other agency, to teach newly elected councillors at least the technical aspect of their new job. Indeed the technical dimension of a councillors' activity in a context marked by the utter absence of transparency explains why a generally high level of education is not sufficient to be a competent councillor: the fact that 82 per cent of women councillors are at least matriculate (the largest group being that of graduates: 48 per cent), just like 83 per cent of men councillors, does not guarantee that they will be able to fulfil efficiently their new functions.

The problem of the lack of acquaintance with the basics of the councillors' function, women representatives say, is such that they need on an average two years to master the rules of the game since the Corporation staff is generally not helpful to teach them the way things work; in other words, 40 per cent of their term is more or less wasted.

How, then, do newly elected women finally learn their job? Most women councillors mention their "personal competence" first, that is, their capacity to be aware of local problems and to learn hands on. They then mention their party colleagues, and lastly their family, especially when they have a relative with some political experience (only 2 per cent of women councillors do not have any relative in politics, as opposed to 79 per cent of men). Indeed, the party seems to be an important training resource, either in the form of a senior party cadre acting as a mentor of the newly elected woman (53.5 per cent of women councillors declare that they have a mentor, as against 46 per cent of men councillors), or through discussions with party colleagues.

But the party can also prove to be a problem in itself. Indeed many women councillors hint at rivalries within the party; they say that reservations have evoked strong resentment among men of their own party. Sexual harassment of the younger lot of women councillors by party colleagues asking for 'favours' is also denounced. Those women councillors who participated in our focus group discussion even recommended that there should be a minimum age set for women candidates so as to avoid sexual harassment.

Male discrimination is also there, they say, when fellow corporators or officials of the Corporation refuse to lend them help. Thus while men representatives mention fellow councillors as the second most important resource to learn their job, just after their personal competence and before party colleagues, women councillors do not mention fellow councillors at all.

What about material difficulties? Money is usually not a problem, women councillors say (they get 65 lakhs rupees per year for the maintenance of their ward), even tough it was mentioned that actually getting funds released is easier for those councillors who belong to the ruling party. The problem is really how to learn the procedures through which the available money can be made use of: how to proceed with tenders, how to deal with contractors etc. The one material problem they face is the lack of facilities such as a secretary or even a typewriter, which compels them to rely, here again, on their family members to play the role of personal assistant etc.

The above list of difficulties faced by women councillors suggests two things. Firstly, while most of the problems they mention apply to male newcomers as well, it appears that the gendered norms of behaviour, as well as male discrimination, make it more difficult for women to use some of the informal training resources open to men.

Secondly, a series of resources also emerge from the list of difficulties mentioned. Education is obviously not a sufficient resource. The party is both a resource and a problem. It provides (informal) training but it is also the site of resentment and harassment. Yet on the whole, the party seems to be more of a help than of a hindrance. Thus, when asked where help comes from, women councillors mention the local MLA, when he/she belongs to the same party. They also declare that having a position in one of the 12 Wards committees (which requires party support since each committee is formed by election), gives one more room to manœuvre. Lastly, they insist that the party is the ultimate resource in times of crisis. During one of the focus group discussions, women councillors declared that "serious councillors" could also benefit from support of the people, and occasionally of government officials.

Age appears to constitute a resource, insofar as (i) it "protects" women from sexual harassment, and (ii) it means that women are more or less freed from domestic responsibilities. To the question "Who takes care of the house and children while you work?" women answered first "myself", then "servants", then only "family members", which suggests that most of them have a limited access to the all important time resource. Indeed, the largest age group among women (as well as men) councillors is that of people being between 41 and 50 years old, i.e. an age at which Indian women's children are generally grown ups.[6]

Finally, family appears as a very important resource. Family provides both informal training and working facilities, that is, intellectual and material support. Moreover, husbands especially are a much needed escort when women have to go out at night for their work. As such, husbands provide both security and respectability, two precious goods in politics.[7]

---

6 One can however note that on the whole the proportion of people below 41 is higher among women than among men councillors.

7 Only 7 per cent of women councillors are single.

WOMEN AS NEWCOMERS, AS MOTHERS AND/OR AS FEMINISTS

The above evidence is obviously limited in three ways. One, it needs to be completed by a more external assessment, based on interviews with partners of women councillors (such as officials of the Corporation and of agencies of urban development, residents' welfare associations, party cadres etc.), on their performance, as opposed to that of men. Two, it leaves aside consequences of the sex of representatives which are elusive but real nevertheless, such as the fact that many female voters may find it less daunting to go and meet their local councillor when she's a woman. Three, it focuses on the very first phase of the implementation of reservations; thus only a follow-up study will allow to distinguish, in the present situation, what owes to the unprepared state of actors such as political parties and women's organizations in front of this new policy, and what is more structurally linked to the nature of urban politics and to the status of women in India.

Yet all the data mentioned here point to one undeniable fact: women councillors *do not want* to make a difference. They want to be seen as competent councillors and reliable party members, that is, they want to be considered as good as their male councillors colleagues. Women councillors are certainly no feminists: even though they are aware of women's problems, they strongly refute any suggestion that as women they might want to defend women's interests more particularly.

What about women councillors as mothers? One observes a marginal difference in the councillors' statement of their priorities, and in the type of issues they raise most frequently during House meetings: women councillors are more concerned than men with schools and gardens, i.e. problems concerning children, and their concern about stray animals may also stem from the danger that these animals represent for people, including children, in the streets. Moreover the words used by women councillors to describe their work strongly evoke the image of dutiful mothers. To compare an electoral constituency to a large household has long been a favourite figure of speech of women politicians, for this metaphor helps them solve the role conflict they find themselves in, as women and as politicians.

But women councillors make a difference, above all, as newcomers, because there are more newcomers among women than among male councillors, and because these women are newcomers in a more radical sense than most of men. The sudden implementation of reservations has indeed led a number of women with very little, if any, political experience, to occupy an elected position. In such a context, the issue of training is a crucial one, but we have seen that in the absence of any formal training, the access of women to informal training resources, such as fellow (male) councillors, Corporation (male) officials and even (male) party colleagues is limited both by the gendered norms of behaviour and by sexual harassment. The one resource available to most women councillors is their family, that is, usually, their husband, father or father-in-law, who are not likely to encourage them to push women's issues forward. The difference made by women, then, is mostly a negative one: women are less assertive, more constrained; they have a more limited access to resources such as training, time and money, than men councillors.

CONCLUSION

One can derive two types of conclusion from these findings. At a pragmatic level, a recommendation emerges from the above series of observations: training sessions must urgently be planned and conducted in all the urban local bodies that have been elected for the second time under the 74th CAA.[8] Indeed, three important potential sources of training must be tapped simultaneously since all three pertain to a meaningful political representation of women at the local level. Some training must be conducted within the Corporation, and by Corporation officials, to acquaint newly elected councillors with the technical and legal aspects of their new functions. Some training should be conducted within and by political parties, to clarify the political dimension of the councillors' work. The women's wings of political parties could here play a facilitating role for women councillors, which would give themselves more importance within the party. Lastly autonomous women's organizations could play a very important role in sensitizing female voters and female candidates to the importance of women's issues as urban development issues, before and during the electoral campaign; they could also mobilize women voters to form support groups for those women

---

8 There is a dramatic contrast here between panchayati raj institutions, to which much attention has been paid ever since 1993 both by academics and by NGOs, and urban local bodies.

councillors who commit themselves to solving at least one problem of importance for the women of their ward.

At a more reflexive level, the above findings show that the presence of women in urban local bodies does not guarantee a gender perspective in urban governance. As Beall put it,

> [...] a gender perspective refers not to a constituency or the participants but to the practice of urban policy-making, planning, management and organisation itself. It refers to recognition of and responsiveness to the different roles and responsibilities of women and men in human settlements and the social relations between them (Beall 1996: 3).

Notwithstanding the fact that urban governance goes beyond the action of urban local bodies, this statement highlights the fact that electoral quotas have a much more limited impact than what is suggested by the debate surrounding them. The reservation of seats does ensure (i) a greater representativity, in terms of sex, of elected bodies, and (ii) a fairer distribution of the symbolic and material benefits of elective office to the individuals concerned. Moreover, one can reasonably expect reservations to have a larger symbolic impact, insofar as they help popularize the idea that politics is not an exclusively male field. But the available evidence refutes the idea that a change in the sex of representatives automatically produces a change in the style and content of politics. The "agenda for change" (Kaushik 1995) attached to the claim for women's quotas must be, can only be, carried by feminists, i.e. by women's rights activists, whether female or male. This implies that feminist organizations confront their own reluctance to engage with electoral politics, and address the major issue of the unacceptability of feminism in mainstream political discourse.

REFERENCES

Bacchi, Carol Lee, *The Politics of Affirmative Action: Women, Equality and Category Politics*, London: Sage, 1996.

Beall, Jo, 'Urban Governance: Why Gender Matters', www.undp.org/gender/resources/mono1.html.

Hernes, Helga, *The State – Women No Entrance?,* Oslo: Universitatforlaget, 1982.

Kaushik, Susheela, *Panchayati Raj in Action. Challenges to Women's Roles*, New Delhi: Friedrich Ebert Stiftung, 1995.

Menon, Nivedita, ed., *Gender and Politics in India. Themes in Politics*, Delhi: Oxford University Press, 1999.

Nanivadekar, Medha, *Empowering Women: Assessing the Policy of Reservations in Local Bodies – A Report*, Mumbai: Rambhau Mhalgi Prabodhini, 1997.

Phillips, Anne, 'Feminism and the Attractions of the Local', in King Desmond and Gerry Stoker, eds., Rethinking Local Democracy, New York: Macmillan, 1996, pp. 111-129.

Pinto, Marina, *Metropolitan City Governance in India*, New Delhi: Sage, 2000.

Sharma, Kumud, 'Power VS. Representation. Feminist Dilemmas, Ambivalent State and the Debate on Reservation for Women in India', in *Occasional Paper* no. 28, Delhi: Centre for Women's Development Studies, 1998.

Tawa Lama-Rewal, Stéphanie, 'Fluctuating, Ambivalent Legitimacy of Gender as a Political Category', *Economic and Political Weekly*, April 28, 2001, pp. 1435-1440.

____, *Women in the Calcutta Municipal Corporation: A Study in the Context of the Debate on the Women's Reservation Bill*, CSH Occasional Paper no. 2, Delhi, 2001.

4

SLUM AS ACHIEVEMENT: GOVERNMENTALITY AND THE AGENCY OF SLUM DWELLERS

MARTIN FUCHS

MARGINALIZATION AND INCORPORATION: THE IN-BETWEEN-STATE OF A SLUM

Slums seem to be the quintessence of marginality, the sum and substance of social and economic uprootedness.[1] Two reasons are usually forwarded for this: First, migration to a slum is seen to occur under compulsion or economic pressure. Second, those residing in a slum are seen as not, or only peripherally integrated into the modern economic (industrial), social (civic) and administrative structures as well as society's social welfare institutions. It has to be added that slums provide residential space and often industrial space too, for such groups especially who have been the victims of *other* kinds of discrimination before, or who represent weaker or so-called minority sections of the population. Slums constitute the spaces where such groups specially cluster when coming to the cities. In the case of Dharavi, the Mumbai (Bombay) slum referred to here, the feeling of marginalization is further accentuated by its (earlier) reputation for being a center of crime.

When it started to develop as a slum, the area of Dharavi actually lay outside the municipal boundaries of Bombay, at the outskirts of the city, and parts of the area Dharavi was later to occupy were used as dumping

---

1 In dictionary definitions the term *slum* refers to a thickly populated usually urban area where conditions of life are squalid and wretched, inhabited by the very poor and marked by social disorganization. Etymologically of unknown origin the term seems to have come up first in England in the early decades of the nineteenth century.

ground by the Bombay Municipality. Many of today's residents of Dharavi are well aware of this original symbolic as well as topographical position of their area, an icon of the non-social, the quintessential waste, but also of the inversion in its later history when Dharavi literally moved into the very center of modern Bombay. This applies not only to its geographical placement but is also mirrored, in a skewed way, in the economy of the slum.

How to describe a slum, or this slum? I take the two-pronged picture just referred to as expression of the inconclusive state slum dwellers, as I know them, find themselves in. The slum represents two oppositional processes, a process of stigmatization and demarcation, pushing the slum and the slum dwellers *outside* society or to its margins, and, at the same time, a movement *into* society, into the very heart of society, into what is considered the mainstream. This dichotomy is not just a reflection of the distinction between an insider's and an outsider's view, rather both aspects are being reproduced *together* in the process of social interaction.

What one finds is a combination or *co*-incidence of marginalization and incorporation (inclusion) – a *conditio* which cannot be captured by the currently popular notion of ambivalence but must be described as simultaneity of two divergent inclinations, refracting one another reciprocally. They contravene yet do not revoke each other. This state of things may also point at larger social processes: the intermission of the formal operational structures of society and state, a kind of "normalization" or annexation of the non-organized, the *informal* modes of life, which still, however, elude the normalizing social science. The failure of all attempts to grasp the social reality of a slum with statistical instruments, the impossibility of enumeration, seems characteristic. But this is only an indicator for the extremely fluctuating and multifarious character of a social reality which mobilizes several registers at a time and thus is difficult to handle (even for NGOs). Even qualitative research, using participatory and hermeneutic methods, seems to be unable to comprehend this reality fully and to represent it in simple terms.

What I propose here, and for which I can only give a sketch, is part of a multi-perspectival approach which is aware of its own fragmentary and incomplete character, and remains sceptical about its own findings (Hansen 2001: 14-15). As point of departure I will take the quest of slum dwellers – the majority of whom are Muslims and Dalits - who in more than one way search for a new placement. To understand this struggle demands to bracket a commonly used concept like "identity". It also requires to handle the term "community" with caution as it covers a range of heterogeneous constellations. The focus will rather be on the local, contextual understanding of dimensions of collective sociality and the relevant practices. I will, furthermore, point out the cultural dimension of a slum, as depicted by Dharavi. Against what every outsider would expect, life in Dharavi shows numerous forms of cultural articulation, in some respect one might even say it is being overdetermined by culture. The interesting question is how the various cultural formations are getting integrated. I will finally indicate that on this background issues like 'governance', 'public space' and 'civil society' have to be repositioned and reformulated. The article provides a preliminary overview over certain results of my fieldwork whose evaluation is in progress.

DHARAVI, THE PLACE: A SOCIO-ECONOMIC SKETCH

Today Dharavi is supposed to accommodate approximately 9 lakhs (0.9 million) people. The area covers about 2 to 2.2 sq. km, depending on where exactly one draws the boundary line. In 2000/2001 according to rough estimates 25 to 30 per cent of Dharavi's residents were claimed to be Muslims, the remaining majority being Dalits and members of other marginalized groups like 'denotified tribes' and some other low caste groups not, or no longer, considered Scheduled Castes or ex-untouchables (like the Nadars from Tamil Nadu).[2]

Modern Dharavi started to develop from 1887 onwards, when the first tannery and the first mosque were established on the south side of the Mahim Creek, using some small islands and a large part of marshy land which was stepwise filled in with garbage, disposed there by the munici-

---

2 Figures vary extremely. Dharavi does not constitute a separate administrative unit nor a census ward of its own. The official census figures are particularly unreliable. My data are based on estimates of several NGOs working in Dharavi. Marie-Caroline Saglio-Yatzimirsky (2002: 47) puts the number of residents at 7 lakhs without mentioning a date, a survey undertaken by the National Slum Dwellers Federation (NSDF) put it in 1987 at 530,000.
An attempt at a regional and/or linguistic breakdown of the population figures seems also futile. The survey conducted by the NSDF in 1987 in Dharavi does not mirror the situation I found 13 years later. It seems especially difficult to compute the number of Muslims who fled during and after the 1992/93 pogroms, some of whom returned later, and the intensified immigration of people from eastern Uttar Pradesh and Bihar in the 1990s, from both Chamar and Muslim background. Deepak Mehta and Roma Chatterji (2001), following Jim Masselos, put the figure of Muslims in Dharavi at 40 per cent.

pality, and with material which the new settlers, the migrants, brought to reclaim land.[3] After Independence, when there still existed some open space, the inaccessible spots around the mangrove trees were used for illegal distillation of liquor, which sold all over the town, providing the chance for some people to make a fortune. For long there was no infrastructure in this newly developing area, a few water taps only, under somebody's control who took money from everyone, and, of course, no toilets.

A prolonged struggle with state and municipal agencies, picking up in the late 1970s, has led to deep changes of living conditions. Now one finds water pipes all over the place, about 80 latrine buildings, electricity and telephone connections, and the open drains, too, have meanwhile been covered to a large extent. This struggle became possible because of new forms of organization, citizens' movements or 'community based organizations' (CBOs) kicked off with the help of newly emerging NGOs and human rights groups. Considering the main demand for residential rights, this struggle by 1983 led to official acknowledgement of security of land tenure for a period of 30 years. This ended the attempts at demolition of hutments in the central parts of Dharavi which its inhabitants had been facing for decades. The decision made it now feasible for the residents to invest into permanent or semi-permanent structures. The latest development is the construction of high rise buildings of five to ten or even more storeys, which provide a standard space and outfit for each family (225 sq. ft per unit). In principle, residents who can prove to have stayed in Dharavi since 1995 can move into these houses.[4]

Economically, the move towards deeper integration into society is reflected in Dharavi's thriving small scale (and a few medium-sized) industries. Its main products are basically made by hand in congested workshops, under deleterious conditions, often on a sub-contracting basis. Dharavi is known India-wide for its leather goods, meant for the national market as well as export. The local outlets are shops in marble with air-conditioning, put up at the outskirts of the slum. Similarly,

---

3 A village of Koli fishermen was the only habitation which had existed here before.

4 In case funds are made available, every 'cooperative society' (formerly 'chawl', i.e. in this case a residential neighborhood which has been registered) has to take an individual decision for construction of a high rise building which implies to give up the current houses or hutments. At least 70 per cent of the co-op society members have to support the decision.

textiles are produced for Indian as well as overseas markets. Dharavi Kumbharwada is known for its pottery. Dharavi also generates bakery products, *papad*, various kinds of savory and other food items for the city's customers and even for the larger hotels. Mumbai's largest *mithai* (sweets) producing company is placed at the outskirts of Dharavi, and one international company also produces wound sutures. Most food stuffs are produced without any control of hygienic conditions. Although the larger tanneries have since the 1980s more or less been closed down because of environmental hazards, a lot of polluting and dangerous processing is still going on, including recycling (e.g. of used engine oil). Labour laws, of course, nowhere apply and many people work something like 80 hours per week. Most (some say 90 per cent) of the production in Dharavi is unlicensed, and thus also not covered by economic statistics.[5]

It is being claimed that about two thirds of Dharavi's workforce work in Dharavi proper. Of those who are employed outside the slum, mostly as semi-skilled laborers, many work in large establishments in the city, like port trust, railways, municipality, earlier also the textile mills. Especially the *safai* workers, engaged in the cleaning of buildings, toilets, roads and sewers, have to work under abominable conditions which contravene all health regulations and which continue to be a mark of stigmatization. A number of them, however, has secure employment in the public sector. The drive for education among Dharavi residents has not only increased the number of graduates but also gained some people better qualified positions and jobs.

The story of Dharavi can be partially presented as a success story, in the field of production, in employment and education, as well as living conditions. But this brings also the danger of gentrification. How precarious the living conditions even for Dharavi residents have become is clear when one looks at social processes in detail. It is an open question, for example, how large the turnover of the population triggered off by the shift to multistorey buildings will be. The new residential setup will not only affect personal interactions, it also means that at least part of Dharavi's residents will lose out again, having to give up the flats they cannot afford (contribution to construction costs,

---

5 For vivid descriptions of working conditions and individual life histories in Dharavi see Sharma 2000. An estimate of the *Times of India* (cited in Masselos 1996: 122) sets the daily turnover in Dharavi before the 1992/93 riots at Rs. 75 lakhs (approx. $375,000 at rates of that time).

maintenance costs) and having to shift once more, to another slum. Some observers envision already the move of (lower) middle class employees of companies being set up in the new commercial zones neighboring Dharavi, into the new "high rise buildings" of Dharavi.

DHARAVI, THE PLACE: SOCIO-CULTURAL COORDINATES

The description of Dharavi given so far can be nothing more than a rough indication of what is usually considered the 'objective' side of things. Such view does not give any clear idea, however, about who the people actually are who live in Dharavi, who energize the area, make it into a 'place'. It is startling how little still slum studies are concerned with the traditions and perspectives of the local residents they talk about, perspectives which go beyond mere economics and the question of civil 'amenities'. Slum studies tend to 'flatten' the life of the people they are concerned with.[6]

To gain an understanding of the socio-cultural coordinates of life in a slum like Dharavi requires an anthropological, hermeneutic perspective. However, a place like Dharavi cannot be studied like the places of earlier anthropological interest: villages or even towns of an older type. Dharavi is too unwieldy and dynamic, and of course too densely populated a ground, spilling over in many directions, as it is itself implicated in many routes and courses of action which have their anchorage elsewhere. The people of Dharavi originate from all corners of India (with the partial exception of the east and north-east), representing most of India's larger and some of its smaller languages, maintaining links of different kind and intensity with their regions of origin and following a wide range of religious denominations, traditions, practices and/or beliefs.[7] Various

---

6 In the case of Dharavi, at least, I can point to two other recent studies which try to overcome the generalist approach in their own ways: while Kalpana Sharma, journalist of the leading English daily *The Hindu*, uses a case study approach to depict strategies of survival, various occupational milieus and the infrastructural development of Dharavi (see fn. 5), Marie-Caroline Saglio-Yatzimirsky's, in a study just released (2002), pays special attention to Dharavi's leather workers. Moreover, Deepak Mehta and Roma Chatterji (2001) look at the 1992/93 riots and pogroms in Dharavi and at the later attempts at rehabilitation through the narratives of Dharavi residents.

7 The word "religion" in its English form is widely used in Dharavi. Even if the term "religion" originally did not suit all Indian forms of sacral practice, today it seems

politicial ideologies and political parties, regional (like the Tamilian) as well as national ones, so-called secular as well as communalist ones, and also Dalit parties are operative, as are symbols of pan-Indian public culture and marks of the metropolitan, national and international economies. All this, yet, should not be set in a static frame.

The composition of the population keeps changing through new influxes, out-migration as well as political interference and commotion. Dharavi shares this with many other places in today's world. However, Dharavi has many facets we would not be able to do justice to if we declare ourselves satisfied with references to global developments. The intercultural complexity of Dharavi has as much to do with the traditional multiplicity of Indian culture *and* with the particular outlook of the people of Dharavi as it has to do with global processes and new patterns of urbanization. The different social factors and developments refract as well as overdetermine each other, so that it does not make sense to differentiate between dimensions of alleged 'tradition' and alleged 'modernity': I approach the constellation as *one* modal configuration of modernity. My own research has centered on Dalits in a broad sense of the term, including 'denotified tribes', Christians and Dalit Muslims. What I present in the following is primarily based on interviews and interactions with people from roughly 25 'communities' with whom I had exchanges and who had never before lived in this combination. The exact number here too depends on how one draws the boundary lines.

One can suggest several feasible perspectives of anthropological analysis of Dharavi which supplement each other. A usual procedure of identification would be to classify the population according to language, religion and filiative community or *jati*. However, even under the spell of modern identity politics, neither the boundaries of communities are always fully clear nor are all communities structured along the same lines. Among Dalits in Dharavi one finds communities with a powerful governing body which tries to exert strict control over its members' conduct of life; others have *sanghas* (corporations) and trusts which are supposed to represent the perspectives and common interests of the community members vis-à-vis the larger public or the state; and there are still other communities which exist in name only and do without a formal institutional body, building on informal networks with certain points at which different strands come together. Of course marriage still

---

the only common comparative denominator of the different "creeds" and ritual practices.

largely conforms to boundaries between filiative communities, but even here one finds increasing numbers, varying in degree in the different communities, of inter-caste or 'love' marriages. When it comes to the more general level of social categorization, like 'Dalit' or 'Hindu', things become even more vague.

There are very distinct ways of being 'Dalit' or 'Hindu', these categories being very differently appropriated and understood. While many set 'Dalit' against 'Hindu', others include Dalits within the Hindu category. Some who are being classified as either 'Dalit' or 'Hindu' do not accept these categories, at least not in all situations. All this indicates the scope of groups and individuals in appropriating and negotiating social meanings and shows the significance of contextual references. It also shows that 'identities', if we use the term at all, can only be seen as *projects*, never as something achieved or arrived at, something 'in hand' (Wagner: 2002). This explains actually why identity has to be constructed or, rather, enforced ever anew. Local residents generally prefer the term *samaj*, which is less specific (meaning in a broad way 'society', 'community', 'association'), to *jati* or other terms.

But even that specification is not sufficient, especially when we turn to religion which has a strong presence all over Dharavi. Limiting myself to the low caste groups, one comes across Hinduism of the folk kind as well as Brahminical or Brahminized deities[8] and new devotionalist Hinduistic movements, but at the same time also oppositional anti-hierarchical movements of Hinduism of the *sant bhakti*-type; furthermore, there are various Christian denominations having evolved from British as well as Portuguese and even German missionary work; some Dalit Muslims; and Buddhism of the Ambedkarite type devised by Dalits themselves. The majority of non-Dalits in Dharavi are Muslims, and there are also a few Jains (who run jewellery shops and act as money lenders). The significant point is that these different religious affiliations are not just identity markers, as it may seem in modern discourse, nor are they to be understood as just and only continuations of the past, the traditional left-over within a slowly modernizing society. Religion is a general *idiom* of modern Indian society as well as politics, which may evoke the image of one broad cultural texture but actually hides very different uses and perspectives.

---

[8] Like Lakshmi, Shankar (Shiva), Ganpati (Ganesh), etc. The worship (*puja*) of all deities is done by Dalits themselves, who are also the ones who have erected the temples. One significant exception is mentioned later in the paper.

What the term 'religion' refers to in the case of Dharavi is a multi-layered field of world-articulation.[9] Religions represent ontologies as they may provide support, relief or transcendental liberation. But in conversations with Dalits residing in Dharavi two other aspects stick out which find expression in religious idioms or are associated with religion: the dimensions of a social ethics and of a social imaginary.[10] The social imaginary, again, has two points of focus: the world of immediacy and the future outlines of society in general. Many Dalits invest the respective religions, preferably universalistic religions, with concepts of egalitarianism and justice, autonomy and self-determination, self-help and solidarity, unity but also segregation, taking as reference either the individual *or* the community. They derive versions of an ethical counter-perspective which informs some of their actions and *at the same time* is used for evaluating and censuring the actions of their social adversaries.

It is important, however, that religious orientations do only partially correlate with boundaries of filiative communities or *jatis*. Religions among Dalits, embedded in a larger (cultural) engagement with the (social) world, in some way resemble floating signifiers, being considered *optional alternatives* with which, between which and through which social actors negotiate their way. What particularly marks the various Dalit engagements with religion in Dharavi, and what allows one to understand the significance of and attitude towards religion in the case of Dalits, is the continuous struggle of individuals and groups for social, *inter*subjective recognition, the quest for a new and better and secure *place in* society and a change *of* society. This often takes the form of a demand for coexistence and equality of all traditions, cultures and communities within civil society. The particular intercultural attitude outlined here entails that many Dalits do not just adapt to the social mainstream or the dominant values, as the notion of 'Sanskritization' suggested, but try to keep or define a perspective of their own and give religion their own shape. Their approach implies the search for new and decent modes of conduct of oneself as also of others.[11]

---

9 I take cultures as different ways of articulating the world. This notion is based on ideas of Maurice Merleau-Ponty as reformulated for social theory by Johann Arnason (see Fuchs 2000).

10 For translation as a social mode of communication and integration see below.

11 The intercultural model of non-exclusive options with respect to universalistic religions as found among Dalits is developed in Fuchs: 2002; see also Fuchs forthcoming. On the Dalit struggle for recognition and the struggle over difference

It thus would be superficial to see the different cultural registers coagulate into clearly separated clusters of traits. *Samaj* or *jati* only partially correlates with a particular cultural attribute. While few *jatis* only come with more than one language, the "internal" diversity of *jatis* or *samajs* is certainly growing with respect to religion, social imaginaries, ideology, and, of course, occupation and economic standing. Those who have opted for a religion other than that of the majority of the earlier filiative community may constitute a group or an association of their own. In other cases, however, the *jati* identity may so much prevail that religious differentiation, even if well ingrained, remains of secondary importance. A factor of some relevance here is the depth of translocal community linkages.

NODAL POINTS OF TRANSLATION AND INTEGRATION: INTERCULTURAL SOCIALITY

One has to think of the cultural as a field of intersecting discourses and practices and should not be content with simplistic notions of pluralism or multiculturalism. It is not so much the differences between communities and between parochial cultures only which are important but the actions and actors mediating between and across differences and their symbolic expressions. It seems requisite for the social sciences to pay larger attention to questions of interculturality or - to use a term recently coined - of '*trans*difference' (Breinig and Lösch: 2002), i.e. to the interlinkages and accommodations but also the conflicts between different socio-cultural registers and layers. It seems even more important to do this by focussing on the level of social interaction.

'Communities' as well as individuals can be seen to represent nodal points at which different routes of action and discourse, different cultural registers meet and associate with self-images and modes of self-organization. Individuals as well as communities have to activate and connect the different registers. It is here, in the last instance, that the various socio-cultural dimensions are being brought into relation with each other. This results, if we only take Dharavi, in a variety of combinations. I briefly describe a few, first 'communal' ones, afterwards individual ones:

---

in general, esp. the religious and cultural dimensions, the tensions and paradoxes see Fuchs 1999.

1. The first example concerns a community engaged in *safai* work which follows a strict Hindu course and, moreover, has opted for affiliation with Hindutva forces, with the BJP and the RSS. This group sticks to its older stigmatising and defiling occupation, which gives them if not a monopoly but at least a strong hold over this secure source of income. They have a strong community tradition with a *panchayat* system that tries to enforce strict control over community members. While also worshipping other Hindu deities, the community has its own separate deity introduced less than a century ago – Valmiki, the mythical author of the *Ramayana* - and has its own understanding of the *Ramayana* as well as Rama, who is not seen as a god. They thus oppose the interpretation of the Hindutva forces in certain respects. Still, affiliation to Hinduism and to the Hindutva forces represents this community's mode of seeking entrance into larger society and recognition by higher caste Hindus. The question to be discussed would be: does the social imaginary of emancipation and equality, not as candidly voiced in this case as compared to others but still clearly audible, conflict with the ideology of segregation and ethnic distinction or can the way the ideology of Hindutva is being appropriated here be seen as a legitimate translation of the social imaginary?

2. The second case concerns an approach found among members of Dalit communities who pursue a line of *communal* equality, i.e. equality which does not only relate to individuals but asks for equality of and among communities, *samajs* or *jatis*.[12] This is connected with a demand for the right to continue with one's own older religious practices, which can for example include animal sacrifices, and at the same time a claim for the right to participate in other, including vegetarian, Brahmanical rituals for the prominent, pan-Indian deities. This position is openly anti-hierarchical and anti-Brahmanical and seeks admission to larger society as well as recognition as equal members via recognition of one's distinctness, one's low-caste traditions. One achievement in this case has been the employment of Brahmin priests in two of the community's temples for doing the *puja* one had for decades done oneself, without necessarily respecting

12 In the sense of Rajeev Bhargava's (1998) 'communitarian egalitarianism' (to be distinguished clearly from 'egalitarian communalism').

the exclusion from the *sanctum sanctorum* the Brahmin priests tries to enforce. Organisationally, the community follows a *sangha* model with an elected committee at its head while manifesting deep ideological fissures.

3. The third option concerns a model which I term 'communal universality'. In this case the religion chosen, Buddhism, centres on a universalist message (liberty, equality, solidarity, justice, compassion) which repudiates all particularist claims of Hinduism. Not only is the introduction, or reintroduction of this religion undertaken by Dalits on their own, who this way try to take the lead and even the authority of a universalist religion, but the everyday religious life is also organised by the lay people themselves. This community builds on a loosely knit network of local centres of communication and prayer (*viharas*) run by its members, but does without any formal institutional structure as met with in the two earlier cases. It does not act as a (communal) body. Although identity as Dalits, and even *jati* identity, continues to be resolutely claimed, the strong ethical premise of this group builds on the assumption of individual equality. Intervention into larger society is grounded in a message which in principle is meant for everyone, Dalits as well as non-Dalits.

The first case refers to Valmikis, originating from the north-western parts of India, who use the name of their main deity as community name, the second to Adi Dravidas, or Paraiyars from Tamil Nadu, who in the case of Dharavi all hail from one part of Tirunelveli district and often are kin to each other,[13] and the third, of course, to Mahars from Maharashtra but also to Jaiswara Chamars from eastern Uttar Pradesh who have recently taken to Buddhism. The different combinations of religion, ideology and social imaginary demonstrate different attempts at gaining entrance into and acceptance in what is seen as mainstream society, which can include ideas of (more or less radical) reform of society. In all cases, communal belonging, however understood, is taken as a premise, and sometimes even as a medium of access. (Mainstream society itself is being differently conceived, as Hindu society, as society of all Indians of different creed and affiliation, or even as humanity in general.)

---

13 This is to be traced back to the Dravidian kinship system.

These 'communal' nodal points or cases of intersection can be taken as representative insofar as large numbers of individuals of these communities take to these models. But many other deviating *individual* mediations and modulations of the different registers, sometimes idiosyncratic, sometimes formative, are possible also. Among followers of the Shiv Narayana *sant* sect, a sect with an egalitarian and universalist message which has its center in eastern Uttar Pradesh, one finds a number of people who also take on Buddhism. Continuous daily worship of Shiv Narayana does not deter them from also declaring their allegiance to the ethical teachings of the Buddha. This can go so far, like in the case of a *pujari* of Shiv Narayana, as to declare Babasaheb Ambedkar '*bhagwan*', meaning the 'god' who really empowered the Dalits, so that they can now go everywhere, sit together with others, give public speeches and receive education. Or one finds the co-presence of four religions in one community, even at one table, as among Adi Dravidas or Paraiyars: namely Hindu, Muslim, Christian and Buddhist, while on the other hand the followers of the different religions share a certain social imaginary of emancipation which unites them.

There is also a man, an Adi Dravida in this case, who combines Lutherian Christianity with Ambedkarite Buddhism, for similar reasons. Someone from the Kunchikurve community leaves his affiliation open and attends services of the Catholic and Hindu as well as Muslim festivals. While cases as the last signify individual search for meaning, others try to link what looks incompatible, like the Mahar who is a practicing Christian and also acts as *shakha pramukh* of the Shiv Sena, which at the time, when I talked with him, voiced a strong anti-Christian rhetoric. Many Dalits, and especially urban Dalits, are on a search for a new social positioning, for social and moral recognition. This results in a constellation in which interpretive frameworks (or worldviews) which seem to exclude each other, and especially those with a universalistic bend, are not just tolerated but respected and seen as possible options one could in principle also take on (Fuchs 2002 and 2003).

These observations can serve as a clue to understand the frame in which residents in a place like Dharavi, and perhaps other modern (so-called hybrid) constellations too, act. Diverse dimensions of action and discursive registers, and even alternative options, are negotiated as well as integrated *situationally and contextually* and even seen to provide *creative* possibilities of self-development. The different configurations illustrate a mode and level of integration neglected badly in social theory: "translation" on the level of everyday interpretive action (Renn 2002). They also allow to contextualize the question of local governance in a new way.

LOCALITY AND GOVERNMENTALITY

The state has a limited presence in Dharavi. Those state agencies with offices in, or links to Dharavi (like police, health centers, slum rehabilitation, area development and housing authorities, electoral registration officers, etc.) look like bridgeheads the state could establish in an unknown territory. They at least provide some interface between citizenry and administration: issuing ration cards, photo passes or entering residents in the voter lists, offering specified services, administering funds to be converted into developmental projects, or, occasionally and unsystematically, undertaking direct interventions. The knowledge state or municipal agencies have of local conditions is often superficial, operational figures (about residential quarters, their residents, productive units, socioeconomic conditions, composition of the population, etc.) are incomplete, voter lists, photo passes and even ration cards do not cover all who reside in Dharavi.

In many respects state agencies are dependent on partners from the residents' and citizens' side. What is actually silently being assumed by the state, are self-organizing or self-organized structures, the process of self-institution of society, to borrow a term from Cornelius Castoriadis (1987). Dharavi, however, does not constitute a self-evident entity, like a village or classical type of settlement, a commune, with a body of representatives or, alternatively, an integrative structure of socio-political dominance. What we come across are certain mediating structures of NGO- and CBO-type, frequently put into the foreground today. But these are focussed enterprises. We also have to learn to take notice of social as well as 'cultural' mechanisms in a broader and more basic sense, which provide some inter-linkage and some shared perspective among the local people, and on whose background only non-formal organizations can thrive.

Michel Foucault (1991) has argued that with the advent of the administrative state in the fifteenth and sixteenth centuries in Europe it was population which became the ultimate end, but also the object and means of governance. The quest for knowledge of all processes related to population is reflected in the significant statistical enumeration gained for modern nation states, however dubious the results may have been in many cases. For India see, among others, Appadurai (1993) and Kaviraj (1995). The current crisis of the nation-state, though, implies changes of the relationship between government and people. In many respects, state governance today appears as not sufficiently effective and the state's knowledge of its population inadequate, a "crisis of redundancy" as Arjun Appadurai (2002) calls it. The answers can be 'privatization', the appropriation of the means of violence by non-state groups, the intervention of transnational agencies like the World Bank and International Monetary Fund, or the takeover of responsibilities by NGOs and citizens' movements (Appadurai 2002: 24). The last option especially is based on the new space created by discourses of democracy, human rights and civil society in recent decades.

Governance is no longer, and in effect was never a concern of the ruler or the state only. Foucault already has reminded us of the question of the government of oneself (or the problem of personal conduct) and the government of souls and lives (or the pastoral doctrine) besides the question of government by the state or the prince (Foucault 1991: 87). This means, we do not only have to distinguish between different agents of governance but also between different dimensions and levels of governance, that is the policy, the self and specific interactive arenas. On each level there can exist differences in the mode of governance and different notions of governmentality. NGOs too pursue different notions of governmentality. Participatory approaches, advocated widely today, can still signify a top-down approach with pre-defined goals and modes of procedure, to be adapted locally.

Partnership approaches, as Appadurai describes them, try to adapt development projects to the experiences, the knowledge and the ideas of the good life of those, the poor, the stigmatized, for whom the projects are meant. I here argue that the salutary work on governance of NGOs and CBOs undertaken by Appadurai with respect to Mumbai (with some reference to Dharavi too) should be supplemented by an analysis of what I would like to call 'social governance': the ways local people in an urban context, and especially slum dwellers who live on the margins of society or in an in-between state, regulate their relationships and organize their (social) lives, outside state or NGO intervention. NGOs and even CBOs, by their very nature, remain issue-oriented and do not take on urban or slum life as a whole.

The key for an understanding of sociality and governmentality in Dharavi lies in the constant little processes of situational and contextual translation – translation *within* a community and *between* communities.[14] Community from this angle means community of discourse, a circle of debate and collaboration which may coincide with a filiative community, or is placed within one, or transverses filiative connections. A characteristic mode, as we have seen, is the ongoing process of translation and retranslation of one's (personal or collective) condition as also of social imaginaries into pertinent discourses (religions). Recurrent too are translations between different discourses (religious options one has or has not taken). Translations allow a certain distance towards and reflection of the respective discourses and, secondarily, identities. Translations are a mode of appropriation of the other, and a way to latch onto the translocal. Translations also are, as we see, a mode of integration (of differences).

Translation also operates *trans*communally as an interactive mode: one can distinguish, in the context of Dharavi, between social networks and social mediation. *Networks* represent an integrative mode, as they explore common denominators and links (common projects etc.) between the actors concerned. The large ones are represented by CBOs, but one finds them also on a smaller scale, in discussion circles, social action groups, informal self-help groups which started especially after tragedies like riots. And congregational bodies of filiative communities may too act as networks, for 'members' only or for a larger public, running schools, co-operative banks etc. *Social mediation* means attempts of bridging gaps of discrimination, finding a third, mediatory point (neutral point, point of agreement).

The paradigmatic figures in Dharavi are, as locals call them, 'social workers'. These are persons, mostly but not exclusively men, who act as social entrepreneurs or brokers, as go-in-betweens, arbiters or troubleshooters, as guides or counsellors for a smaller or larger Dharavi neighborhood or for some other restricted clientele. There is not just one type of 'social worker', but they rather are of very different standing,

---

[14] This is not meant to disregard other aspects of local governance in Dharavi, be it the "public voice" (Roma Chatterji, personal communication), be it the breakdown of principles of governance at certain moments (Mehta and Chatterji 2001), be it the forms of individual and communal self-governance and attempts at guiding the conduct of others already alluded to above. Important as these other modes are, by themselves they would just represent various parallel but separate governmental modes. Together with the situational processes of translation, however, they may add up to a more comprehensive picture of local governmentality in a later analysis.

and every individual develops a different role for him- or herself. Social workers require broad moral recognition in the local public. A second type of a social mediatory institution are peace committees (*mohalla* committees) comprising representatives of the different relevant communities. Such committees were especially instituted after the 1992/93 riots, but today lie largely dormant.[15]

Political parties, which want to be successful in the Dharavi commonwealth, try to replicate or make use of one of these two inter- or transcommunal mechanisms. On the one side are those parties which decided and which managed to build on – i.e. win over or themselves create – more or less widely recognized "social worker" figures, on the other side are those which try to establish their own local network structure. The first is best represented by some Congress politicians, replicated less successfully in case of other parties, the second by Shiv Sena and its *shakhas*. To the extent political parties follow these models, they (or the respective local leaders) do not mediate and intervene only locally, and thus can eventually gain a high degree of legitimacy in the eyes of local residents, but also serve as channels to outside (state) agencies. Parties which cannot adapt to these models do not take deep root in Dharavi.

CONCLUSION

What does all this mean for the question of (social) governance in Dharavi?

1. Dharavi assembles a range of distinct circuits of debate, decision-making and self-governance, some with an ingrained leadership structure (elected representatives of communities, NGO leaders, also church clerics), others more decentralized. The different circuits form an interlocked space or chain of spaces of public (and public-private) interaction. The public, accordingly, is contextualized and differentiated: Dharavi does not represent or signify one common

---

15 While having been introduced to monitor negotiations between communal opponents the police seem to use these committees as a kind of outreach organization: as media and informants for their manoeuvres. The police also tries to replicate the 'social worker' model by nominating certain persons in Dharavi as 'special executive officers' (SEO).

space of public intercourse nor does it have a center. The structure of PROUD,[16] one Dharavi CBO, can be seen as an attempt to provide or develop such an integrated public, with area representatives and a pan-Dharavi elected body.[17]

2. Based on the recognition of differences of circuits of debate and identity, long standing residents of Dharavi, however, share an understanding of occupying a shared place, a place they themselves have created together. Encompassing the chain of circuits which make up Dharavi is the imaginary of a separate, bounded space: '*mini-India*', a term constantly being evoked in Dharavi to mark this slum as quintessential example of intercultural *coexistence*. This implies, even if vague, a certain notion of the 'common good' (cf. Foucault 1981: 94).

3. Conflicts between people of different communal identity, especially among Dalits, are often tackled without recourse to superior authorities, using the mediating and network structures and personalities mentioned. This mechanism becomes ineffective, however, in case of large-scale mobilization, especially if it gets support from outside forces as happened in the 1992/93 pogroms. (The above is in no way meant to paint a harmonic picture. However, the pride in what has been achieved and the importance attached to a space of one's own control should not be minimized. The tensions between Dalit or low caste communities, sometimes resulting in fights, and even the "ordinary" tensions between Hindus (of Dalit background) and Muslims in Dharavi in many cases point at competitive struggles over resources, control of space, etc. The main issue is *not* power over others.)

Dalits in Dharavi again and again contrast the form of governance they experienced in the village (and still experience on their return) with the forms of social interaction found in Mumbai. It is the constant danger of invasion of their personal integrity in the rural context which falls off

---

16 PROUD stands for "People's Responsible Organisation of United Dharavi".

17 While in the high times of Dharavi residents' struggle against demolition and for residential rights as well as infrastructural development in the 1980s PROUD might have served as a public forum and structure of mobilization, today its impact is limited to specified developmental tasks.

when in Mumbai. Local governance in the village meant a tension between internal self-governance of the community and dominance or even oppression and interference by higher castes. Dharavi marks a change of the hierarchical mode, but this change remains limited to the urban space. The hegemonic discourse is brought under control, but this control is confined to a locality. Some local groups are directly integrated into translocal discourses. These are those who pursue an assertive Dalit discourse (on the lines of Ambedkar). Those who stick to Hinduism, on the other hand, hold a more ambiguous position. By appropriating the Brahminic gods and even employing Brahmin priests, who serve them,[18] they at one and the same time affirm the hegemonic scheme and bring it down to their own local circuit (of control). It is the in-between state of Dharavi and its mechanisms of transposing ideas into local conditions and contextual visions, which act as filter and allow for a precarious space of negotiating one's place in a disjointed world.

Acknowledgements:

I deeply thank Pradeep Shinde for his collaboration in the research, on which this essay builds, and Roma Chatterji as well as Deepak Mehta for sharing their experiences of Dharavi with me. I also learned from my talks with Kalpana Sharma, Marie-Caroline Saglio, Ananda Maharajan, Gabriel Britto and many others. The main thank, however, goes to the many interlocutors, NGO workers and friends from Dharavi itself, in particular friends and activists from PROUD, who all contributed with their energy and work to the development of the place I tried to describe, and helped me understand their struggle. They might, however, not endorse all the conclusions drawn here.

Earlier versions of this paper were presented at the 17th European Conference on Modern South Asian Studies, Heidelberg 2002, and at Max Mueller Bhavan, Delhi 2003. Thanks to all who provided comments.

---

18 Adi Dravidas have started to employ Brahmins, one from a traditional family of Brahmin priests from Thanjavur, in two of their temples for about ten years. Before, Adi Dravidas had themselves celebrated the *puja*, as Dalits (or the respective communities) still do in the case of the other Hindu temples of Dharavi.

REFERENCES

Appadurai, Arjun, 'Number in the colonial imagination' in *Orientalism and the Postcolonial Predicament. Perspectives on South Asia,* Carol Breckenridge and Peter van der Veer, eds., Philadelphia: University of Pennsylvania Press, 1993, pp. 314-339.

Appadurai, Arjun, 'Deep democracy: Urban governmentality and the horizon of politics', in *Public Culture* 14 (1) (2002), pp. 21-47.

Bhargava, Rajeev, 'Democratic vision of a new republic: India, 1950', in *Transforming India. Social and Political Dynamics of Democracy,* Francine R. Frankel, Zoya Hasan, Rajeev Bhargava and Balveer Arora, eds., New Delhi: Oxford University Press, 2000, pp. 26-59.

Breinig, Helmbrecht and Lösch, Klaus, 'Introduction: Difference and transdifference', in *Multiculturalism in Contemporary Societies: Perspectives on difference and transdifference,* Helmbrecht Breinig, Jürgen Gebhardt and Klaus Lösch, eds., Erlangen: Universitätsbund Erlangen-Nürnberg, 2002, pp. 11-36.

Castoriadis, Cornelius, *The Imaginary Institution of Society*, Cambridge: Polity, 1987.

Foucault, Michel, 'Governmentality', in *The Foucault Effect. Studies in governmentality,* Graham Burchell, Colin Gordon and Peter Miller, eds., London: Harvester Wheatsheaf, 1991, pp. 87-104.

Fuchs, Martin, *Kampf um Differenz. Repräsentation, Subjektivität und soziale Bewegungen - Das Beispiel Indien*, Frankfurt am Main: Suhrkamp, 1999.

Fuchs, Martin, 'Articulating the world: Social movements, the self-transcendence of society and the question of culture', in *Thesis Eleven* 61 (2000), pp. 65-85.

Fuchs, Martin, 'Soziale Pragmatik des Übersetzens. Strategien der Interkulturalität in Indien', in *Übersetzung als Medium des Kulturverstehens und sozialer Integration,* Joachim Renn, Jürgen Straub and Shingo Shimada, eds., Frankfurt (Main): Campus, 2002, pp. 292-322.

Fuchs, Martin, 'Dalit Struggle for Recognition: Reflections from Dharavi', in *Globalization and Social Movements, Struggle for a Humane Society,* P. G. Jogdand and S. M. Michael, eds., Jaipur: Rawat, 2003, pp. 128-149.

Hansen, Thomas Blom, *Urban Violence in India. Identity politics, 'Mumbai', and the postcolonial city*, Delhi: Permanent Black, 2001.

Kaviraj, Sudipta, 'Religion, politics and modernity', in: *Crisis and Change in Contemporary India,* Upendra Baxi and Bhikhu Parekh, eds., New Delhi: Sage, 1995, pp. 295-316.

Masselos, Jim, 'The Bombay riots of January 1993: The politics of urban conflagration', in *Politics of violence. From Ayodhya to Behrampada,* Howard Brasted, John McGuire and Peter Reeves, eds., Delhi: Sage, 1996, pp. 111-126.

Mehta, Deepak and Chatterji, Roma, 'Boundaries, names, alterities: A case study of a "communal riot" in Dharavi, Bombay', in *Remaking a World. Violence, social suffering, and recovery,* Veena Das, Arthur Kleinman, Margaret Lock, Mamphela Ramphele and Pamela Reynolds, eds., Berkeley: University of California Press, 2001, pp. 201-249.

PROUD (People's Responsible Organisation of United Dharavi), *20 Years of PROUD, 1979-1999*, Mumbai, 1999.

Renn, Joachim, ‚Die Übersetzung der modernen Gesellschaft. Das Problem der Einheit der Gesellschaft und die Pragmatik des Übersetzens', in *Übersetzung als Medium des Kulturverstehens und sozialer Integration,* Joachim Renn, Jürgen Straub and Shingo Shimada, eds., Frankfurt (Main): Campus, 2002, pp. 183-214.

Saglio-Yatzimirsky, Marie-Caroline, *Intouchable Bombay. Le bidonville des travailleurs du cuir*, Paris : CNRS Éditions, 2002.

Sharma, Kalpana, *Rediscovering Dharavi. Stories from Asia's largest slum*, New Delhi: Penguin, 2000.

Wagner, Peter, 'Identity and selfhood as a problématique', in *Identities. Time, Difference and Boundaries,* Heidrun Friese, ed., New York: Berghahn, 2002, pp. 32-55.

Infrastructure:

Technical, Social and Cultural Aspects

5

TOWARDS AN IMPROVED URBAN GOVERNANCE OF PUBLIC SERVICES: WATER SUPPLY AND SANITATION

MARIE-HÉLÈNE ZÉRAH

INTRODUCTION

Towns and cities already represent half of India's gross domestic product and 60 per cent of its national income (GOI 1996: 7) despite a relatively low rate of urbanization (around 30 per cent). As such, they play an increasingly important role in India's economic development. Along with the liberalization and decentralization processes which began in the 1990s, the function of administrations and of local governments is being reinforced. The 74th constitutional amendment on decentralization transfers more responsibilities to local councillors (GOI 1992) while economic liberalization encourages foreign investment. Consequently, States, convinced that cities are engines of growth, develop regional policies favouring new industries (information technology, biotechnology) and investments in the infrastructure of their capital cities. The ongoing transformation of Chennai, Bangalore and Hyderabad bears witness to this process. The positioning of cities towards attracting investment, industries, services and brains demonstrates that they compete amongst themselves to find a significant place on the world map. However, they need to counterbalance these policies with potent actions to reduce economic and spatial inequalities. At the same time, the growing influence of non governmental agencies (industry associations, non governmental organizations, large companies) and the promotion by international organizations of public-private partnerships and civil society engagement become an integral part of the functioning and the making of the city. Adequate coordination mechanisms and negotiation tools between actors and at the various levels of government become essential. To account for this growing complexity, the concept of urban governance is commonly used to qualify the evolution in the management, functioning and rules governing city development. These evolutions have an impact on access and management of basic amenities. This is the reason why I argue that in-depth research on specific sectors contributes to the larger understanding of urban governance.

This chapter, therefore, chooses the water supply and sanitation sector to illustrate some features of urban governance. Our hypothesis is that the combination of a deficient public sector and of the resulting individual response of the public leads both to unsustainability and to a transformation in the methods of managing and delivering services. Our objective is to analyse these changes and to assess their consequences on the improvement of accessibility on sectoral coordination and regulation. This chapter is based on a synthesis of extensive fieldwork comprising of quantitative and qualitative surveys conducted in various Indian cities. It deals separately with transformations involving private operators and those involving the civil society.

PUBLIC SECTOR DEFICIENCIES AND RESULTING INDIVIDUAL RESPONSE

The concept of urban governance can have multiple meanings. Here, I consider that it refers to the transformation in the modes of public action with a focus on concerted and negotiated policies. It implies the role of local government in devising public-private partnership, the emergence of non governmental actors and formal or informal networks and relationships between cities (Le Galès 1995). From a sectoral point of view, the term of governance, in our opinion, is a tool to set the stage rather than an analytical one. Indeed, the essence of analysing a sector is focused on understanding how the sector is managed and regulated. This is the exercise I shall attempt here in the case of intermediary and large Indian cities, where water supply and sanitation services are provided by the municipal corporations or by water and sewerage boards.[1]

---

1 Boards exist in metropolises and they are constituted through special Acts. In Mumbai, water supply and sewerage is still under the responsibility of the municipal corporation.

An Ambitious but Malfunctioning Planning Process

Despite varying demands depending upon the habitat and income characteristics, planning for services is carried out in isolation. For a given population, engineers forecast the future demand, based on consumption norms established by the CPHEEO[2] (GOI 1991) and design new water supply and sewerage schemes. Consumption norms are often overestimated (the Delhi Development Authority officially uses a norm of 363 litres per person per day) and applied as an average for the whole city. In some cases, it can underestimate the needs when an area's development is faster than expected as is the case in some parts of east Delhi. But in most cases, projects are costly (construction of additional treatment plants, booster and pumping stations, extension or building of pipelines) and do not take into consideration the possibility of optimising the actual production and distribution system. Vijayawada, the third largest city of Andhra Pradesh, is a good case in point.

According to the last census, the population of the Vijayawada Municipal Corporation has reached 845,000 people, a number for which the actual water supply and sewerage infrastructure network is inadequate. Consequently, the municipal corporation has devised two new projects to extend services to unserved areas. A recent evaluation of these projects[3] as well as an in-depth analysis of the actual system supports the need for new investments (French Water Club et al. 2002). But overall, this study strongly underlines the deficiencies in operation and maintenance that should in fact be given priority: namely, the collapse of wells, low construction standards, non functioning and unreliable sensors to measure pressure and last though not the least, the defaulting operation of pumping stations. The right mix between improvment and extension needs could easily be estimated with technico-economic calcultations and demand analysis based on detailed surveys. However, the dominant technical culture is not familiar, rather hostile even to such an approach. In some areas, it would certainly show that steps to improve the existing system of public taps through implementation of sound policies, would be more viable than planning costly development plans. Costs are high and wrongly estimated and

---

2 Central Public Health and Environmental Engineering Organization.

3 A team of French companies conducted an analysis of the water supply and sanitation situation in Vijayawada in February and April 2002 with financial assistance from the French government. I was a part of this team supervising the conducting of household and institutional surveys.

projects once begun do not necessarily reach completion due to the shortage of funds and rejection of loans.[4] Delays, unforeseen events, and additional costs needed to ensure the stability and the solidity of the completed civil works, augment the total project cost. This situation might unfortunately lead to a freeze on improvement at a time when new infrastructure are required along with optimization of the actual system.

Concerning the sectoral coordination, the functions of planning, design and implementation, led by the engineers, suffer from a lack of both internal (between departments) and external (between agencies) coordination. To go back to the case of Vijayawada, projects are conceived by two separate technical departments, one for water supply projects and the other for sewerage projects, and without any consultative process with the revenue and the financial departments so as to assess their financial viability. During the conception phase, internal feasibility studies rarely use data already available with other agencies (soil conditions, topography, ground-water level). At the implementation stage, lack of coordination also occur when approvals required from other agencies are delayed as clearly shown by Datta (2002) in the case of Kanpur. The ambitious Dwarka project is another illustration of the defaulting urban planning process. This project, conceived and implemented by the Delhi Development Authority (DDA) aimed at providing housing for 1,400,000 people in the west of Delhi (Jain 1990: Chap. 7).

However, due to electricity shortages and the lack of water available, the rate of occupancy is much lower than expected. This is largely due to a lack of coordination between the DDA and the other agencies to plan infrastructure and assess water availability (the Delhi Water Board, the then Delhi Electricity Board, the Central Ground Water Board). After seeking without success the intervention of the private sector, and as no other alternatives were left, the Delhi Municipal Corporation decided to launch an experimental rain water harvesting project. In the long run, this decision could demonstrate that decentralised production and management of water resources is a feasible option for Indian cities.[5] However, the abundance of actors, the lack of data integration in urban planning and the overlapping of responsabilities, which is not specific to

---

4 HUDCO (Housing and Urban Development Corporation) refused to finance two projects submitted by the Vijayawada Municipal Corporation.

5 The possibility to supplement supply with alternative solutions, especially rain water harvesting, is being raised in numerous forums and generates heated debates on the feasibility and the potential of such options.

India (Jaglin 2001 for an example on Subsaharian Africa), are all factors responsible for the difficulties of urban governance.

A Deficient Technical and Commercial Management

Regarding technical issues, the lack of focus on network systems optimisation is exemplified through the absence of preventive maintenance. Apart from Chennai, most cities have limited programmes to detect leakage, even though they are estimated at around thirty per cent. Engineers and field officers mainly intervene in a case of emergency (important leakage, lack of pressure) and when required by local councillors.[6] Priorities cannot be defined in the long run and are therefore submitted to daily discussions. The number of technical and administrative approvals required for each procedure, the absence of discretionary powers and the rigidity of budget rules, all these contribute to a system that does not favour the use of tools such as cost-benefit analysis to discriminate between various technical choices (such as replacing meters for instance).

A non integrated information system limits the monitoring of indicators, which are necessary for improving the service and to measure the performance of the various departments. In addition, there are no monitoring standards to follow the situation that enable both a time line analysis of the system as well as a benchmarking between various geographical divisions. Finally, in this centralised and technically oriented set up, the best officers and engineers prefer being posted in the constructions department.[7] As a result the actual knowledge and information about service levels and the network is circumscribed to field officers and disappears when they retire. Therefore, the maintenance department remains sidelined despite its importance and cannot see the emergence of innovative or less costly solutions.

Looking at the commercial management side, two aspects stand out. Corporations and boards have no commercial approach, no standardized monitoring tools to generate information about cost recovery and revenue generation and no relationship with their consumers. Cost recovery is often simply estimated every month by dividing the amounts collected (that corresponds to previous months' charges plus arrears) by

6 In Mumbai, a field officer interviewed in 2002 stated that he received three or four requests a day from the local councillor.

7 New projects generate more kickbacks than dealing with maintenance issues.

the amount billed on the same month. Thus, actual cost recovery can not be properly estimated. Relationships with the user are usually not considered to be crucial in Boards or Corporations managed mostly by engineers: complaints are not attended to and information regarding services is not disseminated. There are no conduct of customer surveys or bill analysis to generate knowledge about users' demand and consumption patterns. Even though this feedback could further enlighten municipal officers and decision makers and help them in designing policies, for instance new tariff policies (Ruet, Saravanan and Zérah, 2002: 15-16). The absence of monitoring tools is particularly obvious in the case of low-income areas and this leads to large geographical disparities in all Indian cities. In areas served by public taps or fountains, maintenance is almost non-existent and in unserved areas, officers are totally unaware about the specific demand. There is also very little interaction (to some extent, Chennai, Ahmedabad and Mumbai being exceptions) with non-governmental organizations. Providing services can only be considered when other agencies have recognised these settlements. Despite the ideological importance of "universal service", the low-income situation remains a not so well-known phenomenon for Indian municipalities.

An Individual Response of the Public

The failure of water boards and/or corporations to assess the needs of low-income households results in a scenario where the role of networks as a tool for integration in the urban space (Dupuy 1991) is not fulfilled. Hence, this leads to individual answers from all users despite a forefront discourse built around the notion of universal service. In concrete terms, the service provided is unreliable (limited numbers of hours of supply, low pressure, and uncertainty regarding timings of supply) and as a logical consequence has an impact on behaviours of users.

For households, research based on households surveys in Delhi have demonstrated the extent to which households rely on coping strategies to counter the unreliable supply, irrespective of whether they have an in-house connection (Zérah 2000) or not (Zérah and Llorente 1999; Tovey 1999). Strategies can be extremely diverse and vary from storing water from municipal supply (overhead tanks, buckets), to relying on borewells or handpumps, rescheduling activities, queuing at public taps. For drinking and cooking purposes, households treat water with more or less sophisticated methods or/and use a specific source. Further studies conducted in slums clearly highlight that inadequate supply translates into low levels of consumption (around 30 litres per person per day) and large amounts of time spent to fetch water.

In the six slums surveyed in various parts of Delhi, the average time spent to collect water is estimated at three hours per day (Zérah and Llorente 1999: 39-47). Only eight per cent of the households surveyed spent less than half an hour per day to fetch water. These figures do not reflect the variations between slums but also throw light on the geographical and political conditions. Spatial differences also characterize supply for connected households since variations in the number of hours in Delhi were mostly explained by differences between zones of the city: in the south, sixty per cent of the households have less than six hours of supply per day while in the north, 36 per cent have 24 hours of supply. However, spatial differences *vis a vis* access to water can also be found within zones and even within colonies, and this is partly explained by the structural role of the network.

Results obtained in Delhi are strengthened by surveys conducted in intermediary cities, especially regarding the use of various sources (Table 1, pp. 135-6). In Kakinada, a secondary city of around 300,000 inhabitants on the coast of Andhra Pradesh, the type and number of sources used is very diverse: 45 per cent of the households use a public tap everyday; 6 per cent use a public handpump regularly if not everyday; 57 per cent rely on private sources (borewells, handpumps) on a very regular basis. When a water crisis occurs, other sources are also used: neighbour's water (12 per cent), public water tankers, canals, ponds and some free water tankers provided by a local private company (17 per cent). In Vijayawada, a more recent survey carried out; confirms the use of multiple sources even though on a smaller scale than in Kakinada: almost half the population relied on ground water and around 37 per cent on public tap. Analysis of consumption levels, in Vijayawada, proves the unreliability of figures provided by corporations/boards. As against an official figure given by the municipality of 140 to 150 litres per person per day, the survey highlighted a different reality with an average consumption of around 63 litres per person per day (Zérah 2002).

In Delhi, we calculated the high costs borne by connected households. Aggregated at the level of the city, it amounts to twice the sum spent by the Delhi authorities on water supply every year (Zérah 2000). Kakinada and Vijayawada tell the same story as Delhi. Treatment of water, investment in storage capacities and in motors and pumps to lift water are common strategies among connected households and families with higher incomes. Households with low income levels relying on public taps had to spend more time (than in Vijayawada where tap density is good) to collect water. Consequently, costs of strategies are split between direct financial cost and time opportunity cost mostly borne by low-income households. Reduction of these individual costs could be achieved by integration of non-connected households to the network for those who can afford municipal services or/and by an improvement of the functioning and operation of public taps. These direct costs represent 1.6 per cent in Delhi, 2.7 per cent in Vijayawada and 3 per cent in Kakinada. For slum dwellers and lower income households, most of the cost borne corresponds to time opportunity costs. These results led us and others to compare these costs with the willingness to pay (Zérah 2000 and WSP 1999a). This is partly true but the results obtained in Kakinada,[8] using the contingent valuation method, prove that the willingness to pay is slightly lower than the actual direct costs borne. This highlights the users' lack of confidence in the municipal authorities and their long term strategies which in turn has an impact on their willingness to pay.[9] We argue that these two factors have been undermined by the first studies on the willingness to pay.

These studies further reveal that households, through surveys on water, also express a demand for better sewerage, sanitation and storm-water drainage facilities. This is the case in Kakinada, where the survey clearly showed that the demand was mostly for sewerage and storm water drainage improvement. This is not a surprise as these two services remain major problems in many cities. Kakinada reflects the abysmal situation of secondary towns: households reject waste water in open drain and rarely have septic tanks. Twenty seven per cent of the households, deprived of even collective latrines, go outside for toilets purposes (75 per cent for slum dwellers). The storm water drainage network is deficient and non-existent in some areas, even though it is a priority for a

---

8 For the analysis, assuming that their strategies and their willingness to pay would be influenced by their access to water and their housing characteristics, households were classified as follows: the 43 per cent of the households who had a water connection, the 28.5 per cent who had no water connection and were living in formal settlements, and the remaining 28.5 per cent who had no water connection and were living in slums.

9 For instance, households could state their willingness to pay for a continuous service or for 12 hours of supply. On an average, the increase for a 24 hours service was only Rs 25 per month but more than one third of the households did not increase their bid.

town such as Kakinada hit by regular cyclones and where the southern part of the city is a low lying area and therefore highly prone to flooding. Indeed, around two-thirds of the households face problems during the rains, most of them slum dwellers living in these low lying areas. In Vijayawada, the sewerage system is restricted to the core city and remaining households rely on septic tanks. These are not consistently cleaned, which results in groundwater pollution.

A recent survey conducted in Vijayawada among 20 industries and institutions demonstrates the extent to which municipal water is unable to satisfy non-domestic needs.[10] The sample included twenty non-domestic users of all types: two government institutions (the Indian Railways and the State Bus Agency), both water as well as non-water consuming industries, private offices, five hotels and restaurants, two hospitals and two colleges. All of them, even small water consumers (such as offices) relied on sources of water other than the municipal. Two very large users, the Indian Railways and a milk processing unit relied on their own pumping stations on the river. All other users relied on municipal water, but complemented their supply by ground water (55 per cent of the cases); groundwater combined with bottled water and/or rain water; and water delivered by tanks. Eleven units considered the water supplied from the Vijayawada Municipal Corporation to be inadequate and five of them maintain that they do not want to rely on the Vijayavada Municipal Corporation. This confirms the high probability of exit strategies from the municipal system.

Table 1. Comparison between Delhi, Kakinada and Vijayawada

	Vijayawada	Kakinada	Delhi	Delhi
Date of the survey	2002	1998	1998	1995
Sample size	167	600	110	700
Type of households	all households	all households	only slum dwellers	only households with a municipal water connection

10 The survey was conducted in Vijayawada in June 2002 and the paper presents the first results.

Access to supply	80%	not available	not available	90% for all inhabitants of Delhi
In-house connections	28%	>25%	not available	50 to 60%
HH using one source	64.7%	28.8%	48.2%	40% (1)
HH using two sources	32.9%	63.0%	44.5%	---
HH using more than two sources	2.4%	8.2%	7.3%	---

Note (1): For Delhi, data were analysed to calculate the number of households using a specific compensatory strategy. For instance, use of a borewell (16.5 per cent), of a handpump (12.8 per cent), of a overhead tank (48 per cent) or collecting water from outside on a regular basis (10.7 per cent).

Sources: All the surveys were conducted by the author and by the author and Llorente in Delhi slums.

Despite incurring costs for their private investment, institutions and industries surveyed consider their total expenditure towards water and sewerage as very cheap (Rs 16 for water and Rs 19 for sewerage). This can be partly explained by the absence of payment for groundwater access; the fact that in reality many institutions have domestic connections; and do not have a sewerage system. All these factors contribute to a decrease in the cost of sewerage. This highlights some of the major issues linked to the sewerage situation and the impact of solid and liquid waste disposal systems in Indian cities. The system is inadequate and not very regulated despite norms decreed by the Central Pollution Control Board. In Vijayawada, one of the main hospitals ejects used water in the open drainage system and pharmaceutical industries have no preliminary treatment. Such practices provoke large environmental externalities that could be internalized by a pollution tax.

These analyses demonstrate the extent of public response to inadequate level of services by all type of users, mostly through individual solutions that can even lead to exit the system for some industries and higher income households, but that keeps most other users, especially the poor, captive (or loyal) of the municipal system.[11] Voice options are limited as the low percentage of households who complain (individually or collectively) shows (12 per cent in Delhi, 14 per cent in Vijayawada). On the contrary, exit strategies have considerable consequences as far as potential revenues for a municipality are concerned. Exit strategies are mostly available to companies who can afford large investments. These companies could be an important source for municipal revenues and for financing pollution reduction. Their exit from the system renders the long term sustainability of water supply and sanitation networks even more fragile. Indeed, for a large section of the population, the limited ability to pay means that the mechanisms to balance out will remain. These mechanisms (such as subsidies) can be weakened if large users quit the system. The real core issue it raises is the long term sustainability. As such, even though the terms of the debate are different in developed countries, Barraqué (2003) underlines how the combination of price increases, required investments to renew old infrastructure, removal of subsidies, the impact of environmental directives and decrease or stagnation of demand (increased recourse to private sources, saving water process) all lead to a crisis of municipal services.

EMERGING MARKETS, LOCAL ENTREPRENEURS AND PUBLIC-PRIVATE PARTNERSHIPS

As a result of the inefficiency of the public sector, the individual public response, which emerges exacerbates environmental and social problems. This situation has had two consequences in the last decade. One, the emergence of new actors and, two, the push for large scale private sector participation in order to improve the governance of the sector. Both these phenomena reflect the evolution of the demand for better services and the perception that changes are required.

---

11 The concept of exit, loyal/captivity and voice were introduced by Hirschman (1970) to characterize the level of dependence of users towards the public sector.

Competition and Lack of Regulation in Packaged Drinking Water

In 1997, in Delhi, apart from the famous Bisleri brand and a few other companies selling water in one litre bottles, the market for packaged drinking water was almost nonexistent. Two companies were just commencing their operations by selling water in containers easily accessible for both domestic and non domestic consumption. Since then, this market has undergone a quick transformation all over India. We conducted a survey of the main companies based in Delhi which, apart from an increasing demand, highlighted the main factors that led to an explosion in the number of companies selling packaged drinking water (Llorente and Zérah 1998): the development of joint ventures with foreign companies, the possibility of producing containers at cheap rates and a loose regulation with little specifications on the nature of sources that could be used, the packaging conditions and the manufacturing process itself. Hence, two types of actors found a foothold in the market: companies willing to invest in equipment and quality control to ensure a sound manufacturing process and unscrupulous companies that went to the extent of simply filling bottles with groundwater. The former had usually entered into joint ventures, employed one or two chemists and belonged to an industry association. The latter had poor facilities and used the wrong labels such as "pure mineral water" to market their products.

In the span of a few years, large breweries and beverage companies, relying on their already reputed brand image and their retail network, ventured into this market. They developed production units[12] all over India and garnered large shares of a market worth Rs 6000 million in 2000, and estimated by the CII (Confederation of Indian Industry) to grow at 25 per cent per annum. There are also local producers in many cities. This is the case for instance in Vijayawada, where private producers indicated that the margins were high enough to make a substantial investment to recoup costs quite fast. However, recent surveys on the market shares have highlighted the drastic loss of the market of Bisleri to brands promoted by large domestic and Indian companies. Their production capacity, distribution networks, advertising policies as well as

---

12 Among the famous ones, a leading Indian beer brand, a leading agrofood company as well as Coca Cola and Pepsi. In fact, in its 2002 budget, the Indian Railways decided to launch its own brand to be sold on trains and on railway platforms.

brand names that reassure the consumer are certainly explanatory factors to this evolution.

By 1998, the *All India Bottled Water Manufacturers' Association* had already grouped together 35 companies to lobby for a tax reduction on packaged drinking water and ask the government to ensure the respect of certain norms. In 2000, taking cognisance of the growth of the market and the need to regulate it, water was included in the Prevention and Food Adulteration Act (1954), which involved more stringent rules in the processing and manufacturing. At the same time, it became compulsory to ensure Bureau of Indian Standard norms. This implied additional costs in installing facilities, in conducting regular testing, and in paying on a regular basis to acquire the compulsory standard label. This led to protests by the small manufacturers and in some cases to the withdrawal of labels and the closing down of some units for not conforming to quality regulations (*The Hindu* 30 April 2002).

Water tankers: A Niche Market or a Potential in Building Public-Private Partnerships?

Local water tanker companies have also become a common feature in most Indian cities. By looking at the situation in Delhi, we concluded that the creation of these companies was based upon access to one of the productive factors: trucks for transport companies as profit margins were higher; water for landowners who have property rights on groundwater (Llorente and Zérah 1998). Large profit margins and demands for industrial purposes, marriages and special functions have been the major factors for the growth of this industry, even though it represents less than one per cent of the total water produced at the city level. This reflects the overall situation in India, where contrary to South American countries (Tova Solo 1998), water tankers remain marginal. However, this industry is flourishing as is shows Chennai (WSP 1999b). There are approximately ten companies owning a large fleet of tankers and a large number of smaller ones owning only one or two trucks each (source: interview). Many of these water tankers buy water from farmers therefore putting pressure on groundwater.

The case of Chennai deserves special attention. Parallel to the market for water tapped by independent water tankers, around fifty companies organized themselves into an association that entered into an agreement with the Chennai Water Supply and Sewerage Board. The purpose was to serve areas deprived of water because of the absence of trunk network or lack of pressure in the network (Ruet, Saravanan and Zérah 2000: 16). This contract is negotiated on a yearly basis and payment is based on the number of daily trips. Water is provided by the Board at specific sites in the city. There are problems in respect to speed limits, accidents and the increased vehicular pollution level that the Board is trying to remedy by involving the tankers association in a vigilance committee and recently by the issue of a tender for more eco-friendly lorries (*The Hindu* 21 July 2002). This public-private partnership, however, is more the result of a water scarcity crisis rather than any strategic decision on the part of the Board to opt for a more flexible and decentralized alternative to reach areas for which network would be costly to build. Indeed, no technico-economic cost assessment has been carried out by the municipality especially in comparison with other possibilities of decentralized water supply.

The emergence of these new modes of supply is a testimony to the fact that demand is changing and becoming more and more differentiated. However, water becomes a private good priced according to market rules and affordable only for some sections of society. It reinforces service disparities without improving the overall access at the city level. In addition, consequences on groundwater, environment and on resource appropriation are alarming. In Chennai, private companies have installed their borewells in the vicinity of the city, relying for production on what has traditionally been common village property resources (Kamat 2002). This aggravates even more the conflicts between various users for access to water resources and leads to a competitive deepening of wells (Janakarajan 2000). Despite a Ground Water Regulation Act adopted in Tamil Nadu to license groundwater extraction, loopholes and the lack of enforcement limit its efficacy and raises the question of groundwater regulation and pricing and the enforcement capability of local authorities.

Small Local Contractors: More Effective Management of Services?

Various municipal corporations/Boards have begun to involve small time local contractors to operate services on a contractual basis. This reliance on private partners is largely driven by a freeze on recruitment of municipal employees. Nevertheless, whatever the motivations behind these developments, new forms of service delivery emerge.

In Chennai, private sector participation has been introduced for the maintenance and operation of sewerage pumping stations and of a waste water treatment plant (Ruet, Saravanan and Zérah 2002: 16). The operation and the maintenance of the waste water treatment plant started in 1997. Interviews conducted revealed that, it led to an improvement even though the cost of operation was higher by around 14 per cent (source: interviews). In the case of sewerage pumping stations, savings are estimated to be quite high by the Corporation. The introduction of these private contracts is mostly led by a policy of personnel reduction. Indeed, the Board reduced its number of employees by 3,000 in seven years. The contracts are not well designed, especially regarding labour conditions and indicators to assess the performance of the operator. The lack of expertise on the part of the local entrepreneurs, in addition to the contractual and regulatory loopholes that already exist, are handicaps and can be assessed as minus points.

On the one hand, risks for the public sector are limited (short term contracts) and the drafting of such contracts does not necessitate costly feasability studies to initiate the partnerships. On the other hand, it contributes to the formation of a local industry. It also engages a capacity building process both for the operator and the public sector. Public agencies are forced to develop new competencies so as to be able to clearly define objectives that translate into contractual agreements and monitoring tools and mechanisms. Finally, one can make the hypothesis that such partnerships will accelerate the process of setting up data base and lead to an evaluation of the assets of the public sector. To do this, however, tools to economically validate the technical and organizational options chosen need to be strengthened.

Failures of Large Scale Private Participation

These conditions are necessary if a Corporation/Board wants to engage with large international operators. Since the beginning of the 1990s, the motto of private sector participation is used in most conferences. Many projects, ranging from service contracts to various forms of delegated management failed because of high project costs, lack of transparency both in the process and selection criteria; and the lack of preparation (Mehta 1999). Another commonly acknowledged reason for failure has to do with politics. The case of Pune, where one of the largest projects aimed at attracting international investors was planned, is a good example to explain why large private sector participation failed in India (Zérah 2001). Pune is a typical city where water supply and sanitation facilities are inadequate and where the municipal government has to incorporate neighbouring villages in its jurisdiction. High non-revenue water,[13] intermittent supply, inadequate operation and maintenance were limits to the corporation's efficiency. Changing equations in the political landscape, local and national, explains the staggering political commitment that led to the cancellation of the project and to considerable tension between the Municipal Commissioner and the elected members of the Corporation.

However, beyond the political question, undoubtedly a crucial and complex one, many other issues are at stake in a privatization process. They came out in the open during the couple of years when the project was being elaborated. First, there was a debate on the estimated costs that were considered too high. It reflects the need to develop tools to be able to compare project development between a public and a private sector, taking into account and balancing out both time and cost overruns and the rate of returns expected.[14] In addition it appears that after the project failed, a consensus emerged that local consultants did not consider the potential streamlining of the existing system, which could have actually reduced the cost of the project. Loopholes in project preparation for private sector in India would require the upgrading of skills by consultants and a higher accuracy and quality of data provided by the client as well as its ability to assess the consultant work. Interviews also highlighted the hostility of the local contractor lobby towards the project.

Their influence was strong enough to convince elected representatives to oppose the project, even though, counterarguments demonstrated that the international private sector would rely on local contractors to implement the project. It unveils the reality of the well known nexus between corporators and contractors to get civil works contracts.[15] Above all, the most publicized point of discussion by the media was related to the tariff structure and the rise that were planned and said to

---

13 Non-revenue water represents the percentage of water not billed on water produced.

14 Overall, in India, there is a feeling that private sector participation does not involve operations risks and that overall undue advantages are given to private operators.

15 Tender procedures are often flawed and call for better governance, through more transparent procedures to award contracts and to establish the rates of contractors once a contract is awarded.

be necessary for the project viability. This draws attention to the question of cost recovery as water tariffs are very low and do not even cover operation and maintenance. Finally, within the corporation, some heads of departments argued that the project was too costly and was largely financed directly or indirectly by the Municipality, therefore using most of the finances available that could have been diverted to other projects. This final argument, though not the main explanatory factor for the project withdrawal, broaches a key aspect of governance, that is choice and arbitrage between potential policies and political decision process.

As a matter of fact, credible engagement by political leaders, a precondition to private sector participation is more difficult to gain in case of large projects with strong involvment of international operators. It therefore suggests that a stepwise approach through the development partnerships with local actors is a surer way to reform rather than expecting international investment to solve political and other such sensitive issues.

PARTICIPATIVE MANAGEMENT: INVOLVEMENT OF 'CIVIL SOCIETY' OR THE VOICE OF INTEREST GROUPS?

The trend towards a stronger involvement of civil society results both from the claim of civic movements (association, NGOS, etc.) and from policies in line with the 'guidelines' of international organizations on good governance. It is usually perceived as a progress of local or participative democracy. However, questions regarding the representation of users and of the role of the public sector cannot be left aside.

Co-Production of Services, Networking and Information Circulation ...

The possibility of co-production of services between utilities (publicly or privately managed) in charge of the trunk network, communities and NGOs, who can contribute to the planning and the construction of local networks, gained ground with the example of condominial sewerage system[16] in Brasil or the Orangi project in Karachi where users contrib-

---

[16] The concept of condominial sewage designates a simplified sewerage network. Costs are reduced for two reasons: (i) length of pipelines necessary is less as pipes

uted to the civil works and to some extent to the design of the system itself. This approach is based on the hypothesis that a synergy based on the complementarity between the technical expertise of operators and the social capital of local populations can emerge, under certain conditions, and can lead to a co-production of services (Oström 1996). In India, this mode of management is mostly promoted by NGOs.

The Alliance in Mumbai is a proponent of such long term action rather than project oriented approach. It was created in 1987 based on the coalition of SPARC (Society for the Promotion of Area Centres), an NGO, and two community based organizations: the NSDF (National Slum Dwellers Federation) and an organization of women's collectives, Mahila Milan (Women Together). In a large sewerage project funded through the World Bank, the Mumbai Municipal Corporation introduced a Slum and Sanitation Programme. The usual practice is that the sewerage department builds the toilets while the maintenance is carried out by the conservancy department. Through this programme, new institutional arrangements were thought of which SPARC first disagreed with because of a low implication of communities themselves. Changes were made and with the insistence of the World Bank, SPARC decided in October 2000 to bid for the construction of toilet blocks and won the tender as the price they proposed was lower (Patel and Mitlin 2001: 18). In this scheme, the engineer in charge in the Corporation itself insisted that the programme be demand driven with users forming community based organizations (source: interviews). This example demonstrates how the strategy of the Alliance has enabled it to both engage with the communities and with municipal authorities to improve access to services. The Alliance has also built an extensive network within India and has promoted exchanges between communities in South Africa and other South Asian countries through the Asian Coalition for Housing Rights.

The middle classes and the elites are also getting organized. Local networks, made of personalities, NGOs, resident associations start exerting influence through lobbying and the development of tools to benchmark the public agencies' performance and accountability. The 'report card' system introduced by the Public Affairs Centre of Bangalore is a pioneering effort and is being replicated all over India (Paul and Sekhar 2000). A sample of the population is surveyed and is

---

are installed in the compounds of houses (and not along the houses); (ii) inhabitants contribute in kind to the works, thereby diminishing construction costs.

asked to rate the public agencies and municipal departments according to various criteria. The format followed is simple and carried out again after a few years, allowing a time line analysis. Thus, it brings about an assessment of public service perception over time and accross department agencies. These two features of the report card system can act as an incentive to improve performances. In addition, the reports are published by the Public Affairs Centre and are widely disseminated in monthly meetings on civic issues where around 200 resident associations as well as public agencies are invited to discuss it. It highlights the growing importance of social networks.[17]

... but Questions on Sustainability and Representation

The emergence of civil society raises many questions. We shall here look at two of them. The first one concerns the sustainability and the technical viability of infrastructures built and managed by local populations. International experiences of condominial sewerage have shown the difficulty in sustaining these projects mostly because it requires a strong solidarity and homogeneity within the community. This is not necessarily given and can imply a long capacity building process. In India, social links and shared values, in other words the social capital of communities is often valorised in a romantic vision. But, in cities, some factors are not conducive to the strengthening of horizontal links between populations, among them caste and regional differences. In fact, vertical links between community leaders and local councillors might predominate, inducing political patronage, which does not favour civil engagement. Regularization of colonies, especially the legal land status, is the second condition necessary to ensure sustainability. This cannot be separated from the efforts on service provision. The Alliance in Mumbai stresses the need to ensure right to the land and housing to low-income communities prior to access of basic services. This requires a better urban governance (enhanced collaboration between agencies, clear definition of responsibilities, questioning on the modes of financing).

---

17 Other forms of public protest led by the elites is often found through the tool of the Public Interest Litigation and the recourse to the judiciary system. This procedure is used in the water supply and sewerage sector, especially on pollution issues, but it is not discussed in this paper. However, the growing role of the judiciary, its impact on the sector and implications on democracy would require further research.

At the level of the city, civic engagement can be a source of conflict of interests. For instance, securing land tenure rights (and therefore water and sewerage access) can be opposed by associations concerned with environmental issues. They demand more 'green and public' spaces or they simply oppose the transformation of their living space. Mumbai, where forty per cent of the population lives in slums and occupies only eight per cent of the land is a good example. The NSDF has been involved in conflicts and discussions with municipal authorities and political leaders for more than twenty years in order to secure allocation of land, with property rights, for evicted slum dwellers. Alongside, organizations such as Citispace or the Bombay Environmental and Action Group are principally focusing on the creation of parks, public spaces that they believe are encroached by slum dwellers. These contradictory agendas illustrate the complexity in defining objectives of a sustainable development and raise questions as to who represents whom and also as to exactly where these organizations draw their legitimacy from.

Limits of the participatory approach – praised by international organizations and to some extent recently by the public sector – are compelling. Supposed to enhance democracy, participation can also announce the withdrawal of the State. If participation can provide some answers, it cannot be a substitute to a financial solidarity, institutionalised through subsidies or balancing out mechanisms. Without these mechanisms, the financing of water supply and sewerage would have been impossible in developed countries (Barraqué 2003).

Conclusion: The Unavoidable Reform of the Public Sector

Privatisation and the creation of a regulatory commission for the electricity and telecom sectors, private investments in roads and airports, all this gives the impression that the liberalization process engaged in the 1990s has had a considerable impact on infrastructure. This is not the case for water supply and sewerage. This specific sector, highly capitalistic, in a natural monopoly situation and with a prominent social dimension, remains in the public sphere, despite the promotion of private sector participation by the central government and international organizations. Numerous hurdles to improve the service which range from the weak financial situation of municipalities (despite the law on decentralization), the preservation of a technical culture; a bureaucratic and hierarchical functioning of municipal departments or Boards; and tensions between local councillors and local administrations. The overlapping of institutions add to this scenario, making the thinking (and the implementation) on urban policies, especially regarding land, difficult and secondary. Thus, it reinforces a technical and sectoral coordination or/and an increase in coverage remains slow especially for sewerage in low-income areas. The presence of new actors and the response of the users exacerbate some of these issues.

We believe that these new actors and the emergence of civic engagement are not marginal phenomena. These evolutions will last and require a transformation of the public sector mode of action in its ability to enter into negotiations and constructive dialogue with the civil society and private partners. Being able to develop, strengthen and consolidate contractual relationships is another need. As of today, these changes are still in a nascent stage. The importance of credible commitment of the State in order to create the necessary conditions for a positive synergy between actors imply two levels of reforms: at the macro level as far as the institutional environment and the respective role of the three levels of government is concerned; and at the micro level for the internal functioning of municipal departments and Boards.

At the macro level, the role of the Ministry of Urban Affairs remains too limited. It should evolve towards developing elaborate guidelines and providing institutional and technical support to accompany the process of building capacity at the State and city level to elaborate, monitor and regulate contracts. The intermediary role of the States in defining urban policies should translate into clear and credible policy decisions on which players can base their own strategies. It will certainly involve a change in the subsidies level and the definition of land policies in coordination with municipalities. At this last level, a stronger collaboration between elected councillors and the local administration requires a clear delineation of responsibilities. This could both increase the autonomy of administrations and public agencies and enhance the accountability of elected leaders.

Parallel to this, the transformation of public agencies is essential to reform the public sector. One should however underline that municipalities and Boards are not immovable structures. The combination of a more decentralised environment and the pressure of users groups have had consequences. Recent partnerships with local entrepreneurs and users' groups emerge. Some improvements have been made regarding customer service (information on the service, facilitation for payment, publication of citizen charters). Truly, this responds to the need of middle class groups and urban elites. However, it indicates a shift towards realizing the importance of understanding the demand, even if it is not yet accompanied with integrated tools to collect, follow and monitor information. Except for some cases, like Chennai, where discretionary powers of engineers and technicians were increased, command chains are still based on a bureaucratic control, which are structurally permanent. To transform this would require a change in budgetary rules and human resource management. These changes have to be considered at least as important as increase in investment, tariff reform and financial autonomy, which are comparatively more discussed and put forward.

REFERENCES

Barraqué, B., 'Not too much but not too little: the sustainability of urban water services in New York, old Paris, and New Delhi', in *Sustaining Urban Networks: The Social Diffusion of Large Technical Systems*, edited by Coutard, O., Hanley, R., and Zimmerman, R., Routledge (forthcoming), 2004.

Datta, B., 'Management of Infrastructure Projects in Urban Local Bodies: case study of Kanpur Development Authority', in *India Infrastructure Report 2002. Governance Issues for Commercialization,* 3iNetwork, New Delhi: Oxford University Press, 2002, pp. 206-211.

Dupuy, G., *L'Urbanisme des Réseaux. Théories et méthodes*, Paris: Armand Colin, 1991.

French Water Club et al., Water sector in medium-sized cities in India, Polygraph, 2002.

GOI, Manual on Water Supply and Treatment, Government of India, New Delhi: Ministry of Urban Development, 1991.

GOI, The Constitution 74th Amendment Act 1992 on Municipalities, New Delhi: Government of India, 1992.

GOI, Second United Nations Conference on Human Settlements: Habitat II. Istanbul 1996. India National Report. Government of India, New Delhi: Ministry of Urban Affairs and Employment. Department of Urban Employment and Poverty Alleviation, 1996.

Hirschman, A., *Exit, Voice and Loyalty*. Cambridge: Harvard University Press, 1970.

Jaglin, S., 'Villes disloquées ? Ségrégations et fragmentation urbaine en Afrique Australe', in *Annales de Géographie*, 619, 2001, pp. 243-265.

Jain, A.K., *The making of a metropolis*, New Delhi: National Book Organization, 1990.

Janakaranjan S., 'Competition, Conflicts and Crisis - An Example of Degraded Groundwatwer Regimes and Feckless Governance In South India'. Paper presented in a regional groundwater management seminar, organized by the Global Water Partnership at Islamabad, Pakistan 9-11 October, 2000.

Kamat, A., Water Profiteers. http://www.corpwatchindia.org/issues/PID.jsp?articleid=1604. 28 May, 2002.

Le Galès, P., 'Du gouvernement des villes à la gouvernance urbaine'. in *Revue française de Sciences Politiques*. vol (1), 1995, pp. 57-95.

Llorente, M. and Zérah, M. H., 'La distribution d'eau dans les villes indiennes: quels réseaux pour quels services?', in *Flux, Cahiers scientifiques internationaux Réseaux et Territoires*. no. 31/32. January – June 1998, pp. 83-89.

Mehta, M., A Review of Public-Private partnerships in Water and Environmental Sanitation in India, New Delhi: Department For International Development, 1999.

Oström, E., 'Crossing the great divide: Coproduction, synergy and development', in *World Development*, vol. 24(6), (1996), pp. 1073-1097.

Patel, S. and Mitlin, D., The work of SPARC, the National Slum Dwellers Federation and Mahila Milan, Working Paper Series on Poverty Reduction in Urban Areas. Working Paper 5. Human Settlements Programme. IIED. London 2001.

Paul, S. and Sekhar, S., Benchmarking Urban Services. The Second Report Card on Bangalore. Bangalore: Public Affair Centre, 2000.

Ruet, J., Saravanan, V.S. and Zérah, M.H., The water and sanitation scenario in Indian Metropolitan Cities: Resources and management in Delhi, Calcutta, Chennai, Mumbai, Occasional Paper no. 6, New Delhi: Centre de Sciences Humaines, 2002.

Tova Solo, M., Competition in water and sanitation. The role of small-scale entrepreneurs, Viewpoint no. 165, Washington D.C.: Banque Mondiale, 1998.

The Hindu, Closure notice to four unlicenced water packaging units, Chennai, 30 April 2002.

The Hindu, Metrowater may go in for smaller, eco-friendly lorries, Chennai, 21 July 2002.

Tovey, K., Murky boundaries: Water for the poor, a public, private or collective good? Insights from Delhi's Jhuggi Jhompri colonies, First Year Report, Department of Geography, University of Cambridge 1999.

WSP, Willing to pay but unwilling to Charge. Water and Sanitation Program South Asia, 1999a.

WSP, Improving Water Services through Small Scale Private Providers: Water Vending in Chennai. Water and Sanitation Program South Asia, 1999b.

Zérah, M.H., Water Supply and Sanitation in Vijayawada: Analysis of households' situation towards modes and cost of access, consumption and level of satisfaction, Cerna India, Research Report. Mumbai, 2002.

Zérah, M.H., The Cancellation of the Pune Water Supply and Sewerage Project. Water and Sanitation Program South Asia, New Delhi: The World Bank, 2001.

Zérah, M.H., *Water. Unreliable Supply in Delhi*, Delhi: Manohar, 2000.

Zérah, M.H. and Llorente, M., Institutional Innovations in the Indian Water Supply Sector. Final Report, New Delhi: Centre de Sciences Humaines, 1999.

6

REFLECTIONS ON URBANIZATION IN WATER: INFRASTRUCTURE AND LOCAL DISCOURSE IN A TOWN IN THE MAKING

BETTINA WEIZ

INTRODUCTION

Urban anthropology has widely covered the perception and appropriation of urban space by its inhabitants (Hengartner 2000: 91; Hutchison 1994), but so far it has been less concerned with the discourse about the concrete infrastructure. Yet the setting-up of water mains, telephone lines, transformer stations, gas-pipelines or sewer pipes is not merely a practical and technical process; the infrastructure is shaped in a social discourse on privileges, distribution of assets, rights to access to services, hopes of future possibilities and so on. This chapter focuses on a place in northern Tamil Nadu to explore urbanization; it shows how the development of a municipal water supply comes about with a social process, new spatial identifications and new ways to appropriate resources.

Urbanization has usually come along with the promise of freedom, democracy and new chances. In the 'modern public space' (Caldeira 1999) people of all backgrounds can interact and thereby contribute to the production of an open society. This openness must be especially attractive for many Indians whose society relies so heavily on compartmentalization (Ramachandran 1989: 80-1; Béteille 1997). Yet at the beginning of the new millennium, the metioned promises of urbanization seem to be on the wane. Low, for example, in a review of anthropological research on cities of the 1990s, groups several studies under the headings 'The Divided City' and 'The Contested City' according to segregations of race, class or gender that develop in the cities under research (Low 1999). Marcuse and van Kempen identify the trend towards 'an increase in the strength of divisions in the city and the inequality among them' (Marcuse and van Kempen 2000: 220) and speak of the 'Partitioned City'. These concepts have been developed mainly relating to cities of the Americas. This chapter places them in an Indian context as it shows in which way urbanization patches up divisions and partitions or how it deepens them. Above all it asks for the motivations of people to opt for more or less 'urban' solutions of their problems.

The area under scrutiny in this chapter may be typical for other emerging cities in South India beyond the metro-cities, in the '*mofussil*' area. This notion, other relevant concepts and the setting are presented in part one. Part two starts with a note on the method and introduces the study of the local water supply as a tool to understand the urbanization in a given place. Furthermore, the arrangements to supply water are of interest because they present one of the most pressing tasks of governance in the study-region, an area that suffers from frequent droughts. Part three traces signs of urbanization in the changing arrangements to supply water and shows how this issue has contributed to the social and symbolic production of what could be understood as 'urban space' and to the emergence of a sense of locality.[1] This leads, in part five, to the answer of the question for the motivations and finally to the conclusion.

THE 'MOFUSSIL'

Social scientists have been debating for at least six decades the question of how to define 'city'. Some have reached a point at which they recommend to drop the term altogether and substituting it, for example, with concepts like 'Functional Community Area'. (Frey and Zimmer 2001: 31) Several authors and especially administrators concerned with Census procedures or with the governance of cities have proposed a dichotomy of the urban and an 'other', mostly called the rural. One of the problems that emerge with such dichotomies relates to the settlements of different size (Rao 1983: 88-94) and to areas at the fringes of cities. Denominations for these zones beyond the city limits abound: 'City-region', 'urban fringe', 'the peri-urban zone', 'primary umland' and 'secondary umland', 'periphery', 'urban shadow zone', 'perishables supply zone' to name but a

[1] 'Locality' occurs in the anthropological debate mostly in the context of migration, groups in diaspora, and globalization (Kokot 2000: 197-8). This paper supposes that the perception of 'locality' can change as time goes by even among people who continue to live in the same place.

few (Rao 1983: 130-52, 186-95; Friedrichs 1995: 99-114). To cope with this 'blurring of the urban-rural distinction' (Jones and Visaria 1997: 13), new concepts of cities such as 'desakota'-region (McGee 1991), 'conurbation', 'metropolitan area', 'edge city', 'urban agglomeration' cropped up (Champion 2001). The Indian Census adopted the latter in 1971. Yet these demarcations seem to be often arbitrary (Ramachandran 1983: 113).

The study area is an example thereof. On one hand, Tirukkalukundram in Kanchipuram District is influenced by the proximity (70 km) of Chennai, South India's biggest metropolis. It also fulfils the official criteria of a city itself as it acquired the status of an Urban Town Panchayat and has been the headquater of a *taluk* since 1997. On the other hand, Tirukkalukundram's inhabitants do not perceive it as a town. According to the statistics of its Panchayat office, Tirukkalukundram had 34,000 inhabitants in 1999. It stretches out over 15.63 sq. kms and comprises five revenue villages. It grew steadily in the past century, starting with less than 6,000 inhabitants in 1901.

Table 1. Population Growth of Tirukkalukundram

Year	Inhabitants	Growth in per cent
1901	5,728	
1911	6,838	19.38
1921	7,957	16.36
1931	8,623	8.37
1941	9,505	10.23
1951	11,407	20.01
1961	12,881	12.92
1971	16,593	28.82
1981	19,804	19.35
1991	23,333	17.82

Source: Census of India 1991. Note: The growth between 1961 and 1971 is in part due to the incorporation of outlying villages in the area of Tirukkalukundram.

There is a constant influx of people who come to work in Tirukkalukundram – immigrants from other states as well as daily commuters. As the latter get out of the buses that brought them from the villages as far as

20 km away, other commuters take their seats and proceed to Chennai for the day, to work in factories or to puzzle over software-solutions for customers in the USA or in Europe. In 1879, Charles Stewart Crole, collector of Chingleput District to which Tirukkalukundram belonged at that time, wrote: 'The neighbourhood of the Presidency town which the people have not yet learned to turn to their real advantage, is at the bottom of most of the unsatisfactory conditions, which have caused the district to be described with too much truth as the "most backward in the whole Presidency" ' (Crole 1879: 65). He deplored what would nowadays probably be called braindrain: The well-to-do, apt people of the district move to Chennai and exploit the region from the distance not bothering about the state of its agriculture and other economy. More than one century later, new dimensions have been added to this picture. Emigration of skilled people continues. But many rather dwell in Tirukkalukundram and endure rides of at least six hours per day in noisy buses than shift to Chennai. A number of ambitious inhabitants have learned to turn the ever spreading presence of Chennai to their real advantage, e. g. to use the markets in the state-capital to sell their products or to get supplies, to send their children there for education, or to use the hospitals.

As to the perception of Tirukkalukundram by its inhabitants, the statement of a local lawyer may be paradigmatic: '[Tirukkalukundram] is neither a village nor a town. It comes in-between'. The lawyer has spent enough time in Chennai and elsewhere to be able to tell the difference. A senior staff worker of a local kindergarten compares Tirukkalukundram with the place of her birth, a village in the vicinity. '[That one] is very rural [*romba graamam*]', she says and shudders a bit as she imagines how it would be to live there again. She prefers Tirukkalukundram because it provides all the amenities she needs: a wide variety of shops, a daily and a weekly markets, cinemas, telephone lines, medical practitioners, five banks and artisans of all crafts. On the other hand, she – like many inhabitants of Tirukkalukundram, especially the women – does not like travelling to Chennai. She fears it as being too hectic, anonymous, stressful and even dangerous. She points out that Tirukkalukundram is small enough so that people know each other and that everything is within walking distance. It enhances the rural aspect of Tirukkalukundram that many of its inhabitants invest their money in agricultural lands and gadgets such as motor pumpsets to have rice or sugarcane cultivated by their tenants or by daily wagers.

Nobody would have contradicted the statement that Tirukkalukundram is neither *graamam* nor *nagaram*, neither village nor city. So what is it then? How could this space in-between city and village be designated? I got a clue from a conversation I had with a 23-year-old divorcée of Tirukkalukundram. After her home had broken, she returned to her parents' house. Since then she has been avoiding to visit even the temple as she knows that she is the target of much gossip. Her dreams of starting all over again will only come true in a town, never in Tirukkalukundram, she said with a deep sigh and hissed, the area is '*mofussil*'. The first evidences of *mofussil* (or corruptions of this term) being used in Indian English stem from 1781 (Yule and Burnell 1986 [1886]). Today it is a word in colloquial Tamil as well as of local English. In Arabic, where it originates, *mufassal* means 'separate', 'distinct', 'particular' (*Ibid.*; Wilson 1855: 349; Temple 1897: 81). Inhabitants of Chennai employ it to refer to the area that lies beyond the metropolis and its faceless suburbs. Through their lenses, it has a tinge of backwardness and provincialism. However, it does not refer to agrarian sites alone, but may include towns - as far as they are distinct from the capital of a province (Whitworth 1976 [1885]: 208). In the wake of urbanization, the *mofussil* attains a quality of its own.

Anthropologists have frequently warned not to 'essentialize' the concept of 'city' and to keep in mind the various and shifting contexts in which cities are positioned and present themselves. The 'urban' should be viewed rather as a process than as a type or a category (Low 1999: 1-2; Kokot 2000: 200). Yet if 'urban' is understood as a process, it should be clearly demarcated from the concept 'urbanization'. This in turn has various meanings. It can signify both, the increase of the population per square kilometre, and the concurrent changes in values, cultural and behavioural patterns (Barnett 1973). In addition to that, in the Latin American context, anthropologists have introduced the concept of 'social urbanization' which refers to the ideological extension of the urban system to the former hinterlands, that is 'urban' ideas are taken to exist far outside a location that would fulfil the first mentioned criteria for 'urbanization' (Bommer 1993: 120-35 and Wildner 1993: 2-6).

A multitude of approaches to the 'city' and 'urbanization' revolve around notions of concentration and integration,[2] which is ultimately in

2 Cf. Tisdale (1942: 312) "Urbanization is a process of population concentration. It proceeds in two ways: the multiplication of the points of concentration and the increase in size of individual concentrations.", and Leeds (1979: 231), where he depicts cities as "concentrations of more or less large ranges and arrays of certain

line with two of the oldest definitions, both of 1938, namely that of Mumford: 'The city [...] is the point of maximum concentration for the power and culture of a community' (Mumford 1938: 104), and Wirth: 'a city may be defined as a relatively large, dense, and permanent settlement of socially heterogeneous individuals' (Wirth 1938: 8). Thus in this chapter, for practical reasons, I use the term 'urbanization' whenever I refer to a process of concentration and integration of people, resources, ideas, infrastructure, services, and capital in the locality in question. This allows to differenciate between activities and praxes that are more or less urban, even though all of them may occur inside what is usually called a city. For example if a person in Chennai draws his water from his own well at home, I would label it less urban than the case of an inhabitant of Tirukkalukundram who obtains his water from the outlet of a centralized, integrated municipal water supply scheme in pipes. By *mofussil*, I refer to places that develop a distinct character as being less urban than mega-cities.

URBANIZATION REFLECTED IN THE WATER SUPPLY

As this chapter scrutinizes why people opt for more or less urban solutions for their problems and as it explores appropriations and perceptions of places, it is in the ambit of the much debated 'anthropology of the city'. It considers a given city as a whole and aims at finding out how it 'works' and relates to the wider social, cultural and historical context (Bommer 1993: 137-46). A successful approach to an anthropology of the city results from considering the urban space no longer as a delimitation of the ethnographic field, but as the object of the perception and appropriation of its inhabitants (Kokot 2000: 199-202). 'Theorizing the city [...] is a necessary part of understanding the changing postindustrial /advanced, capitalist /postmodern world in which we live', writes Low (Low 1999: 2). Yet how can urban dimensions be grasped with the traditional tools of anthropologists? Among the most

---

types of specialties" as well as Hannerz (1992: 173) "In the city we find in the most concentrated form within a limited space, the kind of cultural complexity that this book is about..." or Sassen (2001: 256); she highlights the role of cities in the global process of concentration and integration: "There is growing agreement about the fact of a network of major cities cutting across the North/South divide, cities that function as centres for the coordination, control and servicing of global capital." and observes, p. 258, "a new cross-border geography of centrality."

fascinating as well as saddening and maddening features of cities, especially of those in countries of the south, is their monstrosity in terms of population, required infrastructure, and economic output. Twenty-three cities of a population of more than one million emerged in India in the twentieth century, three of which had a population of 8 million or more and therefore met the United Nations criterion to be termed 'mega-cities' (Visaria 1997: 270). An entire metropolis can hardly be covered with participant observation, and this is true for *mofussil* areas as well.

To cope with that problem various anthropologists have confined their fieldwork to certain aspects of a given city – for example to single streets or neighbourhoods, to specific groups or subcultures within cities. So methodologically they created 'their villages' within the cities, running danger of losing the context in sight (Welz 1991: 29-43; Hannerz 1980; Mitchell 1987). This approach amounts to what is being discussed as 'anthropology in the city'. Others resort to the sphere of figures and formulae as e. g. in network analysis that has a certain tradition in urban anthropology (Schweizer 1988). Additionally, the general trends of medialization and the preoccupation with signs and representations in post-modern anthropology come handy for researchers of cities who have to grapple with the monstrosity of their objects of research. Symbols, symbolic acts, 'fictions' or narratives, and representations in the media condense meanings and experiences and serve to depict how a city as a whole 'works'.

For example, real estate advertisements in the local newspaper can serve as mirrors of the lifestyles and give cues to understand patterns of social differentiation (Caldeira 1999: 88). 'Mental maps' (Lynch 1960), explorations in planning processes, the analyses of specifically meaningful situations and occurences as well as of names of locations make use of representational or iconic material (Wildner 1993: 11-17). This chapter focuses on the water supply.[3] The arrangements to provide the households with water serve as symbolic tools to understand urbanization in Tirukkalukundram. This shall prevent the risk of constructing a 'village within the city', because the water supply concerns everybody in Tirukkalukundram, irrespective of social standing, age, religious affiliation, or gender. Moreover, the quality of the water supply is an indicator of the equitability of a society and of the quality of its governance.

---

3 I conducted fieldwork intermittently between December 1998 and November 2000, partly financed by a scholarship of the Indian Government and by the German Academic Exchange Service.

The most conspicuous feature of Tirukkalukundram's water supply – apart from wells – are open water reservoirs within the settlement. In the study area, they are called *kulam*.[4] They are typically rectangular with more or less clearcut edges. Flights of stairs – or at least rough slabs – on one, two or all four sides provide a rather riskfree access. The smallest *kulam* of Tirukkalukundram measures 27 by 27 metres, the biggest about 170 by 220 metres. Most range in the middle between these extremes. They receive the rain that precipitates on the spot, the surface runoff, often helped by small earthen channels which are connected to the groundwater stream. Some *kulam*s hold water all year round, especially if they have wells in their beds.

A typical picture of such a *kulam* would show lots of people taking baths. It would be set to the beat of women doing the laundry and resound with the merrymaking of children. They use the *kulam*s as playgrounds and swimming pools. There might be basket-makers soaking their canes, or herdsmen would be watering cows, buffaloes, goats or flocks of ducks. Somebody might be washing his bicycle. The surroundings of *kulam*s are often replete with materials of all kinds that people find convenient to store there – stacks of straw, leaves of palmyrah-palms, bricks or sand to construct huts. The public space compensates for the lack of storage room in the private houses and huts. There may be public threshing-floors, oxen may be relaxing in the shadow of trees that surround the *kulam*s, benches invite to sit down or to alight one's headload on them.

The *kulam*s also serve various ritual purposes. For example, during ceremonies like weddings or bestowals of the sacred thread, sprouted grains are being thrown into the *kulam*. There are certain ritual ablutions on special days of the year. Many families visit the *kulam* for the annual commemoration ceremony of the ancestors. The obsequies after a death culminate in a rite in which the son of the deceased symbolically hands over his father's or mother's soul to the *kulam*. Hence *kulam*s are reservoirs of both, water and the souls of the ancestors. Two of Tirukkalu-

4 In Indian English, they figure as 'tanks'. This term is confusing: Firstly, it glosses over important distinctions among different types of water reservoirs in Tamil Nadu (Mukundan 1992: 2). Secondly, outside of India the standard usages of 'tank' are 'closed container' or 'armed car', both of which is very different to what *kulam* means. On 'tank', Yule and Burnell (1986 [1886]: 683 – 85) write: "This is one of the perplexing words which seem to have a double origin, in this case one Indian, the other European" and trace it to Gujerati roots. Laping 1982: 83 assumes a Sanskrit background. For clarity, I will stick to the word *kulam*. Ganesan (1995) provides a long list of Tamil terms for water reservoirs with explanations.

kundram's *kulams* are sites of floating festivals, during which the images of the local form of god Shiva and his various companions are taken around *kulams* on huge decorated rafts. One *kulam* of Tirukkalukundram is situated inside a temple compound, and it is there that the temple festivals usually begin and end. Other *kulams* may have shrines or little temples at their sides. Several *kulams* are called *theertams*, that means holy places or holy water. But the profane usages dominate clearly. The sacred is but one aspect of *kulams*.[5]

A striking feature of *kulams* in Tirukkalukundram – and in most other settlements I came across in Tamil Nadu – is their high number. I found 14 *kulams* in Tirukkalukundram. However, whenever I asked inhabitants of Tirukkalukundram for the number of *kulams* or *theertams* in their place, the answer was invariably 'twelve'.[6] Yet few people were able to enumerate these *kulams* exhaustively, and if so, the lists differed. Obviously the sheer number is important in itself. Also in other places in Tamil Nadu, set numbers of *kulams* are reported, for example seven each in Tiruttani and in Kanchipuram, relating to the seven days of the week. Thanks to the high number of *kulams* in Tirukkalukundram each neighbourhood has at least one reservoir of its own. This amounts to a water-supply network that is highly de-concentrated and thus non-urban in the above defined sense. It also enriches the identification with one's neighbourhood: If people use the *kulams* of their neighbourhoods for many everyday activities such as doing the laundry, this is the chance to interact with their neighbours. They also establish a physical relationship with their neighbourhoods as they take bath in their *kulams*, drink its water and probably eat the fish that were raised in them. As the souls of the ancestors remain in the *kulams* of the neighbourhoods, the sense of identity touches even the historical dimension.

The people of Tirukkalukundram classify the *kulams* generally as *pothu idangal*, public places, but their access and utilization are restricted. These restrictions apply firstly to specific purposes. There are *kulams* to bail drinking-water from. Other *kulams* serve to water animals, yet others to take bath after witnessing a cremation. Certain *kulams* were used mainly by washerpeople. I found no *kulam* that would have been set aside exclusively for one purpose, just predominantly so. *Kulams* are basically

---

5 On the sacredness of *kulams* see C. P. R. Environmental Education Centre 2002.

6 This number also figures in a palm-leaf-manuscript on Tirukkalukundram, the age of which is not clear; the first paper edition I found of it dates from 1938 (republished in Vetacalam 1999: 28-9). Several informants advised me to refer to books to find out the exact names of the *kulams*.

multi-purpose institutions. However, separating *kulam*s for various usages surely helped to keep the bulk of them clean. Much stricter are caste-based restrictions of access to *kulam*s. It is always clear which neighbourhood a *kulam* belongs to, even if it lies at the boundaries of two neighbourhoods.

I use the term 'neighbourhood' firstly in a spacial sense – refering to the households in the vicinity. Neighbourhoods (and *kulam*s, too) usually have proper names. Secondly, it involves a certain degree of corporate organisation. This shows also in the right to exploit the *kulam*s' produce – for example, the fish, the firewood that grows on their banks, the mud which is moulded to bricks. These rights would be auctioned off. The headman of the neighbourhood, the non-elected *naatar*, would do it, or the committee of the neighbourhood's temple. They invest the money for the benefit of the neighbourhood which may include the maintenance of the *kulam*. I recorded stories of collective action of the neighbourhood towards the *kulam*. For example in cases of torrential rainfalls people of the neighbourhood assembled to hurriedly fortify the banks or to clear the inlet channels in order to prevent their houses from being flooded. In one instance the youngsters of one of Tirukkalukundram's neighbourhoods reportedly armed themselves with sticks and chased away a man who had started to build his house on the public place of the *kulam*'s flank. He had come from a different neighbourhood.

Thirdly and most importantly, people of Tirukkalukundram associate neighbourhoods with castes. In everyday conversations 'a person from M. N. Kuppam' will be synonymous with 'a *Naicker*', 'someone from Desamukipettai' will be tantamount to 'a *Mudaliyar*', or 'a man from Ayarbady' will refer to an *Itaiyar*. The reports of people of castes other than that of the respective neighbourhood being banned from its *kulam* are galore. This pertains particularly to *Paraiyar*s and to other 'SC-people'.[7] Older informants remember that such scenes happened in Tirukkalukundram as well, even though I have not witnessed one myself. Various *kulam*s in Tirukkalukundram are said to have been guarded by watchmen until recently. In some adjacent villages the institution continues to exist. In one case, a Brahman couple that resides at the banks of a *kulam* has pushed the rule through that only *Brahman*s are allowed to

---

7 In the study area, nobody would call them 'untouchables' openly. After all, this would be unconstitutional. The common term (by SC as well by non-SC-people) is 'SC' or 'SC people' after the administrative category 'scheduled castes'. Yet it is exactly the question of exclusion or inclusion of that group which is at stake in this conflict - as this is meant by 'untouchability', I use the term here.

bathe in the *kulam* and that the other inhabitants of the village may at most draw drinking water from it.

The separation of castes is a means to keep *kulam*s not only physically clean but also ritually pure (Dumont 1999 (1970): 46-60). In sum, deep-rooted notions of purity and pollution helped to perpetuate the multitude of *kulam*s in Tirukkalukundram. At the same time they reflect the divided and partitioned nature of south Indian villages and towns such as Tirukkalukundram in less urban contexts.

SIGNS OF URBANIZATION

In 1966, a municipal water supply was installed in Tirukkalukundram. It carried the urban promise of democracy and equality: It implied that everybody will drink water which stems from the same source, which flows in the same mains and which pours out of the same type of taps for people of all castes, classes, genders, religions and other affiliations. It stands for an era which has overcome the times when only *Brahman*s had the right to take bath in *kulam*s with good-quality water. The municipal water supply system is pumping water from the Palar river in a 20 km-pipeline to an overhead-tank in Tirukkalukundram and distributing it from there through a system of mains to taps. These are either located in private homes or in public areas such as street corners. Since 2001, two new overhead tanks have been constructed and more mains and pipes laid to integrate into the system neighbourhoods and people who until that date had relied on *kulam*s or on wells to get their water.

There are no reliable data on the condition of *kulam*s before this more urban system of water supply was introduced. Judging from the statements of the inhabitants, several *kulam*s have deteriorated in the past decades. For example an 84 year old lady who resides at the *kulam* in a market street remembers that its water used to be clean at the time of her marriage. At the time of the fieldwork, it is the filthiest *kulam* of the study area. It is emitting a dreadful stench, is full of faeces and rubbish, and its flanks are completely ramshackled. Pigs love to wallow in it.[8] In an even more extreme case, a *kulam* was filled up and a temple dedicated to Gangai-Amman, a massive cement structure, was erected on the spot. One *kulam* has become the area where Tirukkalukundram's municipal dustmen dump bazaar waste. Many parts of the network of channels that

8 See the chapter by Bellwinkel-Schempp in this book for more on the cultural significance of pigs in Indian cities.

feed the *kulam*s are silted up, full of refuse, or houses and streets have been built on them. Yet most *kulam*s prevail, albeit in dilapidated conditions. Eight are (at least occasionally) used to do the laundry.

Among the few *kulam*s that are fairly well-kept, *Sangu theertam* stands out. It is the biggest *kulam* of Tirukkalukundram and the most elaborate one, equipped with pillared halls, granite slabs, parapet, shrines and a special entrance which is said to once have been reserved for elephants during festivals. Today no animals are taken into *Sangu theertam* anymore; the most frequent of the manifold usages of *Sangu theertam* are washing and doing the laundry. Especially before noon there is hardly any place left at the stairs to float *saree*s or *loongies*, men's wraps. Women not only from the neighbourhood but from all over Tirukkalukundram, including from distant streets, are taking the laundry there. For many of them, this entails time-consuming, strenuous walks with heavy loads on their heads and hips. But the water in the *kulam*s of their vicinities is spoilt. A barber is offering his services at the *Sangu theertam.* Boys are coming from far away streets of Tirukkalukundram to catch fish. One flank and patches of the others is stinking awfully. Obviously people are using them as toilets.

There is more to *Sangu theertam* than these profanities. A lot of myths and stories focus on it. It receives the runoff of the hillock on top of which towers the ancient temple of Shiva. As in many other *kulam*s of Tamil Nadu, *Sangu theertam*'s water is said to have medicinal and miraculous qualities. Every twelfth year a conch (*Sangu*) is believed to emerge from the water. Priests of the big Shiva temple are locking them carefully away and worship them. Judging from the amount of conches collected so far the custom is not older than a century. There is also an annual grand floating festival. Many Hindus are making use of *Sangu theertam* for rituals: For instance they are going there to perform the prescribed last rites after a death or on the commemorative days. Notably in summer people are taking vows which is usually accompanied by dramatic ceremonies at the sides of *Sangu theertam.* Its water serves for all kinds of ritual baths. For these purposes, *Sangu theertam* draws people from far flung neighbourhoods of Tirukkalukundram and sometimes even from other villages. Thus the souls of the ancestors are put to rest in a central place of Tirukkalukundram nowadays instead of decentrally, near their families.

Hence *Sangu theertam* is gradually absobring the functions of other *kulam*s of Tirukkalukundram. It embodies the reverse of the lacklustre medal of their decay. As a process of concentration and integration, it is a sign of urbanization in Tirukkalukundram. Moreover, *Sangu theertam* has become an issue in local politics, or, vice versa, it offers an arena for various local groups to distinguish themselves. Several parties are laying claims to the *kulam*. Examples include

- the administrators of the local temple. *Sangu theertam* comes under their official administration, yet they are lacking the necessary means for its maintenance.
- a religious movement which a pious man of Tirukkalukundram has founded on the lines of the popular Aiyappan- and Adi-Parashakti-cults. He claims to have organized groups of young men to guard and clean *Sangu theertam*.
- representatives of the local political parties, including the Member of the Legislative Assembly, the mayor and representatives of opposition parties. Whenever anything good is to be done towards *Sangu theertam*, they are quick in claiming it as their success.
- different denominations of Hindus declare *Sangu theertam* to be 'theirs'. Followers of vaisnavism argue that the conch belongs to god Vishnu's paraphernalia and that the apparently most ancient of the shrines at *Sangu theertam*'s flanks is dedicated to Hanuman, Vishnu's companion. The anointment of Vishnu's idol with the help of a conch is an integral part of vaisnavite ceremonies and is called, like the *kulam*, *Sangu theertam*. Followers of Shiva contest that and maintain that *Sangu theertam* belongs to the grand Shiva-temple of the place, that it is there where the conches are kept and that important processions for god Shiva encompass *Sangu theertam*.
- a recently constituted group of committed citizens who want to promote the welfare of Tirukkalukundram, *Ur nala peravai*. Its members are present at important rituals in the big Shiva temple and at important instances of public life to check that everything is done according to the rules and incorruptibly so. They, too, publicize their concern with the *Sangu theertam*.
- Finally, the contested *Sangu theertam* has become an issue even beyond the *mofussil*: A Member of Parliament from Chennai, respectively New Delhi has allotted 10 lakhs, that is a million rupees for its renovation.

The people of these parties have various things in common. They usually belong to the local middle or upper classes, and many of them have wells at home. Some can even afford private connections to the municipal water supply or (for drinking) water in bottles or cans. A typical statement would be 'Why do I need the *kulam*? I get the water from the tap.' They are almost invariably men – and as such customarily not in charge of doing the laundry or supplying water to the household. Thus the vast majority of those who actively take part in the contest over the responsibility for *Sangu theertam* hardly ever use *Sangu theertam* for day-to-day purposes.

Many of the men attended the same schools. Tirukkalukundram has a girl's and a boy's high schools and number of middle and elementary schools which pupils from the outlying villages attend as well. Their caste-backgrounds[9] may be diverse: They belong predominantly either to merchant's (*Cettiyar*), the administrative (*Kanakkuppillai*) and the priestly (*Brahman*, *Gurukkal*) castes which traditionally enjoy quite a high esteem in vast parts of the population. Or they are members of a farmer's (*Vanniyar, Naicker, Vellaalar*) or the weaver's (*Sengundar*) castes which are showing a strong upward mobility in Tirukkalukundram. But obviously they tend to set aside the caste differences that exist among each other when it comes to distinguish themselves *vis a vis* the SC-people.

Leaders of the local dalit parties also claim rights to *Sangu theertam.* They argue that the Panchayat should take better care of its surroundings and dispose of the refuse that amasses at certain flanks. The dalit leaders would seamlessly shift to the topic of free access to streets and other public amenities. Thus their approach is fundamentally different from that of the above sketched parties in Tirukkalukundram, and I know of no case in which a Paraiyar would openly act and be publicly recognized as a member of them. I will call the people behind these parties the 'mainstream society'. Even though they do not numerically form the majority of Tirukkalukundram's population, they are the men who have the means to make things happen in Tirukkalukundram. It is them who promote *Sangu theertam* and the municipal water supply scheme and who withdraw their support from most *kulam*s so that it becomes difficult or impossible to maintain them.

---

9 Caste understood as a group that is putatively endogamous and competes with other such groups for social status and privileges. Some authors tend to replace the word 'castes' with 'communities' (Singh 1999). However, as 'community' in the Indian context has come to be used to label different religious groups such as Hindus, Muslims and Christians, I find it too confusing to use it here. In Tamil, there is no equivalent term for caste. The word *jaati* is used in that sense. But it has a broader meaning: Signifying 'category', it can be applied to a whole array of phenomena, including various types of rhythmical patterns.

However, a plethora of people in Tirukkalukundram still depends on non-urban ways of getting water, because the municipal water supply scheme has severe drawbacks. It supplies water only on an hourly basis once in two or three days. There is no fixed schedule when the water will be available, so the women and the children of the neighbourhood have to stand long vigil at the taps in order not to miss the release of water and queue up to get their turns. Many households belonging to the mainstream society have tanks at home to store water for days where there is no supply, but poorer people lack these resources. In the year 2000, there remained 1,800 connections to be built to reach the goal of one public tap per 30 households – for which the money was not available.[10] Only the happy few of Tirukkalukundram afford to pay Rs 25 per month (soon to be raised to Rs 35 per month) plus the installation charges for a private water connection. Streets in which active members of the mainstream society live who can make powerful representations at the office of Tirukkalukundram's Executive Officer can count on sooner connections to the municipal water supply and on better maintenance and quicker repair of damages. I heard most of the complaints about bad supply in a neighbourhood of Tirukkalukundram that is chiefly inhabited by SC-people.[11]

MOTIVATIONS

Within Tirukkalukundram's mainstream society, various motivations to opt for more urban modes of the water supply can be singled out. Firstly, there are financial interests. Denying any direct responsibility (or agency) towards *kulam*s, borewells and other elements of the public water supply, members of the mainstream society argue that they pay their taxes and expect the Panchayat Union to see to the repair and maintenance. Most of them will prefer to suffer for years together from stinking ditches or leaking valves, loudly complaining about the Panchayat, to taking action themselves, that is to taking a spade and cleaning the ditch or fixing the valve. From the perspective of members of the mainstream society, this is no fatalism, on the contrary: It is them who

---

10 Information given by the Executive Officer of Tirukkalukundram.

11 Above all these complaints reflect the subjective feeling of being neglected by the municipality. In fact many taps had run dry when I inspected them, but due to the general intermittency of supply it was impossible to prove for how long this situation persisted.

after all profit greatly from the situation. Whenever the Panchayat Union does something towards the upkeep of the water supply, money from higher echelons of the state pours into the local economy.

The technical contraptions and constructions involved in pumping, storing and distributing the water, in lining of wastewater channels with concrete etc. devour enormous sums. For example, the extension of the system during my fieldwork cost Rs 174.58 lakh. New jobs are created, for example in the local health department: The neglect of teh *kulam*s and their inways results in waterlogging and the emergence of breeding places for mosquitoes, the transmitters of diseases. Filaria (the 'elephant-foot-disease') is rampant, and the Panchayat created four jobs of workers who tour Tirukkalukundram and spray poison in a hopeless battle against the disease. The local contractors and administrators who share these jobs and this money among themselves belong to the mainstream society.

A necessary prerequisite to agree with this shift of control from the neighbourhood-level to the level of Tirukkalukundram as a whole would be that Tirukkalukundram is small enough. Unlike in a metropolis such as Chennai, in Tirukkalukundram it is quite easy to meet the Executive Officer who is in charge of the minor public works in Tirukkalukundram, or the responsible persons of the Public Works Department, or the ward members, or the mayor. Their offices are constantly flocked by people who want to stay in touch with the decision-makers. The distances are short, the relevant people well known, they belong to the local mainstream society themselves. Hence giving up one's control over the resources such as the *kulam* in one's neighbourhood, this does not necessarily mean disposing of every access to control over resources. On the contrary, there will be many members of the mainstream society for whom new possibilities emerge, and on a bigger scale than in less-urban contexts. This is what makes it attractive for them to stay on in the *mofussil* area and not to move to more urban places where they would have no influence.

Those who are not part of the mainstream society find themselves devoid of their agency in the more urban context in which it requires administrative acts to get things done or to prevent them – which is more complicated and takes much longer than to take direct action oneself. Once a poor weaver showed me round the construction site of a new water mains in his area. His weaving-pit was regularly inundated because water stagnated in his area during the monsoon. Some years before, he said, he and some neighbours would have picked up spades and dug channels to lead the water away. Probably not everybody in the neighbourhood would have come, but certainly enough men to finish the work reasonably soon. At the time of the fieldwork, new water supply mains were being laid in shallow ditches that on many spots crossed the lines of drainage, obstructing them rather than helping the water to find its way.

Furthermore, the weaver spotted hundreds of metres of expensive tubes that were completely superfluous. The contractor who executed this work was a distant relative of the weaver and lived just round the corner, but the weaver had no means to stop this waste of money as the decisions were not taken on the level of the neighbourhood anymore but of Tirukkalukundram as a whole, in circles to which he did not have access. If he and his equally affected neighbours picked up spades and cleared the drainage lines (workforce they would be ready to contribute free of charge), they would damage the expensive pipes and cause trouble with the locally powerful.

There is another motivation for the mainstream society not to use the water of their respective neighbourhoods, even though it would often be available in sufficient quantity, easy to get and also cheaper. This is due to the very same notions of purity and pollution which were shown before to be instrumental for the upkeep of the multitude of *kulam*s. The above cited rhetoric conveying the impression that Tirukkalukundram's neighbourhoods are castewise homogenous is unrealistic – perhaps it reflects the situation of bygone times, perhaps wishful thinking. House-to-house surveys show that the neighbourhoods are becoming castewise more and more diverse. The mentioned influx of people from other parts of the country as well as the outflow of those who leave the *mofussil* area make themselves felt. Houses change hands. It becomes more and more uncontrollable which kind of person uses the water of the *kulam* in one's neighbourhood.

During my fieldwork, I kept asking my informants for their opinion on the *kulam*s and what could be the reason for their decay. Off-handed answers would mostly be 'because of the population growth', 'because of cultural change', 'because times are changing' or the like. As I got better acquainted with the informants and inquired in more detail, they would become more outspoken. They explained that all kinds of people live now in their respective neighbourhoods. How could they make sure that there was no menstruating woman defiling the water? One family recalled the time before their own well was dug in the backyard of their new house. They spared no pains and carried their heaps of dirty clothes on a bicycle over a distance of three kilometres to where they owned a paddy field with a well. There they did the laundry – to keep it from mixing with *kulam*-water that impure persons could have defiled. In several instances, my informants lowered their voices and said, the *kulam*s of their respective neighbourhood could not be controlled anymore as even SC-people had moved to the area.

In spite of the apparent mixing of people of diverse castes in the neighbourhoods, the study area remains deeply divided on the lines of caste. There are especially many clashes between *Paraiyar*s (belonging to the SC-category) one one hand and *Vanniyar*s or *Naicker*s on the other hand. During the period of my fieldwork it happened frequently that the hustle and bustle of Tirukkalukundram's bazaar came to a sudden standstill because there was trouble brewing between these castes: stone throwing in the streets, fistfights, blocked roads, buses set to fire. In the past decade there had been even deaths. The above described filthiest of all *kulam*s of Tirukkalukundram lies at the heart of the erstwhile *Brahman*s' neighbourhood of Tirukkalukundram, the *agraharam*. Albeit many *Brahman*s have left, several stay on, and some *Jain* families moved in. They are usually not less fussy about purity than the *Brahman*s. Yet they obviously do not see a chance to control the *kulam* and prefer to wall themselves in and to not even look at the *kulam* any longer. The above mentioned statement on the water quality by the 84-year-old lady tells as much about social changes as about the water.

As for the *Sangu theertam*, people of all kinds of castes dwell around it. Strangers come frequently as they visit the marriage halls, the post office, the court or the schools that are built at the flanks. It is easily accessible on all four sides. This traffic – adding to its sheer size – makes its utilization hardly controllable. When I asked members of Tirukkalukundram's mainstream society on their opinion about that, they argued for example that *Sangu theertam* is so big that it is hard to pollute the water. Furthermore it contains holy water. Others admit that they do not use the *kulam* for day to day purposes, just for religious ceremonies. It becomes clear why *Sangu theertam* is such a contested *kulam*. Some very articulate members of the mainstream society promote a special plan: When I return to Tirukkalukundram, they promised, I will find *Sangu theertam* cleaned and fenced in. It shall not be accessible but through a heavy gate which will be opened only for pure usages. In short, they reduce *Sangu theertam* to a religious place, stripping it of its multipurpose-character. At the same time, they promote it even beyond the *mofussil* as a symbol of Tirukkalukundram, that is of the locality which they chiefly constitute by their own activities. For example the temple authorities had multicoloured leaflets printed to advertise for Tirukkalukundram and to solicit donations among pilgrims who frequent the place. In these broshures *Sangu theertam* ranges prominently as a touristic spot. For those who turn to this *kulam* because they have no other sources of water, the proposed fencing of the *Sangu theertam* will be disastrous.

Furthermore, in the short run, the municipal water supply scheme makes governance easier as it relaxes the strong linkage of water with locality embodied by *kulam*s. In seasons of sufficient water, I often came across leaking valves and taps that somebody had left open with the water running waste. The municipal water system offers local politicians, members of the mainstream society, the opportunity to export problems that are created by the carelessness towards water resources or in its over-exploitation in one's own locality. To see what this means one has to trace Tirukkalukundram's pipeline towards the Palar river. Surprisingly, it does not tap the riverwater at the nearest point, which would be the easiest and comparatively cheapest way. It takes a deviation of about two costly kilometres until it reaches Vallipuram. Vallipuram's mayor complains that since more and more water is pumped away to Tirukkalukundram, the water level in the area has gone down so remarkably that farmers nearby the pumping station find it difficult to carry on cultivating. Asked why he does not defend the village against the thirst of Tirukkalukundram, he shrugs and explains, that Vallipuram is chiefly inhabited by SC-people, that he belongs to the communist party and that all this means that he has no good standing in regional politics. And if he would stand up? He shrugged again and said, in such a case there would be menaces and quarrels.

Finally, some wealthy members of the mainstream society have found their way to even evade the democratizing aspect of the municipal water supply that is the fact that everybody drinks the same water. In late 2002, the first dealer of water in cans started to operate in Tirukkalukundram. The labels on the plastic-cans promise that the water is pure according to international ISO-norms through '100 percent double reverse osmosis', 'UV-disinfection' and other treatments the names of which must, in the ears of most inhabitants of Tirukkalukundram, sound at least as mysterious as verses in Sanskrit. As 25 litres cost Rs 30 plus Rs 100 deposit, only few people of Tirukkalukundram can afford this water, a fact that bequeaths to it an exclusivity like that of the erstwhile separate *kulam*s for *Brahman*s. Currently there is a boom of bottled water in India; the market is expected to grow at a rate of 40 to 50 per cent every year.

Beverage companies from abroad are especially active in this field: The Coca Cola corporation for example, has been selling table water since 2001 and reached a market-share of 38 percent within two years.[12] Yet table-water is no solution for the unsolved problems of the water supply: Let alone ecological considerations, canned table water is economically out of the reach of 98 percent of the Indian population.

CONCLUSION

This chapter has used its focus on the water supply to explore a form of urbanization that occurs outside the metropolises in India. Tirukkalukundram in Tamil Nadu has served as an example of these vast '*mofussil*' areas. Tirukkalukundram is developing a distinct urban character and is set off against the mega-city – and not just because it has its proper water supply based on old local reservoirs and a new municipal system of pumps and pipes. The times are gone in which men of means neglected what could be found in Tirukkalukundram and oriented themselves exclusively around the capital city. The newly emerging powerful persons in the locality are not moving to bigger cities; many of them are staying on and asserting their standing in the *mofussil*, and thus the standing of the *mofussil*. They acclaim its advantages versus the disadvantages of living in a bigger city and speak up for its points of interest, which include Tirukkalukundramís biggest water reservoir.

This development, which on the regional level can be understood as partitioning or decentralization, accompanies a process of centralization on the local level. In the wake of urbanization, the grip of neighbourhoods on their local resources relaxes. Water reservoirs that were reportedly cared for by people in the vicinity are now managed on the level of Tirukkalukundram as a whole. Hence, a new political arena is levelled in the locality. It offers fresh opportunities to assert power and to lay claims on resources. Along with that, a *mofussil* city like Tirukkalukundram becomes a more important focus of identification and action than the erstwhile caste-based neighbourhoods, many of whose restrictions vanish in the course of urbanization. A mainstream society develops, adding to 'old' identifications based on neighbourhood, caste or class. Members of castes like weavers, shepherds or petty farmers whose ancestors may not have had much of a say in local politics have a chance

[12] Interview with Nantoo Banerjee, spokesperson of Coca Cola India, 10.03.2003

to become powerful political agents. They lose the control over the resources in their immediate neighbourhood, but they probably gain influence over the resources that are central to Tirukkalukundram as a whole. They often have the opportunity to choose, for example, whether they want to be connected to the municipal water supply system or whether they would rather continue using their private wells and the local old water reservoirs. In that sense, urbanization in a place like Tirukkalukundram creates a 'modern public space' as referred to above. This is mirrored by the dilapidation of the decentralized neighbourhood-managed water reservoirs and the comparatively good condition of the big, central reservoir.

However, a closer look at the process of urbanization in Tirukkalukundram discloses how well it matches the picture of the 'Partitioned', 'Divided', 'Contested City' mentioned at the outset of this chapter. First, the population is divided along lines of income and wealth. The well-to-do inhabitants of Tirukkalukundram can afford to use other sources of water than the nearby water reservoirs and evade their responsibility to maintain them, so that it is hard or impossible to keep them in shape. Yet their poorer neighbours still rely mainly on those non-urban, decentralized sources of water, especially as the municipal supply is far from sufficient. Women, who are generally in charge of provisioning their families with water, have to cover longer distances to get water from the big, central water reservoir if the little reservoirs in their neighbourhoods have become too dirty or dilapidated to use. The alternative is to spend long hours waiting for the scant municipal supply.

Second, as notions of purity and pollution prevail, new partitions emerge in the process of urbanization, replacing the old ones. For example, if people have lost control over the water reservoir in their vicinity to the point that others whom they would like to keep out use it, they tend to wall themselves in and get water from the tap or a well if they can afford it. Furthermore, they use their political influence in the emerging political arena of the locality to have areas of purity preserved. An example is the proposed fencing of the big, central water reservoir of Tirukkalukundram. This would be detrimental to those who need it for everyday purposes.

'The process is an active one, driven by concrete actors advancing concrete interests against concrete opposition, rather than the perhaps unfortunate result of some immutable laws of development', observe Marcuse and Kempen, and my findings in Tirukkalukundram demonstrate that. They write that partitioning has extremely negative results for a vast number of people. 'It increases inequality, threatens democracy, and ultimately undermines the viability of democratic society' (Marcuse and van Kempen 2002: vii). In my study area, the new variety of partitioning would never have been possible without attempts to democratize society.

This chapter has shown that in both arrangements to supply water – the more urban one and the less urban one – space is partitioned and subdivided, the access to resources is restricted, and groups of people are excluded. The motivations do not differ much, even though the more urban water supply system comes along with the worn-out promise of new technology to overcome social cleavages. It is also ecologically questionable, as it relies on importing water from a distant place instead of using the rainwater that precipitates on the spot, forgoing the knowledge involved in decentralized arrangements to obtain water. (IETC 1999; Agarwal and Narain 1999). In sum, urbanization – here explored in a region outside the metropolises – brings about new arenas of politics, new spatial identifications and new groups of powerful people, but it does not unify a partitioned society.

REFERENCES

Agarwal, Anil and Narain, Sunita, eds., *Dying Wisdom: Rise, fall and potential of India's traditional water harvesting systems*, New Delhi: Centre for Science and Environment, 1997, rpt. 1999.

Barnett, Steve, 'Urban is as urban does: Two incidents on one street in Madras city, South India', in *Urban Anthropology*, vol. 2, 1 (1973), pp. 127-160.

Béteille, André, 'Caste in contemporary India', in Christopher J. Fuller, ed., *Caste Today*, New Delhi: Oxford University Press, 1997, pp. 150-179.

Bommer, Bettina, *Entwicklungslinien des Forschungsgebietes Urbananthropologie: Eine Untersuchung der Zeitschrift Urban Anthropology*, Bonn: Holos Verlag /Mundus Reihe Ethnologie, vol. 64, 1993.

C. P. R. Environmental Education Centre, ed., *Sacred Tanks of South India*, Chennai: The C. P. Ramaswamy Aiyar Foundation, 2002.

Caldeira, Teresa P. R., 'Fortified enclaves. The new urban segregation', in Setha M. Low, ed., *Theorizing the City. The new urban anthropology reader*, New Brunswick et al.: Rutgers University Press, 1999, pp. 83-107.

Caminataiyar, Ve., *tirukkalukkunrattu ulaa*, Madras: kesari accukkoodam, 1938.

Champion, Tony, 'Urbanization, suburbanization, counterurbanization and reurbanization', in Ronald Paddison, ed., *Handbook of Urban Studies*, London et al.: Sage Publications, 2001, pp. 143-161.

Crole, Charles Stewart, *The Chingleput, late Madras, District. A manual compiled under the orders of the Madras Government,* Madras : Lawrence Asylum Press, 1879.

Deliège, Robert, *Les Intouchables en Inde. Des castes d'exclus*, Paris : Editions Imago, 1995.

Dirks, Nicholas B., *Castes of Mind. Colonialism and the making of modern India,* Princeton: Princeton University Press, 2001.

Dumont, Louis, *Homo Hierarchicus: The caste system and its implications*, 1970; rpt, New Delhi: Oxford University Press, 1999.

Frey, William H. and Zimmer, Zachary, 'Defining the City', in Ronald Paddison, ed., *Handbook of Urban Studies*, London et al.: Sage Publications, 2001, pp. 14-35.

Friedrichs, Jürgen, *Stadtsoziologie*. Opladen: Leske und Budrich, 1995.

Ganesan, Sa., 'nir nilaip peyarkalum vilakkamum', in Godumudi Sa. Shanmugam, ed., *pantaip paacanap poriyiyal,* Chennai: tenolai, 1995, pp. 146-9.

Government of India, *Census of India 1991*, Madras: Government Press, 1991.

Hanklin, Nigel, *Hanklyn-Janklin or A Stranger's Guide to Some Words, Customs and Quoddities Indian and Indo-British,* New Delhi: Banyan Books, [4]1994.

Hannerz, Ulf, *Exploring the City: Inquiries toward an urban anthropology*, New York: Columbia University Press, 1980.

idem, *Cultural Complexity. Studies in the social organization of meaning,* New York: Columbia University Press, 1992.

Hengartner, Thomas, 'Die Stadt im Kopf. Wahrnehmung und Aneignung der Städtischen Umwelt', in Waltraud Kokot, Thomas Hengartner, Kathrin Wildner et al., eds., *Kulturwissenschaftliche Stadtforschung. Eine Bestandsaufnahme*, Berlin: Dietrich Reimer Verlag, Kulturanalysen Band 3, 2000, pp. 87-105.

Hutchison, Ray, ed., *Research in Urban Sociology. New directions in the United States,* vol. 4, Greenwich and London: Jai Press, 1994.

International Environment Technology Centre (UNEP-IETC), *Proceedings of the International Symposium on Efficient Water Use in Urban Areas. Innovative ways of finding water for cities*, Osaka /Shiga, 1999.

Jones, Gavin W. and Pravin Visaria, 'Urbanization of the third world giants', in *Urbanization in Large Developing Countries. China, Indonesia, Brazil, and India*, Gavin W. Jones and Pravin Visaria, eds., Oxford: Clarendon Press, 1997, pp. 1-23.

Kokot, Waltraud, 'Diaspora, Lokalität und Stadt. Zur ethnologischen Forschung in räumlich nicht begrenzten Gruppen', in Waltraud Kokot, Thomas Hengartner, Kathrin Wildner, eds., *Kulturwissenschaftliche Stadtforschung. Eine Bestandsaufnahme,* Berlin: Dietrich Reimer Verlag/ Kulturanalysen Band 3, 2000, pp. 191 - 203.

Laping, Johannes, *Die Landwirtschaftliche Produktion in Indien. Ackerbau-Technologie und traditionale Agrargesellschaft dargestellt nach dem Arthasastra und Dharmasastra,* Wiesbaden: Franz Steiner Verlag, Beiträge zur Südasienforschung Band 62, 1982.

Leeds, Anthony, 'Forms of urban integration. 'Social urbanization' in comparative perspective', in *Urban Anthropology*, vol. 8, no. 3 /4 (1979), pp. 227- 47.

Low, Setha M., *Theorizing the City. The new urban anthropology reader,* New Brunswick et al.: Rutgers University Press, 1999.

Lynch, Kevin, *The Image of the City*, Cambridge, Mass.: MIT Press, 1960.

Marcuse, Peter and van Kempen, Ronald, eds., *Globalizing Cities. A New Spatial Order?,* Oxford: Blackwell Publishers, 2000.

_____, eds., *Of States and Cities. The partitioning of urban space,* Oxford: Oxford University Press, 2002.

McGee, T. G., 'The emergence of *desakota* regions in Asia. Expanding a hypothesis', in *The Extended Metropolis. Settlement transition in Asia,* Norton Ginsburg, Bruce Koppell and T. G. McGee, eds., Honolulu: University of Hawaii Press, 1991, pp. 3 - 25.

Mitchell, J. Clyde, *City, Society and Social Perception. A central African perspective,* Oxford, 1987.

Mumford, Lewis, *The Culture of Cities,* New York: Harcourt, Brace, 1938, rpt. in Douglas L. Miller, ed., *The Lewis Mumford Reader,* New York: Pantheon Books, 1986.

Partridge, Eric, *A Dictionary of Slang and unconventional English: Colloquialisms and catch-phrases, solecisms and catachreses, nicknames and vulgarisms*, ed. Paul Beale, New York: Macmillan Publishing Company, [8]1984.

Ramachandran, R., *Urbanization and Urban Systems in India,* Delhi et al.: Oxford University Press, 1989.

Rao, Vadhiparti Prakasa, *Urbanization in India. Spatial dimensions*, New Delhi: Concept Publishing Company, 1983.

Sassen, Saskia, 'Cities in the Global Economy', in Ronald Paddison, ed., *Handbook of Urban Studies*, London et al.: Sage, 2001, pp. 256 -72.

Reiniche, Marie Luise, 'The urban dynamics of a caste. A case study from Tamil Nadu', in Christopher J. Fuller, ed., *Caste Today,* New Delhi: Oxford University Press, 1997, pp. 124-49.

Schweizer, Thomas, *Netzwerkanalyse, Ethnologische Perspektiven,* Berlin: Dietrich Reimer Verlag, 1988.

Singh, K. S., *Communities of India*, New Delhi: Oxford University Press, 1999.

Temple, G., *A Glossary of Indian Terms relating to Religions, Customs, Government, Land and other terms and words in common use*, London: Luzac & co., 1897.

Tisdale, H., 'The process of urbanization', in *Social Forces*, vol. 20 (1942), pp. 311 - 316.

Vetacalam, Ti. Ca., *tirukkalukkunram tala varalaaru,* Tirukkalukundram: T. M. Pattapiraman veliyeetu, 1999.

Visaria, Pravin, 'Urbanization in India. An overview', in: Gavin W. Jones and Pravin Visaria, eds., *Urbanization in Large Developing Countries: China, Indonesia, Brazil, and India,* Oxford: Clarendon Press, 1997, pp. 266-88.

Washbrook, David A., 'Caste, class and dominance in modern Tamil Nadu. Non-brahmanism, dravidianism and Tamil nationalism', in Francine R. Frankel and M. S. A. Rao, eds., *Dominance and State Power in Modern India. Decline of a social order,* vol. 1, Delhi: Oxford University Press, 1989, pp. 204-64.

Welz, Gisela, 'Sozial interpretierte Räume, räumlich definierte Gruppen. Die Abgrenzung von Untersuchungseinheiten in der amerikanischen Stadtforschung', in Waltraud Kokot und Bettina Bommer, eds., *Ethnologische Stadtforschung. Eine Einführung* Berlin: Dietrich Reimer Verlag, 1991, pp. 29-44.

Whitworth, George Clifford, *An Anglo-Indian Dictionary: A glossary*, London, 1885, rpt. New Delhi and Gurgaon: Indian Documentation Service, 1976.

Wildner, Kathrin, '"Picturing the City": Themen und Methoden der Stadtethnologie', in *kea* no. 5 (1993), pp. 1-21.

Wilson, H. H., *A Glossary of Juridical and Revenue Terms and of useful words occurring in official documents*, London: W. H. Allan and Co.,1855.

Wirth, Louis, 'Urbanism as a way of life', in *American Journal of Sociology*, vol. 44, no. 1 (1938), pp. 1-24.

Yule, Henry and Burnell, A.C., *Hobson-Jobson*, first published 1886, revised 1903, 1985, rpt. New York: Routledge and Kegan Paul, 1986.

7

WASTE AND THE CITY: PUBLIC RESPONSES TO THE PROBLEMS OF MUNICIPAL SOLID WASTE MANAGEMENT IN INDIAN METROPOLITAN CITIES

MICHAEL KÖBERLEIN

INTRODUCTION

The emergence and existence of highly developed civilizations have always been associated with a high degree of social development and an advanced standard of public health and sanitation. Accordingly, people in the prehistoric times had already learnt to dispose wastes[1] outside their settlements in order to protect their habitat from unhygienic conditions and the consequential spread of parasitic diseases.

The Harappa Civilization which emerged around 2500 BC in South Asia was the first civilization with a well planned garbage collection system, which was managed by an efficiently organised city cleaning brigade. Other than the first garbage collection system, the water closet and other sanitary techniques were also invented during the times of the Harappa Civilization (Palmer 1977: 5). However, with the decline of the Harappa Civilization, the skills to capably organize a waste disposal system got lost, and in the aftermath cities in South Asia had to cope with carelessly littered refuse and the consequent spread of common water and vector borne diseases, of which the most appalling were the plague and cholera. It was only during the twentieth century that these

---

1 The terms waste and refuse are used synonymously and refer to unwanted materials which are discarded and disposed off by people. Garbage refers to household and kitchen wastes, rubbish refers to inorganic wastes like plastic bags, papers and other packing material. Municipal solid waste includes refuse and residues generated from households, commercial and institutional areas as well as street sweepings.

water borne diseases were reduced to a relatively manageable level in India due to fundamental improvements in water supply and sanitation.

Solid waste management, however, continued to be the most neglected area of urban development over the years and accounted for severe urban health problems all over urban India. Accordingly, in the last two decades the outbreak of water and vector borne diseases were reported from numerous cities in India.[2] For instance, the devastating pneumonic plague in Surat, Gujarat, which occurred in September 1994, was largely associated with uncollected garbage which facilitated the growth of the rat population which is the primary source of plague-infected fleas. Only after this incident, urban solid waste management was publicly discussed with determination, put on the political agenda and accepted as an essential field of research and urban development in India.

This resulted in governments at the central, state and city level, non-government organizations (NGOs), individuals as well as research institutes paying enhanced attention to the continuously annoying problem of garbage and launching various waste management projects or special cleaning drives in order to counter the prevailing problems pertaining to waste disposal (Köberlein 1998). But all these political efforts soon slackened due to the common lack of public concern towards garbage and filth. Hence, even at the beginning of the 21st century, litter and uncollected refuse are an everyday sight and persistent nuisance for people living in Indian cities.

Accordingly, the objectives of this chapter are to examine the complexity and comprehensiveness of the current problems pertaining to municipal solid waste management in urban India, and to subsequently illustrate the responses of the public to this omni-present problem. The major focus here is on civic engagement and community based initiatives.

Conceptual Issues of Urban Solid Waste Management

Urban solid waste management is a tricky and delicate subject matter which involves various stakeholders and concerns all sections of the society. Hence, it is important to review some conceptual issues of urban solid waste management.

---

2 See for example the various reports in 'The Hindu Survey of the Environment 95' (*The Hindu* 1995).

Solid waste management is a crucial component of the urban infrastructure and an essential public health service, mandatory for the provision of sanitation and hygiene in an urban area. The execution of solid waste management is usually entrusted to municipal agencies, and is subsequently a part of urban governance. Urban governance, yet again, refers to "both the formal and informal political processes which determine, or at least influence, what happens in the city" (Devas 2002: 207).

Figure 1: Stakeholders in Urban Solid Waste Management in Developing Countries

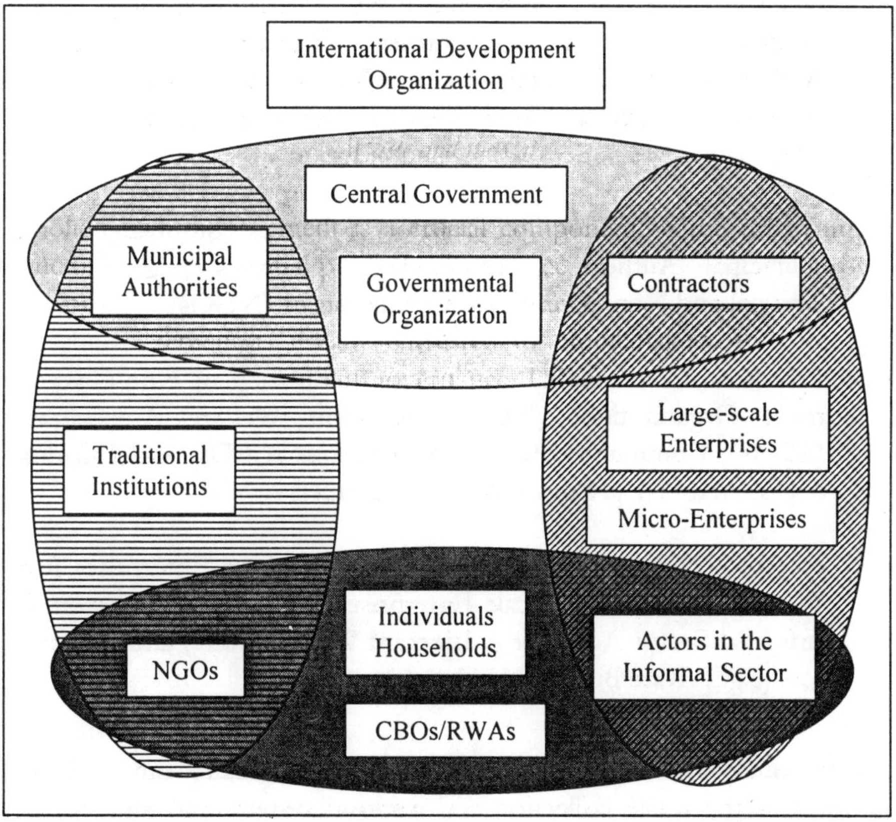

Draft: Köberlein 2004

Taking this definition into account, urban governance with reference to solid waste implies that all processes and activities concerning waste in the city form a part of urban solid waste management. However, this fact is widely ignored by those who are in charge to manage municipal solid waste in Indian cities, and hence not all processes and activities concerning waste in the city are performed by the municipal agencies. In fact, the contrary is the case, and solid waste management strategies in India do not take into account that apart from governmental institutions a wide range of other stakeholders are actually involved in urban solid waste management in Indian cities (see Figure 1, p. 179).

The entirety of stakeholders involved in urban solid waste management in Indian cities can generally be distinguished as:

- Policy Making and Administrative Institutions comprising of the Central Government, Government Organizations, Municipal Authorities and Contractors (e.g. Quasi-governmental Agencies such as the National Environmental Engineering Research Institute)

- Executive Institutions and Supervisory Bodies comprising of the Municipal Authorities, Traditional Authorities (e.g. Sweeper Unions) and Non-government Organizations (NGOs)

- Private and Community Institutions comprising of Non-Government Organizations (NGOs), Resident Welfare Associations (RWAs), Community Based Organizations (CBOs) and Informal Sector Actors (e.g. Private Waste Collectors)

- Private Sector Stakeholders comprising of Micro-Enterprises (e.g. Waste Dealers), Large Scale Enterprises (e.g. Recycling Factories), Informal Sector Actors (e.g. Itinerant Waste Buyers) and Contractors (e.g. Private Business Undertakings)

The various stakeholders play different roles and carry out different activities in the waste collection and disposal system, and also pursue different objectives and approaches with regard to urban solid waste management. The activities related to the waste collection and disposal system are best demonstrated by the 'so-called' waste disposal chain which encompasses a complex layout of interconnected activities associated with the generation, storage, primary and secondary collection, haulage, transportation, processing and final disposal of solid waste (Holmes 1984 and UNEP/IETC 1996).

In Indian cities, as a rule, the conventional concept of solid waste management is applied. This concept is very technically oriented with the primary objective being merely disposing of the generated waste for reasons of public health and hygiene. Solid waste as assessed in this concept is an omnipresent menace and a severe public health hazard. The modern concept of solid waste management, however, is a much more complex subject matter, comprising not only the technical aspects of the conventional concept, but also incorporating economic, ecological, institutional, political, social and cultural issues.[3] Environmental protection, economic feasibility and the common acceptance of the operational waste disposal system are the first priorities of this new concept. The implementation of the modern concept of solid waste management demands sophisticated institutional arrangements with a set of laws and regulatory instruments which define the obligatory institutional, technical and financial standards ensued by a high technological, logistic and sanitary know-how to operate an efficient waste collection and disposal system.

Causes and Effects of Inadequate Solid Waste Management

The causes of inadequate solid waste management and the resulting detrimental effects are illustrated in this chapter in order to understand the complexity and comprehensiveness of the current problems pertaining to municipal solid waste management in urban India.

Haphazard urbanization is seen as the basis of all the difficulties and complications with regard to the management of solid waste, followed by the incompetence of the governmental institutions to design and implement appropriate waste management systems and to amend and optimise the inadequate and 'antique' waste collection and disposal systems which are currently put into operation (see Figure 2, next page).

[3] In the technical jargon the term 'Integrated Solid Waste Management' is used for circumscribing the modern concept of solid waste management.

Figure 2: Causes and Effects of Inadequate Urban Solid Waste Management in India

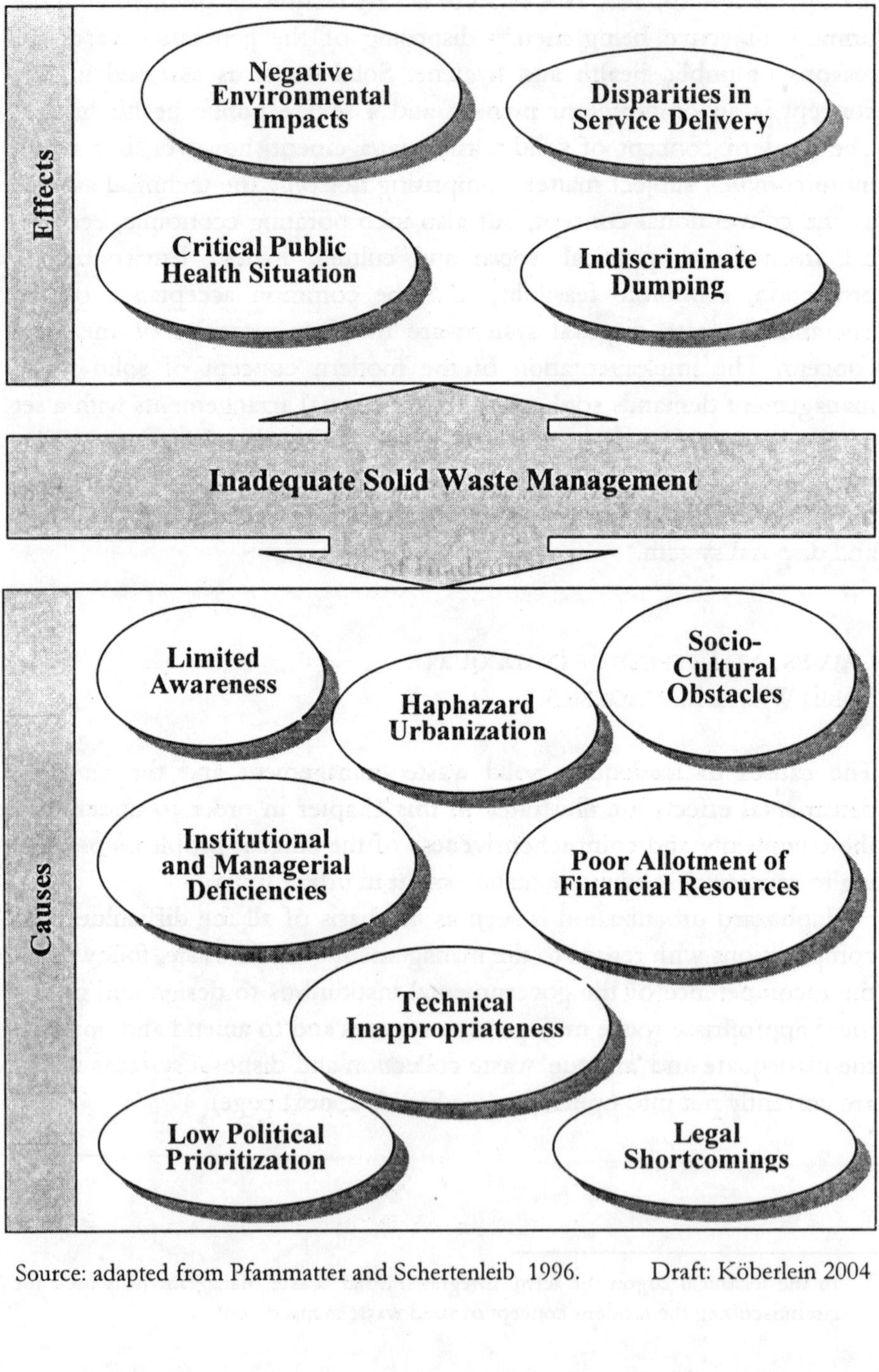

Source: adapted from Pfammatter and Schertenleib 1996. Draft: Köberlein 2004

Urbanization and its Impact on Urban Solid Waste Management

India has experienced rapid urbanization in the recent decades, which has brought about a rapid population growth, massive spatial increase in the urban areas as well as a substantial growth in the number of urban areas. At present, more than 300 million people live in nearly 3,700 urban areas, a quarter of whom live in unauthorized squatter settlements. The total urban population is estimated to increase to approximately 395 million by 2011 (Committee on Solid Waste Management 1999: 17). This rapid urbanization process has caused a tremendous lack in the delivery of urban services, which again is responsible for the immense ecological and social problems prevailing in Indian cities. Growing amounts of solid waste represents just one of the problems associated with haphazard urbanization, but it is a very apparent and repugnant one. The rapid urbanization has been accompanied by industrial growth and economic development which has led to an increasing per capita consumption and a growing generation of solid waste since Independence. As a result, Indian cities are nowadays confronted with an unprecedented amount of refuse and the consequential difficulties relating to waste collection and disposal. Yet, calculations predict that waste generation rates will even more rapidly increase in the near future and as such increasingly put pressure on the waste management systems which are in operation (see Figure 3).

Figure 3: Population Growth and Waste Generation in Urban India

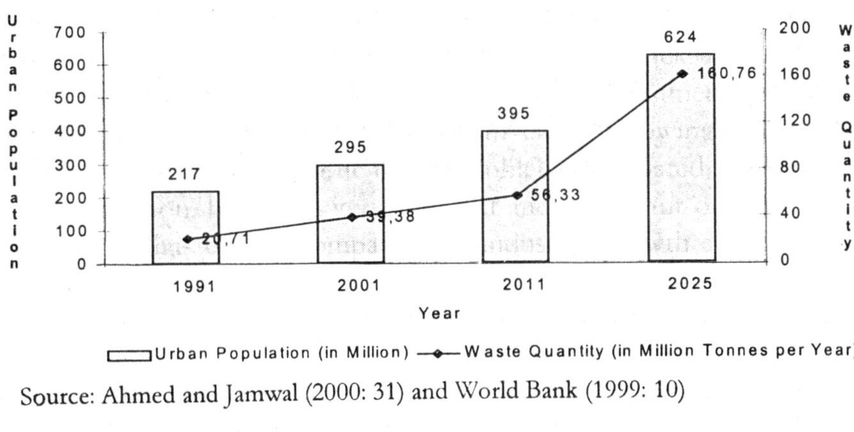

Source: Ahmed and Jamwal (2000: 31) and World Bank (1999: 10)

Furthermore, the task of managing solid waste has become more and more problematic and complicated as new types of waste, such as hazardous chemicals or different kind of plastic materials, have been introduced into the consumption cycle in the recent years. In the last decades, especially after 1991 with the commencement of the economic liberalization process, globalization and expanded international trade, which have led to growing per capita income and better living standards in the metropolitan cities, have also contributed to increasing waste generation rates, rising levels of uncollected solid waste, and the consequential unsanitary living conditions in many parts of the Indian cities. Rubbish which is scattered all over as well as untidy heaps of garbage are a vision of annoyance in most parts of Indian cities, and represent a severe health hazard for the greater part of the urban population. Even high income residential areas are affected by inadequate solid waste management as the cleaning of the back lanes and the areas around transfer points is usually neglected, and thus these areas are constantly littered with rotting garbage.

Moreover, Indian cities nowadays not only have to cope with the low quality of waste management services, but also suffer from enormous disparities in the level of services delivered between high income and low income residential areas, not to mention peri-urban areas and squatter settlements. In times of structural adjustment with diminished financial resources for municipal agencies, priority of waste collection services is exclusively given to high and middle income residential areas, thus increasing the already existing inequalities in urban service delivery. As documented by Chaplin (1999), it is the urban middle class who obstructs necessary sanitary reforms as they have been able to monopolize the basic urban services provided, and actively support the exclusion of the poorer section of the society. Several studies have revealed in detail the poor quality of waste management services provided to low income groups, and the deplorable unhygienic conditions prevailing in the majority of the urban squatter settlements (Ali 1992 and NIUA 1991).

Deficiencies in the Current Waste Management System

The deficiencies in the current waste management system can be attributed to various reasons, which act coactively and pertain to all involved stakeholders. The initial sources of all the deficiencies in the current waste management system stem from the various short-comings in the existing legislation. Although new rules and ordinances have been passed lately, the current legislation, apart from being inadequately enforced, is not comprehensive enough to cope with the whole spectrum of problems relating to urban solid waste management. The present legislation focuses mainly on the technical issues pertaining to municipal solid waste management and omits the other essential criterions such as the role specification of the various stakeholders or the definition of other regulatory standards. Moreover, existing by-laws are antiquated as some of them are still relics of the British colonial government, and are thus certainly inapt and obsolete (Bhide 1994: 24). For instance, no responsibilities or incentives are delegated to the citizens with respect to waste segregation or participation in community based waste collection schemes in the current rules, and as a result the whole task remains the responsibility of the municipal agencies who in turn consider solid waste management as "their domain" (Ahmed and Jamwal 2000: 37).

The personnel in charge of the sanitation departments[4] are in general not adequately trained, and are thus barely competent enough to fulfil the complexity and multifacetedness of the assigned task. The frequent transfers of executive personnel additionally hamper effective long term planning or the introduction and implementation of new and appropriate waste management systems (Ali, Olley and Cotton 1999: 497).

The auxiliary personnel employed in the sanitation departments often have only low qualifications and literacy standards, but they are routinely promoted from the lower sections of the department, based solely on the number of years served in the department. In-service training, if carried out, is often inadequate, and hence most of the employees are not proficient enough to handle more demanding jobs or take individual decisions.

In addition to the lack of qualified staff, the institutional and administrative framework also suffers from various deficiencies. The overlapping of jurisdiction and functions between different departments of a municipality, as well as between municipalities, State and Central Government, obstructs the effective performance of waste collection and disposal activities. Furthermore, the interdepartmental co-ordination is unsatis-

4 In small and medium size cities, the personnel in charge are usually public health officers who have a medical background, and thus often lack the technical and managerial know-how. In larger cities (Class I) the municipalities are provided with a separate solid waste department which are usually managed by civil engineers.

factory as there is often much antagonism among the various municipal departments (Köberlein 2005).

In matters of applied technology, it has been generally assessed that the equipments used and operational structures applied are inappropriate or deficient and in many Indian cities also insufficient with respect to actual waste management problems (Bhide 1994, Köberlein 2005 and Mehta 1995). Sanitation departments, for instance, are rarely provided with adequate long term plans concerning solid waste management. The lack of basic data about quantity, composition and characteristics of solid waste is one of the major deficits, since a good database is the key for operating a prolific and efficient waste collection and disposal system. Long term planning for municipal solid waste management, if contrived, is usually done on a very technical basis, hinging rather on the technologies and know-how developed in western countries than on Indian concepts and appropriate technology.

Waste processing methods such as composting, bio-gas generation or pelletization are widely neglected and only seven to ten per cent of the waste collected in Indian cities are utilised by the municipal agencies as a resource.[5] This fact implies that about 90 per cent of the refuse collected is just dumped without any processing (Central Pollution Control Board 1995: 11). The most critical deficits, however, exist in the field of final disposal. There is not a single sanitary landfill in India which deserves the name `sanitary´. Refuse is usually just dumped and levelled at designated landfill sites which normally do not have any modern technical facilities such as bottom layers with impermeable linings, leachate collection and treatment, and a gas control system.

One of major reasons for the technical inappropriateness of the waste collection and disposal system is that the sanitation departments in general suffer from a deficient budget, due to the fact that the majority of the municipalities carry large debt obligations and cannot assign any extra funds required for the improvement of the waste management systems. Apart from the lack of financial resources, the administrative structure is often set up very inefficiently, as up to 85 per cent of the available budget is spent on the salaries for the employed staff

---

5 Processing and recycling activities are mainly carried out by informal sector actors. On account of an elaborate and very efficient system, accessible recyclables (paper, glass, metal and plastics) are sorted out of the waste stream and find its way back into the production and consumption cycle (Köberlein 2003). Still, the greater part of the recyclables are not salvaged from the waste disposal chain, but merely dumped at the landfill sites.

(Committee on Solid Waste Management 1999: 143). Only a minor part of the budget can thus be used for the maintenance of the equipment and hardly any capital remains for investments in new equipments (Ali, Olley and Cotton 1999: 501).

The largest part of the employed staff belongs to the Balmiki community[6] who are traditionally obliged to carry out all cleaning work owing to their caste status. Even nowadays all inferior activities in the sanitation departments, such as street sweeping or manual loading of refuse onto the waste collection vehicles, are undertaken by members of this particular community. Sweepers usually have a low social status and minor promotion prospects in the municipalities, but their socially discredited occupation, their huge number within municipalities, along with their capability to organise collectively through labour unions makes them a very strong and influential group. Their collective power is one of the most important reasons for the restricted involvement of the private sector in waste collection activities, as sweepers see privatization as a direct threat to their livelihoods. Attempts have been made in various cities to introduce a less labour intensive waste management system or change the prevailing waste collection scheme, but all of them have failed due to massive resistance by the sweepers, usually in the form of strike actions.

Apart from technical, financial and operational issues, attitudinal or behavioural aspects also add to the current appalling situation in Indian cities. Many people lack environmental consciousness and have no understanding on handling refuse. The high rate of illiteracy and especially the widespread ignorance of the people further intensify the current difficulties. The sanitation departments hardly conduct any public awareness campaigns in order to fill this gap and moreover, there is very little environmental education at school and other educational institutions. A great number of citizens take urban services for granted as they perceive that the entire legal and obligatory responsibilities of waste collection and disposal lie with the civic authorities. Moreover, people are unwilling to collaborate with civic authorities and are reluctant to participate in the new approaches initiated by the municipal agencies as they have lost their trust in any government organization. Apart from that, many people have adapted a kind of Western lifestyle and have

---

6 The Balmiki or Valmiki community comprises of different groups like Bhangi, Mehtar, Lalbegi, Chura and other castes. This community is historically associated with scavenging work and the collection of refuse in North and Central India (Singh 1999).

acquired the distinctive throw away behaviour, which also accounts for the litter visible in most Indian cities (Mehta 1995: 66).

PUBLIC RESPONSE

Urban solid waste management, like most other urban services, is entrusted to municipal authorities in India. These municipal authorities, however, have proved to be incompetent in systematically countering the negative effects of inadequate solid waste management as illustrated above. Taking these circumstances into consideration, the question arises as to which strategies or initiatives have been taken up to respond to the difficulties in the management of solid waste and the concomitant deterioration of the public health conditions.

The Government responded to the detrimental effects of haphazard urbanization with the preparation of new policies which were to enhance the quality of urban governance. The most important developments in urban policy making, which also had a significant impact on the operation of the solid waste management systems, are the decentralization process, the quest for improved public participation and the move towards the privatization of urban services.

However, apart from government institutions, also the public in the form of dedicated citizens became active and responded to the ever present problem of waste. Among the various initiatives and activities, which have been commenced, two different kind of public responses, that is the 'Civic Engagement' and 'Community Based Initiatives', have been acknowledged in this chapter, and are subsequently assessed in detail.

Civic Engagement

In the last decade, the deteriorating public health situation incited extensive public protest throughout India which finally instigated several initiatives carried out by individual citizens.

A few committed citizens took judicial action against the local and Central Government in order to legally compel the municipalities to provide adequate basic urban services all over the country. In Delhi, for instance, several Public Interest Litigations[7] were filed against the Delhi Government for improper solid waste management. The most famous case was of Dr B. L. Wadhera, a retired advocate of the Supreme Court, who filed a Public Interest Litigation in the Delhi High Court in 1996 against the Government of Delhi for inappropriate waste collection and disposal in the city. The case was finally forwarded to the Supreme Court of India and the Government of India was directed in the verdict to "appoint an expert authority to monitor the actions taken by the agencies ameliorating the situation" (Ghosh 2000: 64). As a consequence of this verdict, the Central Pollution Control Board (CPCB) was appointed as the monitoring authority, and the National Environmental Engineering Research Institute (NEERI) was hired by the Municipal Corporation of Delhi for designing a technical and managerial action plan to modernise their waste management system and to recommend proficient solutions to the city's waste problem.

Apart from the Delhi case, Ms Almitra Patel, a retired engineer and environmentalist from Bangalore, together with Jai Velu filed another Public Interest Litigation in the Supreme Court of India in 1995, accusing the Government of India of inadequate sanitation and solid waste management practises in all Class I cities.[8] After several hearings, the Supreme Court constituted a 'Committee on Solid Waste Management for Class I Cities' involving practitioners in the field of solid waste management. The Committee was directed to submit a report on all aspects of solid waste management in Class I cities in India. Accordingly, the Committee prepared two reports; an Interim report in June 1998 and the final report in March 1999, after conducting four regional workshops in different cities with members of the municipalities, national and international organizations, NGOs and Trader's Associations. The final report includes a description of the unhygienic situation in Indian cities and a whole range of recommendations for technical and management improvements of the present waste management system and is seen as the "comprehensive policy-frame for cleaning up India's cities" (Anon 2000).

However, the final report, which nowadays serves as the ultimate regulatory framework for urban solid waste management in Indian

---

7 Public Interest Litigation is a method of vindication of the rights of the people who are unable to seek redress through judicial action due to political exclusion, helplessness or disability, social or economic disadvantageous position.

8 Class I cities refer to all cities which are populated by more than 100,000 inhabitants.

metropolitan areas, lacks the necessary depth because the development of a new administrative set up, the improvement of the current legal framework at the national and municipal level, and the involvement and role specification of the various stakeholders such as private sector or community institutions were not conferred the much needed significance. Moreover, the report also failed to consider measurements on controlling or reducing the rising waste generation in future.

Community Based Initiatives

In December 1992 the Central Government passed the 74th Amendment of the Constitution[9] to invigorate city administration. Based on the 74th Amendment Act, Ward Committees, District Planning Committees and Metropolitan Planning Committees were constituted, political and administrative functions as well as financial resources were transferred to local government authorities and an increased participation of the people in civic affairs was sought (Ghosh 2000: 4). This participatory and community based approach also influenced the municipal solid waste management system throughout the country, stressing the fundamental and active role of communities[10] in managing their refuse.

Subsequently, Community Based Organizations (CBOs), Resident Welfare Associations (RWAs), Non-Governmental Organizations (NGOs) or even dedicated citizens became active and started various programmes and projects based on community participation and self-reliance in terms of primary waste collection in several cities, as they recognized the need to adjust the waste collection system to their community structure and the necessity to involve the entire neighbourhood (Venkateswaran 1996: i).

As the main reasons for the initiation of these programmes were the filthy, often unhygienic conditions in the neighbourhoods due to the lack of house to house waste collection schemes and the resultant uncollected garbage, most of the approaches targeted only at the organization of an efficient primary refuse collection scheme based on waste collectors on

[9] The 74th Amendment Act of 1993 is presumed to be the major step to the decentralization process of local governance in urban India. It provides the legal framework for the States to formulate legislation governing the composition, powers and role of the municipal agencies in the respective States and Union Territories.

[10] A community in this context refers to the residents of a particular neighbourhood or of a certain informally defined area.

contract who pick up household waste from house to house, and dispose it off at the provided municipal waste bins. Most of the programmes included environmental awareness campaigns attempting to better the waste handling practises of the residents or to enhance the general civic responsibility. Only very few programmes included an ecological approach, focusing on waste segregation and processing activities such as composting (Nunan 1999, Pitot 1999 and Venkateswaran 1996), or included social targets such as the involvement of waste pickers or the increase of the social acceptance of the waste collectors (Huysman 1994 and Venkateswaran 1996).

The most illustrious and successful of all these programmes is promoted by Exnora, a NGO based in Madras, which involved the community by forming neighbourhood associations managed by local volunteers or an elected Committee for organising the primary refuse collection. The conception of self-reliance, participation of the whole community and the involvement of the municipal agencies has established a platform which made the whole approach sustainable. More than 450.000 people in Madras, including slum-dwellers, are covered by this scheme as the programme has been converted from a grass-root project into a movement spread all over the city (Anand 1999: 162).

POTENTIALS AND LIMITATIONS OF COMMUNITY BASED INITIATIVES

Though community based initiatives have been glorified in the academic body of literature, by the media, as well as by the public as the ultimate solution of the cities' garbage problem, it is necessary to critically assess both the potentials or significance and the limitations or failures of community based initiatives in Indian cities.

Potentials

The potentials of community based initiatives pertain to technical, organizational and social aspects as illustrated in Figure 4.

The implementation of house to house waste collection schemes in residential areas, which directly serve the citizens, is considered as the most noteworthy potential of this approach. The main technical improvements ensuing the introduction of community based approaches are that the efficiency of primary refuse collection substantially increases, and less waste is indiscriminately dumped in the respective neighbourhood. Furthermore, the deficiencies in the organization and performance of local waste management are resolved as a result of community initiatives, especially through the initiation of partnerships between different stakeholders such as community institutions and executing institutions as fundamentally demonstrated by a programme in Hyderabad (Venkateswaran 1996: 30 - 34).

Figure 4: Potentials of Community Based Initiatives

Technical Potentials
• Implementation of House to House Collection Schemes • Improvement of the Efficiency of Primary Waste Collection • Streamlining of Operational Aspects
Organizational and Managerial Potentials
• Initiation of Partnerships with Different Stakeholders • Monitoring of Municipal Waste Disposal Activities • Change of the Negative Mindset towards Solid Waste • Improvement of Citizens' Waste Handling Practises • Enhancement of Civic Responsibilities
Social Potentials
• Employment Effects on 'underprivileged' People • Creation of more Hygienic and Clean Residential Areas

Draft: Köberlein 2004

Furthermore, community based approaches are the ideal base to monitor and positively influence the waste handling practices of the municipal authorities in a neighbourhood, such as loading and haulage of refuse. Besides, households and individuals, who are the actual victims of inadequate urban solid waste management, are actively included in the local waste handling practises as well as in local decision making. Community initiatives are also of social significance as they help in creating employment for 'underprivileged' people, such as waste pickers or jobless sweepers. Another undeniable potential lies in the improvement in the 'quality of life' of the residents owing to the establishment of clean and hygienic neighbourhoods.

Moreover, community initiatives facilitate the creation of environmental awareness among the citizens and thus a general improvement in the attitude towards waste and the people working with waste. The enhancement of civic responsibility, which means that citizens acknowledge their responsibilities as well as their active role in the realization of an efficient waste collection and disposal system, is the crucial point of community based approaches.

Limitations

The failures of many community based initiatives can be attributed to technical, organizational and social aspects as illustrated in Figure 5.

Figure 5: Limitations of Community Based Initiatives

Technical Limitations

- Improvements only Relating to Primary Waste Collection
- Lack of Capacities in Terms of Expertise and Financial Resources
- Lack of Social or Ecological Objectives

Organizational and Management Limitations

- Dependency on Dedicated Activists or NGOs
- Conflicts Among Various Stakeholders about Roles and Powers
- Lack of Legitimacy
- Lack of Linkages with the Municipalities
- Lack of Management Skills of People in Charge
- Insufficient Involvement and Education of Households
- Lack of Motivation and Commitment of the Concerned Citizens

Social Failures

- Exclusion of Low-Income Areas and Squatter Settlements
- Absence of Women in Waste Collection Crews
- Lack of Occupational Health Standards and Sanitary Facilities for the Employed Waste Collectors

First of all, it has to be acknowledged that community based approaches have only a limited impact on the whole waste management system, as community initiatives principally improve merely the primary refuse collection. Then again, not all schemes have been successful as the people in charge, both in RWAs, CBOs and NGOs, who have attempted to implement these schemes, often lack the necessary managerial and technical know-how. Additionally, many of the community institutions lack financial resources, and hence the purchase and maintenance of appropriate high quality equipments are by and large not realisable.

A very common management failure, which has been regularly observed, is that women running the households or servants who are the 'real managers' of waste at the household level have been insufficiently included in community based approaches, and hence the most important actors at the community level are missed out. Furthermore, community based approaches often are not comprehensively outlined, as they do not incorporate social and ecological objectives. The omission of social objectives refers on the one hand to the exclusion of women in waste collection schemes, although women constitute a large part of the sweeper community (Karlekar 1982: 5), and also form the majority among the waste pickers (Huysman 1994: 50). On the other hand, the omission refers to the non-inclusion of awareness campaigns in order to fight against the social stigma attached to the occupation with waste materials (Puerbo, Sicular and Supardi 1984: 99).

Furthermore, health and safety standards pertaining to the work of the employed waste collectors are neglected and the requirement of sanitary facilities for the staff is not complied with. The omission of ecological objectives refers mainly to the fact that waste segregation at source as well as waste processing activities on a regular basis are not integrated into community based initiatives.

A general problem is that community based initiatives lack the legal means which are required to efficiently enforce the implementation of waste collection schemes in a community or put the objectives pertaining to these approaches into practice; as such there are no enforcement mechanisms or punitive measurements which can compel people of a community to participate in local waste collection schemes or get involved in community initiatives. The lack of regulatory standards also often leads to conflicts among the various stakeholders about their specific roles and powers in urban solid waste management.

A substantial limitation of community initiatives is that its functioning is entirely dependent on external NGOs or dedicated activists of CBOs or RWAs who manage and monitor the procedures of the respective waste collection scheme, and the withdrawal of these actors usually makes the whole initiative a failure. The unwillingness of a critical amount of citizens to pay an extra fee for primary refuse collection or to accept their civic responsibility poses further difficulties in the smooth functioning of a community based waste management system (Human Settlement Management Institute 1996: 190, Köberlein 1998: 64, Pitot 1999: 71). Another constraint of many community initiatives is the missing linkage to the civic authorities. As a consequence, community based waste collection schemes are often carried out in entire isolation without any connection to subsequent working steps such as secondary storage, haulage or transfer to the disposal sites. A significant mistake, however, is that there are only very few attempts to install appropriate and effective waste collection schemes in low-income residential areas or squatter settlements, and thus the deplorable, insanitary living conditions of the urban poor still continue.[11]

CONCLUSION

Civic engagement or community based approaches alone cannot change the pathetic sanitary conditions prevailing in Indian cities. Community based approaches represent only a part of the solution for the 'sheer unmanageable' waste problem, as the positive effects of community initiatives on the entire waste management system are limited. However, with clean neighbourhoods and enhanced civic responsibility among the involved citizens, community based approaches represent an ideal initial step in changing the common negative attitude and perception towards refuse. Community initiatives, as successfully exemplified by Exnora in Madras, can be an impetus for a sanitary movement which is requisite for implementing waste management systems or strategies targeting at the overall sanitary improvement of a city. The proper integration of local community based waste collection schemes into the city's entire waste management system is hence a prerequisite for achieving 'integrated solid waste management systems'. For this reason, partnerships between the executing institutions and community initiatives

[11] There have been very few projects initiated in low income and slum areas; however, apart from the Exnora programme none has proved to be sustainable (see for example Pitot 1999 and Venkateswaran 1996).

through NGOs, CBOs or RWAs must be further evolved and better coordinated.

Consequently, the main functions of community based initiatives in future will be:

1. Implementation of house to house collection schemes in all parts of the cities, including all low income and squatter settlements
2. Promotion of waste segregation at source which are to facilitate more efficient waste processing and recycling activities
3. Education of citizens on the health and environmental implications of undesirable waste disposal practices.

However, it has to be acknowledged that private and community institutions can never substitute civic authorities or even render them superfluous. Governmental institutions, especially the municipal agencies, will always remain the most significant stakeholder in urban solid waste management. But their roles and tasks have to be amended and more specified in future. Governmental institutions will always hold the responsibility of law and policy making, and hence their foremost task will be to precisely define the roles and jurisdiction of all the involved stakeholders in urban solid waste management.

In future, municipal authorities more and more will have to take up the role of a supervisory body and law implementer, rather than carrying out the role as an operational and executing body. Their duty should be to coordinate contractual arrangements with private sector stakeholders or with community institutions in order to upgrade the respective waste management systems, and subsequently the monitoring of the contracted arrangements and operational performances. Furthermore, aside from the recognition and assistance of community based approaches, the municipal authorities will have to amend their institutional set-up to make a smooth integration of these schemes possible. Then again, while integrating new stakeholders in the urban waste management system, social and environmental objectives are not to be neglected.

Furthermore, it has to be acknowledged that the appalling public health conditions in Indian cities will show significant progress only when all involved stakeholders improve their collaboration and give the necessary priority to urban solid waste management.

To recapitulate, it is more the political will and the human resources than the technical or financial resources which "constitute the key of change" in urban solid waste management (Ali, Olley and Cotton 1999:

505). The conventional technical oriented approach to solid waste management applied in Indian cities has to be broadened, and all relevant stakeholders and aspects which encompass a modern solid waste management system will have to be integrated in an approach applied henceforth. Accordingly, the existing legislation has to be reassessed, amended and updated to be competent enough to cope with the full dimension of the current solid waste management problems.

Regulatory instruments to monitor the required technical and financial standards have to be formulated and added to the existing legislation, and subsequently the implementation of these standards has to be strictly enforced. The vital organizational step in improving the efficiency of urban solid waste management systems in Indian cities will be to achieve a sound balance between the move from the municipal agencies as the sole service providers to the involvement of private sector stakeholders and the inclusion of community institutions in the waste collection and disposal system.

Accordingly, the low political prioritization given to urban solid waste management will have to change significantly and the common public apathy towards filth and refuse has to dissipate in order to get a broad platform of all involved stakeholders for a sanitary movement which is the essence of the overall improvement of India's wretched public health situation.

REFERENCES

Ahmed, Kazimuddin and Jamwal, Nidhi, 'Garbage: Your Problem', in *Down to Earth*, 31 January (2000), pp. 30–42.

Ali, Mansoor, Snel, Mariëlle and Cotton, Andrew, 'The Challenges ahead - Solid Waste Management in the Next Millennium', in *Waterlines*, vol. 17, no. 3 (1999), pp. 2-5.

Ali, Mansoor, Olley, Jane and Cotton, Andrew, 'Public Sector Delivery of Waste Management Services: Cases from the Indian Sub-Continent', in *Habitat International*, vol. 23, no. 4 (1999), pp. 495-510.

Ali, Sabhir, 'Garbage Collection in Two Resettlement Colonies in Delhi', in *Social Change*, vol. 22, no. 1 (1992), pp. 140–145.

Anand, P. B., 'Waste Management in Madras Revisited', in *Environment and Urbanization*, vol. 11, no. 2 (1999), pp. 161-176.

Anon, 'Good News about Garbage', in *The Hindu*, 19 March (2000), New Delhi.

Baud Isa and Schenk, Hans, eds., *Solid Waste Management. Modes, Assessments, Appraisals and Linkages in Bangalore.* New Delhi: Manohar, 1994.

Bhide, A. D., 'Solid Waste Management in Urban Areas', in *Nagerlok*, vol. 26, no. 4 (1994), pp. 17-24.

Central Pollution Control Board, ed., *Management of Municipal Solid Wastes*, New Delhi: CPCB, 1995.

Chaplin, Susan E., 'Cities, Sewers and Poverty: India's Politics of Sanitation', in *Environment and Urbanization*, vol. 11, no. 1 (1999), pp. 145-158.

Committee on Solid Waste Management for Class I Cities in India, *Solid Waste Management in Class I Cities in India*, Report of the Committee Constituted by The Hon. Supreme Court of India, New Delhi, March 1999.

Devas, Nick, 'Urban Livelihoods – Issues for Urban Governance and Management', in Carole Radoki and Tony Lloyd-Jones, eds., *Urban Livelihoods. A People-centred Approach to Reducing Poverty*, London: Earthscan, 2000, pp. 205–221.

Fritz, Jack J. and Misra, Girish K., 'Comparative Issues in Solid Waste Management in India and China', in *Nagerlok*, vol. 23, no. 1 (1991), pp. 1-16.

Gosh, Archana, *Solid Waste Management in Delhi. An exploratory study on local government-community interface*, Institute of Social Science Manuscript Report 14, New Delhi: Institute of Social Science, 2000.

Hasan, Samiul and Khan, M. Adil, 'Community-based Environmental Management in a Megacity: Considering Calcutta', in *Cities*, vol. 16, no. 2 (1999), pp. 103-110.

Holmes, John R., ed., *Managing Solid Wastes in Developing Countries*, Chichester: John Wiley & Sons Ltd., 1984.

Human Settlement Management Institute, 'City Wide Best Practices in Solid Waste Management in Collection, Transportation and Disposal', in B. N. Singh, S. Maitra and R. Sharma, eds., *Urban Environmental Management. The Indian Experience*, New Delhi: HUDCO, 1996, pp. 151-205.

Huysman, Marijk, 'The Position of Waste Pickers in Solid Waste Management in Bangalore', in Isa Baud and Hans Schenk, eds., *Solid Waste Management: Modes, Assessments, Appraisals and Linkages in Bangalore*, Delhi: Manohar, 1994, pp. 46–104.

International Environment Technology Centre and United Nation Environmental Programme, *International Source Book on Environmentally Sound Technologies for Municipal Solid Waste Management*, IETC Technical Publication Series 6. Osaka/Shiga: International Environmental Technology Centrem, 1996.

Karlekar, Malavika, *Poverty and Women's Work: A Study of Sweeper Women in Delhi*, New Delhi: Vikas Publishing House, 1982.

Köberlein, Michael, *Solid Waste Collection and Disposal in Delhi: An Applied - Geographical Analysis of the Problems faced by an Indian Metropolis with Managing its Refuse*, M. A. Thesis, University of Bamberg, Germany, 1998.

Köberlein, Michael, *Living from Waste: Livelihoods of the Actors Involved in Delhi's Informal Waste Economy*, Saarbrücken: Verlag für Entwicklungspolitik, 2003.

Köberlein, Michael, 'Cities of Waste: Urban India and its Garbage Problem'. (forthcoming 2005, in Susan E. Chaplin, ed., *Contemporary Issues Confronting Urban India*, New Delhi.)

Mazumdar, N. B., 'Municipal Solid Waste Management: The Indian Perspective', in *Energy Environment Monitor*, vol. 12, no. 2 (1996), pp. 57-69.

Metha, Dinesh, 'Urban Waste Management. Future Portents', in The Hindu, ed., *The Hindu Survey of the Environment 1995*, Madras, 1995, pp. 65-69.

National Institute of Urban Affairs, ed., *Basic Services and the Urban Poor*, Research Study Series No 46, New Delhi: NIUA, 1991.

Nunan, Fiona, 'Improving Farm Soil Using Urban Organics', in *BioCycle*, April (1999), pp. 77-78.

Pachauri P. K. and Sridharan, P. V., eds., *Looking Back and Think Ahead. Green India 2047*, New Delhi: Tata Energy Research Institute, 1998.

Palmer, Roy, *Auch das WC hat seine Geschichte*, München: Pfriemer, 1977.

Pfammatter, Roger and Schertenleib, Roland, 'Non-governmental Refuse Collection Systems', in *Sandec News*, vol. 2, October (1996), pp. 1-9.

Pitot, Hanns Andre, 'Source Separation of Organics in Delhi', in *BioCycle*, August (1999), pp. 70–71.

Puerbo, Hasan, Sicular, Daniel and Supardi, V., 'An Approach to Development of Informal Sector: The Case of Garbage Collectors in Bandung', in *Prisma*, vol. 32 (1984), pp. 85-100.

Sharma, V., 'Environmental Management Concern for the City: Some Initiatives in Solid Waste Management, in *Shelter - Cities for all*, vol. 2, no. 3/4 (1999), pp. 46-49.

Singh, K. S., *People of India, National Series Volume II: The Scheduled Caste*, New Delhi: Oxford University Press, 1999.

The Hindu, ed., *The Hindu Survey of the Environment 95*, Chennai 1995.

Venkateswaran, Sandhya, *Community Sanitation: Alternative Solid Waste Management Systems*, New Delhi: National Institute of Urban Affairs, 1996.

World Bank, *What a Waste: Solid Waste Management in Asia*, Washington DC: Urban Development Sector Unit, 1999. Available at: http://www.worldbank.org/html/fpd/urban/publicat/waste.pdf

8

PIGS AND POWER: URBAN SPACE AND URBAN DECAY

MAREN BELLWINKEL-SCHEMPP

PUBLIC ARENAS AND DALIT IMAGERY

Mary Douglas started her fundamental insight into the study of purity and danger with the fairly blunt observation that dirt is substance in the wrong place. This chapter will deal with dirt as well but mainly with pigs on garbage heaps in the wrong place: that is in public. Mary Douglas' second observation about dirt is more interesting. She claims that the things we abhor or detest develop a power over us. The fear of dirt or pollution has a transformative quality as it empowers the culturally dfined realm of man, animal or substance (Douglas 1966: 165). Starting point in time for the narrative of pigs and power was a visit to Kanpur after a time gap of nearly 20 years. Two things stunned me: The pigs on the garbage heaps along the roadside, even in the best localities, and a new and for me unknown Dalit assertiveness. The Dalit had gained a place in public, not only through numerous Dr Ambedkar statues, but also through public arena activities. What did it mean for Kanpur, India's first and oldest industrial town, the former 'Manchester of the East'? Can one derive the one from the other? Is there a Dalit narrative on urban development or industrial decay? Or is there more than one narrative?

In this chapter, I will try to show why the pigs in Kanpur multiplied and in what respect their appearance is linked with Dalit assertion in Kanpur. Assertion is employed on the one hand as social movement of underprivileged groups (Fuchs 1999: 59) in their fight for recognition as well as their fight to be different. In Uttar Pradesh, Dalit politics and Dalit imagery have been in the foreground during the present and fomer rule of Mayawati and the Bahujan Samaj Party. During her short spells of rule in 1995 and 1997, she multiplied the representation of Dalit culture, especially of Dr Ambedkar through statues, parks and *ghats* – river banks.

It led to a "foregrounding of the Dalit issue" (Froystad 2000: 265) and has been more pronounced since the elections in 2002 when Mayawati became chief minister of Uttar Pradesh again.

Intertwined with the discourse of Dalit assertiveness is the narrative of pigs and power, which entered public awareness during the so-called post Ayodhya riots of 1992. These Hindu-Muslim riots broke out after the destruction of the Babri Masjid in Ayodhya by fundamentalist Hidus. In Kanpur, the riots were machinated and carefully planned by the Bharatiya Janata Party (BJP), and the agency of this unabated and pointed murder of Muslims was attributed to a Khatik swineherd and city councillor with the meaningful name 'Kala Bacca'. For the BJP he was a hero but for the police and administration he was "not only a 'criminal type' but a 'thief' as well who made money by stealing 'whatever unclaimed pigs were roaming around'" (Brass 1998: 249). Through him the pigs reached a level of perception, although it took a long time before public action followed.

The support for the BJP was very much in line with the overall political development in UP and Kanpur as well. In Uttar Pradesh the BJP formed the government in 1991 and in Kanpur, the BJP had a landslide victory (Brass 1998: 213). The Kala Bacca episode was not a singular derailment from the path of Dalit politics but rather a long entanglement with Hindutva as the dominant political discourse. It actually lasted from 1993 till 2002, when Rakesh Sonkar was elected as BJP MLA from Ssamau reserved constituency. His only qualification was that he was the son of a pork butcher; and he was very much in the mainstream of Dalit identity. The infatuation of the Khatik with the BJP is even more surprising, as they were once at the forefront of the Dalit movement in Kanpur (Bellwinkel-Schempp 1998: 193).

Concerning the pigs, there are only scanty references to this species. The pig is considered to be the animal of Dalits and Adivasis, which is why it is juxtaposed to the 'holy cow' and essentialized as an abomination for *savarna* Hindus and for Muslims as well (Harris 1988: 84). According to Manu, the domesticated pig is looked down upon as the animal of the dung heaps (Doniger 1991: 100). The pig is symbolically frozen as the heraldic animal of the sweeper (Searle-Chatterjee 1981: 36), both of them scavenging, removing garbage, dirt and faeces of the *savarna*. It deserved the same fate as its master, and there is barely any recognition of its nutritional value, only by courageous veterinarians (Shukar 2000). There is a colonial discourse on pigs, which is closely connected with Kanpur and the Khatik. It is at the root of the present day's problem of pigs in public, urban governance and civic response.

The focus of this chapter is on the Khatik, a caste of untouchable masons and butchers. I am deliberately taking an approach which focuses on one particular caste, although most research on Kanpur has been accentuating the class dimension of industrial development, most prominently in two recent studies (Gooptu 2002; Joshi 2003). Religion, culture and politics transform the representations of class and lead, according to Nandini Gooptu, to the following subaltern manifestations: "The untouchables drew upon a religious tradition of heterodox nirguna bhakti in their self-assertion, while the shudras elaborated upon a martial past and *saguna* tradition of devotionalism, which had been more prominent in their own history." (Gooptu 2002: 198). For her, the Khatiks and Pasis belong to the lower Shudra agricultural castes (*ibid*, 192).

The caste approach helps to understand the complex interplay of urban governance, politics, public response and violence more minutely than the class approach. However, it leads to a critique of the subaltern class construction of Shudra and untouchable castes with respect to their religious and political orientation. Besides, it serves as reassessment of the colonial construction of caste (Cohn 1987; Charsley 1996) in its political as well as religious dimensions. This chapter serves the purpose of showing the positioning of the Khatiks within Dalit assertion and Shudra militancy and to deconstruct the juxtaposition of heterodox *bhakti* and orthodox *saguna* devotionalism.

'MANCHESTER OF THE EAST'

Kanpur has 4.1 million inhabitants according to the Census of 2001. It is still the biggest city in Uttar Pradesh. Kanpur was founded as a British army camp in 1778 (Yalland 1987: 42). For a long time, the origin of the name was contested between Kanaiyapur city of Krishna, - and Kampoo – the etymological deduction from camp (Majumdar 1960: 19) but recently Kanaiyapur has been given the preference with the rise of Hidutva (Froystad 2000: 48). It was to become the oldest and most renowned industrial town of India. Kanpur's industrialization was born out of the 'Great Rebellion' of 1857, which led to the annihilation of the British civil and military population. The 'Great Rebellion' supplied the trope (Mukherjee 1998: 4) of treason and treachery and the script for Kanpur's industrialization.

The British transformed the 'white man's tragedy' into the 'white man's triumph' with textile and leather industries. Blueprint, machinery and foremen were imported from England (Nevill 1909: 82) and raw material (cotton, hides, bristles, sugar, oil seeds), capital[1] and labour were Indian. Kanpur's industries diversified into sugar, brushes, engineering and ordinance and in the 1930s chemicals and metals (Singh 1990: 16). Kanpur became the 'Manchester of the East', India's first industrial town. Not only that, Kanpur developed into a wholesale market for grains and pulses, hides, bristles and raw cotton. This was due to the fvourable traffic network. Kanpur was situated on the navigable Ganges and the Great Trunk Road connecting Kanpur with Lahore to the West and Calcutta to the east. The town became one of the major railway junctions in northern India with three different railway lines (Majumdar 1960: 16).

Had it not been for Kanpur's industrialisation, the so-called 'Cawnpore massacres' - as they were called in colonial historiography, would have been long forgotten. Now, through the industrial and commercial eminence of Kanpur, the events at 'General Wheeler's entrenchment' got transformed into 'All Soul's Church' in cantonment and 'Bibi Ghar' into 'Memorial Gardens' right in the centre of town. These places of "horrors and valour" (Yalland 1994: 3) were full of cloying Christian symbolism, barred to the Indian public. British mourning was regularly enacted through the drive to church on Sunday morning (Yalland 1994: 2) or through conducted tours, organized by Thomas Cook. The 'Great Rebellion' became frozen in the marble angel and remained ever present.

Not only that, the trope of the 'massacres' of Kanpur did not only linger on but gained notoriety through its frequent riots (1905, 1923, 1927, 1931, 1939). During the Khilafat and Non-Cooperation Movement, tesions built up between Hindus and Muslims (Freitag 1989: 234), and burst in the 1931 Hindu-Muslim riot,[2] which was considered to be the most severe in pre-independence India (Rai 1999: 16). The riot reinforced the trope of Kanpur as "city of violence" (Molund 1988: 32) and left a major imprint on Kanpur's urban landscape and on the minds of its people. Since the beginning of the trade union movement, and even before that, riots were interspersed with strikes, police firing and lock outs, the most militant ones being under communist leadership in

---

1 The capital came from landed property, salaries paid in India and a minor portion of the capital was borrowed from Indian bankers. The most prominent, Juggilal, became an industrialist later on as well.

2 About 400 persons killed, more than 1200 injured, 18 mosques, 42 temples, 248 homes of Hindus and 101 homes of Muslims destroyed (Brass 1998: 209).

1937/1938, which gave Kanpur the fame and name of "Lal Kanpur" (Joshi 2003: 208).

Before the 'Great Rebellion', the town of Kanpur had consisted of a hypertrophied cantonment and a densely populated 'black town' (Molund 1988: 39). After the 'Great Rebellion', the western part of the cantonment beyond the railway lines and parallel to the Ganges was given to the civil authorities. The Civil Lines were set up with broad streets, single spacious bungalows in huge gardens, surrounded by high walls. It became the seat of administration, police and industry. As an extension of the Civil Lines in the western direction along the Ganges, the factory area developed. The factories were huge brick structures with majestic gates, which had their own charm. The woollen factory Lal Imli even built a replica of Big Ben in London, which rang out at every hour.

The 'black town' came under the jurisdiction of Kanpur municipality in 1861. "The natives were allowed to live as they pleased and to build in a way that suited their fancy, so long as they were separated from the civil station by a broad shopping mall" (Srivastava 1996: 111). The 'native bazaar', as it used to be called from the 1880s onwards, became proverbial for its congestion, overcrowding and appalling sanitary conditions. Already in the 1870s, a broad thoroughfare was laid through the 'native bazaar' (Yalland 1994: 166) and sewage canals were built.

The native town sheltered Hindus, Muslims and Scheduled Castes. Already before the riots of 1931, these groups clustered along community and caste lines, because, due to migration, "bonds of community and ties of religion" (Joshi 1985: 278) were strong. After the Hindu-Muslim riot of 1931, the cleavages between caste and religious communities became even more accentuated (*ibid.*, 279). The Dalits too were affected, most noteworthy the Chamars, but the Khatiks withstood the clashes, which was to become a part of their self-definition.

The Dalits used to live in so-called *hatas* – enclosures, which were privately built wards. They sprouted around the factory areas and gave Kanpur the additional notoriety of "city of slums" (Majumdar 1960: 35). Industry and city were well planned and the factories set up housing for the labouring classes. These 'model labour colonies' with school, health centre, and open space stood in marked contrast to the congestion and squalor of the *hatas*. Although there were considerable efforts for town planning, especially after the Improvement Trust was set up in 1909, these exemplary measures were usually too little or undertaken too late. They could never compete with the influx of migrants, caused by famines in the countryside in the nineteenth century, and in the twentieth by the depression and war production during two World Wars.

For the 'white sahibs', decolonization was a slow but steady process in Kanpur, as it took them nearly ten years to hand over their factories to the Indian merchants who were in second rank. But the symbolic reorganisation took place at a much faster rate. Memorial Gardens were opened to the public. The 'weeping angel' and the entire memorial were removed to All Soul's Church in the cantonment. During this process, the nose of the angel got damaged (Mukherjee 1998: 2). Memorial Gardens became Nana Rao Park, named after the nobleman who led the rebellion. The former 'traitor' became the 'hero'. Tantia Topis' bust (he was Nana Rao's able military commander) was put up instead of the angel. Nana Rao Park became the focal point of the early morning walk of Kanpur's citizens from all genders, castes and creeds. As soon as the British were out, the Americans set up the Indian Institute of Technology in 1959, far out on the outskirts of Kanpur beyond the municipal boundaries. The campus became a modern township in itself and was only incorporated into city administration in 1991.

30 per cent Muslims resided in Kanpur in 1941. After partition there was a substantial shift of population. Muslims migrated to Pakistan and Punjabi refugees swelled the ranks of the Sikh community. Since the 1950s, Muslims from eastern Uttar Pradesh had been migrating to Kapur to work in the leather industry. Nowadays, the Muslim population of Kanpur constitutes 18 per cent. Population growth has been at par with the overall development, but Kanpur lost its rank as sixth largest city of India which it held in 1961. In 1991 it had dropped to rank 9 and according to the Census of 2001 to rank 10.

Initially, independence brought a diversification of industry with light engineering, transport equipment, electric goods, chemical based industries, cold storage, fruits and vegetables (Singh 1990: 54). Besides, there was also expansion, noteworthy is J. K. Rayon in Jajmau in 1959 with a well-planned labour colony attached. Nevertheless, the percentage of workers employed in industry decreased continuously from 45.1 per cent in 1951 to 28.5 per cent in 1991 (Srivastava 1996: 111), which was due to a number of factors. Already in the early 1950s, it became obvious that the machinery was outmoded, necessary investments had not been made and there was little demand for country cloth. Besides, Nehru favoured other growth centres and decentralisation became the industrial policy.

The U.P. government intended to increase productivity through rationalisation. But rationalization schemes faced stern opposition (Pandey 1970: 128) from Kanpur's trade unions. Old memories of 'Lal

Kanpur' resurrected, which were channelled into frequent strikes and unrest (1955, 1981, 1989). By the mid 1970s, the Government took over the old textile mills, and subsequently they served as income schemes for a laid-off working class. Production stopped at the beginnings of the 1990s. When Narasimha Rao opened India's economy for the world market in 1991, there wasn't much to finish as the old and renowned factories set up by the British had already closed. The newer ones followed the same lead.

Leather industry in the private sector under predominantly Muslim entrepreneurs took a different turn from the end of the 1970s onwards. Encouraged and streamlined by various Government schemes (Bannerjee, Nihila 1999: 185), the leather industry could meet the quality standards of the global market. Labour costs were low and tax-free export secured high profits because labour was recruited on a contract basis, therefore undermining labour laws and trade union representation. On an all-India scale, the region Kanpur and Unnao procure 13 per cent of all leather exports (Council for Leather Exports 2001: 28). Besides, Kanpur is one of the main suppliers of *chappals* – sandals and manufactured footwear.

The dominant theme during the first two decades of independence was housing for the labouring classes, which was undertaken by Development Board and Labour Office. New colonies in south Kanpur sprang up (Babupurwa, Juhi, Govindnagar and Kidwainagar) and slums were cleared in old labour areas like Benajhabar and Khalasi Lines (Singh 1990: 29). A total of 27,744 houses were constructed. Many Dalits and Muslims, usually those better off, moved to those areas. However, nearly 40 per cent of Kanpur's population were still living in slums (Awasthi 1985: 24). In the 1980s and 1990s government policy changed. With the help of UNESCO, slum improvement schemes (Lavigne 1984: 72) were launched. The upgrading of *hatas* had a positive effect but did not solve the slum problem. New slums developed and with them a new terminology: they are called *malin bastis* – dirty hamlets.

Other southern suburbs, which were developed in the 1950s or 1960s, were decaying already and people were moving back to their old localities. This shift of population had political reasons too. After the severe Hindu-Muslim riots of 1992, many Muslims from South Kanpur moved back into Muslim majority areas either in the old part of town or to the tannery area Jajmau. Ghettoization is nearly complete nowadays. On the other hand, the newly affluent began moving to Civil Lines where high rises, boutiques and restaurants convey a modern western flair – apart from pigs and the roaring sound of the Diesel generators needed in case of a power cut. Whereas originally 'The Mall', warded off the Indian part of town from the residences of the 'white sahibs', nowadays urban segregation is different. Houses in Civil Lines and other upper middle class areas are fortified by high walls and solid gates to ward off poverty, communalism and squalor.

These various streaks of industrial decline were accompanied by urban deterioration on the administrative level, which could only partially be cushioned through World Bank, UNICEF and Indo-Dutch Government Projects. Housing, water and sanitation were the tasks, which were on the agenda, but only effluent treatment for the Jajmau tanneries was partially successful, administered through the Indo-Dutch Project. Besides, not only lower middle class housing, but also new factory areas were developed in Unnao district, which led to a shift to these new growth centres and an even greater loss in the budget of Kanpur's municipal corporation. Since the introduction of the self-assessment tax in 1986, there was a drastic decline of income and the Kanpur Municipal Corporation is literally bankrupt and municipal workers are not paid regularly. This leads to an atmosphere of mistrust and obstruction, which is accompanied by further deteriorating civic and sanitary conditions

MASONS AND BUTCHERS

The Dalits in Kanpur constitute 15.5 per cent, much less than in Uttar Pradesh as a whole, where they comprise 22 per cent. The *Khatiks* are a comparatively small *jati*, only constituting 5.8 per cent of all Scheduled Castes in Kanpur, according to the Census of 1961 (Bhatnagar 1965: 62).[3] In Kanpur, they reside in two areas of the old part of town, which are named after a street and a ward. It is La Touche Road Khatkiana and Colonelganj. There are smaller Khatik settlements in Khalasi Lines, Gitanagar, Kalyanpur and Babupurwa, which have only recently branched off from the two original settlements.

Let us start with the Colonelganj Khatiks, an *upjati* – subcaste of

[3] The most numerous are the *Chamar* (leather workers 37.3 per cent), *Kori* (weavers 16.8 per cent), *Pasi* (vegetable sellers 11.2 per cent), *Balmiki* (sweepers 10.8 per cent), *Dhanuk* (pig rearers, 4.5 per cent), *Dhobi* (washermen, 4.3 per cent), *Shilpar* (stone cutters 2.1 per cent) (Bhatnagar 1965: 62). The *Chamars* supplied most of the workers in leather and textile industry (Niehoff 1959: 18) but their proportion of educated spokesmen is quite high (Ram 1988: 35). The *Kori* are a highly urbanized caste and work in textile industry and bristle dressing (Molund 1988: 119).

masons and building contractors who are intrinsically connected with the development of industrial Kanpur, because as experienced masons and building contractors, they set up the mills. They were endogamous and only recently started exogamous relationships with the other *upjati* of Khatiks living on La Touche Road. The Colonelganj Khatiks consider themselves to be the original inhabitants of this area, which was according to their narrative a village around which the town grew. Before the 'Great Rebellion' this area belonged to the cantonment.

The present settlement in Colonelganj is an amazing manifestation of Khatik skills and craftsmanship: Most of the double storied houses were constructed at the end of the nineteenth century. They are huge mansions, solidly built and beautifully decorated. They prove the Colonelganj Khatiks' glorious past as masons and contractors. During the 1931 riots, there was also an exchange of population: upper castes and Chamars moved out[4] and Muslims from other localities moved in.

Today there are 150 households of Khatiks, 30 Chamar, 40 Teli and 30 Pasi households. The Muslim population is said to constitute 750 households. In Colonelganj, there is the Barhe Masjid, the main mosque in Kanpur for the Id prayers. Besides, the Bakarmandi goat market, slaughterhouse for buffaloes and the Muslim graveyard is not far away from there. The Colonelganj Khatiks do not keep pigs and claim that they have given up eating pork a long time ago. The Gassa *akhara*[5] – wrestling stadium – tells the story of Muslim and Khatik cooperation and competition in a brotherly – *bhaiband* – manner. But still, this area is known for its Khatik and Muslim strife, hooliganism and petty disturbances. Whenever there is a curfew, it is certainly imposed on Colonelganj, although during the post Ayodhya riots of 1992 there was only one incident reported from there (Brass 1998: 218).

The people of Colonelganj quickly learned how to build factories. The British respected them for their craftsmanship, their entrepreneurial acumen and skills and maintained friendly and respectful relationships with them. "The British paid us great respect, and on Christmas they sent baskets full of dry fruits and nuts as a present. We were rich and affluent, and on Sundays our men used to take the buggy and drive

---

4 Interview with Advocate Tej Saxena on 20.2.2000. He is an old gentleman of over 80, the only *savarna* – upper caste – resident still residing in Colonelganj.

5 We attended the celebrations of all *akharas* on Nag Pancmi on 25.7.2001. The Colonelganj *akhara* was just celebrating its Diamond Jubilee with an impressive *kusti*- wrestling competition, a procession to the Hindu graveyard and a sword dance on the grave of Bihari Lal.

down the 80 miles to Lucknow just to eat pan, that was our life."[6]

Their professional status as contractors (*thekedar*) elevated them above the normal and put them into a different status bracket. The profession as such had a very wide connotation and was an all-inclusive category: it could be trading in raw hides, making shoes, recruiting labourers, supervising construction work, conservancy work or procurement of cattle and slaughtering. On the one hand, the term had an ennobling quality as it pointed to an elevated position; on the other hand it covered up polluting tasks and messy business. In the case of the Colonelganj Khatiks, they pursued a 'clean' profession, but were still regarded as untouchables.

The most famous person was Bihari Lal (1820-1905), who built Muir Mill and erected the Shiv Narayan *math* – monastry in Colonelganj. The *gurdwara* is consecrated to Swami Shiv Narayan (1716-90), a *bhakti* saint in the tradition of Sikhism. Swami Shiv Narayan was a Thakur by caste but he had an exclusively Dalit following, especially amongst the Dhusiya and Jaisvara Chamar in Eastern Uttar Pradesh and Western Bihar. Amongst the Khatik, his following was confined to Bihari Lal's extended family in Colonelganj. The temple became the centre of the early Dalit movement under Swami Achutanand (1879-1933) in Kanpur. Swami Achutanand was the founder of the Adi Hindu movement (Khare 1984: 83) who claimed that the Dalits were the original inhabitants of India, driven off their land by Aryan conquest and enslaved by Brahmanism.

The Khatiks from La Touche Road are of different stock. There is a general agreement that they were there already before the turn of the nineteenth century.[7] La Touche Road[8] is one of the major thoroughfares through the old part of the town, which was constructed in 1905 (Majumdar 1960: 21). Substantial three storied commercial buildings line La Touche Road. It is the main bazaar for agricultural tools, spare parts and machinery.

Around La Touche Road there are approximately 250 households of Khatiks, 30 Balmikis and 60 Chamars. It is an area, which is highly congested with a concentration of 562 persons per acre (Singh 1990: 27).

---

6 Interview on 8.2.2000

7 A tombstone in a Hindu graveyard, mentioning one Khatik Bhawanideen Chaudhuri Anwarganj Cawnpore who died on 30 July 1894, confirms this. His tombstone is not as elaborate as Bihari Lal's but still impressive. Visit to the Hindu graveyard behind Idgah Colony on 10.11.1999.

8 It was named after the then governor of the United Provinces, James La Touche.

Solid buildings were only established rather late in the 1940s but this was done by the rich. There was also a slum clearance drive in the 1980s with UNESCO money (Lavigne 1984: 72), which led to the reconstruction of Khatik lane with two blocks of municipal housing and sanitation.

Muslims constitute 1000 households. The close proximity of Khatiks and Muslims on both sides of La Touche Road triggered off frequent communal disturbances in the past. Besides, there is considerable professional rivalry because both groups are vegetable vendors. They sit at the same markets side by side. Their agency – the Muslims' as well as the Khatiks' – is well recorded for the 1931 riots[9] and during the post Ayodhya riots, although only three incidents were recorded (Brass 1998: 218). The whole area is known for its high incidence of crime, hooliganism and communal disturbances.

The La Touche Road Khatiks are pork butchers, vegetable vendors and brush manufacturers. They are proud to be self-employed and much prefer to employ others: Kori for bristle dressing and Pasi for pork butchery. The Khatiks in La Touche Road are very much part of the mainstream Hinduism with a strong veneration for the *devi* – goddess. In the 1930s, a number of them came under the influence of the *shuddhi* – purification – movement of the Hindu Mahasabha (Rivariya 2000: 48). Although they did not reform their eating habits – pork is still their cherished meat and alcohol their cherished drink to date – a number of them considered themselves to be Shudras, whereas few supported the early Dalit movement of Swami Achutanand. In the caste dimension they oscillated between Dalit and Shudra identity. In the religious realm however, there was interplay between religious and secular identities.

What is most stunning is that the La Touche Road Khatiks consider themselves superior to the Colonelganj Khatiks, although with their 'piggery' and 'bristle' they were pursuing a 'defiling' job according to Hindu norms of purity and pollution. They use the English terms, because the Hindi terminology sounds derogatory (Molund 1988: 195). The Colonelganj Khatik had a 'clean' profession. Until the 1950s, there were no marital relationships between the two *upjatis* – subcastes, and the first one – between the son of a La Touche Road *chaudhuri*–headman and the daughter of a Colonelganj contractor – led to the social boycott of the later. It required a formal decision of the 'Akhil Bharatiye Khatik Sangh', an all-India body of Khatiks from Rajasthan, Madhya Pradesh,

9 Interview with Nazar Mohammed, owner of the Pioneer Tannery on 17.11.1999. He was a 12 year old boy and used to live on the Cooliebazaar side of La Touche Road.

Bihar and Punjab, in 1969 to abolish subcaste endogamy.[10]

Babupurwa is a residential area which was constructed by the government as a labour colony in 1954. The Khatik population is said to comprise 150 households (Singh 1990: 29) but a closer look discloses that this is sheer exaggeration. After the post Ayodhya riots, many Khatiks and Muslims left. It was the area with the highest number of incidents due to the agency of Kala Bacca. Nowadays, there are only 12 Khatik households and 80 Muslim households left.[11] The Khatiks in Babupurwa are said to be an offshoot of the La Touche Road Khatiks, kinship relations exist between these two groups. The same applies to the Khatiks living in Harshnagar (20 Hh). The 20 Khatik households in Khalasi Lines and the households in Gitanagar (30 Hh) are said to be from the same stock as the Colonelganj Khatiks.

Piggery and Bristles

Let us probe into the intricacies of piggery and bristles, which is at the core of the problem. The British were well aware of the fact that pigs are despised animals, both by *savarna* Hindus and Muslims. But they realised soon that it would be better to use the peculiarities of Indian culture and commerce to their advantage. The ravines around Kanpur were full of pigs and it was a risky waste of energy only to use them for pig sticking, which was the favourite and violent sport of Kanpur's youthful 'white sahibs' (Yalland 1994: 359). As British animal husbandry had just turned to breed hogs for consumption, there was a shortage of bristles for the expanding British brush industry. Why not export those bristles as the Indians had no use for them? It did not escape their attention that the 'Depressed Classes' and 'Depressed Tribes' traditionally kept pigs, which had a great resemblance to the wild species: They were black, long legged and above all, endowed with long and stiff bristles along the spine.

With an infallible sense for business and profit, the British put the Khatiks to the task of procuring those bristles. From the 1860s onwards (Yalland 1994: 330), bristles were exported to London, even before the British opened the 'Pioneer Brush Factory' in 1896 (Nevill 1909: 82). The commodity was so eagerly sought after, that even a special auction was set up in London. Kanpur became the Indian centre for bristle

10 Interview with Sunder Lal Sonkar, president of the Kanpur Khatik Mahasabha, on 16.3.1999.

11 Interview with Chunnu Bacca, the younger brother of Kala Bacca, on 27.2.2000.

manufacturing, and its product was called 'Calcutta' bristle, because the leading British trading firms had their head offices in Calcutta.

In the 1930s, after the Great Depression, when it became feasible for Indian capital generally to venture into industry, the Khatiks from La Touche Road established firms. At that time Kayasthas, Punjabis and a few Parsis got into that line as well, sensing the profit. Due to the Chinese civil war, supplies from China were seriously hampered and 'Calcutta Bristle' came into even more prominence. Although the British middlemen and agents deducted a good share from their profits, the Khatik bristle manufacturers invested in real estate and built substantial houses during the war years.

Four firms rose into prominence[12] and many more made a good living as traders, dressers and agents. Mitthu Lal, one of the big bristle dealers, was casually and with the ironical undertone of British humour named "King of Bristles" by a British customer in the 1940s. He took it as an invitation to crown himself. He got a coloured photograph made with the caption 'King of Bristles' in quotation marks.[13]

They could not translate their rise to riches into esteem within society at large but among the Dalit castes of Kanpur they were assigned the highest rank. Ram argued that this is due to the fact that they were pursuing a "clean occupation" (Ram 1988: 42). This does not hold true because only the rich bristle dealers could delegate the polluting task to other Scheduled Castes. The 'piggery' business posed additional problems, which were clearly spelled out by George Trevelyan in 1864:

> Along the gutters wanders the hideous foul Indian pig. It is only necessary to watch the habits of the animal for five minutes to understand why the eaters of swine-flesh are held unclean throughout the East. In this respect Englishmen have adopted what is generally looked upon as an oriental prejudice; and no pork appears on a Calcutta table except such as has been sty-fed by hands in which the host reposes the most perfect confidence. (Trevelyan 1992: 22).

---

12 There were initially only four registered: Mitthu Lal & Roshan Lal; Masterji Bandi Din & Bake Lal, Makund Lal & Dori Lal and Ram Lal & Shoba Nath,. They became founding members of the 'Indian Bristle Merchants Association' which was established in the 1930s. Interview with Suresh Saxena, the former Secretary of this association on 22.11.1998.

13 Visit to La Touche Road and the house of Satish Chaudhuri, Mitthu Lal's youngest son who keeps the photograph in his *puja* corner on 12.2.1996.

How to obtain sty-fed pork? Teaching the Khatiks what they called 'piggery' was not enough. Cleanliness, supervision and handling had to be done under British eyes to avoid any deviation from their understanding of hygiene. Besides, the Indian public, Hindus and Muslims alike, for whom the pig was an abomination, had to be bypassed. Although abattoirs were constructed in the 1880s, one in Fazalganj industrial estate for pigs and the other at Colonelganj for cows and buffaloes, it was better to place the bloody business of the butcher into the cantonment.

Besides, the job of the butcher was camouflaged as *thekedari*, meaning procurement, slaughtering and processing of pigs for the needs of the British civil and military population.[14] Veterinary doctors did the inspection. Besides, the Aligarh Dairy Farm added a pig breeding section to their cow stable from where ham and sausages were supplied which were regularly advertised in the Pioneer, the leading newspaper. Kanpur had four pork shops on the Mall, which predominantly served an English public.

While doing 'piggery', a semantic change occurred for the Khatiks. The pig was no longer the defiled animal, which marked their untouchable status, but the cherished food of the 'white sahibs'. Slaughtering of a pig was not done any longer in veneration for the goddess to heal a sick child (Briggs 1920: 138) but according to veterinary considerations and health inspection. The semantic shift and the expertise worked well and enabled individual mobility and social recognition. Ram Avatar, a pork butcher doing 'piggery' for the British, bought a substantial mansion in Etawah Bazaar, an area inhabited by Banias, Brahmins and Kayasthas. Living on the top floor of his house, he has rented the other apartments to Brahmin and Kayastha families. Asked about the quality of inter-caste relations, he described their neighbourly exchange as amicable and full of mutual respect.

Besides, cow protection had a great impact on the Khatiks. Ideologically, the cow protection movement was quite strong in Kanpur, as Pratap Narain Misra's monthly *The Brahmin* was published in Kanpur. "Misra put forward in 1880 'that cow protection was the supreme dharma of the Hindu, that the wealth of Hindustan too was largely dependent upon the welfare of the cow, and that without cow protection the 'Hindu nation' and the country of Hindus could never prosper'...The religious appeal focussed on cow as mother" (Pandey 1992: 179-80).

---

[14] Interview with Ram Avatar at Etawah Bazaar on 1.2.2001. He has his pork shop on King's Bazaar, the only British-style pork butcher left.

The notion of cow protection was adopted by the Khatiks wholeheartedly and pitted against the Muslims and even to a lesser extent against the Chamars. They strongly incorporated into their belief system the conviction that the cow is the incorporation of mother India and he who eats beef is committing matricide. These two streaks of reasoning developed, which were paradoxically juxtaposed against each other. For the Khatiks, bristles became ennobled as commodity and lost its defiling status, on the other hand, cow protection sanctified even animal by-products from the cow. The British went on happily slaughtering cattle for their flourishing tanneries and leather industries, semantically camouflaged as "commissariat cattle" (Roy 1999: 176). The Khatiks knew very well that it was the Muslim *kasai* - butchers on the other side of La Touche Road who slaughtered cows, and although cow slaughter was banned in Uttar Pradesh in 1955 (Lensch 1987: 64), the notion of cow protection is still at the core of Khatik - Muslim resentment.

"King of Pigs"

The 1970s were years of economic decline for the old British-founded textile and leather industry. There was also a political set back through the emergency. For the Khatik bristle manufacturers, the export boom was over when Nixon renewed trade relations with China (Bellwinkel-Schempp 1998: 194). Kanpur could not compete with the cheaper and greater quantities of Chinese bristles. The economic decline of the Khatiks began, when the constraints of the textile industry became obvious. Bristle trade was on the decline, and the final blow came in 1984,[15] when the Chinese flooded the international market with their cheap and good bristles, which made Indian bristles obsolete. The former bristle manufacturers turned brush makers.[16] But the Khatiks lagged behind the more experienced Kayasthas and Punjabis who were able to cater for the Indian market as a whole.

The Khatiks resorted to vegetable dealing where they faced the swelling numbers of the laid off and unemployed industrial workers who were doing the same. Their former monopoly was broken. Apart from this, in the wholesale market, the Khatiks could not compete with the Muslims.[17] Piggery was also on the decline. When the British left, the

---

15 Interview with Tilokchand Sonkar on 26.10.1998.

16 Interview with Rakesh Saxena on 4.11.1998.

17 In Kidwainagar 75 per cent of the business is in Muslim hands. Visit with

demand for high quality pork subsided. Most of the Mall road pork shops closed. With increasing buying capacity, chicken became the craze for the middle classes. Pork became the meat of the Dalit poor[18] and buffaloes the meat for the poor Muslims.

At the end of the 1970s, one Khatik family started a new business venture: pig rearing in public. It was facilitated by the garbage collection system of the municipality which only had primary and secondary collection. Primary collection is the sweeping of roads, drains and the collection of garbage from open garbage dumps along the roadside. A few are containers, others are walled compounds, but most of them are open dumps. Secondary collection is done once or twice a week with lorries and bulldozers. The garbage is then dumped at the outskirts of Kanpur as landfill.[19] The new entrepreneur used the gaps between primary and secondary collection to his advantage and put pigs on Kanpur's garbage heaps, The pigs multiplied quickly, although their fertility rate was severely hampered by traffic, toxic refuse and climate.

When I started with my enquiry into the technicalities of pig farming on public grounds, I was quickly led to Romi Sonkar, who is known as 'King of Pigs', because he owns 20,000 pigs in Kanpur. Pig farming is done in the whole of Kanpur and it is especially rewarding in the 'posh' localities, where the nutritional content of the garbage heaps is high. An inspection tour on the back of Romi's motorbike proved to be very illuminating. The whole of Kanpur is divided into four zones, which are 'farmed' by his brothers and uncle. The pigs in each zone get a specific brand for designation. Inspection is done on motorbike early in the morning and it consists of enumerating the pigs which have died during the night. Pig farming depends on networks of so-called 'friends', who turn up from nowhere to do odd jobs for Romi. These *lumpen* elements get no salary from him; instead they extract dues and fines from the car drivers if a pig is run over. Romi commands high authority, a whisper and raised eyebrows are followed. He himself claims to do *pahlwani* (wrestling) but not in the *akhara*, but privately. *Pahlwani* is often blended with *badmashi* – petty criminals, hooligans – (Freitag 1989: 241) and his 'friends', the muscle men, belong to that category.

Mohammad Ahmad and Babar to Kidwainagar on 2.12.1999.

18 According to an estimate, which I got at the slaughterhouse from the Khatiks, there are still 300 pork butchers in Kanpur, whereas the health inspector claims that there are only 90 left.

19 Interview with Dr Girdhani, Chief Health Officer of the Nagar Nigam Kanpur (NNK) on 9.2.2000.

For Romi and the Khatiks in general, pig farming certainly means money, authority and urban development, when one takes Romi's five storied building as proof of that. The Khatiks define themselves as Hindus, which makes them susceptible to the BJP who use their traditional animosity with the Muslims for their own end. Public pig farming on the premises of Kanpur Urban Agglomeration had the effect that the meaning of Hindu amalgamated with these representations of Dalit culture. It showed Dalit assertiveness on a different plane, an extension of the boundaries of locality, which left an imprint on the town as a whole. They were also an expression of solid waste mismanagement and the negligence of urban authorities.

Kanpur's public took a long time to realize what had happened. But slowly, public opinion turned against the pigs. It started with small articles in the Hindi press, in the hot season of 1999, about various mischief done by the pigs (*Dainik Jagran*, 18.4.1999). The municipal authorities took legal action and issued orders that the pigs had to be kept in sties. This led to an immediate protest by the Khatiks,[20] who pointed out that the pig issue might be drawn into the forthcoming Lok Sabha election campaign. The municipal authorities gave in, because they knew very well with whom they were dealing. As the Khatiks had BJP backing at local, state and centre level, the municipal authorities were not keen to get entangled. The outcome of the election showed a new and unprecedented alliance: a Congress candidate won the Lok Sabha seat supported by Khatiks and Muslims alike.

The new millennium came and with it a new trial. The mayor issued orders that the slaughterhouse should be auctioned to the highest bidder. As the slaughterhouse was situated right in the middle of town, it was to be moved to the periphery. This scheme stirred up a big commotion and brought the whole Muslim community against the mayor. Right into the imbroglio with the slaughterhouse, another onslaught came from a fairly unexpected side. The young lawyer's association, which had nothing to do, filed a court case against the mayor (*Times of India*, 9.2.2000).

20 Satya Prakash Sonkar, Congress politician from La Touche Road formulated the objection with a threatening undertone in a well-versed letter to the Mukhya Nagar Adhikari ; communication on 17.11.1999.

"Let's clean Kanpur Together"

The mayor did not know how to respond until Anna came. She was young, energetic, a civic engineer and an expert in solid waste management. She joined the ranks of 'Indo-Dutch Ganga Institutional and Community Development Project', a bilateral government project, which had gone through several phases since 1988. Started under the Ganga Action Plan, it was to set up an effluent treatment plant in Jajmau to recover highly toxic chromium. This was only partially successful, because the plan had used the wrong technology whilst frequent power cuts hampered the whole process. The water was pumped untreated into the fields, damaging the standing crops (*Pioneer,* 15.2.2000). Lately, Indo-Dutch, as it was called colloquially, was helping out the city administration with computer billing to recover the outstanding tax-arrears. The Kanpur municipality was bankrupt.

Anna wanted to do some real work. She came with the clear intention to free Kanpur from the pigs. Her scheme was simple and convincing. She intended to deprive the pigs of their feed, which would make them disappear in no time. So the sweeping and lifting of garbage had to be organized in such a way that the pigs could not get hold of any garbage. However, the municipal administration already had some experience with 'door to door collection'. Repeatedly, they had tried on a NGO-basis to privatise sweeping. But before long sweepers were beaten up by Romi's 'friends' and the whole project collapsed. The KNN knew very well who the big *badmash* was, although they never met Romi personally.

The KNN were thrilled about Anna. Not so much about the plan but with Anna, her youth and vigour. Her help became even more necessary because the reports in the Hindi press got even longer and more precise (*Dainik Jagran*, 5.7.2000). Suddenly all kinds of animals were targeted. The more the journalists probed and inquired, the more complaints were issued. Besides, there were 'People for Animals' a NGO projecting the cause of the animals. They were blaming the littered polythene bags for endangering the health of the cows. The KNN reacted in the usual manner, promising to remove stray animals from the streets (*Times of India*, 13.3.2000), especially Romi's pigs. But who could catch pigs if not Romi's friends? They were hired to do the task. The KNN was not keen on keeping the pigs and they were sold for a small sum to 'deserving people'. Romi's friends were certainly deserving, so the pigs were back on the streets again.

At the same time, the KNN under Anna's guidance started with the new project. To enable door-to-door collection and the installation of new garbage pits, Anna wanted to know exactly, how much garbage Kanpur produced. She went on to weigh the daily garbage disposal, which put the authorities under considerable strain because she supervised the weighing herself and noted down the tonnage. This led to an estrangement between the truck drivers and the health inspectors because the result was that the total garbage was much less than estimated. There were superfluous trucks, too many truck drivers and wasted petrol. Squandering of public resources happens every day but one loses one's face if that becomes public news through a foreign expert. As a consequence, the whole project was considered to be too ambitious and stopped.

A small model scheme on self-help basis was thought to be better. So "Let's clean Kanpur together" was born. A poster showed how cows and pigs were driven out of their urban grazing grounds. New uniforms and new charts would give additional incentives to the sweepers. Everything was well prepared and the administrators and workers were happy and optimistic. The day of the inauguration came. The mayor was there, the municipal authorities and the journalists. Suddenly, the sweepers union turned up, threatening the assembly with their *jharus* - brooms. They put forward that the whole project was nothing else but a clandestine privatisation, and they would strongly object to it. The mayor fled immediately, and Anna left for a long vacation. The cleanliness drive was over. Six months later, Indo-Dutch's solid waste management was terminated, because there was no other scheme to justify their presence.

The corporation elections were coming. Romi Sonkar and Chunna Bacca, Kala Bacca's brother, were standing on a BJP ticket. But public opinion turned against them.

> The biggest pig holder in Kanpur, Romi Sonkar, is standing for the corporation elections in Kanpur… . The pigs are feeding on garbage and spreading dirt. After the death of Kala Bacca, Romi has become the biggest pig holder in town. It is estimated that he has got more than 10,000 pigs. He has beaten up many people. In this respect, criminal cases are filed against him. Romi does the supervision of the pigs on his motorbike and he gives orders with the help of his mobile. At the last elections, the BJP put up another pig holder with the name of Chunna Bacca who was threatening the voters and never did anything against dirt and

disorder in his constituency" (*Dainik Jagran*, 8.9.2000).

Neither Romi nor Chunna Bacca was elected. And the BJP mayor lost her seat against the Congress candidate. The people were looking for a more gifted administrator. So the choice fell on Anil Sharma, whose father was a long time MLA on a Congress ticket, known for his competence, impartiality and skilful political manoeuvring. High hopes accompanied the election of his son. The dominance of the BJP was broken at the city level. The state elections in 2002 resulted in Mayawati and the BSP forming a coalition government with the BJP (Pai 2002: 267). Dalit assertion became prevalent on the political plane as well.

BACK TO CITIZENSHIP

Amongst the Khatik too, the tide was turning. The moderates gained ground, not so much because they resented what Romi was doing but more from a vision of a better future for their *samaj* – society. They felt left behind in comparison with the upwardly mobile Chamar who were securing most of the posts in the highest echelons of administration. The Khatiks had only one IAS officer in the Class I bracket. Neither brush manufacturing nor contracting opened an avenue for progress and prosperity and pig rearing led to criminality. The educated and enlightened amongst the Khatik began projecting the three tenets of Dr Ambedkar "educate, unite and fight" for the well being of their own society.

Nawal Kishor was the leading figure behind this. He was the son of a rich bristle dealer Makund Lal who had educated his sons well. Makund Lal was convinced that progress was only possible through the equalizing effect of trade, commerce and modern education, which would eventually overcome discrimination arising from the caste system. His sons were the only ones among the La Touche Road Sonkars who knew English fluently. When the bristle boom was over, Nawal Kishor managed to transform his trade into brush manufacturing, placing his son and nephew into the business. Now, at the age of 60, he was in a position to fulfil himself a dream: In 1998, he had started a magazine called *Brushes, Hairs and Fibres*.[21] Swimming against the current of Sonkar

21 His magazine was a replica of the English bristle merchants magazine: 'Bristles, Hairs and Fibres', which stopped publication at the end of the 1970s. His father had been a regular subscriber to that magazine.

resentment, he employed two Muslims as office staff, and with the help of his secretary and a young computer specialist, he got in touch with the world at large through the internet.[22] This was his response to globalisation, and the Khatik had been linked with global economy for more than 100 years.

On 16 March 2001, the last day of Holi, a riot broke out (*Times of India*, 18.3.2001). The Islamic Student's Union (SIMI) was protesting against photos which were circulated on the Internet showing the Koran being burnt. In the course of their demonstrations, an Additional District Magistrate got shot, which triggered off a riot. But neither Khatiks nor Hindus participated. Looting and burning of shops and brutal harassment of Muslims was the police reaction, against which a broad citizen forum of all social groups and denominations protested in a silent demonstration (*Times of India*, 26.3.2001). Nawal Kishor lost his Muslim office staff as they gave notice after these events.

There was not only growing resentment against the pig holders in Kanpur but also against Rakesh Sonkar who was accused of having contributed to the deteriorating urban conditions.

> The increasing number of pigs has created a great chaos in different localities. 'We are fed up of the pigs. Our *puja* – prayers – has become useless. The moment we leave the house, the filthy pigs are coming up from the sewers and garbage heaps and cheek us. It is like hell – *narak.*' Road decay, brain disease, cancer and other severe diseases are attributed to the pigs. Not only that the pig herders and their families are also getting chronic diseases. 1000 people are connected with this business and it is very lucrative. Mr Sonkar agreed to build pig herders colonies outside the city with the help of the government, the municipal authorities and the Kanpur Development Authority. He was also confronted with the fact that the popularity of the BJP is going down because they are pursuing group politics. When he was questioned that he acquired schools and *dharmshalas* and misappropriated public property, he just denied but could not argue the case (*Dainik Jagran*, 16.7.2001).

Misappropriation of land, urban property and corruption were the charges against Sonkar. He lost the candidature in the 2002 State elections and a candidate on a Congress ticket, Sanjay Dariawadi, a Khatik as

[22] While working on this paper, I got the sad news that Nawal Kishor died suddenly on 31.1.2000.

well, won the constituency seat reserved for Sisamau. Nawal Kishor raised funds for the election campaign and actively supported him. Sanjay's father had been Makund Lal's partner in bristle manufacture. He had been a businessman for many years and set up the *Jauhar* temple on La Touche Road. Following his father's sudden death, Sanjay's mother became an MLA, also on a Congress ticket. During her legislative period, the slum clearance scheme in La Touche Road Khatkiana was set into motion (Lavigne 1984: 72). Apparently, the Khatiks had gone back to the Congress.

SWINE HERDER'S ASSERTION

Pigs in the Indian contexts are considered an abomination, closely connected with pollution and danger and a signifier of untouchable culture. Let us go back to Mary Douglas' observations about substance at the wrong place, in this case about pigs at the wrong place. Has the public appearance of the pigs changed their cultural meaning? In the mapping of urban space, pigs are synonymous with Hindu localities. They show an extension of untouchable culture to the whole town. Pigs are equated with the concept of Hinduness in structural opposition to Muslimness as the other. Besides, they had an equalising effect on the town as a whole, because so called 'posh' localities were affected as well as poor localities. Pigs were not the only ones creating havoc in town. Dogs, cows and buffaloes were a security and health hazard as well. But all efforts to contain them, starting from slaughterhouse campaigns to repeated schemes to settle them at the outskirts of Kanpur, did not help.

The failure of urban governance to contain the live-stock on Kanpur's streets seems to be symptomatic of a variety of factors (de-industrialisation, economic decline, communal tensions) although they do not explain the complex interface of different segments of the public and the power relations involved. The rather helpless manoeuvring of the administrative set up and the NGO involved shows the failure of the 74th Amendment. Urban governance depends on the power relations at the centre and state level, which is openly discussed and reckoned with. The political constellation on the different levels of electoral authority is important, not the administrative measures, schemes and projects.

Engaged journalism was voicing the complaints of the citizens against animal menace. Detailed enquiries presented differentiated reactions to all kinds of animals, which reiterated the notions of purity and pollution as well as superseded them, thereby elevating a religiously contained animal symbolism on to a secular platform. Newspapers as a forum of citizens' concerns beyond communalism and in pursuance of common objectives (health, cleanliness, safety) presented a public awareness for the common good.

But how did that semantic shift occur from the pig as an abomination to the so-called 'clean' profession the Khatiks are pursuing? Piggery and bristle manufacturing were a break with the untouchable past, because the colonial understanding of the pig ennobled that business and changed the meaning. The Khatiks derived their self-respect and self-definition from the centre of colonial power, the London auction, where they sent their bristles. They turned to Hindu culture without reforming their eating habits in which the seeds for their susceptibility for Hindutva and its anti-Muslim appeal lay. Cow protection is at the core of their belief system and the pig was pitted against the Muslims as a provocation.

The Khatiks have grown out of two endogamous groups into a 'caste', what they call *samaj* in a shifting and oscillating understanding of 'caste' as *jati*, as caste association, as the community of Dalits in Kanpur and society at large. Apart from this, they are also oscillating between Shudra and Dalit identity and notions of purity and pollution do not explain their status, which also represents the paradoxical part of their history. I could also show how militancy was subsiding and how the Khatiks were coming back to a civic understanding of political propriety.

Neither Nandini Gooptu's construction of Dalit and Shudra castes with distinct characteristics holds true, nor the deconstruction of caste as a colonial machination. The Khatiks of Kanpur were oscillating between Dalit and Shudra identity, between secular and religious notions, between fundamentalist and progressive political orientations. Throughout their history, there was a continuous foregrounding or backgrounding of their multiple orientations and attributes of status. The Khatiks of Kanpur were followers of a *bhakti* saint as well as of Shudra militancy.

The Khatiks were closely associated with the British and derived their identity from the tasks they were assigned to. I could show how on the one hand the British 'fixed' the Khatiks into something they considered to be their hereditary occupation but they were also pragmatic enough to accept what was offered. The Colonelganj Khatiks were skilled masons and the British used their mastery to get their factories and houses constructed. Caste stigmata were used and ignored at the same time, they were fixed and superseded, all as a part of the colonial discourse. The

Khatiks of Kanpur are a good example of constructing and deconstructing of caste, along and beyond pollution lines. The semantic shift to piggery and bristle from the abomination of the polluted animal is an amazing finding. This lies at the bottom of their power and their appropriation of the public realm through their pigs.

REFERENCES

Awasthi, Rajendra Kumar, *Urban Development and Metropolitics in India*, Allahabad: Chugh Publications, 1985.

Bannerjee, Nirmala; Nihila, Millie, 'Business organization in the leather industries of Calcutta and Chennai', in Bagchi, Amiya Kumar, ed., *Economy and Organization. Indian institutions under the neoliberal regime*, New Delhi: Sage Publ., 1999, pp. 147-187.

Bhatnagar, P.P., *Special Report on Kanpur City. Census of India 1961*, vol 39 (2), New Delhi: Government of India Press, 1965.

Bellwinkel-Schempp, Maren, 'The Khatiks of Kanpur and the Bristle Trade: Towards an anthropology of man and beast', in *Sociological Bulletin*, 47, 2 1998, pp.187-206.

Bellwinkel-Schempp, Maren, 'Kabir-Panthis in Kanpur: From Sampradaya to Dalit identity', in Horstmann, Monika, ed., *Images of Kabir*, New Delhi: Manohar, 2002, pp. 215-232.

Brass, Paul R., *Theft of an Idol. Text and context in the representation of collective violence*, Princeton: Princeton University Press, 1998.

Briggs, George Weston, *The Chamars*, Calcutta: Associated Press, 1920.

Charsley, Simon, 'Untouchable, what is in a name?', in *Journal of the Anthropological Institute*, 1996, pp. 1-23.

Cohn, Bernhard S., *An Anthropologist among the Historians*, Delhi: Oxford University Press, 1987.

Council for Leather Exports, *Facts and Figures of Export of Leather and Leather Products during 1999-2000*, Chennai: Leather Centre, 2001.

Doniger, Wendy, *The Laws of Manu*, New Delhi: Viking, 1991.

Douglas, Mary, *Purity and Danger. An analysis of concepts of pollution and taboo*, Hammonworth: Penguin: 1966.

Freitag, Sandria B., *Collective Action and Community. Public arenas and the emergence of communalism in North India*, Berkeley: University of California Press, 1989.

Froystad, Kathinka, Beneath Hindu Nationalism. Caste, class and shifting faces of 'Hinduness' in a north Indian city, Ph.D. Dissertation, Department of Social Anthropology, University of Oslo, June 2000.

Fuchs, Martin, *Kampf um Differenz. Repräsentation, Subjektivität und soziale Bewegungen. Das Beispiel Indien,* Frankfurt: Suhrkamp, 1999.

Gooptu, Nandini, *The Politics of the Urban Poor in Early Twentieth-Century India,* Cambridge: Cambridge University Press, 2002.

Harris, Marvin, *The Sacred Cow and the Abominable Pig. Riddles of food and culture,* New York: Touchstone, 1988.

Joshi, Chitra, *Indian Labour and Its Forgotten Histories,* Delhi: Permanent Black, 2003.

Khare, R.S., *The Untouchable as Himself. Ideology, Identity and Pragmatism among Lucknow Chamars,* Cambridge: Cambridge University Press, 1984.

Lavigne, Jean Claude and Milbert, Isabelle, *La réabilitation des bidonvilles de Kanpur (U.P. Inde).* Lyon: Ministère de l'Urbanisme, du Logement et des Transports, 1983.

Lensch, Jan, *Problems and Prospects of Cattle and Buffalo Husbandry in India with special Reference to the Concept of the 'Sacred Cow'*, Hamburg: Seagull Publishers, 1987.

Majumdar, D.N., *Social Contours of an Industrial City. Social survey of Kanpur 1954-1956*, Bombay: Asia Publ. House, 1960.

Molund, Stefan, *First we are people. The Kori of Kanpur between Caste and Class,* Stockholm: Stockholm Studies in Social Anthropology, 1988.

Mukherjee, Rudrangshu, *Spectre of Violence. The Kanpur Massacres,* New Delhi: Viking Penguin India, 1998.

Nevill, H.R., *Cawnpore, a Gazetteer*, Allahabad: Government Press United Provinces, 1909.

Niehoff, Arthur, *Factory Workers in India,* Milwaukee: Public Museum Publications in Anthropology, 1959.

Pai, Sudha, *Dalit Assertion and the Unfinished Democratic Revolution. The Bahujan Samaj Party in Uttar Pradesh,* New Delhi: Sage Publications, 2002.

Pandey, Gyanendra, *The Construction of Communalism in Colonial North India,* Delhi: Oxford University Press, 1992.

Pandey, S.M., *As Labour Organizes. A study of unionism in the Kanpur cotton textile industry,* New Delhi: Sri Ram Centre for Industrial Relations, 1970.

Rai, Vibhuti Narain, *Combating Communal Conflicts. Perception of police neutrality during Hindu-Muslim riots in India,* Allahabad: Anamika Prakashan, 1999.

Ram, Nandu, *The Mobile Scheduled Castes. Rise of a new middle class,* Delhi: Hindustan Publ. Corp., 1988.

Rivariya, Man Chand, *Khatik Samaj ka Itihas. History of the Khatik community*, New Delhi, 2000.

Roy, Tirthankar, *Traditional Industry in the Economy of Colonial India,* Cambridge Studies in Indian History and Society 5, Cambridge: Cambridge University Press, 1999.

Sahukar, Chandra Shekar, *Piggery India Year Book 2000*, New Delhi: Scientific Publishers and Distributers, 2000.

Searle-Chatterjee, Mary, *Reversible Sex Roles. The special case of Benares sweepers,* New Delhi: Oxford and Pergamon Publ., 1981.

Singh, S.N., *Planning and Development of an Industrial Town. A study of Kanpur,* New Delhi: Mittal Publications, 1990.

Srivastava, R., 'Uttar Pradesh, Sectional Politics in an Urban Constituency. Generalganj, Kanpur', in *Economic and Political Weekly*, 31, 1996, pp. 111-120.

Trevelyan, George, *The Competition Wallah,* New Delhi: Harper Collins, 1992.

Yalland, Zoe, *Traders and Nabobs. The British in Cawnpore 1765-1857*, The Chantry, Wilton, Salisbury, Wiltshire: Michael Russell, 1987.

Yalland, Zoe, *Boxwallahs. The British in Cawnpore 1857-1901*, Wilby Hall, Wilby, Norwich: Michael Russell, 1994.

In Time and Space:

Urban Settlements and the State

9

PLANNING URBAN CHAOS: STATE AND REFUGEES IN POST-PARTITION DELHI

RAVINDER KAUR

INTRODUCTION

The overriding theme addressed in this chapter is the "urban degeneration" (Das 2002) afflicting Delhi city. The term 'urban degeneration' in a narrow sense points to severe breach in civic order over an immediate time span whereas in this chapter it helps provoke a larger discussion around the institutions of state, processes of history and their combined impact on creating and filling urban spaces. In the case of Delhi, it is Government of India that played a dominant role in earmarking a variety of sites for urban expansion following the territorial division in 1947.

However, it's a paradox that in most recent studies of urbanisation in Delhi, the year 1947 often remains amiss (Dupont et al. 2000).[1] It is a paradox because 1947 Partition is one such process that has most remarkably shaped the contours of the city in 20th century. The partition of British India into the new states of India and Pakistan was accompanied by unprecedented communal violence and forced migration that started as early as the month of March. An estimated 10 to 12 million Hindus, Muslims and Sikhs migrated across the international boundary between India and Pakistan. The city of Delhi was affected particularly with the mammoth influx of refugees the enormity of which was clearly manifested in the dramatic increase in city's population along with its expanded urban boundaries. Though Partition and its aftermath are clearly etched in popular social and political discourses, it has failed to

---

1 Of the 41 articles in Khushwant Singh (2001) *City Improbable: An Anthology of Writings on Delhi*, only one article 'Delhi 1947' by Yashpal touches the theme of Partition and displacement.

permeate the academic concerns about urbanisation in Delhi. It is this lacuna – of employing ahistorical approaches to urbanisation – that this chapter aims at addressing. Any understanding of the process of urban development in Delhi city needs to be imbued with historicity of political events that took place half a century ago. As the imperial capital of British India and later independent India, Delhi has been at the centre of political upheavals

The largest intake of Partition refugees for a single city is one of the most significant claims that Delhi city can make. The trickle of refugees that had started after the Rawalpindi riots in March inundated into never ending columns of refugees by the summer of 1947. The exact number of dead, injured or those forced to migrate in either direction, though, has been a source of contention among historians. The conservative estimates emanating from British sources about the number of casualties put the figure at 200,000 (Moon 1961), while the Indian estimates peg the number at around 400,000 to 500,000 (Khosla 1950). The estimates in some of the recent studies, that rely on oral historiography extensively, put the figure at 800,000 (Butalia 1998). The number of migrants is, thus, equally contested. For the purpose of this paper, population censuses of 1941 and 1951 conducted in Delhi are used to compare the decadal demographic shifts and the corresponding extent of movement.

The total population of Delhi in 1941 was counted at 917,939 which at an unprecedented decennial growth rate of 106 per cent increased to 1,744,072 in 1951.[2] In absolute numbers, the increase amounts to 1.1 million people making it the highest ever increase in the city's census history, more so, when the increase does not take into account the outward migration of approximately 300,000 Delhi Muslims to Pakistan. Even if we assume that not all the increase was due to influx of Punjabi refugees owing to the factors of usual rural-urban in-migration and natural growth at the natural growth rate of 4 per cent, the massive increase can be largely attributed to the Partition related events. This makes it imperative for any meaningful research that the single event that has characterized city the most – Partition – is not glossed over entirely.

While the foremost task has been to establish post-Partition migration as the point of departure for this chapter, the other is to delve into the intricacies of refugee resettlement and the consequent expansion of the city. The aim of this exercise is to extricate and then examine the role of Indian state in the course of post-partition urban development. The

2 Census of India 1941 and 1951.

events of 1947 are often cited as a reason for the haphazard growth of the city due to the influx of a large population. It would seem that the refugees were responsible for the emergence of the "vast sprawling, multicoloured soulless monster of today which we continue to call by the same name" (Khosla 1985: 37). Yet most of it was 'planned' by the Ministry of Relief and Rehabilitation along with the Town Planning department. The Master Plan of Delhi emerged long afterwards Lajpat Nagar, Jangpura, Ramesh Nagar, Moti Nagar and Tihar colonies had been established. The 'soulless monsters' were not entirely the refugee's own creation. The new rulers had earmarked these sites for them. The over crowded colonies with narrow lanes often have leaking sewerage systems, a lack of sufficient water or electricity and illegal constructions that generally define them. The refugees and their descendants who inhabit these colonies are routinely examined for the causes of apparent decay of the city. The state is seldom a part of this examination since much of the discourse about the city's cultural decay evolves around the Punjabi refugees.

This chapter looks at the state rehabilitation schemes and the inherent class biases therein that sowed the seeds of the 'soulless monster'. The state was creating a new citizenship through its permanent rehabilitation schemes where one's place in the new hierarchy was largely decided by one's social status in the pre-partition order. The discussion is located around the unexplored areas of Delhi which lie outside the periphery of both the old city as well as the Imperial British capital. It examines the negotiations between refugees and the new state, an entity which controlled most of the resources and thus held a key to the refugee's future. Two separate examples referring to the (a) Purana Qila refugee camp and (b) the autobiographical notes of an Indian Civil Services (ICS) will be examined to show how urban expansion of Delhi was planned, executed and presided over by the state through the process of Partition refugee movement and resettlement.

Retrieving Delhi from a Nostalgic Cul-de-Sac

> Meanwhile, the city was growing imperceptibly in a totally chaotic manner. Builder settlements developed in all directions swallowing up the old *lal dora* villages in their wake. A big land grab operation was on. With the land sharks at work, the Municipal Corporation was totally out of its depth and by the time the authorities began to

> wake up to the impending urban disaster, they were able to do too little much too late. (Menon 2002)
>
> This is not the Delhi I grew up in. That Delhi was quiet and innocent, with very few cars, no television, many trees, and a routine rhythm of school or work, and leisurely walks on wide car-less streets. (Caur 2002)

The common tendency in most discussions on Delhi's urban career is to swing between the pristine past and the chaotic present. The defining features that mark any given sample of such writing are that (a) the authors belong to the upper middle class, (b) the chaotic growth of Delhi is attributed to some clandestine projects designed by illegitimate faceless forces, and (c) finally, a highly studied effort and a politically correct approach is employed to stay clear of pointing to the perceived culprits. The tumultuous events of Partition are not often mentioned directly in this context, but do surface from time to time in the form of nostalgia that invariably accompanies such popular and, at times, even academic discourses (Dupont et al. 2000). It is the seemingly innocuous and stray remarks like the following that point to the underlying tensions:

> By the '90s, a loud and noisy population of *nouveau riche puppies* (my italics) had taken over this other Delhi, flouting all those values that the Dilliwallahs had held dear. Worse still, this loudness and vulgarity began to impinge on 'establishment' Delhi as well, fed by the growing corruption and money culture that had begun to be all-pervasive. (Menon 2002)

The singular mention of 'nouveau riche puppies' is the lone indicator to the vastly held perception that Partition migration drastically changed the face of Delhi. The phrase itself needs to be explained here since it not only compresses a historically significant episode but also entire generations of forced migrants, their descendants and their efforts at restarting their lives. Puppy is an improved acronym derived from yuppies – young urban professionals – with a pronounced letter P that stands for Punjabis. It was the Partition migration that brought Hindu and Sikh Punjabi refugees to Delhi city in such large numbers that made them numerically conspicuous. Unsurprisingly, these accounts do not accrue from the refugees themselves but the pre-partition 'locals' who routinely lay claim to the original Delhi as it was before the arrival of refugees; intellectuals who despise the aesthetically unappealing architecture; and the upper middle class residents accustomed to the wide-shaded-avenues-part of the city.

The nostalgic mourning can vary from the 'lost charm' of the old part of the city called Shahjahanabad, a contempt for the new areas where "Tilak Nagars and Nehru Roads proliferate, and hardly anyone knows of the poetry of Mir and Zauq, the humour of Ghalib, the quality of life that Chandni Chowk once symbolised" (Gupta 1981: ix), or better still the invasion of the city in 1947 by the 'ugly Punjabi'[3] whose 'migrant mentality' (Baviskar 1998: 3102). robbed Delhi of its culture and sense of community. This nostalgia endows upon Delhi titles such as 'the city that nobody loves' (Dupont et al. 2000: 16) that help conjure up an image of a city that is culturally and architecturally dead. The loop of such nostalgic discourses holds Old Delhi and Lutyens Delhi in clear contrast to the post partition expansion areas of the city. These areas are something that one does not talk about, they are not meant for display or discussion for they possess no architectural beauty or cultural significance. They are the faceless habitations of the Partition refugees for whom mass housing was constructed by the Indian Government in the early fifties. In these colonies 1947 remains a crucial date, as most of the inhabitants are either Partition refugees or their descendants. They are among the millions of people who were forced to migrate during the Partition violence in Punjab, Sindh, Bengal and North-West-Frontier Province (NWFP). Despite this collective amnesia that prevails outside these colonies, Partition remains the single most important historical process that changed the city decidedly. Through this enquiry, one aims at extricating the city and its inhabitants from the 'nostalgic dead ends' for these dead ends effectively prevent any probing questions and uncomfortable challenges.

State, Class and Urban Space

To understand how the post-partition urban expansion in Delhi created some well laid out, spacious areas – like Nizamuddin, South Extension on the one hand and highly congested areas – like Old Double storey, Nirmal Puri in Lajpat Nagar on the other, one needs to look at the resettlement policy pursued by the Government. The role of the state is significant since it became, through a number of property laws, the sole

---

3 A regular reference in the city newspapers to the 1947 Punjabi migrants. They are considered brash, loud, unsophisticated and nouveau riche.

claimant to the refugee property. The state could then decide how and to whom these fixed assets should be distributed.

The refugees on both sides left behind substantial immoveable assets like houses, workshops, factories, shops etc. in the urban areas. These assets were declared as state property under the 'East Punjab Evacuee (Administration Property) Ordinance of 1947' with the state proclaimed as the guardian of the assets until the original owner claimed it back (Husain 1954: ix). The Ordinance was amended a number of times before it was passed as a parliamentary act in the form of 'The Administration of Evacuee Property Act, 1950'. Under this law, an office of the Custodian General of Evacuee Property in India was created with the proclaimed object of providing for the "administration of evacuee property and that this property has to be ultimately used for compensating the refugees who had lost their property in Pakistan".[4] An 'evacuee' was defined as a person who "on account of the setting up of dominions of India and Pakistan or on account of civil disturbances, leaves or has, on or after the 1st day of March 1947, left any place outside the territories now forming part of India".[5] The evacuees seldom came back[6] and the property effectively came to belong to the state. The state through the custodian's office could use, rent or allot it to incoming refugees.

The role of state in the urban expansion of Delhi became more pronounced when it embarked on its project of providing permanent rehabilitation to the refugees. The acquisition of evacuee houses provided accommodation that was far from adequate, as for every two Muslims who left India, at least three Hindus and Sikhs came in from Pakistan (Rao 1965: 56). The skewed proportion was worse in Delhi where for every outgoing Muslim refugee there were three Hindu and Sikh refugees who sought shelter instead. The options available were, one, to distribute evacuee accommodation and, two, to create new housing colonies for the ones without a roof. Both these options were exercised at different levels but both were preceded by similar administrative processes. It started with the arrival of the refugees at the old Delhi railway station where a refugee reception centre was opened. All

---

4 Administration of Evacuee Property Act, 1950, Chapter 1 (Para. 1).

5 Ibid. Chapter 1 (Para 2).

6 A few evacuees, though, did come back as the records in the office of Custodian General suggest. There were several cases where litigation was taken course to for the restoration of property. For example, Mohammad Habibudin Vs Government of Hyderabad , 1953, Hyderabad 1957.

the disembarking refugees were registered and given a number and a card. They were then directed to refugee camps if they had nowhere to go. There were four big camps in the city at Kingsway, Rajindar Nagar, Purana Qila and Pul Bangash.[7] The biggest camp was the Kingsway camp comprising of an estimated 30,000 refugees[8] spread over and around the old British barracks called Hudson, Reeds, Edward and Outram Lines. Thereafter they could approach the Ministry of Relief and Rehabilitation to file for compensation against lost property in Pakistan. The Ministry would assess the application and make a recommendation for compensation in terms of cash or *in lieu* property.

The most vital pre-requisite for compensation was that the refugees should have owned some form of property to be eligible. This effectively barred the homeless and poor from staking any claim in the new scheme of nation building. They could continue to live on the margins just as before while new territories were being carved for the middle class refugees. Of those who did own properties, their success in getting compensation depended on their social networks, literacy and ability to bribe the clerks and officers at the Ministry's various departments. So, the second most important pre-requisite was to have knowledge of the official procedures, skill in filling up many lengthy forms and some reserve capital that could be used to grease palms at an opportune moment. It was important to break the codes that state had invented and only those who managed to feel the state at an intimate level were able to do that. The elite comprising of high level government officials, non-farming landlords, merchants, university teachers and other such people with dominant positions in the society had a far better understanding of the state than ordinary people. They were less in awe of the state for they had in one way or the other, as employees, contractors or tax-payers, dealt with its machinery.

Those, especially, at the higher level of bureaucracy came from the rich and socially well connected families because the Indian Civil Services was an exclusive preserve of those who could afford to travel and study in England. They were in a privileged position to move their persons and belongings in a number of ways and then lay claims against the immoveable property left behind. The official influence could be exerted not only to protect one's family and friends but also to recover one's personal articles down to the knick-knacks. The troubled months

---

7 All India Congress Committee (AICC) Records (2nd Instalment) File no. 3(XV).

8 Personal Interview with Mr H. K. Dhawan, a retired Assistant Custodian at the Minsitry of Relief and Rehabilitation on 15 December 2000.

of the Partition process provided an opportunity to measure one's importance and influence in the society. The ones who scraped through unscathed with their lives and properties intact were indeed the most influential as the following narrative will show.

THE LOST CARPET

Justice Gopal Das Khosla was a member of Indian Civil Services having taken his ICS exam in London in 1926. His father was a Punjab Civil Service officer and Gopal Das was sent to England to carve a similar career path for himself. In 1947, he was placed at the Punjab High Court seat in Lahore as a judge. During the communal strife in Punjab, his wife and children were safely in Mussorie for summer vacations as was the custom with British or anglicised Indian families to retire to the hills to escape the searing summer heat. Justice Khosla describes the communal situation in Lahore city during the summer of 1947 in his autobiography *Memory's Gay Chariot* (Khosla 1985: 156-8).

> One day I accompanied Prem Thaper, Commissioner, Lahore Division, on his tour of inspection in the walled city, and saw horrifying holocaust beyond Shahalmi gate. The entire bazaar had been reduced to rubble and ashes, and we could feel the heat radiated by the cinder and the mounds of grey dust lying on either side of the street. That day, I realised that we would have to leave Lahore, our home town, and seek safety elsewhere in India. (...)
> Four days remained from the closing day of the High Court session. I received a letter from Shakuntala in Mussorie, that I must withdraw all her jewellery from the bank locker in Lahore, take it to Delhi and deposit it there in a locker without fail. (...) I had never had any fears or misgivings that any of my belongings in Lahore were in any danger from the consequence of the fast approaching partition, and I thought Shakuntala's anxiety about the safety of her jewellery wholly unreasonable and uncalled for. But it was her jewellery and not mine and women often have a hunch about matters that concern them intimately. (...)
> So after a moment's deliberation I sent my trusted peon, Munna Lal, to Mussorie. He returned, two days later, with the keys and I extracted Shakuntala's entire jewellery from the locker and packed it in the trunk that was to accompany me to Delhi and Mussorie.

> Shakuntala was of course right. The Government of Pakistan later froze all bank and locker assets, and I should not have had another opportunity to gain free access to the locker. To recover the jewellery, I should have had to go through the tedious and complicated procedure of applying to the Custodian of Evacuee Property in Pakistan, instead of taking it out and carrying it away lawfully and without restrain.

In this account, intimate knowledge of political events comes handy in making the vital decisions. Here, the most difficult decision for everyone in Punjab was whether to stay or to leave. There was utter confusion on the border areas as no one knew how far the national boundaries would extend. Many people were ill-informed and did not have a full grasp of the fast unfolding events.[9] The word 'Pakistan' was often heard but not fully understood. The class that understood the gravity of the situation fled to safety before being chased out. Justice Khosla had first hand knowledge of the situation and as a judge of the high court he could tour the sites of violence. Many had access to those sites but they were the ones who were involved as victims, perpetrators or bystanders who could both turn into potential victims and perpetrators. Few could tour those sites without being involved and as bearers of the state authority Justice Khosla and the Commissioner of Lahore were at a minimal risk. This knowledge of impending greater calamity made Justice Khosla decide that it was time to leave. His family was already out of danger zone due to the custom adopted by well-off Indians to move to cool climate of hills in summer. The retrieval of jewellery was not the only feat that Khosla's managed. Once they were in together in Mussorie the news reached them that their house in Lahore had been occupied by the Pakistan authorities. His friend Manzur Qadir, a fellow judge from Punjab High Court managed to intervene and remove his silver and small valuables to his house. In his letter to Justice Khosla, Manzur "concluded with an expression of his distress that my Persian carpets had not been traced." (Khosla 1985: 161; 167). Justice further narrates in his memoir,

> Shakuntala was very upset (…) she parried "But, how shall we get our things back?" [Gopal Das replied] "We will manage somehow, and if we can't, we'll start all over again, as lakhs of other Hindus

9 Personal interview with Mrs H. Kaur in Delhi.

> will be doing. All of us are alive and safe, and I still have my job." [But] It was not easy to philosophise and reconcile ourselves to the loss of our ancestral house in Gowal Mandi, three acres of valuable land on the Mall and all our furniture, clothes, carpets, crockery, cutlery, silver and so much besides. But we had to resign ourselves to the inevitable and hope that we might be able to redeem something by virtue of my official status. (*Ibid.*: 161-2)

But Khosla's did not have to start their lives all over again like other Hindus. The magic of 'official status' that Justice Khosla was hoping for did work. He decided to go to Lahore to retrieve his personal belongings. He got a place in a car that carried newspapers from Simla to Amritsar everyday. The car broke down on the way but

> my free and unashamed use of the prefix 'Justice' was rewarded by a lift to the spot where Colonel Kochhar was camping with his army unit. He very kindly offered to me a seat in a jeep leaving for Amritsar. (…) The next day I called on Brigadier Mohite, who was arranging and supervising the transport of refugees to and from Pakistan, and explained to him the nature of my mission. He was most obliging and helpful, and at once, assigned a weapon carrier and an armed Gurkha security force to conduct me to Lahore and bring me back along with six trucks which would carry, from Amritsar, Muslim refugees waiting to go to Pakistan and transport my personal affects and those of my two brother judges on the return journey. (…)
>
> [In Lahore] I had met several of my old friends, Mueen-ud-din and Majid of the ICS, Qurban Ali, the policeman who, despite his reputation as a devout Muslim, had been a very good friend and now readily conceded my request to release my father-in-law's car on the (transparently fictional) [text in parenthesis not mine] ground that I needed the vehicle for my official use. (...)
>
> The three days assigned to my stay in Lahore had grown to four. By noon, all trucks were ready, packed to capacity, their loads towering above the side-walls, in precarious piles of chairs, tables, side-boards, and boxes which seemed ready to leave their eminence at the slightest tilt in the vehicles balance or a jolt in its passage over rough and bumpy roads. (…)
>
> It was 5 p.m. when the weapon carrier was seen entering the drive way. (…) Behind came the long line of trucks ostensibly

> with High Court records for that is what the paper handed me by Brigadier Mohite declared, with official authority. It was quite dark when we reached the check-post, halfway to the Wagah border. He [a Pakistani official] looked up and asked: "High Court records. You are Justice Khosla?" "Yes, I replied. High court records....and personal property of judge." The official signed the paper, stamped it and handed it to me, with an expressionless face. (*Ibid.*: 170-1)

The 'official status' surely has its uses as this account shows. While a large part of the population was struggling to get out of the violence prone areas, the people well connected with authority of the state managed to retrieve their personal belongings from crockery to carpets, silver, clothes, books, furniture etc. Justice Khosla managed to get his father-in-law's car along with the belongings of his 'brother judges'. The networks of influential people grew on such acts where everyone is aware of the importance of the other and hopes to make use of it some day. These bonds of class based brotherhood helped earn a future security against some misfortune or trouble. Justice Khosla was helped first by a fellow judge who despite his nationality – Pakistani – helped him because of a common professional bond. Then it was army officers who at various points felt obliged to accommodate a high court judge. Brigadier Mohite put six trucks at his disposal on the return journey from Lahore which could have been easily used to bring across a number of ordinary refugee families. Many accounts suggest that people had to wait for days to get a place in the trains or motor trucks to get safely across the borders.[10]

The official accounts also recount the shortage of essentials like petrol, motor trucks and trained drivers to run transport for evacuation purposes. "At every point they [?] strained our resources in men, money, and materials almost to a bursting point" (Rao 1965: 13). It does come as a surprise that in such an emergency situation, the Commander of evacuation operation could spare several trucks and a vehicle with armed guards to recover Justice Khosla's personal possessions. The official authority was again utilised to show the personal articles as court records to let it pass the border unhindered. Only those in such positions of

[10] I have described this in another paper entitled 'Unequal Refugees: Migration narratives from the 1947 partition', presented at 17th ECMAS at Heidelberg University.

influence could benefit from such arrangements. Otherwise most had to leave their homes almost empty handed.

The point in this narrative is that people with socio-political capital found it easier to relocate in material terms. The emotional loss of a sense of belonging is beyond measurement and definitely not a point of discussion here. The networks minimised the material as well personal losses. The resettlement laws favoured the once who possessed prior capital and could demonstrate it to the authorities in the form of authentication from a well known person. So, higher one was in the hierarchy, official or otherwise, the easier it was to authenticate the possessions. The authentication then formed the claim for compensation and resettlement. The old class order was, thus, allowed to continue. Many of the policy makers, both politicians and bureaucrats, especially from Punjab, held substantial properties and came from wealthy families.

Planning Chaos

The second level of permanent resettlement was the construction of housing colonies for the refugees. It was for those refugees who had found no place in evacuee houses, vacant military barracks and other available *pucca* buildings. The Ministry constituted the Rehabilitation and Development Board under the chairmanship of Aftab Rai in 1948. The Board proposed a number of sites on the periphery of Delhi city for the rehabilitation colonies and preliminary planning work was started right away (see Tables 1, 2, and 3). The government set the monsoon season of 1951 as the target date for completing the first phase construction (Rao 1965: 11-12). The target was to construct dwellings for the top-priority group, i.e. the ones who lived on roadside pavements, tents, school, or in temple buildings. The was to be a "modest affair with one living room (14 ft x 10 ft), a verandah with an improvised kitchen, a bathroom and a lavatory" (*ibid.*: 12). The estimated cost for these dwellings was between Rs. 2400 to Rs. 3500 in a city like Delhi. But there were many who could not even afford this rent. For them the "Ministry developed certain sites on an austerity basis, parcelled them out into 100 square yards plots to be given away on a nominal lease. With each of these plots went a building grant of up to Rs 500 to enable the refugees to construct houses" (*ibid.*). Such gestures suggest that the state led building activity was strictly functional in its approach. But state planning had larger visions attached to it, we are told:

> (...) it would be a great mistake to imagine that putting up of cheap tenements and the development of building plots represented the sum total of the Ministry's housing effort. Government's planning was more ambitious, comprehending every aspect of the urban refugee's needs. (...) Government's aim was not merely to set up a conglomeration of houses, but to assist with everything that goes to make community life happy and purposeful. (*Ibid.*: 61)

The state vision was obviously not realized as further evidence will suggest. Most of the resettlement colonies have come to symbolize the 'disorder' of urban living like cramped living spaces, lack of water and electricity, filth and squalor and the accompanying lack of social status for the residents. However, by the Government's own accounts nothing could be further from the truth since,

> (...) by the end of 1954, one was conscious of the change that was rapidly coming over the capital. The city seemed to be spreading out endlessly, new colonies were springing up everywhere, each one equipped with a market or shopping centre and provided with ample civic amenities. To a visitor who had last witnessed the Delhi landscape in the dark days of 1949 the transformation must have had a breath-taking quality? Few of the ugly patches of squatters that disfigured the Old city remained. Instead, wherever he wandered, he beheld new house, modest may be, but neat and comfortable. New colonies throbbed with a vigorous life. The misery and the squalor of the early days of migration had been all but erased from the memory. (*Ibid.*: 62)

The comforting picture of neat and orderly expanded city is marred by a state document entitled "Policy regarding provision of various services in the Rehabilitation colonies".[11] It reveals the differing standards that the government adopted right at the beginning creating housing for people of different economic levels. The document refers to these colonies as DP colonies (Displaced Persons) and alternates it sometimes with Cheap Colonies. Each area earmarked for construction could have more than one type of housing that fell into A, B or C category. Some colonies like

11 File no. 90(1) 54 -H1 (A) Ministry of Relief and Rehabilitation, 1954. The following quotes refer to this file.

Tehar and Ramesh Nagar were completely categorized as cheap colonies. The essential difference in the categorisation besides quality and area of construction was the provision of civic services like providing water, electricity, sewerage, garbage disposal and drainage etc. The document as a matter of fact states that "the ministry of rehabilitation has developed certain cheap colonies Ramesh Nagar and Tehar".

The Ministry decided that services in such 'cheap colonies' are to be provided on 'austerity' standards, viz., there will be no provision for under-ground sewerage and street lighting and water supply will be by means of hand-pumps. Other colonies in this area will have normal standards subject to the availability of out-fall sewers and water main on the Nazafgarh Road. The Ministry had received an opinion from the Ministry of Health that "services in the cheap colonies should also be brought to the same standard as in the other colonies". It was also pointed to the policy makers that "no local body will be in a position to take over and maintain these colonies unless the services are brought to the proper standards." Rest of the document details the various conflicts and negotiations that the Ministry had with different government bodies especially municipalities in order to convince them to take over the resettlement colonies, DP and cheap colonies. The fragile infra-structure of these colonies must have been a deterrent to most authorities because of the costs involved. Therefore, the ministry even suggested that it "will consider representations from the local bodies for tapering grants to them for a period of six months for running essential services like sanitation after which they must be able to tax the inhabitants, if they have already not done so."

The conflicts between the state bodies and the refugees are particularly well illustrated with the case of Purana Qila camp settlements. The less than comfortable relationship that refugees shared with the state officials is sufficiently documented in a collection of written exchanges entitled "Settlement of Claims of Quarters at Purana Qila". Significantly the rapprochement stems from the refugees, a constituency for whom the ministry was set up in the first place.

Purana Qila

Most historical monuments were put to use as camping sites for Partition refugees, Purana Qila (Old Fort) situated south of New Delhi became a temporary home to refugees from Punjab. According to the established state practice, the refugees were meant to be provided with permanent housing facilities as soon as possible. In most instances the permanent construction was delayed and the temporary sites assumed greater permanence. The camp residents started petty businesses around the site, and as the times passed, became more reluctant to move to distant areas like Lajpat Nagar where alternative mass housing was underway. In the meanwhile the civic conditions in the camp housing deteriorated as the municipal authorities treated the place as a makeshift arrangement not fit for durable civic facilities. What ensued was a minor battle between the authorities and the quickly assembled refugee association. A series of letters were exchanged between the Rehabilitation branch of the Ministry and Nanak Singh, the President of Purana Qila Congress Committee.

The following petition addressed to the AICC President sums up the entire conflict and show how state aid to refugees was not being laid out on a platter. It was something that refugees often fought for and had to enter into negotiations with the local officials at various levels.

To

The President AICC

Sir,

Most respectfully I, as a Representative of the residents of Purana Qila Refugee camp lay down the following few facts for your kind and sympathetic consideration:-

The refugee camp in Purana Qila was established in January 1948 and at that time the Government declared that those who could afford to live at their own expenses were eligible to stay in the camp. Necessary tents would be provided for the occupants. We all agreed to the above proposal and shifted to the camp after obtaining the necessary permits from Delhi Municipal Committee. At the time of occupation the local officers helped us a lot and for which we are very thankful to them. They further suggested us to form a committee of all the residents to enable them to hear our grievances and suggestions through the committee. The suggestion was warmly welcomed by all of us and accordingly we formed a committee.

On occupation of these tents we found that tents were not safe against fire and theft and therefore we suggested to the authorities concerned that some pucca rooms should be built for all of us. But it was pointed out by the officials that our proposal was not acceptable as the necessary funds were not available with the authorities since all the expenditure to be incurred during the year had already been catered for in the budget that year. Realizing the difficulties put forward by the officials we further proposed that since enough building material was available with the Government the same may be utilized for building of the rooms. The charges for the labour would of course be paid by the individuals concerned. This proposal was accepted by the officials and it was estimated that a room will cost about Rs 750 including Rs 150 a labour charges. We are NOT aware as to what transpired between the officials and the higher authorities concerned. It was also decided that a sum of Rs 750 should be paid in 5 yearly instalments of Rs 150 each. It was further decided that those who could not afford to pay Rs 150 at a stretch may pay it in 12 monthly instalments of Rs 15 each. We were made to understand that after paying the above amount the rooms would belong to the individual concerned and that Government would have nothing to do with it. The last date for depositing this amount was fixed as 15 May 1949. We accordingly paid the amount and obtained the necessary receipts, a copy of which is attached for your information please. Necessary rooms were built and were allotted to us after a period of 4 or 5 months. Necessary receipt is attached.

After a period of two years we were surprised to see the authorities concerned forwarded us the bills as rent for those rooms which was NOT justified as we were the owners of the rooms according to the previous decision. Members of the Committee have approached the authorities concerned several times and every time the reply was "something is being done very soon". Instead of giving us a satisfactory reply and a final decision they have started evicting some of us which is NOT reasonable on the part of the authorities concerned.

Since we are unable to get a satisfactory reply from the authorities concerned we approach your honour to please mediate in our case and give your personal attention to our grievances which are quite reasonable. We do not want that our Government should suffer due to our account but at the same time we too do not want to suffer for no fault of ours.

In the circumstances explained above we hope that your honour will kindly take personal interest in our case and will approach the authorities concerned at an early date to meet our demands which are apparently very reasonable.

Thanking you,

Yours faithfully

NEW DELHI

NANAK SINGH

Dated the 25 Mar 1954

(President, Congress Committee, Purana Qila)[12]

While this petition is filed in the ministry's archives and is supplemented with short official replies, the notes on the margin throw a better light on official reaction. A hurriedly scribbled note says that Nanak Singh, the president of Purana Qila committee visited the ministry yet another time and he is pushing his unreasonable demands a bit too much. In a typed note the officer denies that any promises of ownership were ever made and that "it has been explained to the displaced persons on (*sic*) Purana Qila on more than one occasion that Government cannot accept the position that the tenements were constructed there as a relief measure."[13]

The residents continued their battle with the Ministry though the president ship of their association had been passed on from Nanak Singh to Dr. S. K. Saluja. The new president also complained that the "tenements are without any cross-ventilation, without a kitchen, without a bathroom and without a latrine."[14] He alleged that they "contributed a sum of Rs 60,000 in cash to cover the construction charges of these tenements, thereby giving an excellent and unique example of co-operation with the Government. Apart from the above sum of Rs. 60,000, we have paid other amounts also from time to time. We had also volunteered our services for levelling the site where the present Nizamuddin

12 Ministry of Relief and Rehabilitation, 25 March 1954.

13 Ibid. 21-7-1954.

14 Ibid. December 1955.

Extension Area houses stand,[15] on a call by the then Rehabilitation minister, Shri Mohan Lal Saxena who had promised that houses would be built there to settle us permanently, and then the Government would not charge anything from us for the tenements. We toiled there free of any charge, but we were not rehabilitated at the Nizamuddin site.[16]

The last part about promised movement to Nizamuddin is not officially corroborated and could have been a verbal assurance. But it must seem ironical to the former camp residents that the promised land that they never got has become a piece of high value real estate while the place where they eventually got moved is often termed an urban jungle. The refugees from Purana Qila camp were resettled in several DP colonies but most of them came to live in the Lajpat Nagar area.[17] This area is now the hub of 'illegal construction' as few can afford to move out to better localities. The children and grand children of Purana Qila camp residents are now engaged in a different battle with the authorities. It is paradoxical that while refugees are blamed for the 'urban disorder', the authorities remain beyond scrutiny. These conflicts and negotiations that the Ministry was engaged in show that ugly buildings and filthy streets did not emerge from nowhere but were produced by the new state. While a sort of 'official sympathy' existed for the refugees and their plight, its translation into reality was seldom smooth.

In February 2002, Delhi witnessed a series of road blocks, sit-in-strikes outside municipality offices. The protest was organised by the residents of 'old double storey' quarters in Lajpat Nagar area because municipal authorities had started demolishing 'illegal construction' in the area. The double storey flats were built for the Partition refugee families in 1950s as part of the permanent resettlement scheme. Each flat is no more than 100 square yards (86 sq. ft) with one living room, verandah, and a kitchen. The bathrooms and toilets were built commonly for every four flats in one corner of the building. Over the years, the verandah had been converted into a room, toilets/bathrooms had been carved out and extension areas built out on the street. The children in refugee families had grown into adults and had now children of their own.

Some families who had achieved a better economic status moved to better localities, others sold the flats to realise profit from fast rising real

15 Nizamuddin is an upper middle class colony where the rich refugees could buy plots ranging from 500-1200 sq. yds.

16 Ibid., RHB / 122 (2) / 54, December 1954.

17 I met several refugees in various colonies of Lajpat Nagar during my fieldwork survey, who had lived in Purana Qila camp in 1948.

estate value of the area, while the remaining partitioned the same living space to accommodate two or more families. The extensions to the buildings had converted the old double storey area into a four storied complex while it continued to be called by the same name. The changes in the structures were not entirely the making of the residents but in an unofficial collaboration with the municipality's employees as they were made over a period of twenty years. The residents and the municipality continued making charges and counter-charges and both sides eventually approached the courts. That is where the matter still is. This litigation is clearly rooted in the resettlement schemes that were being planned in early years of post-Partition construction boom.

CONCLUSIONS

The entire foundation of Delhi city, as we know it today, is a result of post-Partition negotiations between the state and the refugees. While the negotiating prowess of the state accrued from a series of ordinances that made it the sole owner of the abandoned property of the fleeing Muslim refugees, the basis of bargain for refugees varied widely depending on their pre-Partition social class and status. The refugees who had brought along some capital from Pakistan had better prospects of resettlement. They were the ones who could anticipate the coming events through their intimate knowledge of the political/communal events, often in their official capacity. The state policy of resettlement was based on compensation against previous ownership. The proof of ownership was also tricky, either one possessed property documents or verification was necessary from a well known person, normally an officer of the state or a political leader, from the refugee's area of domicile in Pakistan. This led to corrupt practices as some could file false claims with false verifications and genuine claimants due to lack of verification could not do the same. Most people who were forced to migrate came with little of their belongings. And very few could remember to bring their property documents because no one knew that it was a permanent journey that they were making.

In a way, the fate of the migrants in their new home was largely decided even before they had set out on their last journey. The response of the state in offering interim relief and later permanent resettlement options was influenced by the social class of the migrants. This explains why new colonies did not have uniform standard of civic facilities, but were instead divided into different class groups. The much derided lower middle class areas like Old Double Storey in Lajpat Nagar were planned by the state agencies. Therefore, the 'planned' chaos in post-Partition Delhi needs to be focused upon as much as the 'unplanned' growth that characterizes the post-Emergency expansion in Delhi.

Table 1: Housing Colonies for Refugees

	Name of Housing colony	Number of dwellings
1.	New Delhi northern extension	3200
2.	Rehgarpura (Harijan) huts	500
3.	Shadipur extension	101
4.	Kingsway mud houses	2000

Table 2: Development of land for sale of plots to refugees

	Name of the area	Number of plots
5.	Shadipur extension	3889
6.	Malkaganj	275
7.	Nizamuddin	249
8.	Jungpura	2000
9.	Western extension	357
10.	Delhi Mathura Road	60

Table 3: Township schemes around Delhi planned in 1947-48

	Name of the scheme	Remarks
11.	Mehrauli expansion	Given up due to water shortage
12.	Tihar township	Given up due to drainage difficulties
13.	Kalkaji township	Being pursued
14.	Golf Links	Being pursued
15.	Sheikh Sarai	Being pursued
16.	Accommodation surplus with Army	Being pursued

Source: Table 1, 2 and 3 are complied from the Annual Report 1947-48, Ministry of Relief and Rehabilitation, GOI.

REFERENCES

Baviskar, Amita, 'Towards a sociology of Delhi: report on a seminar', in *Economic and Political Weekly* 33: 49, 5 December, 1998.

Butalia, Urvashi, *The Other Side of Silence: Voices from the partition of India,* Delhi: Penguin Books, 1998.

Caur, Arpana, 'The art of living', in *Seminar* 545 (2002).

Das, Aupreeta, 'First City', in *Seminar* 515, July 2002, issue on Delhi.

Dupont, Veronique, Tarlo, Emma and Vidal, Denis, eds., *Delhi. Urban Space and Human Diestinies*, Delhi: Manohar, 2000.

Gupta, Narayani, *Delhi between two Empires 1803-1931: Society, Government and Urban Growth,* Delhi: Oxford University Press, 1981.

Husain, Syed Mohammad, *The Laws and Practice Relating to Evacuee Property in India being Commentaries on the Administration of Evacuee Property Act, 1950 and Allied Acts,* Delhi, 1954.

Jain, A. K., *The Making of a Metroplolis: Planning and Growth of Delhi,* Delhi: National Book Organisation, 1990.

Khosla, G. D., *Stern Reckoning: A survey of events leading up to and following the partition of India*, Delhi: Oxford University Press, 1989.

Khosla, G. D., *Memory's Gay Chariot: An autobiographical narrative* Delhi: Allied Publishers, 1985.

Menon, Anjolie Ela, 'The age that was', in *Seminar* 545 (2002).

Moon, Penderal, *Divide and Quit*, Delhi: Oxford University Press, 1998.

Rao, U. Bhakshar, *The Story of Rehabilitation*, Ministry of Relief and Rehabilitation, Delhi: Government of India, 1965.

Singh, Khushwant, ed., *City Improbable: An anthology of writings on Delhi,* Delhi: Oxford University Press, 2001.

10

TOWN PLANNING AND URBAN RESISTANCE IN THE OLD CITY OF DELHI, 1937-1977

MICHAEL MANN

CONTESTED URBAN SPACE

The history of urbanization is also the history of organising and re-organising the space of changing and expanding human settlements. On a global scale this becomes particularly apparent during the nineteenth and twentieth centuries, when towns started to grow beyond their artificial or natural limits. The influx of rural migrants into industrialising towns in nineteenth century western Europe, north America and also India saw new concepts of town planning taking a more significant role within expanding municipal administrations. Urban planning had to address both the layout of new quarters of rapidly growing cities and correspondingly rapid environmental decline in the densely populated old wards. Town planning, mainly consisting of the distribution of residential and industrial quarters, public and private land, street layout and settlement strategies, became a major focus of modern urbanism, beside the provision of amenities like sewerage, transport, and social systems.

Another focus was the new scientific ideas of urban hygiene and health that had been developed in Europe. Overpopulated and congested old wards in the industrialising cities became areas where the poor segments of society were forced to live because only here could they afford the rent. Yet 'western' politicians and administrators generally regarded these quarters as hothouses of dearth and dirt, disease and decay wherever they emerged, which had to be accordingly regulated by administrative and political measures. Therefore, 'modern' town planning had and has a lot to do with organising, policing and disciplining the urban poor whilst a large part of the municipal fiscal income is spent on securing the general well being of the urban middle classes and the rich (Pickstone 1992; Dossal 1991).

Capital cities received special attention not only from town planners, but of course from politicians too. Beside problems of security, questions of architecture and design topped the 'representation' agenda. Paris and Berlin epitomise how city planners and architects like Haussmann and Schinkel became responsible for drastic re-organizations of urban space along aesthetic lines during the nineteenth century. In British India the new Imperial Capital, New Delhi, was designed by architects Baker and Lutyens, both referring to the latest town planning concepts like large open spaces, public greens, easy traffic systems for motor-vehicles, coupled with the representative functions of a capital city.

New Delhi is also an example of colonial town planning, with its emphasis on the segregation of British rulers and Indian subjects or, in the contemporary idiom, separation of the different races and civilizations. New Delhi, as opposed to Old Delhi,[1] was modelled on British colonial settlements in India, the Cantonments and the Civil Lines, which generally formed an artificial annex to an existing Indian town (Grewal 1991). Apart from this typical characteristic, New Delhi's layout was certainly of extraordinary dimensions. New Delhi reflected contemporary notions of modern town planning and lifestyle, whilst Old Delhi and its population soon stood for a traditional, backward Indian society living in congested, dirty and filthy *mohalla*s (wards) within the walled city of former Shahjahanabad and its few urban extensions towards the west (Metcalf 1989; Irving 1981).

However, urbanization is not just the history of town planning and administrative measures, but above all the history of urban inhabitants, both long resident as well as recent in-migrants. For this reason, two discourses dominate urbanization. On the one hand we have the literature on planned urban development which portrays the city as a more or less peaceful and prosperous entity. On the other, we can observe

1 The British gradually named Delhi or Dilli 'Old Delhi' after the 'Great Rebellion' of 1857-59, when they extended the Civil Lines in the north of the city towards the 'Ridge' (present-day campus of the University of Delhi) thus transforming and reducing the walled city or former Shahjahanabad to a distant and picturesque scenery. Henceforth Delhi and its surrounding old towns, forts and fortresses as well as 'ancient' monuments were summarily called 'Old Delhi', particularly in tourist guides. The capital name 'New Delhi' originates from this peculiar history of power, politics and aesthetics to signify the historic place's new metropolitan and imperial function. In this chapter the term Old City refers to the walled city.

'urbanization in progress' as people on the move search for employment and a place to live, with associated tensions, frictions and violent upheavals. The two histories resemble two antagonistic principles if not paradigms. Therefore, as has recently been pointed out, it becomes important to examine the relationship between project and progress, between structure and event. Urban history is not concentrated or condensed in the glimpse of a moment but unfolds with the changes in individual lives in a wider political environment; the development of urban space over time. Put differently, urban planning reflects national politics through local politics, whereas, vice versa, public protest demarcates the limits of all town planning, urban visions and political concepts (Tarlo 2000: 52). Moreover, the tension of these two antagonistic principles causes multiple social dynamics and, in a more general sense, propels history.

In British India, systematic town planning in terms of health and sanitation took shape only after the plague had ravaged many of the subcontinent's large towns at the end of the nineteenth century, and even then largely as a response to the colonial regime's needs. Sub-standard dwellings and the unhealthy habits of the poor were held responsible for outbreaks of epidemic disease. Mid- to late-Victorian notions of poor health and hygiene gained special prominence in the Indian colonial environment where racial segregation was seen as the only preventative measure against contagion and contamination. For sanitary as well as security reasons, the British kept a distance from their Indian subjects. Only during the 1920s was the British policy of caution towards the indigenous urban population reversed when the increasingly crammed and congested settlements and wards of the poor were identified as seedbeds of disease and squalor. This 'unhealthy' development was soon to justify harsh and even violent public action against the labouring poor, who were regarded as a constant threat to an 'embryonic' Indian civil society and were thus evicted from their homes and habitats and kept away from core urban areas (Gooptu 2001: 66, 73-4).

British health and hygiene rhetoric was well received by the emerging Indian middle class who had an aversion to manual labour and physical work, further helping stigmatise the working poor of India's towns. British colonials and Indian nationalists both viewed the urban poor as an object to be uplifted and civilized. To successfully pursue the self-imposed duty of a 'civilising mission', the poor had to be subdued, policed and educated to cleanliness for their own betterment. Literacy programmes were to promote these educational attitudes. It was Patrick

Geddes, touring several Indian cities at the beginning of the twentieth century who with evangelical zeal recommended the 'Revivance of Cities' with respect to health, hygiene and order to reform society at large. He gave special attention to the history and environment of a city as well as the realistic planning objectives appropriate to social, economic, spiritual and aesthetic principles (Meller 1979: 342-5). Nevertheless, Geddes' opinion remained a silent cry in the desert since 'official opinion' was convinced that constant in-migration of rural labourers permanently threatened public health. In keeping with their rustic habits, new arrivals chose to settle in the urban environment's open spaces, close to open drainage and in preference to overcrowded and dilapidated houses. The British regarded densely populated bazaars as the locus of sexual promiscuity, intoxication and criminality, in short: of social depravation and degeneration. Habits and habitats were closely linked so, not surprisingly, the transformation and reorganization of paupers' living quarters was seen as a justified step in improving their lot and, on a more general level, along the path of civilization (Gooptu 2001: 67-70, 77-82).

Geddes was not able to reap the fruit of his town planning schemes for India. This was left to his successors like H. V. Lanchester with their more radical approach towards the treatment of congested urban areas, suggesting a root and branch approach towards public health problems which included the wholesale demolition of slum areas (Meller 1979: 338-9). However, it was only the British retreat from public institutions in the inter-war period which opened offices and space to operate for Indian officials then taking charge of numerous municipal and governmental posts. With the aid of the legal framework and the power structures of their colonial superiors, the Indian political and administrative elites implemented British notions and principles of modern town planning. Meanwhile, British planners and Indian administrators generally preferred more decisive measures to clean and sanitise the towns through speedy general clearance of congested areas. Financial loss, material damage and personal suffering was the price which had to be paid for modernization.

Members of the Indian middle class were particularly happy to see slums, dirt, filth and poor people disappear from town centres and areas close to middle class living quarters. It became the task of the municipal institutions to reclaim town centres for commercial activities and to protect them from the increasing, spreading, and hence barely controllable poorer classes. Within a few decades, the modern Indian city became a contested field with fierce ongoing conflicts over diminishing urban space, scarce housing facilities, land reclamation and the dispossession of the poor (Gooptu 2000: 83-4).

In 1919, the provincial government passed the United Provinces Town Improvement Trusts Act and within a couple of years local Town Improvement Trusts were established in Lakhnau, Kanpur and Allahabad. Originally, the main function of the Improvement Trusts was to buy non-built up lands on the urban fringes and to provide town planners and municipal corporations with concepts to improve sanitary conditions, especially drainage and sewerage systems, and provide potable water in the expanding urban quarters new and old. However, in the 1920s, this agenda of basic amenities was extended to housing conditions, the demolition and clearance of slum areas and the creation of public open spaces which was thought fundamental to urban cleanliness, health and the general improvement of living conditions. Both issues topped the municipal priority list when the Delhi Improvement Trust was established in 1937, shortly after the relocation of the capital from Calcutta (Mehra 1991: 162-5). As the old and new imperial residence, the Old City attracted tens of thousands of job-seekers in-migrating from the adjacent regions of north India. Between 1921 and 1931, the population of Delhi increased from 247,000 to 348,000 indicating an exorbitant annual growth rate of 10 per cent and an absolute increase of almost 41 per cent (BSS 1958: 5).[2]

This demographic development caused Delhi's municipal authorities to implement drastic measures against congested and unhealthy *mohalla*s of the walled city and overcrowded and unsanitary *basti*s[3] in the adjacent nineteenth-century quarters. In the aftermath of India's independence from British colonial rule, urban politics seem to have been guided by the same paradigms as those developed by the British authorities and their collaborating Indian middle class administrative elites. The very same attitude towards sanitary and health aspects of Delhi urban politics

---

2 After the British occupied Delhi/Shahjahanabad in 1803, the population of the city was approximately 100,000 inhabitants. During the nineteenth century, population slowly increased to about 200,000 in 1891 (Census figures). After the King-Emperor's announcement to shift the imperial capital from Calcutta to Delhi in 1911, the demographic growth accelerated dramatically after building activities were taken up. In 1911 about 225,000 people lived in Delhi. For the figures in 1921 and 1931 see the text above, and in 1941 the number of inhabitants was calculated at 522,000 (BSS 1958: 215)

3 A *basti* can be described as a little village or a large cluster of houses within a city indicating a segregated area of small shacks with its own lane system and generally lacking any sort of amenities like public latrines, sewerage, water, electricity etc.

can also be observed during the 1960s and particularly during 'Emergency Rule' in 1975-7 when slum clearances were declared 'beautification' measures. For this reason it will be argued in this chapter that Independence did not cause a break with colonial urban politics. On the contrary, Indian governments and municipal corporations repeated, continued and intensified British categories of space, congestion, sanitation and health, the well known catalogue eventually being enriched by aesthetic aspects.

This kind of urban planning (and politics) was met with fierce resistance by the local population. It is the variety of actions and reactions that demonstrate poor peoples' ability to plan and elaborate effective forms of resistance against forceful eviction from their homes. Hitherto, hardly any of the various forms of urban resistance towards colonial, and in a few instances post-colonial governments in India had attracted scientists and particularly historians from the so called Subaltern School. Whilst the conceptualization of rural or peasant resistance found plenty of attention, a concept of urban resistance categories is still missing, particularly that of the 'lower classes'. These are commonly and uniformly described as the urban poor. In case of violent resistance, they are indiscriminately and summarily characterized as the 'mob' devoid of any rational action. However, in comparison to a rural setting, the urban space offers different opportunities and strategies of organising, challenging and resisting town politics. For this reason, we will attempt with this sketch to roughly conceptualis forms of urban resistance.

Setting the Administrative and Ideological Context

Immediately after the Delhi Darbar of 1911, British authorities in Delhi regarded the city as overpopulated. Earlier comments on the congestion of the city dating from the beginning of the twentieth century went unheeded. In 1912, Colonel Beadon, the then President of the Delhi Municipal Corporation (DMC), stated that 'the people in Delhi have been huddled into a totally insufficient area so that the streets have been encroached upon, slums have been built and the land has become so valuable that even capitalists cannot build' (BSS 1958: 215). Originally, Shahjahanabad or the present-day walled city of Delhi was able to accommodate about 60,000 inhabitants covering an area of 1,240 acres. Yet during late Mughal rule, the city was already inhabited by more than 200,000 people when the Mughal fortress-residence was still regarded as a beautiful and busy city, even by contemporary European travellers and traders (Gupta 1981: 1-5; Blake 1993: xiii).

Taking into account that at the time of the capital's relocation, about the same amount of people lived within and without the wall, the categories of congestion and overpopulation seem to be rather arbitrary and clearly indicate the political intention of such a statement. This is proven by the fact that before 1911, the British were barely interested in Delhi's internal municipal affairs as they had 'pacified' the city with the wholesale clearances in front of Lal Qila in the aftermath of the 'Great Rebellion' and the subsequent entrenchment of the city by railway lines in the north and the west (Gupta 1981: 62; King 1976: 268-70). The 'cordon de securité' was completed by the Jamuna in the east.[4]

Not until 1935 was A. P. Hume appointed to prepare a comprehensive report on the 'Relief of Congestion in Delhi'. He came to the conclusion that about 28 per cent of the previous decade's population increase was directly due to the construction of New Delhi. To cope with the constant influx of in-migrants and the dire need for housing, Hume, suggested the formulation and execution of town expansion schemes which eventually led to the establishment of the Delhi Improvement Trust (DIT) in 1937. According to the legal stipulations of the UP Town Improvement Act, the DIT's main task, amongst others, was to elaborate a comprehensive slum clearance and re-housing programme for Delhi. This clearance scheme provided for the closure and demolition of dwellings or parts thereof unfit for human habitation. Additionally, it recommended an improvement scheme for any buildings regarded as unfit for human habitation or those that were seen as a danger to the health of inhabitants, caused by the narrowness, closeness or bad arrangement of streets, or the want of light, ventilation or sanitary facilities in such areas.

The DIT and the DMC were basically empowered to demolish and clear, to rebuild houses and resettle inhabitants *ad gusto*. Initially, the DIT defined large parts of the walled city of Delhi as slum and marked specific areas for an immediate re-building programme. Among them was the Delhi-Ajmeri Gate Slum Clearance and Development Scheme which was treated as a kind of 'pilot project' for future programmes. Due to administrative difficulties, the project had to be postponed several

---

4 A look at the current map of Delhi and a drive from whatever direction into 'Old Delhi' demonstrates that actually nothing has changed during the last 150 years. The walled city has been 'preserved' as an isolated town amidst a vastly expanding urban agglomeration.

times. Nevertheless, by 1943 the DIT had built almost 3,000 new houses (Bopegamage 1957: 87-91).

Yet the pace of construction was far too slow to cope with the constant influx of 'normal' migrants from north India, plus refugees from Pakistan following the partition of British India in 1947. Accelerated in-migration started in the decade 1931-41 with an annual arrival of roughly 25,000 people, but partition in 1947 proved disastrous not only for the subcontinent but, for demographic reasons, for Delhi in particular. Between 1947 and 1951 alone, 325,000 Muslims left the city. In return, 495,000 people from Pakistan came to Delhi marking an absolute population increase of 166,000 inhabitants. Immigration led to an additional demographic growth of 206,000 people, amounting to a net surplus of 372,000 inhabitants within only five years (Rao and Desai 1965: 54-5).

The Old City was severely affected by this development. Though figures on demographic change in the Old City must be viewed with some reservation, an overall trend is nevertheless discernible and gives a fairly good impression of the dramatic circumstances. In 1941 the Old City had about 180,000 inhabitants, going up to 381,000 people in 1951 and about 420,000 people in 1961. Not until 1971-1981 was the demographic trend reversed and population figures decreased from approximately 410,000 to about 362,000 inhabitants (Krafft 1993: 66; Mehra 1991: 45). Approximately 100,000 Muslims left the Old City during the above mentioned five years, yet between 1951 and 1961 the Muslim population recuperated from the remaining 100,000 to 155,000 inhabitants (Mitra 1970: 17). It is easy to imagine how this demographic growth must have hampered the work of the municipal institutions.

Shortly after Independence, in 1951, the Government of India appointed the members of the Delhi Improvement Trust Enquiry Committee, also called 'Birla Committee', to evaluate and assess the work of the DIT. The commission came to the conclusion that the achievements of the DIT were not at all impressive, on the contrary, 'the story of the Trust is the story of failure' (BSS 1958: 218). The DIT was accused of not having been able to develop concepts of town planning that comprised a civic survey and a master plan. The Slum Areas Improvement and Clearance Act of 1956, which regulated the eviction, re-location and occasional compensation of slum-dwellers must be viewed as the major legal framework that was initiated by the DIT.

However, instead of implementing its own criteria for re-construction, the DIT had erected huge buildings along the Asaf Ali Road further walling up the Old City from New Delhi and disobeying principles of ventilation. Lack of funding and administrative limitations were cited as excuses for the misconception (Jagmohan 1975: 29-30). As a result, the DIT was abolished in 1957 and replaced by the Delhi Development Authority (DDA) under the provisions of the Delhi Development Act of the same year. Together with the Ministry of Health and a staff of eight from the Ford Foundation, the DDA presented a Master Plan for Delhi in 1961, covering the two decades from 1962 to 1981 (*Delhi Gazetteer* 1976: 755-9).

Certainly, the Delhi Master Plan (DMP) must be judged as a major piece of town planning, pioneering in its scale with far-reaching schemes hitherto unprecedented on the Indian subcontinent. Although deficient in many respects such as the organization of public transport, it foresaw urban development based on estimated demographic development and planned a decentralized capital region for the end of the century. For the Old City of Delhi or former Shahjahanabad, however, the DMP did not develop a framework for re-building and re-housing. In this respect, ideas and measures remained fairly vague, which was in contrast to other zones of Delhi (Jagmohan 1975: 30).[5] There are various reasons why the whole projected development failed, but this cannot be discussed here. Of more importance is the fact that with the implementation of the DMP, operations for slum clearances were transferred from the local municipal councils and centralized under the authority of the DDA. Additionally, under section 144 of the Criminal Procedure Code, police were given the right to fire on what might resemble a crowd, giving the DMC and the DDA the opportunity to enforce speedy clearances and demolitions (Tarlo 2000: 58).

Preliminary guidelines for slum clearances set up in the 1950s found their way into the DMP. For example, the Bharat Sevak Samaj had already stated in 1958 that the *katras*[6] of the Old City being older than 25 years "deserve, on this account alone, to be discarded so far as healthy

5 The DMP divided Greater Delhi into eight zones which were to be connected by arterial roads, ring-roads and bridges crossing the Jamuna.

6 Typical *katra* tenements consist of single storied houses in rows forming a compound with one common entrance. The tenements comprise one room with a single door to the front and a kind of verandah which serves as cooking place. The roof is generally used as additional living space. Sometimes the *katra* has a second floor with another room of the same size as the one on the ground floor. Often this additional room is rented out to a separate family. According to a study at the end of the 1970s, 72 per cent of the families living in slum *katras* had a monthly income less than Rs 100 (Mehra 1991:54).

and comfortable human habitation is concerned." However, the same category, namely that of age, was not in the same sense applicable to the *bastis*[7] because, 'in general, they constitute a later development' which is the reason why they could be instantly demolished (BSS 1958: 20-1). Studies by the DDA in the preparation of the DMP classified 52 per cent of the houses in the Old City as in poor condition or dilapidated. Only 42 per cent of the buildings were regarded in a fair or even good condition. Basically, this statement repeated the opinion of the DIT of 1937 which had actually turned Delhi/Shahjahanabad into a single slum area. Further elaborated and more detailed preparatory investigation for the DMP reproduced this approach when introducing three categories, namely the *Conservation Areas*, the *Rehabilitation Areas* and the *Redevelopment Areas* which were supposed to guide urban renewal (Jain 1990: 156-7).

The *Conservation Area* with more than 75 per cent of its houses in good condition comprised almost 40 per cent of the Old City and about 100,000 inhabitants who, it was said, needed protection from the spread of slums. The *Rehabilitation Area* comprised roughly 36 per cent of the intramural town, its buildings having partially deteriorated due to neglect. 141,287 persons lived in these houses. Finally, the *Redevelopment Area* which covered almost 25 per cent of the area under investigation and containing little more than 100,000 people, was classified as generally dilapidated and physically beyond repair and must, therefore, be cleared (Mehra 1991:68). Again, at least one quarter, in fact it was a third of the Old City was declared a slum area whilst the residential areas of the 'better off' deserved protection from contamination by the virulent areas of dearth, dirt and disease. Neither perception nor paradigm had changed between 1937 and 1960 with regard to slums, slum dwellers and the Old City .

Backed by strong legislative regulations like the Slum Areas Improvement and Clearance Act of 1956 and the DIT/DDA recommendations as well as the central government, the DMC cleared several slum areas within and around the Old City, among them B. N. Nagri (1963), Delhi Gate (1963, 1964 and 1965), Rajghat (1964), behind Lal Qila (1964), Sher Shah Road (1965), Jamuna Bazaar (1965, 1967, 1968 and 1969) (Tarlo

---

7 A *basti* is situated in an open piece of land within or at the fringes of a town forming a separate entity within the urban settlement area. Whilst a *katra* is mostly built from *pakka* materials (stones, bricks and tiles), the house constructions in a *basti* mainly consist of *kacha* materials (bamboo, tin-sheets, thatch and mud). It was estimated that within the Old City more than 50,000 people lived in slum *katras* and about 12,000 in four *bastis* (Krafft 1993: 71)

1995: 2928). This first wave of clearances was followed by a second and even more drastic one in the 1970s. To make further clearances more viable, the duties of the DMC were transferred to the DDA in 1974. In the following year, a seminar on the Redevelopment of Shahjahanabad convened by the Ministry of Works and Housing came to the conclusion that a comprehensive approach towards an integrated redevelopment of the Old City ought to have top priority since all planning so far had lacked macro as well as micro strategies, in short: a comprehensive perspective was demanded (Jain 1990: 161-3). However, this overall redevelopment scheme contained nothing more than a polished form of the three categories of the early 1960s and the resettlement of the Old City's 'unauthorized settlers' on distant trans-Jamuna plots of land. Not surprisingly, large parts of the intramural city were again declared slums, with only slight differences concerning the measures to be taken for re-housing and re-development. In particular, the whole area between Turkman Gate and the Jama Masjid was deemed a clearance area (Krafft 1993: 71).

Special provisions under the Emergency Rule (1975-77) gave the central government and the DDA additional power to pursue their resettlement and redevelopment policy even more stringently. The Lieutenant-Governor for Delhi was ex-officio chairman of the DDA. He was appointed by the central government and vested with a veto over any decision of the democratic urban institutions, effectively a relic of the centralist un-democratic colonial administration. Jagmohan, the acting vice-chairman of the DDA during the Emergency, made slum clearance, resettlement and beautification of the capital, and particularly the 'rebuilding' of Shahjahanabad his personal political object. Examples from old European cities like Paris, Warsaw and Bologna were used to demonstrate the benefits of rebuilding and reconstructing old cities for cultural self-understanding and objects of identification for their residents as well as the nation. Quoting Napoleon Bonaparte ("War is easy, it is waging that is difficult"), Jagmohan made it clear that he was willing to initiate a determined and uncompromising battle against the poor quarters and the poor people in Delhi, especially in the Old City (Jagmohan 1975: 47-59, 109).

In her "Twenty Points" laying out the programme of Emergency Rule, Indira Gandhi promulgated the "[s]tepping up provisions of house sites for the landless and the socially weak" going along with the "[s]ocial ownership of urban and urbanisable land." Journalists echoed this statement praising the programme as the "beginning of a vigorous battle against poverty, for mitigating the suffering of the deprived, vulnerable and weaker sections of society' as well as for 'improving the living conditions of the poor people." Whilst the Prime Minister condemned the lethargy of previous years, she called upon the Indian people to "get on with the job of nationbuilding." (Drieberg and Mohan 1975: 76-9). It was thus the context of Emergency Rule which turned slum clearance and resettlement, particularly in the national capital, from the sphere of social responsibility of the municipal institutions into the challenge of a national project within the wider discourse of 'nationbuilding'.

Clearance Schemes and Resistance Strategies

During the period under consideration, several municipal attempts were made to deprive poor people of their poor habitat and housing within and in the immediate vicinity of the Old City. In most cases, people affected by the clearances were not able to organise nor to show any resistance towards the gruesome and forceful eviction from their living quarters. However, people did take up action against police forces, clearance commandos and bulldozers. In fact, the poor classes in particular developed highly sophisticated strategies of resistance to prevent their eviction or to get the re-housing and redevelopment schemes reformulated or substantially altered, if not completely cancelled. Beside the incompetence of the municipal administration which, in quite a few cases, rendered attempts to implement the clearance schemes null and void from the very beginning, it had been the various forms of resistance ranging from everyday 'avoidance strategies' (Adas 1998) to open and even violent actions which delayed or in some cases prevented the imposition of 'improvement schemes'.

Of the many redevelopment projects and clearance actions that took place from late colonial rule until Emergency Rule, some outstanding events will be selected to exemplify the forms of resistance the affected population took up in response to the forcefully implemented urban schemes. In 1958, slum clearance and resettlement ideas being more in an experimental state, the Advisory Committee appointed for Delhi recommended the so called Jhuggi Jhompri Removal Scheme.[8] Its plan was to remove unauthorized dwellers from government land within the

[8] The term *jhuggi-jhompri* is derived from Hindustani meaning clustered ramshackle hutments of a temporary character. Often *jhuggi-jhompri*s turn into stable and permanent settlements: *basti*s.

city and to compensate them with plots of land at subsidized rates in resettlement areas that provided basic amenities like water taps and latrines. Demolitions began in 1960. The scheme, however, soon ran into unexpected difficulties since the resettled people developed unpredictable strategies. Many of the resettled people sold their plots and re-migrated to the inner city where they erected new *jhuggi-jhompri*s. This scheme attracted new in-migrants into Delhi settling on government land, getting removed and re-selling their plots. The Delhi municipal authorities reacted in 1962 distinguishing between in-migrants before and after 1960 to counteract and discourage squatting within the city (Tarlo 2000: 55).

Without doubt, the Delhi-Ajmeri-Gate Slum Clearance Scheme is the most famous example of an ambitious urban design, and it is also well remembered by the people. The redevelopment scheme stands for administrative arrogance, popular protest and the failure of the redevelopment concept as such. Originally, a plan for the general improvement of the area came up in 1926, but it was only after the monsoon of 1933 when the city wall on that section partly collapsed that the removal of the entire wall between Delhi and Ajmeri Gate was considered. Eventually, the clearance scheme for the Delhi-Ajmeri Gate area was notified by the DIT in 1938 and submitted to the Government of India for approval three years later, but the entire improvement scheme was only sanctioned in 1946. Principally, the scheme envisaged the extensive clearing of an area 400 yards wide running parallel behind the city wall as well as the wall's demolition between the two gates. However, at this very moment the execution of the scheme was halted due to uncertain political prospects (Mehra 1991: 42-3, 58-9).

More than 3,400 families would have been affected by the clearances, while government felt responsible to re-house just 2,377 of them. The plan proposed new communication means and new roads. Quite striking was the idea of extending Minto Road up to Jama Masjid to open up the Old City because the British, so far, had strongly opposed any such suggestion. Instead of the city wall, some eighteen blocks of modern buildings housing apartments and shops were designed to face New Delhi. But the scheme ran into difficulties from the very beginning. When the municipal authorities started with the acquisition of properties, both the form of acquisition as well as the amount of compensation became heavily disputed. Influential people and owners of houses in affected *mohalla*s organized themselves in the Improvement Scheme Union (Ajmeri Gate). Their Chief Secretary pleaded that the DIT had never replied to the objections against the scheme since its notification in 1938 and that the re-housing programme was insufficient even if less than 3,000 families had to be evicted. This proved to be the crucial point of the scheme as the DIT failed to develop proper arrangements for the displaced people. Influential inhabitants and property owners organized the local resistance movement seeking legal advice and aid which enabled them to successfully fight court cases. These actions were further aided by the local people's refusal to move to the re-housing camps because they did not trust the re-development plan. Therefore, the DIT was unable to take possession of all the properties necessary for the realization of the whole scheme.

Only the multi-storeyed commercial-cum-residential replacement for the city wall and the filling of the old ditch was completed at the beginning of the 1950s. However, this part of the project fuelled the doubts of local residents with respect to the credibility of its intention. Filling the ditch required the eviction of the Balmikis,[9] people from the lowest stratum of Indian society who had settled there. Since these people were given neither financial nor spatial compensation, they became displaced people within the urban area of Delhi. Despite this circumstance, the major argument for demolishing the fifteen yard high city wall was that it prevented ventilation. This was, of course, regarded as one of the foremost reasons for the unhealthy conditions of the people living behind the city wall. Yet the new building complex was thirty yards high. (Mehra 1991: 59-62) Both parts of the re-development scheme which originated from early British plans were designed to remove poor and "unsightly" people along with their hutments and obscure one of the worst slum areas of the Old City with an even higher wall of functional (commercial) house constructions. Old problems of poverty were to be solved by a 'wall of modern money-grubbing' (Evenson 1989: 198) and by aesthetic ideas of modern housing.

The clearance of the notorious slum called Jamuna Bazaar (the official name is Yamuna Pushta) situated between the city wall and the river was resolved in 1960 by India's then president, Dr Rajendra Prasad, who was worried about the impression the stench and filth of the place would make on the international guests taking part in the cremation of one of his family members at nearby Nigam Bodh Ghat. Officially, the people in Jamuna Bazaar were told that it was the smell of the burning place and the threats from monsoon flooding which made resettlement absolutely

[9] See Michael Koeberlein's article in this volume.

necessary. However, it took the municipal institutions another seven years to carry out the scheme. Party politics caused the delay because politicians from the Jana Sangh and Congress wanted the votes of the 'slum dwellers', who were promised that their habitations would not be destroyed. However, in 1967 demolition started. In the beginning, people were offered plots in Seelampur (resettlement) colony across the river but the inhabitants of Jamuna Bazaar refused to move.

Eventually, residents were forcibly removed from the area and resettled in worse conditions than initially offered. The new legal powers vested in the DDA[10] provided for a swift clearance of the slum within a couple of days. And within weeks, the whole area between the city wall and the river was transformed by gardeners and engineers developing the river front into a modern traffic zone dotted with some greenery (Tarlo 2000: 56-8). Apparently, this urban design, with the pollution and noise of modern traffic was not in contradiction to the holiness of the burning *ghat*. A set of reasons was created to make the demolition viable: Party politics, national politics, aesthetic considerations and modern traffic concepts were the major ingredients of the formidable town planning 'cocktail' which the members of the (mobile) middle classes as well as the political and economic classes were all too willing to swallow whilst the inhabitants of Jamuna Bazaar were left thirsty.

During the 1960s, the so called Dujana House Rehabilitation Scheme (Bazaar Matia Mahal) was one of the DIT's putatively successful re-development projects. The buildings of and within the former city palace were so dilapidated that it was resolved to have the entire site cleared and re-built. Its residents were shifted to transit camps and four new apartment blocks constructed to provide new homes for 120 families. The modern construction not only marks an alien architectural element in that part of the Old City but contains major misconceptions and misconstructions with regard to the climatic conditions and the way of living of the predominantly Muslim population. Despite the fact – or maybe because of it – that only parts of the scheme were implemented, the whole project is generally classified as a good example for the re-development intentions of the DMC and the DIT. However, the evictees did not give up and within a few years either they together with new in-migrants settled again on that spot and also occupied the open park created by the clearance measures. Even unauthorized workshops have

---

10 The Government of India decided to transfer all clearances schemes from the Delhi Municipal Corporation to the DDA. Additionally, section 144 of the Criminal Procedures Code was enforced for slum clearances (see above).

been established since then (Krafft 1993: 74-5). Administrative ideas and measures of proper housing and living were ridiculed by the 'mobility' of the people who came back to re-take possession of their former habitats. This mobility is only possible within the urban area, for in similar and comparable situations peasants would have to leave the region to resettle elsewhere. From the municipal point of view, Dujana House is now in a worse condition than it had been before the clearances which clearly indicates the power of 'long term' resistance strategies.

As part of the Delhi-Ajmeri Gate scheme, the re-development of the Turkman Gate area became another field of dubious municipal politics met by fierce resistance from local inhabitants. Though plans for re-developing the site had been elaborated in the pre-Independence period and the entire area confirmed by the DMC as a slum in 1957, the scheme was actually carried out during the Emergency. Only Emergency Rule provided the special legal conditions under which the scheme could finally be implemented. At the beginning of April 1976, bulldozers guarded by hundreds of policemen demolished the old *mohalla*s, occupied by a small number of Muslims who had been living there for generations, and a larger number of Muslims settled there after Partition. About 150 houses were torn down and more than 700 families made homeless. After a few days, demolition work had to be halted due to the fierce resistance of the evictees who had organized a *hartal* and stayed in the vicinity of the area demonstrating against the measures. Within days, protests turned into violent riots. What exactly happened remains open to speculation.

On 19 April, about five hundred people from families selected for removal gathered at Turkman Gate and demonstrated against the demolition. In spite of, or rather because of official attempts to calm down the situation, the crowd swelled to about 3,000, who started throwing bricks, bottles and acid bulbs against the police guards. The police post itself was surrounded by outraged people. Tear gas and *lathi* charges did not halt the protesters, on the contrary, the situation deteriorated and eventually ran completely out of control when the riots spread into Asaf Ali Road. The police sustained several casualties, which is why at 5.30 in the afternoon it was resolved to open fire. Numerous protesters were injured and six killed (Bakshi and Sharma 1995, 4: 196-7). Meticulous public investigations claimed twelve dead (Dayal and Bose 1977: 35-65). During the following night policemen broke up houses, raiding and raping in the Turkman Gate area. The action was followed by bulldozers which demolished most of the houses, and the rubble was disposed of behind the Ring Road where it stank, for days, of rotting flesh. People claim, that more than 400 people were killed during darkness (Tarlo 2003: 40, 58).

Rumours said that Indira Gandhi's son and designated successor (who had neither a party office nor any governmental functions), Sanjay Gandhi, was deeply involved in the Turkman Gate action, particularly in speculation in urban land and other machinations, beside his ambition to carry out a long pending and continuously suspended urban project. However, the action is also said to have been intended as a blow against the compact living quarters of the Muslim community within the Old City (Singh and Dhamija 1989: 73-6; Krafft 1993: 76-7). When Muslim families turned up at Jagmohan's office asking if they could be re-settled together in a new colony, he is said to have replied, "Do you think we are mad to destroy one Pakistan to create another Pakistan?" (Tarlo 2003: 39). Hence, the displacement and further marginalization of Muslims who had remained in north India and returned to Delhi in even larger numbers after Partition was part of the plan of nationalist forces within government and the administration to comprehensively weaken Muslim identity and foster communal strife.

Still other aspects need to be taken into consideration. As has been pointed out in Emma Tarlo's article, "Welcome" resettlement colony's history reflects the history of Delhi's municipal and national politics after Independence. For example, in various cases during the Emergency, evictees under the regulations of the Slum Clearance Act became only entitled to plots of land if they agreed to sterilization thus helping to implement the Government of India's sterilization programme launched in the 1970s. Even today, people from this re-settler generation live in the then built wards of 'Welcome' colony (Tarlo 2000). Jagmohan, Vice President of the DDA, stated that the riots at Turkman Gate were not the violent outburst of the evicted and desperate people but instigated by the Muslim inhabitants of the nearby *mohalla*s and diverse Muslim political organizations[11] who feared that government authorities would enforce sterilization upon them at Dujana House Family Planning Camp (Jagmohan 1978: 144-9). In fact, the people staying at Dujana House were relatives and friends of the inhabitants of Turkman Gate and two hitherto more or less independent dramas were converging into a tragic end. In the aftermath of the Turkman Gate incident, Jagmohan tried to separate what actually belonged together. Despite his elaborate tactics of

---

[11] Particularly the Indian Union Muslim League and the Muslim Personal Law Board

distraction the convergence of national and urban programmes was well understood by the local population at the time of the resettlement actions – and reactions (Tarlo 2003: 38-9). For this reason and on a more general level, local urban politics do indeed reflect national programmes, in this case the Hinduization of Indian society and nationalising of India's politics and polity.

The same kind of 'communal politics' by the DMC, the DDA and the Government of India can also be observed with the Mina Bazaar re-development scheme. Preliminary action to prepare the clearances was taking place in November 1975 against the Muslims residing within the Old City. Placed in the Delhi Master Plan under the rubric of "beautification", the project actually involved the complete clearance of the buildings surrounding Jama Masjid. The area was mostly inhabited by Muslims. Six-storey modern commercial-cum-residential constructions were to replace the old houses, even covering from view parts of the three domes of India's largest mosque. People protested strongly and perhaps not in vain against this architectural design for the project was never realised in full.[12] Local shopkeepers criticized the proposal from the very beginning and particularly pointed out the absence of a proper road connecting the new buildings with the main arterial roads of the Old City. Since better re-development plans by Jawaharlal Nehru and Maulana Azad were never considered seriously (Mehra 1991: 102; Krafft 1993: 75-6), it seems that the Muslims within the walled city were either to be displaced or disconnected from Delhi's urban sphere. This, again, indicates that the Indian Union's initial policy of strict secularism was gradually substituted by elements of communalism.

It is also quite significant that the DIT and the DDA in fact continued the regulations as well as the ideas of the colonial Town Improvement Trust during the 1930s and 40s, supporting primarily urban Indian middle and upper class interests. This included the clearance of centrally located slum settlements and the forceful eviction of the 'urban poor' through armed police forces and the acquisition of these "new" plots of land by the said governmental organisations paying insufficient compensation to evictees to cover the high rents in the newly erected tenements. Like the colonial Town Improvement Trusts, the DIT turned into a profitable undertaking for the improvement of the city's centre which mainly served the commercial prospects of the 'monied interests'

12 Eventually, about 600 shops were demolished and replaced by 344. Without proper resettlement plans, people were forcibly removed and only a few families could, later on, return to their old living ward.

(Gooptu 2001: 91-101, 109, 119-24, 135-6). The protagonists of Emergency Rule have definitely strengthened this political approach which caused much discontent, deprivation and eventually violent resistance among the poor segments of the urban population.

According to an official survey on the condition of the country one and a half months after Emergency Rule had been proclaimed, police no longer had to deal with agitation and demonstrations and life in the villages and cities seemed to be absolutely normal (Drieberg/Mohan 1975: 96). This was, indeed, true for the first few months but within six months more violence than before was spreading in the cities, above all in Delhi. Particularly the urban middle classes were impressed by the speedy success of the emergency regime, thus legitimising the extraordinary constitutional measure. However, the Gandhi regime proved successful only in the political core of the country, that is Delhi, Uttar Pradesh and Haryana (Dhar 2000: 265-7). Indira Gandhi, her son and her government seem to have been completely ignorant about the effect of Emergency Rule on the Indian population. Positive about the results of her politics, she announced general elections to take place in 1977. Yet, the Indian voter took that opportunity to protest against the suspension of democracy and rule of law and the electorate punished the Prime Minister and the Congress Party with a landslide victory for the major opposition parties, these being, for the first time, united in the Bharatiya Lok Dal (BLD).

In Delhi, and particularly in the Old City, the election disaster was extraordinarily striking for the Congress Party (INC). All seats of the seven Delhi constituencies formerly held by the Congress were gained by the BLD. In the constituency of Chandni Chowk only 64 per cent of the electorate voted in the general elections of 1971 with 64.15 per cent of all votes for the Congress Party and 31.52 for the BLD. In the 1977 elections, 68 per cent of the electorate polled and 71.91 per cent voted for the BLD whilst only 27.03 per cent voted for the Congress Party. This was the worst result for the INC among all seven constituencies of Delhi and worse than the average votes of all these constituencies, where the INC received 30.15 per cent and the BLD 68.15 per cent of the votes (SRGE, 1971; SRGE, 1977). Urban politics including the town planning schemes of the central government and the Delhi municipal authorities, particularly with regard to the clearances within the Old City during Emergency Rule were adjudged by voters with a dramatic loss of power for a political regime that lacked legitimacy from the very beginning and that had turned violent the longer it stayed in power. The general elections of 1977 demonstrated and maybe founded India's reputation as the world's largest democracy when state violence was met by the voter's verdict.

Concepts of Town Planning and Conceptualising Urban Protest

During the twentieth century, British Indian as well as Indian governments were united in characterising the Old City of Delhi as overcrowded and congested. The main aim as well as challenge of Delhi's town planners was to reduce the population density within the walled city. An average of ideally 200 up to a maximum of 250 people per acre (ppa) was viewed as the optimal density for the Old City (Mehra 1991: 67-70). However, the post partition population increase to 607,000 inhabitants within the walls would have made it necessary for more than 300,000 people to move (Jain 1990: 153, 156). So far, efforts to reduce the population density had failed completely. Even the drastic measures during the Emergency when more than 200,000 ha were cleared in the Old City alone and more than 700,000 inhabitants of Delhi evicted and partly resettled on the outskirts of the city (Dupont et al. 2000: 232) did not lead to a decrease in population figures since the Census of India in 1981 places the population of Old City at 622,000 inhabitants.[13] As before, average density figures for the different *mohalla*s and wards varied extremely showing 286 ppa in Chandni Chowk and 807 ppa in Lal Darwaza near Jama Masjid. Even worse, deprivation seems to have increased dramatically from the 1970s onwards as the Census of 1971 listed about 10,000 homeless people for the Old City while twenty years later, the number of homeless people had almost doubled (Krafft 1993: 72).

Since the British had decided to shift the capital of their Indian empire from Calcutta to Delhi, the latter meanwhile sunk into the deplorable state of a 'provincial' and 'ancient' town in north India , the city was seen

[13] Yet it has to be acknowledged that the overall demographic trend shows a significant decrease of the Old City's population from 1961 onwards. In that year, about 420,000 people lived in the walled city, the figures for the decennial censuses show 409,000 (1971), 399,000 (1981), 350,000 (1991) (figures for 2001 are still not available from the internet Census of India). This development reflects the consequences of the subcontinent's partition in 1947 and the commercialisation of the Old City since the 1960s driving out its inhabitants continuously ever since (Krafft 1999: 103).

in constant decline. From the 1920s, British officials and scientists, and from the 1960s and 70s onwards, also Indian town planners and scientists (and still at the end of the 1980s, Jain 1990: 155) lamented the decay and decline of the once beautiful Old City of Delhi thereby continuously and uncritically reproducing a colonial cliché. They rediscovered the former Mughal fortress-residence Shahjahanabad for their arguments with respect to clearing houses, evicting people and, above all, re-building that 'abominable' urban place (Jagmohan 1975: 1-2, 38).

For the declining urban environment, politicians and planners constantly demanded an improvement scheme be implemented at once. As has been pointed out, it was particularly the sanitary and health conditions that headed the improvement agenda. Often, therefore, the old parts of Indian cities were regarded as 'plague spots' to signify the undesirable places of poor human habitat rather than the locus of the disease itself. The Improvement Trusts of the colonial government constantly repeated this view which is why in the 1930s the spatial separation between the better residential and the poorer quarters had become standard guidelines within the municipal institutions (Gooptu 2000: 86).

This attitude towards their own cities was perpetuated by Indian politicians and administrators. In a speech at the end of the 1950s, Jawaharlal Nehru picked up the metaphor of disease as feeling 'feverish whenever I think of slums.' As a remedy he prescribed a radical cure: "We should burn down these slums wherever they are" (cited in Bopegamage 1957: 92). These ideas on the epidemic and highly infective character of slums – interestingly enough nobody talked about the dwellers – were echoed by the authors of the Master Plan for Delhi in 1962, stating that "[t]he ugly hutment colonies pox-mark practically every part of the city. The majority of the occupants live in huts or filthy shacks built of poor material. They are mostly located in forsaken and insanitary places, bordering railway lines, open drains, open spaces earmarked for dumping refuse, etc." (cited in Birdi 1995: 1.52 para. 3.23).

Apparently, it was still believed by urban people that rural immigrants preferred to live on dump heaps. This must have been the reason why, in the course of the clearances, these people were brought out of town and sometimes removed, or should one say 'dumped', at Delhi's urban fringes. Finally, the *Delhi Gazetteer* of 1976 mentions 'slum clearances' under the heading 'Medical and Public Health', as done since the establishment of the Delhi Municipal Corporation in 1957 (DMC 1957: paras 355-9) indicating that slums still have to be treated as a stronghold of disease and that the only appropriate treatment possible would consist of comprehensive 'clearance-cum-beautification operations'. A list of 33 successfully treated and cured 'patients', among them Jamuna Bazaar, Jama Masjid and Asaf Ali Road, concludes the 'report' (*Delhi Gazetteer*, 1976: 920-1).

Continuity rather than change signifies the urban politics of the colonial and post-colonial era. Officials and official reports repeatedly mention British categories and concepts of town planning such as congestion (of houses and of people), sanitation, public health, open land and improvement. Initially, even the educational concept of the colonial civilising mission with regard to urban health and sanitation was reproduced by many politicians of independent India. Jawaharlal Nehru thought a "lack of desire and a lack of training" responsible for the misery of the slum dwellers, again emphasising the uncivilized "rural backwardness" of these "ignorant" city inhabitants (BSS 1958: 7). However, at least some colonial officials of the interwar period had the vision that Indian towns could still be rescued and reformed (as the Indian people at large) though the majority of the British in India thought Indians, their morals and their character beyond redemption.

After Independence, former British 'idealistic' educational attitudes were discarded too and town administrators instead demanded an "intellectual and cultural stimulation", accompanied by a simultaneous removal of the 'dead parts' of the Old City (Jagmohan 1975: 71-2). After the 'patient' had been declared dead, slum improvement plans turned into simple slum clearance programmes disposing of the corpse. Indian politicians and administrators seem to have completely abandoned at least the slum dwellers, despite occasional official lip-services during election campaigns and before law enactments (Birdi 1995: 1.77).

As political and economic measures were never seriously taken into consideration, slum improvement schemes proved political failures, economic setbacks and overall human disasters. Politicians, planners and administrators never consulted the local people when elaborating 'rebuilding' or 'reconstruction' schemes for the Old City. A survey compiled at the end of the 1980s showed that a quarter of the walled city's inhabitants had no idea at all of what was actually meant by the term 'rebuilding'. Most people believed that 'rebuilding' is just another term for demolishing which did not include the re-building of the site. Therefore, some inhabitants strictly opposed the demolition of the old *mohalla*s without being offered a realistic concept asking whether the improvement of a ward could not have been realized without the destruction of its old yet in many cases not dilapidated buildings.

Apparently, people had clearly realized the conceptual deficit of Delhi's town planners and city administrators. Apart from this, the government agencies' lack of concept and cooperation was seen as the major cause for the conflicts going along with the demolition works (Mehra 1991: 105-9).

Administrative ignorance coupled with political arrogance urged the inhabitants of the Old City to develop multifarious strategies of protest and resistance and thereby to establish their own agency. Analysing this agency through the examples given above, several sorts of reactions, actions and strategies become evident and help conceptualise resistance in an urban environment. Firstly, to avoid open confrontation, people agreed upon government re-housing schemes on the urban periphery only to resettle on their former land within weeks or months, and additionally to make some pecuniary profit from the sale of the allocated plots which they had been given as compensation. Many evictees resettled on their former sites, thus annihilating government re-housing, rebuilding and beautification efforts.

This kind of strategy is predominantly individual (single male persons as well as family units). However, groups of dispossessed people also re-migrated into the core of the city. In any case, this kind of resistance does not need a specific form of organization. The same is true for the general elections in 1977, when the electorate expressed its dissent, not only in general with Emergency Rule but also in particular with Delhi urban politics. This form of protest is, without doubt, highly individual and does not need organizational skills. However, discussion (by definition not an individual action) in private as well as in public may happen accidentally but in many cases has to be arranged, and this may certainly have influenced the voting.

People from all sections including the lower classes of the social strata were able to organise and represent themselves. As the Turkman Gate incident shows, inhabitants from the most densely populated *mohalla*s behind the city wall joined and acted commonly against government 'rebuilding' plans for that area. It had been the middle (influential and possessing) classes of these wards which successfully presented their demands, seeking legal advice and eventually suing municipal institutions. In some instances, government had to give in, which in turn strengthened the position of the local population and its organization. More open forms of resistance took place when the inhabitants of clearance areas did not leave their habitat and stayed in the vicinity during demolition works. As soon as it had become clear that rebuilding did not mean building after destruction, people started protesting and ultimately fighting.

It seems very likely that most of the protesters came from the ranks of the poor within the area, yet it is not clear to what extent, or if at all, landlords and tenants acted together. However, to successfully fight the police as the 'rioters' did until gun fire quelled the protests, certainly demands elaborated strategies if not pre-arranged tactics. This observance contradicts ideas of a 'spontaneous' and 'unorganized' protest by an undisciplined urban 'mob' and, in fact, indicates the organizational skills of the demonstrators. Additionally, the ability to reshape and appropriate institutions and ideologies of elite politics for their own purposes documents the autonomy of the subaltern urban population to participate actively in the public sphere of a larger urban environment in terms of their "distinctiveness of practice" (O'Hanlon 1988: 197).

For this reason, popular protest in Delhi as well as on a general urban level can be characterized by personal, individual action and also by a highly diversified group response. In addition to rural and perhaps more common forms of resistance based on immediate mutual communication and cooperation, urban and certainly more individual(ized) protesters join together in groups to represent their interests and organise their resistance. This also shows people's ability to utilise forms of urban organization and representation for their own purposes and to counteract political as well as administrative urban designs. Though quite similar in its structures and appearances, urban resistance ought to be distinguished from rural or peasant resistance as it has similar yet not identical forms of action and counteraction. Apart from informal strategies of resistance, people in the urban environment tend to use rather formal strategies of protest. This slight but nevertheless important distinction seems not only to be justified by the different environmental settings but also by the different inner-urban mobility and the different competences with respect to the organization of non-violent and violent forms of resistance.

REBUILDING SHAHJAHANABAD: PERSPECTIVES, VISIONS AND UTOPIAS

As a reaction to the general elections of 1977, the new Indian government shifted the Slum Clearance and Improvement Scheme and the

Jhuggi Jhompri Rebuilding Scheme from the DDA to the DMC in 1978. However, two years later the departments were again transferred to the DDA. The frequent transfers had adverse effects paralysing town planning and slum improvement and particularly financial liabilities between the departments for mere administrative reasons (Birdi 1995: 1.47-8). As a consequence of the harsh clearance politics during the Emergency, the Delhi municipal authorities changed the demolition programmes into a scheme for the Environmental Improvement of Urban Slums. EIUS, though already started in 1972 but suspended for almost a decade, laid emphasis on the improvement of existing slums with basic amenities like latrines, sewerage and electricity instead of their wholesale clearance (Ali 1995: 41-4). This change in politics did not reflect a deeper understanding of the living conditions of Delhi's poor and was, therefore, not guided by humanitarian aspects but resulted from the economic insight that the slum dwellers provided an indispensable cheap workforce within the city. The overall attitude towards slums as a disease did not change too since as long as they are devoid of basic civic amenities they are still seen as 'cancerous growth in the urban centres.' (Birdi 1995: 1.79)

Rebuilding Shahjahanabad is also still on Delhi's urban planning agenda. Jagmohan had envisaged a tidy, pedestrianized intramural town directly linked with New Delhi via an extended Minto Road towards Jama Masjid as suggested by the original plan of Lutyens. Additionally, the Old City would be enlarged by a 'second Shahjahanabad' between Minto Road and Bahadur Shah Zafar Marg providing space, housing and various public institutions for approximately 60,000 people that formerly lived in the Old City (Jagmohan 1975: 63-71; 82-102). Plans from the middle of the 1980s suggested that 'revitalization should be taken up keeping in view the traditional character and style of the buildings.' (Evenson 1989: 191). Parts of the local population even argue in favour of a literal "reconstruction" of Shahjahanabad opting for an overall face lift in what they believe to have been Mughal Delhi: a city consisting of splendid houses with arches and pink façades, spacious *haveli*s with courtyards, fountains and restaurants serving traditional food (Mehra 1991: 110-1). Recently, this very same attitude has been revitalized by a city architect romanticising the walled city of Delhi (Mohan 2000), and turning a lively and bustling urban space into a quiet and pacified, in short: a 'disneyfied' open air museum.

Of course, the Old City does need some fundamental improvement. But so far plans and projects only oscillate between clearances and conservation, between rebuilding and reconstruction. Realistic re-housing schemes and sensible town planning for the Old City are still missing. Voices demanding basic amenities for the *mohalla*s and a halt in continuing commercialisation within the Old City have still not been taken into consideration. As long as the demands of the local population differ so widely from the urban visions of the political and economic classes, the problems and solutions of the inhabitants of Delhi's walled city will remain and urban resistance to town planning schemes will doubtless continue for some time.

REFERENCES

Adas, Michael, 'From avoidance to confrontation: peasant protest in precolonial and colonial Southeast Asia', in Michael Adas, ed., *State, Market and Peasant in Colonial South and Southeast Asia,* Aldershot et al.: Ashgate, 1998.

Ali, Sabir, *Environment and Resettlement Colonies of Delhi,* New Delhi: Har-Anand Publications, 1995.

Bakshi, S. R. and Sharma, Suresh K., eds., *Delhi through Ages*, vol. 4, Capital of India, Delhi: Anmol Publications, 1995. Press Information Bureau, Government of India, Turkman Gate incident, Deputy Home Minister's statement, 27 April 1976, pp. 196-7

Birdi, H. D., *Slum Law and Urbanization,* New Delhi: Vidhi Publishing, 1995.

Blake, Stephen, *Shahjahanabad. The sovereign city in Mughal India, 1639-1739,* Cambridge, Cambridge University Press, 1993.

Bopegamage, A., *Delhi. A study in urban sociology,* Bombay, University of Bombay, 1957.

BSS – Bharat Sevak Samaj Delhi Pradesh, *Slums of Old Delhi. Report of the socio-econmic survey of the slum-dwellers of Old Delhi City,* Delhi: Atma Ram & Sons, 1958.

Delhi Gazetteer, Delhi Administration, Delhi: Ministry of Information and Broadcasting, 1976.

The Delhi Municipal Corporation Act, 1957, Act No. 66 of 1957.

Dayal, John and Bose, Ajoy, *For Reasons of State. Delhi under emergency,* Delhi: Ess Ess Publications, 1977.

Dhar, P. N., *Indira Gandhi, the 'Emergency' and Indian Democracy,* Delhi: Oxford University Press, 2000.

Dossal, Miriam, *Imperial Designs and Indian Realities: The planning of Bombay city, 1845-1875,* Delhi: Oxford University Press, 1991.

Drieberg, Trevor, Jag Mohan, Sarala, *Emergency in India,* New Delhi: Manas Publishers, 1975.

Evenson, Norma, *The Indian Metropolis. A view toward the west,* Delhi: Oxford University Press, 1989.

Gooptu, Nandini, *The Politics of the Urban Poor in Early Twentieth-Century India,* Cambridge: Cambridge University Press, 2001.

Grewal, Reeta, 'Urban morphology under colonial rule', in Indu Banga, ed., *The City in Indian History. Urban demography, society and politics,* Delhi: Manohar, 1991, pp. 173-190.

Gupta, Narayani, *Delhi between two Empires, 1803-1931. Society, government and urban growth,* Delhi: Oxford University Press, 1981.

Irving, Robert G., *Indian Summer. Lutyens, Baker and Imperial Delhi,* New Haven and London: Yale University Press, 1981.

Jagmohan, *Rebuilding Shahjahanabad. The walled city of Delhi,* New Delhi: Vikas Publishing House, 1975.

Jagmohan, *Island of Truth,* New Delhi: Vikas Publishing House, 1978.

Jain, A. K., *The Making of a Metropolis. Planning and growth of Delhi,* Delhi: National Book Organization, 1990.

King, Anthony D., *Colonial Urban Development. Culture, social power and environment,* London: Heneley and Boston, 1976.

Krafft, Thomas, 'Contemporary Old Delhi: Transformation of an historical place', in Eckart Ehlers and Thomas Krafft, eds., *Shahjahanabad/Old Delhi. Tradition and colonial change,* Stuttgart: Steiner Verlag, 1993, pp. 65-91.

Krafft, Thomas, *Von Shahjahanabad zu Old Delhi: Zur Persistenz islamischer Strukturelemente in der nordindischen Stadt,* Sankt Augustin: Asgard Verlag, 1999.

Mehra, Ajay K., *The Politics of Urban Redevelopment. A study of Old Delhi,* Delhi: Sage Publications, 1991.

Meller, Helen E., 'Urbanization and the introduction of modern town planning ideas in India, 1900-1925', in K. N. Chaudhuri and C. J. Dewey, eds., *Economy and Society: Essays in Indian economic and social history,* Delhi: Oxford University Press, 1979, pp. 330-50.

Metcalf, Thomas R., *An Imperial Vision. Indian architecture and Britain's Raj,* Berkeley/Los Angeles: University of California Press, 1989.

Mitra, Ashok, *Delhi, capital city,* New Delhi: Thomson Press (India), 1970.

Mohan, I., *Delhi: Development and change.* Delhi: A.P.H. Publishing Corp., 2000.

O'Hanlon, Rosalin, 'Recovering the subject: Subaltern Studies and the histories of renaissance in colonial South Asia', in *Modern Asian Studies* 22 (1988), pp. 189-224.

Pickstone, John V., 'Dearth, dirt and fever epidemics: Rewriting the history of British "Public Health", 1780 – 1850', in Terence Ranger and P. Slack, eds., *Epidemics and Ideas: Essays on the historical perception of pestilence,* Cambridge: Cambridge University Press, 1992.

Rao, V.K.R.V, and Desai, P. B., *Greater Delhi. A study in urbanization – 1940-1957,* London: Asia Publishing House, 1965.

SRGE, 1971: *Statistical Report on the General Elections, 1971, to the fifth Lok Sabha,* vol. 1, New Delhi: Election Commission of India, 1973.

SRGE, 1977: *Statistical Report on the General Elections, 1977, to the sixth Lok Sabha,* vol. 1, New Delhi: Election Commission of India, 1978.

Singh, Patwant and Dhamija, Ram, eds., *Delhi. The deepening urban crisis,* Delhi: Sterling Publishers, 1989. [Publications from the *Design* magazine]

Tarlo, Emma, 'From victim to agent. Memories of Emergency from a resettlement colony in Delhi', in *Economic and Political Weekly* 30, no. 46 (1995), pp. 2921-28.

Tarlo, Emma, 'Welcome to history: Resettlement colony in the making', in Veronique Dupont, Emma Tarlo, Denis Vidal, eds., *Delhi. Urban space and human destinies,* Delhi: Manohar, 2000, pp. 51-74.

Tarlo, Emma, *Unsettling Memories: Narratives of the Emergency in Delhi,* London: Hurst & Company, 2003.

11

URBAN VILLAGES OF DELHI

AJAY K. MEHRA

INTRODUCTION

Delhi, an eternal capital city and the capital of modern India, inheres many contradictions. The existence of villages, known in policy and planning circles as 'urban villages', within the sprawling metropolis is just one of them. The so called 'urban villages' constitute a paradox for a variety of reasons. First, rural and urban constitute two ends of civilizational continuum. Despite complementary coexistence since the beginning of human civilization, they continue to maintain distinct socio-economic identity. Only transitional settlements retain the features of both. Therefore, if settlements visibly combining the features of both continue to remain an integral part of a metropolis for decades, they certainly constitute paradox. Second, the concept of an 'urban village' poses a serious dilemma for policy makers and urban planners alike, for it requires reconciling contrasting policy and planning ends. Third, 'urban village' presents a serious challenge for urban governance and management too, because the two kinds of settlements require different management strategies. Finally, howsoever, adroit the policy measures and planning exercise may be, such a paradoxical characterization of a settlement would definitely pose an identity crisis and an existential dilemma for the inhabitants.

This study seeks to examine economic, social and policy consequences of the unique urbanization process in Delhi that has reduced most of the villages inducted into metropolitan Delhi into slums. It proposes to review the changes taking place in such villages as a consequence of urbanization policy. What kind of future role the urban planners visualized for these 'urban villages' in the economy and life of the metropolis? Was the existence of 'urban villages' thought of as a transitory measure, or they were supposed to remain as enclaves for certain specific purpose? Has the development of the villages conformed to the future envisaged for them? Have the villages played the role they were supposed to play in the economy of Delhi?

This essay proposes to look into policy dimension of 'urbanization' of these villages. Acquisition of agricultural land is a normal process of urban expansion. What had the policy makers in mind when they decided to put these villages in *lal dora*?[1] Did they ever ponder over location of the 'urban villages' in the overall system of Delhi? Has there been any well thought out policy towards them, or have they just been left alone to degenerate?

It would be worth while to clearly understand the concept and phenomenon of urban village in theoretical and locational contexts. The distinction between an urbanizing village and an urban village, for example, is crucial to this essay. For, the process of urbanizing, i.e. the process sociologically defined as adopting and adapting to urbanism, or an urban way of life, would be visible both in an urbanizing village and an urban village. Nevertheless, there would be qualitative as well as quantitative difference in this process in the two different settings. An urbanizing village reflects the natural process of transformation of a human settlement from one economic order to the other and one way of life to the other. Thus, socio-economic and morphological changes taking place in natural process bring about attitudinal as well as socio-cultural changes gradually and naturally. An urban village, on the other hand, represents a process in which a rural settlement is caught in the process of rapid urbanization of a metropolis.

Thus, while such a settlement suddenly loses the source of it's livelihood, it has to adjust to new types of economic activities it has not hitherto been familiar with. Attitudinal and socio-cultural changes do not come overnight. Naturally, as such changes take place, people go through a process of ambivalence and confusion. We can see these changes taking place in the context of Delhi. The villages in the region have been losing their land to the expanding capital of India since the 1950s. In fact, soon after independence the ceaseless influx of refugees from Pakistan necessitated expansion of the limits of the national capital. Partly due to

---

1 *Lal dora,* literally a red cord, is an interesting concept used in the context of 'urban villages' in the Delhi Development Act and the Master Plan for Delhi. It is an imaginary boundary line, usually marked by a road, that separates the village *abadi* (inhabitation) from the urban neighbourhood. Fixed at the time of regular settlement operation, land-use in the village *abadi* within the *lal dora* has been reserved strictly for residential housing. However, as low-rent neighbourhood, they have attracted trade, commerce and small enterprises. Moreover, in this paper we study a situation wherein commercialization of built space was inherent.

this process and partly due to the natural process of urban expansion, Delhi had been growing at a fast pace since 1947. The impact of the haphazard growth was felt by the mid-1950s and the decision was taken to prepare a Master Plan for Delhi in 1956. The task of preparing a plan and implementing it in the next two decade was entrusted to Delhi Development Authority (DDA) created in 1957. The Master Plan of Delhi was ready by 1960 and aimed at a planned development of Delhi until 1981.

The Master Plan of Delhi, 1961 used the expression 'urban village' in a special sense to designate the clusters of villages chosen on the fringes of urban Delhi to relocate certain small industries with village-like character, e.g. pottery, handloom weaving, tanning, rearing milch cattle. However, in later years the DDA did not use the term in the specific sense it had defined. It used the term to denote all the villages which had lost their agricultural land either to the DDA, or to a private agency in the process of urbanization. This is the sense in which this paper looks at the 'urban villages'.

DEFINING URBAN VILLAGE

For our study it is important to locate urban villages in the contexts of the process of urbanization and larger urban system. Rural-urban mobility in migratory sense would mean movement of population from villages to towns and cities, which consists the core of the urbanization process. Suburbanization and rururbanization, on the other hand, present population movements in the opposite direction. If a city overflows its boundaries and builds housing estates in its surrounding country area then the houses may well be located in the 'X' rural district, but the result is not a movement from urban to rural, rather it is urbanization of what was previously a rural area. In the case of professional and business people who choose to live outside the city in country villages, it is a further aspect of urbanization of the rural (Mann 1970: 21).

However, in case of urban villages, particularly the case being discussed in the present study, it looks to be a case of false mobility. For the population has not moved from its rural environs to an urban one, it is the city that has come to them. Having been engulfed by urbanization, they have not changed their life styles overnight. In fact, while most of them have apparently adopted an urban life style, kinship, family ties, ambience and daily chores reminiscent of country are still present in many, if not most, cases. Transformation is, of course, taking place, but, for one, it is slow and, for another, its result is producing a curious mix. From this point of view, urban villages would appear to be an appendage to the city they are part of as well as an anomaly in socio-cultural terms. Within the village community, the contacts and interactions are close, intense and personal. In the context of the larger city, the contacts acquire an urban character. The inhabitants of these villages still live in two different worlds, as it were.

It is easy to distinguish a rural from an urban settlement, but it is not easy to differentiate between an urbanizing village and an urban village. This distinction, however, is crucial to our study. For the process of urbanizing, i.e. the process sociologically defined as adopting and adapting to urbanism, or an urban way of life, would be visible both in an urbanizing village and an urban village. Nevertheless, there would be qualitative as well as quantitative difference in this process in the two different settings. We shall, therefore, attempt not only to clarify this distinction, but also to underline its importance for the present study.

An urbanizing village reflects the natural process of transformation of a human settlement from one economic order to another and one way of life to another. Thus, socio-economic and morphological changes taking place in natural process bring about attitudinal as well as socio-cultural changes gradually and naturally. An urban village, on the other hand, represents a process in which a rural settlement is caught in the process of rapid urbanization of a metropolis. Thus, while such a settlement suddenly loses the source of its livelihood, it has to adjust to new types of economic activity it has not hitherto been familiar with. Attitudinal and socio-cultural changes do not come overnight. Naturally, as such changes take place, people go through a process of ambivalence and confusion.

This study seeks to examine economic, social and policy consequences of urbanization process in Delhi that has led to the induction of villages into metropolitan Delhi. This phenomenon is unique to Delhi. What kind of future role in the economy and life of the metropolis have the urban planners visualized for these villages? Has the development of the villages conformed to the future envisaged for them? Have the villages played the role they were supposed to play in the economy of Delhi? The study proposes to look into policy dimension of 'urbanization' of these villages. Acquisition of agricultural land is a normal process of urban expansion. What had the policy makers in mind when they put these villages in *lal dora*?

The three villages sampled[2] for the study have been 'urbanized' during three different periods, though their land might have been acquired almost simultaneously. Among the oldest urban villages, Masjid Moth, which gave away its land to South Extension II was urbanized during 1951-61. The land from Munirka, also in South Delhi, was acquired for Rama Krishna Puram, a housing colony for government servants, during 1951-61, but its 'urbanization' took place during 1961-71. Jawala Heri, located in West Delhi, lost its land during 1961-71. However, urbanization in its vicinity took place during 1971-81.

VILLAGES IN A GROWING METROPOLIS

The modern history of Delhi as a metropolis and the national capital of India is linked to the twin cities of Delhi (Shahjahanabad) and New Delhi since the shifting of the capital of the British Raj from Calcutta to Delhi in 1911. However, the growth of this administrative and commercial city was still slow till independence and partition of the country. Provisions for resettlement, both physical and economic, had to be made for the millions uprooted by partition of the country. Thus started the continuing process of Delhi's urbanization which engulfed not only agricultural land but also several villages that came in its way.

During 1951-61, Delhi consumed 131 sq. kms of land. The next decade, i.e., 1961-71, witnessed the city adding another 119 sq. km. to its boundary. Its urban limits reached hand-shaking distance with adjoining states of Uttar Pradesh and Haryana by the end of the 1980s. Had the proposed concept of National Capital Region (NCR) been on target, Delhi would have by now become a megalopolis, spreading its tentacles even to a state like Rajasthan, which does not have a common boundary with the city. Adjoining towns and suburbs of Haryana and UP are already parts of Delhi's urban system.

The population of Delhi has grown rapidly during this century, particularly after Independence. From just over 200,000 at the beginning of the twentieth century, it crossed 300,000 in the 1920s, when the capital of the British Raj was shifted from Calcutta to Delhi. It turned into a million-

2 The sampling of these three villages is both random and purposive. It was random because they were not sampled after an intensive look at the socio-economic features of all the urban villages. It was purposive to the extent that in order to study adaptation to imperatives of 'compelled urbanization' three villages urbanized in three different decades were sampled.

city in the wake of Partition, registering a phenomenal 106.58 per cent growth during the decade 1941-51. The 1981 census reported Delhi's population as 5.23 million, a 43.4 per cent increase over 1971. Registering 46 per cent growth during the next decade, Delhi's population grew to 8.42 million in 1991. Adding over 4 million people during the next decade, Delhi's population stood at 12.8 million in 2001. Delhi maintained its third rank in terms of total population (behind Kolkata and Mumbai) in 2001 census too. Naturally, in order to accommodate the swelling population, the urban limits of Delhi had to increase. However, in this process not only agricultural land had to be acquired, but also a large number of villages had to be incorporated within its boundary. Before 1931, only 25 villages had been identified within Delhi's urban limits, but its growth since then (also including the critical period of partition) has engulfed 132 villages.

An Acquisitive Metropolis

A census of villages around Delhi undertaken in 1921 mentioned 314 inhabited villages that year. A similar exercise in 1931 gave a record of 381 revenue villages, of which 307 were inhabited, 49 were uninhabited (i.e., revenue estates) and 25 were merged into Delhi's urban area. Eighteen out of these 25 were merged into Delhi city, six were included in the new capital city built by the British, i.e. in New Delhi and one was included in Shahadara town. Out of 162 villages urbanized until the mid 1980s, many lost their identity completely. Six villages were totally obliterated and their population relocated during the establishment of capital city New Delhi. As per official records during 1931-51, 1956-61, 1961-71 and 1971-81, 22, 48, 40 and 27 villages respectively were urbanized (India 1987: 284-85).

However, systematic acquisition of land belonging to villages in the urbanizable limits of Delhi began after the creation of the DDA in 1957 and the preparation of Delhi Master Plan by it in 1961. The Master Plan for Delhi defined urban land policy for Delhi. The orders passed on 2 May 1961 envisaged the acquisition of entire urbanizable land as indicated in Master Plan for Delhi, except those already developed and committed with a perspective until 1981. When the measures recommended by the Master Plan were enforced in 1962, the developed urbanized area in Delhi was about 18,000 ha. Another 26,000 ha. was proposed for acquisition and development. This brought 112 villages within the new urbanizable limits as indicated in the Master Plan.

Acquired land was to be developed and provided for public and private institutes, public utilities, community facilities and industrial and commercial uses. In addition, housing plots were to be allotted to individuals whose land had been acquired (provided they did not own residential plot or building). A suitable percentage of housing area was to be reserved for the low-income groups. Undeveloped land was earmarked for industrialists' cooperative societies. These orders were amended in July 1967 and February 1970 (Jha 1978).

This policy of planned urban development for Delhi nevertheless had two negative aspects. First, numerous housing colonies created and sold in semi-planned and unplanned state without any civic authorization by unscrupulous real estate developers to the unsuspecting middle class, mushroomed in different parts of the city. Subsequently 'authorized' on political considerations, they continue to be planners' nightmare.[3] According to the government's estimate in 1985, about 200,000 families were residing in these unauthorized colonies (India 1987: 288).

Second, because of large-scale acquisition of agricultural land the villages have undergone a physical and socio-economic transformation. In urbanization process, the agricultural land in most of the villages was left out for secondary dwellings and public buildings. This private land in most of the villages, according to the government's own estimate, has been put to use as single family tenements, or for the inner zone of villages comprising compact old houses and a homogenous community has remained almost intact, the outer zone has completely changed and has acquired a heterogeneous character (India 1987: 288).

VILLAGES IN DELHI'S URBAN LAND POLICY

With the realization that urbanization of Delhi would engulf villages coming in the way, villages were also included in the planning process. Even though there were very few villages in that category, there was a realization of the phenomenon of 'village enveloping' or 'village engulfing' and the planners were aware of its ill-effects. The Work Studies devoted a full chapter to 'Rural Delhi'. The basic thrust of their recommendations was to identify 'community of interest areas' based on socio-

---

3 Ashish Bose studied land speculation in Delhi for the National Building Organization in 1968. His study brings out the *modus operandi* of colonizers, developers and real estate agents in the expanding national capital during the crucial decades of 1950s and 1960s (Bose 1980: 225).

economic considerations, after delimiting planning areas within the four physical divisions[4] of rural Delhi. The method adopted in delimiting the 'community of interest areas' was to recognize the important centres of rural activity and to determine their spheres of influence. The Work Studies team was of the view that with suitable modifications 'community of interest areas' could be adopted as planning areas for the countryside. While the Work Studies presented a comprehensive framework for planning rural Delhi, it recommended detailed studies for the preparation of detailed master plans for the villages wherein proper delineation of land uses would be made to improve the village *abadis* (Delhi Development Authority 1962: 382).

Since the DDA did not succeed in its effort to implement the Master Plan for Delhi as promulgated on 1 September 1962, the villages, or 'urban villages' as they had come to be known as, also grew as unplanned rural islands in the national capital. The review of the Master Plan by the DDA in 1985 also took cognizance of the existence of urban villages and stressed the need to integrate them in the planning of Delhi. Delhi 2001, a perspective plan for Delhi formulated in the mid 1980s to extend the perspective of the original Master Plan to the end of the century had the following to say about urban villages:

> Presently there are 106 villages within the urbanizable limits, more villages would be added into the urban area because of its extension. The settlements having a completely different life-style for centuries are now getting merged into the urban environment and need a sensitive treatment in the planning and development process. The settlement should get the modern services and amenities and should also be catered for their traditional cultural styles. (Delhi Vikas Varta 1985: 18)

The perspective gathered from the official memo of the Ministry of Works and Housing and the Master Plan for Delhi indicates that villages did not get the attention they deserved from policy makers and planners. The Ministry of Works and Housing was concerned only about checking speculation in land in Delhi and the availability of land at a reasonable price for the expanding capital. Although it was clear that the land for

---

4 The four physical divisions in Delhi's countryside were identified as the reverie tract or *Khadar*, the low lying tract or *Dabar*, the hilly tract or *Kohi* and the level tract or *Bangar* (Delhi Development Authority 1962: 351).

Delhi's swelling population would come only from the surrounding villages, the fate of the villages was not discussed at all.

The Master Plan cannot be accused of ignoring villages in its eagerness to plan Delhi. The planners involved in the exercise were aware that the 'village enveloping' or 'village engulfing' in the process of urbanization of Delhi would not be a desirable situation for the populace that would sacrifice its livelihood and confront an uncertain future. They, therefore, kept space for planning the villages and 'rural activities'. The Master Plan eventually advanced the concept of 'urban villages' to relocate 'rural activities' like dairying, tanning and so on in some villages selected on the fringe of the city. Their approach, however, was both impractical and condescending. The acquisition of land was looked at purely as administrative, legal and managerial issue. Land for Delhi's urban development requirements had to be acquired, compensation for the acquired land had to be paid to the rural owners and the land developed and allocated. How the people, who had only agriculture related skills, would cope with their uncertain future with some cash in hand, was not considered. Even the lofty objectives incorporated in the planning process were not sincerely implemented.

ACQUISITION IN SOCIAL PERSPECTIVE

The process of urbanization is recognized to be the most unplanned among the general forms of social change.[5] Urban planning is intended to contain or neutralize several consequences, particularly the negative ones, that follow from urbanization. Acquisition of land is an essential component of planning. Acquisition of rural land in this process takes place in two ways. Rural land is either submerged silently and voluntarily as urbanization flows into its rural hinterland, as it were. Alternatively, land is acquired in the process of planned urban change by private or public agencies. In either case, the transformation of a habitat from rural to urban is a major qualitative as well as quantitative change. Naturally, significant human and socio-economic changes follow when such a major change, with qualitative as well as quantitative implications, takes

---

5 Social scientists have pointed out that urbanization is one of the four components of 'the whole process of social change'. The other three components are (i) industrialization, (ii) the emergence of a middle class, and (iii) the rise of nationalism. Urbanization could either be a consequence of the three components mentioned above, or part of a continuous interaction as the fourth component with the other three.

place in the lives of people living in the affected areas. However, the changes in case of gradual transformation of the habitat in course of natural growth, either its own, or that of a proximate urban area, are evolutional. Therefore, the changes are slow enough to be absorbed gradually, without any major problem of any kind for the inhabitants.

There are some analyses of socio-economic changes in villages affected by urbanization available. We have referred to such an analysis for Delhi earlier in the chapter. Once the agricultural land belonging to an agrarian rural community is acquired for urbanization by a public agency, suddenly the community is compelled to look for an alternative source of livelihood. The rural community with only traditional skills for agricultural pursuits, or for related occupations, is suddenly forced to fend for itself in a different economic and social setting.

Even if it is agreed that the community has been adequately compensated for its land and the 'adequacy' of compensation is not in question, it is little satisfaction that it has money to fend for itself. For the people do not have the requisite skills to use that money gainfully (Bose 1980). If they use that money for their immediate needs, they would certainly be jeopardizing their future. Unless they are helped with proper counseling on investment and alternative economic opportunity, the community would go through confusion and psychological uncertainties.

The fact of the matter, however, is that the adequacy of compensation, on most occasions, has been in question. Even though people have lost the Fundamental Right to property since the abrogation of Article 31 of the Constitution of India, and consequently the right to question adequacy of compensation in case their property is acquired for public purpose, the relevance of adequate compensation, in case the acquired property is the basic and only source of livelihood of the owner, remains. In fact, the balance between public good and individual right to property has always been hard to reconcile in India, for even when the Right to Property was a fundamental right the Indian State argued that the adequacy of compensation should not be questioned where a public purpose was involved.

It is not surprising that under the circumstances a large number of acquisitions for the general purpose of urban expansion, which largely meant urban housing, came under dispute on the ground of just compensation. In Delhi alone, a large number of cases were filed by villagers against inadequate compensation and many of the cases dragged on for decades. This, on the one hand, slowed the planning for urban development and, on the other, led to haphazard growth in certain areas.

The villages, which protested against the inadequate compensation, were unfortunately left out of the planning process due to disputes involved. Naturally, urbanization of villages remained a myth. This certainly could have been avoided, had the cases of compensation been looked at slightly differently, taking into account the fact that the villages were not merely losing their land, they were also losing their source of livelihood.

Socio-economic Changes

The process of urbanization undoubtedly brought physical and socio-economic changes, particularly changes in the livelihood pattern inherent in the loss of agricultural land in the Delhi's 'urbanizing' villages. K. V. Sundaram studied the process of socio-economic change in the mid-1970s in Kotla Mubarakpur, an urban village next to South Extension I and Defence Colony, two of South Delhi's posh residential neighbourhoods.[6] He identified four important elements, which give to a Delhi village its substantial character:

> (i) the village square or chopal,[7] as it is called, with its shady tree and little platform; (ii) the village well, which is very often the meeting place for women; (iii) the peculiar street pattern which is often narrow and winding with its numerous small dead-end streets or alleys; and (iv) the typical mud houses with flat roofs. To these, we may perhaps also add the neatly and even elegantly constructed 'piles of cowdung cakes' (known as *bitauras*), which are found in all Indian villages and which give to the village scene its characteristic look and odour. (Sundaram 1977: 105)

Sundaram found that despite being 'subject to urban influences on an intensive scale during the last more than two decades, it – Kotla Mubarakpur – has managed to retain all the above mentioned village characteristics. It has its separate *chopal* (...) and in one case, even a *chopal* earmarked for the lower castes. These *chopals* continue to serve some

---

6 It must be pointed out to make the context clear that the Delhi Master Plan studies undertaken in 1958, recognized Kotla Mubarakpur as a densely occupied low rent neighbourhood, meriting the description of a slum and requiring urgent attention. The MCD prepared a Redevelopment Plan for the village in 1967, which envisaged building some roads and earmarked sites for certain civic amenities like parks, playgrounds, schools and shopping centres.

7 *Chopal* or *chaupal* is a centrally located meeting place in a village. Usually, it is easily accessible from outside and located at a prominent place in the village.

community functions' (Sundaram 1977: 105). This description indicates that despite changes, the village retained some of its rural characteristics not only in physical structure, but also in its social organization and structure.

There is, however, a slow and gradual, at times strenuous, shift from rural occupation to urban occupation as 'the villages lying on the outskirts pass through certain stages of transition, from an interior village into a fringe village and then into a 'rural enclave' engulfed by urban growth' and the rural urban interaction increases. Sundaram further describes the process:

> As urban expansion proceeds, some cultivated lands pass into urban use, but in the remaining lands cultivation is still possible, and villagers may exploit such economic opportunities as market-gardening, dairy-farming and poultry-keeping. Some of them may also seek employment in the city and start commuting. The peasants who have been deprived of their land and who get cash compensation may invest in land in far-off places or in commerce or squander the money. But slowly and steadily, the villagers tend to practice urban-oriented occupations or seek urban employment. (Sundaram 1977: 95)

Sundaram has mentioned two possibilities of investment of compensation received by the peasants in the urbanized villages – investment in land in far-off places, or in commerce. A study of investment pattern of the compensation money in a village on the fringe of New Delhi by Ashish Bose in 1969 revealed that illiterate Jat cultivators did not withdraw the money paid to them by account payee cheques for six months. Not surprisingly, faced with uncertain future and lacking any institutional or governmental advice on investment, they consulted each other over their future. There were stray investments, successful or otherwise, in business and commerce. Most of them, however, invested in land in far off places. Since land they purchased was cheaper, they acquired more than what they had in Delhi and saved some money. The compulsion of distance made them change from cultivators into landlords, leasing out their newly acquired land for cultivation. The next generation was thus educated and turned away from farming (Bose 1980: 241-4).

Of the 115 villages urbanized between 1951-81, the data from 1971 census were analyzed for 113 villages to look at socio-economic changes taking place in the villages due to urbanization, for the Gazetteer of Rural Delhi. The changes taking place due to urbanization were analyzed in terms of participation rate, economic activities, sex ratio and age structure. Change in occupation structure meant that the work force in such villages took to urban occupations. There was a fall in number of workers in agriculture while the number of workers in other occupations such as manufacturing, construction, trade and commerce and transport showed an increase. In construction work the proportion of workers increased from 3.2 per cent to 7.9 per cent and in trade and commerce from 4.4 per cent to 10.7 per cent of total workers. A visible reduction in sex ratio in this process indicated the entry of migrant workforce into urban villages for want of cheaper accommodation. It was found that there was proportionately lower population of children in the age group of 1-14 years, a higher population of adults in the age group of 15-60 years and lower population in the 60 plus category (India 1987: 285-7).

However, P. B. Desai's study of 115 'urbanized villages' out of 214 in Delhi's expanded metropolitan limit for the Gazetteer of Rural Delhi revealed:

> These village people lost their traditional agriculture and allied occupations and they could seek no employment avenues that the expanding metropolis provided. In this new expansion of city's economy, they did not fit in squarely as they neither had general, not any kind of vocational education or training. They could only swell the rank of footloose unskilled labor. Some of them were probably lucky in getting unskilled jobs in the great variety of industrial, commercial and service establishments, but most were pushed into informal sector to scratch uncertain livelihood. *There was a disintegration of their well-knit abadis and their social fabric was shattered.* The already unhealthy ecology of these abadis further worsened and each of them was transformed into a veritable slum. (India 1987: 430; *italics* intended)

The benefit from the appreciation of land values, mentioned by Bose (1980), also helped only a few. The villagers also did not have the skills to take advantage of the tremendous appreciation of land values within and around *abadis.* Barring a few who had the will to survive and even prosper, most of the people of these urbanized villages fell prey to speculative private developers who cheated them (India 1987: 430) .

CASE STUDIES

Masjid Moth

Moth ki Masjid is the name of a medieval mosque located near an upper class South Delhi residential neighbourhood, South Extension II. The mosque is surrounded by, apart from other such residential colonies as Udai Park, Gulmohar Park and Niti Bagh, a dense 'urban village' named after the mosque – Masjid Moth.[8] The village has been losing its agricultural land to meet the housing demand of urban Delhi since the 1950s. South Extension II, built entirely on the land of this village during the 1950s and the 1960s by the Delhi Land and Finance (DLF) Ltd., a real estate developer, now forms frontage of the village in the north. The village land has also gone to other residential colonies in its vicinity mentioned earlier, which now surround the village in the northeast. The All India Institute of Medical Sciences flanks it in the West. In addition, in the southwest lies a small *qasba* (town) Gautam Nagar.

According to the 1961 census Masjid Moth had 298 acres of land. According to its inhabitants, the village occupied about 240 acres of land in 1990.[9] This difference shows how much of agricultural land Masjid Moth lost in the process of urbanization. The census data for Masjid Moth creates problems for us in understanding the demographic changes taking place in the village over the years. The 1961 census shows total population at 2270 and households at 440. The 1971 census, on the other hand, gives total number of household at 82 and population as 627. Obviously, such a decline in population or households is unbelievable. This clearly looks like a case of changes effected in the census area for administrative convenience. The task is made more difficult since 1981, when Masjid Moth is not shown as a village in the census. It becomes a part of charge 64 of the census. Naturally, the population of the charge 64, which includes other adjoining area as well, is enumerated as 105,907 in 1981 and 49,573 in 1991. Clearly, a re-delineation of the census area took place in 1991 as well.

---

8 There is another posh housing colony of the same name further south from Masjid Moth the village. The two should not be confused with each other. The village is an old inhabitation, as the name suggests dating back at least to medieval times, whereas the housing colony has been named after the historical monument by some historically inclined residents of the locality. Our concern here is obviously not with the housing colony.

9 Since the village in 1990 meant only the inhabitation and no agricultural land, the area denoted the land on which the inhabitation was settled.

Traditional styles of buildings mingle with the modern in the village. While some old structures built in the traditional mansion style still exist, new extensions in several such structures presented a curious architectural mix. Some of these buildings belonged to the dominant family of the village. Though most of the houses had inverted open space in the form of courtyards, the village did not have much community open space or a park. The villagers regretted this neglect, as also the use of such allotted space for other purposes. However, the traditional *chowk*[10] of the village was reported to be the traditional meeting place, with a mix of shops around. Metalled road inside the village, lying in a state of disrepair, narrated the tale of neglect.

Though sewer pipes had been laid in the village years ago, uncovered stinking drains are a common sight on all the streets of Masjid Moth, which get clogged very often and spilt filth all over in the village. Bumpy lanes and roads, and uncovered drains and filth littered around narrated the story of civic neglect of villages in urban Delhi. The road in front marking the *lal dora* and bordering South Extension II has been a small market catering to the daily needs of the village as well as of the urban neighbourhood for years. Pandit Leela Ram Market, as it is popularly known after the most prominent personality of the village, whose family owned most of the real estate in the village, has seen a tremendous face-lift since 1988. It has been transformed into a massive market complex, with multi-storied shopping arcade and commercial complex. A multi-storied deluxe apartment complex had also been constructed around the same place. Obviously, aside from adding to congestion, these constructions had changed life and lifestyles in the village.

The Sharmas, who came from Rajasthan, owned bulk of land in Masjid Moth. Many villagers leased land for cultivation from them and in return gave some amount of the yield to them. For example, the land on which the residential neighbourhoods of Lajpat Nagar and Andrews Ganj now stand, were set up in 1948 to resettle refugees after Partition and in the 1950s to house central government servants, was usually leased out for five years by the land owners. In the 1950s the DLF decided to develop residential colony around this area and purchased land for the purpose from the villagers at Rs. 10 per square yard.

When the DDA acquired land in Masjid Moth in 1962 in order to develop residential quarters for government servants, it offered compensation at measly rate of Rs. 4 and Rs. 5 per sq. yd. When the

---

10 Literally, an intersection of four roads, a square. In a traditional Indian habitation, it also has an importance as a meeting place.

villagers appealed, the Additional District and Session Judge revised the amount to Rs 6 per sq. yd. The DDA in its turn appealed to the Delhi High Court. For the next three decades,[11] the matter remained subjudice. The big landlords like the Sharmas received interest running into lakhs, but the smaller land holders suffered due to this delay in payment of compensation.

Those villagers whose land was acquired by the government found themselves at a loss. Whether their land holdings were small or big, the villagers suffered financially while dealing with the government. Those with small land holdings suffered most. Small compensation, smaller installments, legal disputes involving the quantum of compensation, or delayed payment made investment in profitable ventures difficult. The grievance was that they had received the entire compensation in a single installment they could have made profitable investments.

The main source of earning for the villagers before urbanization was trade and occupation linked with agriculture. Naturally, the acquisition of their land for urbanization took away their source of earning and brought a fundamental change in the source of livelihood in the village. The low rate of compensation offered by the government and consequent litigation led to a great financial hardship for the villagers. The payment in installments made things even worse as those who received the money had to spend it on accumulated necessities. As the compensation came in small install-ments, most villagers could not invest it in any profitable ventures. Even awareness of mechanisms of investment was lacking. Very few villagers adjusted to the changes brought about in their economic life by urbanization. The villagers also seemed apprehensive of seeking bank loans. Yet, some of them did approach nationalized banks for loans for self-employment, but complained that they were told that they were not eligible for loans.

Only a few families in the village were economically well off. The standard of living of other villagers had not improved much since urbanization of the village. Those who sold their land to the DLF could invest the money either in small business or in purchasing land in some other places. Five or six villagers could purchase agricultural land in other villages. One started a brick-kiln business. Three could purchase taxis and three wheeler auto rickshaws. One person purchased a truck lorry. Two opened tea and milk shops on pavements. Most of the landless persons took up jobs as domestic servants, or worked as labourers. Five villagers

---

11 We are talking of 1989-90 when the data for this study was being collected. We have no information whether the case has finally been decided.

secured jobs as drivers and conductors in the Delhi Transport Corporation. One of the residents of the village secured an MBBS degree from England. The villagers were proud of a young man employed in the Meteorology Department of the Government of India because he was part of the team that visited Antarctica.

Leaving aside the posh urban neighbourhoods that have surrounded the village from all the sides, the outer ring of Masjid Moth adjoining the South Extension II has become a bustling market with high rise commercial complexes and shopping plaza since 1988. However, this portion along the road that constitutes *lal dora* has been a small market since 1946. With the construction of residential houses in South Extension II during the 1960s, the small town Leela Ram Market began supplying daily provisions to the residents. It provided employment to some of the villagers. However, the construction of the Southex Plaza by a young and dynamic scion of the Sharma family has changed the economic life of this sleepy village. Though the new complex has brought in traders, businesspersons and commercial establishments from all over the city, it would be wrong to assume that it has not affected the local residents. First, all the shopkeepers who were dislocated in the course of construction of the new complex were given the option of being relocated on the completion of the complex. Second, it opened new opportunities and horizons for the enterprising among the villagers. Third, so much of economic and commercial activity in the vicinity would naturally open up new opportunities for the local residents in the informal service sector. Finally, it would also push up demands for residential space, creating opportunities for future rentiers.

The process of construction of the new commercial complex in Masjid Moth in 1987-88 needs to be recorded here, for it is not difficult to construct such buildings on a vacant plot of land, but it is not easy at a place where there are already tenants. The young and enterprising scion of the Sharma family referred to above gave two options to the tenants in his old buildings in the Leela Ram Market. Either they could get a shop of the same size in the new complex, or enough money to set up a shop somewhere else. Most of them agreed to settle for a shop there itself. Those who did not, were given compensation.

However, the initial economic plight of the villagers was expressed in the remark of a citizen that every farmer cannot run a business. It is not surprising that nearly four or five villagers trying to set up a business lost the money received as compensation. Naturally, no one tried to set up any kind of manufacturing or repairing unit. Only those who set up shops or purchased landed property could gain something. Obviously, one of the main effects of urbanization, at least in the initial stage, was increasing unemployment among the youth in the village. The village elders recalled that before the acquisition of agricultural land belonging to the village in 1962, hardly anyone was seen idle, or even at leisure, during the day. All the young men, rather all the able-bodied men were occupied either in cultivation or other allied occupations. It must be pointed out here that the problem of unemployment was mentioned to us during the course of research in 1989-90. Apparentliy, this problem was not sorted out even in 27 years.

As described earlier, Masjid Moth is literally surrounded from all sides. The moment one crosses the *lal dora* limits from the village to one of the urban, rather metropolitan, neighbourhoods, one is struck by the difference – relatively open roads, green parks, neatly arranged and maintained houses, and so on. Crossing the limits of *lal dora* from the metropolitan end would be shocking, as one will be surrounded by filth.

The spillover of the economic deprivation in the social field bothered the village elders. The rising graph of crime and violence in the village and involvement of youngsters of the village in such activities worried every one, but it seriously disturbed the elders. The glitter of the neighbouring urban pockets, felt some, added to the feeling of deprivation. Rising unemployment further aggravated such feelings. Rise in the crime in the vicinity has resulted in growing suspicion of the residents of the village in the urban neighbourhoods. Worse, still, as one villager pointed out, some nearby schools refused to admit children from the village because of the bad image.

In its journey from a village dotting the territory of Delhi to an urban village in Delhi Metropolis, Masjid Moth has witnessed, apart from changes in its morphology and social texture, a number of changes in the lives, surroundings and life-styles of its residents. The most fundamental change is that the basis of their economic livelihood has changed. A few have gained or just been able to maintain their old standard, but most seem to feel that they have been losers. They have a feeling that, not only the village, but also they as individuals have been simply reduced to a mere adjunct to the neighbouring urban pocket. There is a feeling of loss not merely of independent economic status, but also of an independent identity. Many seem torn between a placid village life and the highly competitive metropolitan life.

Munirka

Munirka is located in South Delhi. Situated on the Outer Ring Road, the village was once the outer fringe of Metropolitan Delhi in the south. The southern boundary of Metropolitan Delhi has now extended several kilometers beyond the outer ring road. This has left Munirka surrounded, rather engulfed, by urban sprawl. The core of the village is now enveloped by residential colonies like Rama Krishna (RK) Puram, Vasant Vihar and various clusters of multistoried DDA flats and institutions such as Jawaharlal Nehru University (JNU), Institute of Family Welfare, a five star hotel and an upmarket commercial centre.

With a total area of 1527 acres, Munirka is a rather sprawling village (District Census Handbook, Delhi, 1961). In 1961 the total number of houses in the village was 1161 and households 1170, which means nine households lived in shared accommodation, either as joint family, or as tenants. According to the villagers, the total number of houses had increased to 2500. All the houses were *pukka*, i.e. brick and concrete constructions. A few houses had beautifully carved ethnic wooden doors, very common in rural India. Clad in traditional attire, senior members in many families could be seen smoking *hukkah* either in the courtyard of their houses,or outside with others in the village *chaupal.*

The built space in the commercial area of the village was put to mixed use, but not in any planned manner. Hence, no regular pattern could be seen in it. The tendency was to let the ground floor or a portion of it. However, the first and the second floors were also let, though mainly as office premises. Thus, residential use of space could be witnessed, either on the ground floor, or on a portion of it, or on the first or the second floors. In some buildings, for example, a couple of shops had been carved out in the front. A narrow passage led to the inner verandah, which led to different rooms. In many cases, there was a courtyard adjacent to the verandah.

The available data on demography of the village is rather thin. The reason for this weakness, as explained in the earlier case, is definition and redefinition of census areas. According to the estimates of the villagers, total population of the village was 15,000 in 1990. If the estimates are correct, Munirka registered 334 per cent growth since 1961 (over 4496 persons in Mohammadpur Munirka) and 2542 per cent since 1971 (over 590 persons in Munirka alone). The total number comes to 1,025 households, or approximately 5,000 persons. It leaves a gap of 10,000 persons from the estimated 15,000 people. The number of tenants, who were not counted in the village population, made up this shortfall. The number of tenants in Munirka in 1990 was estimated to be 10,000 by a group of village elders.

South-Indians were reported mainly to have rented houses for residential purposes, whereas Panjabis rented premises for shops. Despite the fact that rapid commercialization of space took place after 1975 and most of the Munirkaites had income from rent in 1990, many in the village felt that they did not have much spare space to let. Many bemoaned the lack of more space to put to commercial use for more income, as rent was reported to be the only source of income for a significant number of the villagers. We found a confirmation for this as many admitted that loss of agricultural land due to urbanization left little option for them but to rely on rent. The loss of agricultural land and the consequent end of farming as the main economic activity had an impact on related economic activities too. There were very few cattle left in the village. Neither did the villagers have space left for cattle, or for their feed anymore. Dairying as an economic activity ended with urbanization.

Munirka became 'urbanized' as a result of the formation of South Delhi Municipal Committee vide Chief Commissioner's Notification dated 4 March 1954. Thus, it is among the few of the earliest urbanized villages of Delhi. R.K. Puram and Vasant Vihar occupied most of its agricultural land. It was in 1958, informed the villagers, that their land was acquired through compensation ranging from Re. 1 to Rs 3 per sq. yd. Not satisfied with this, they appealed and the Sessions Court awarded them Rs. 5 per sq. yd. A few of the villagers, who could afford going to the High Court, got the compensation revised to Rs. 10 per sq. yd. Cases filed by some of the villagers were still reported to be in Court. Thus even after knocking at the door of the judiciary for over three decades, some villagers had still to receive full payment of the compensation.

The villagers also went to the then Prime Minister, Jawaharlal Nehru, and requested him to relocate the village to some other site. Teen Murti House (then the Prime Minister's residence) and the office of the Prime Minister were also *gherao*ed (sit in protest) by the villagers, they were '*lathi*-charged'. But nothing came of it. Meanwhile the court cases swallowed the scarce resources of the villagers. Some of them said that they tried all avenues without much 'knowledge' of what was to be done. Some of them were reported to be still fighting legal battle in the Supreme Court.

There was an anguish and frustration among the senior citizens in Munirka against the deliberate neglect of the village by planners and policy-makers. They seemed mystified as to why Munirka, and other villages, which parted with their source of livelihood – agricultural land – have been left to decay and fend for themselves while other areas of Delhi were developed since the 1960s. They said that after the notification of acquisition, the village land remained vacant and unutilized for many years, while the villagers were groping in the dark to find new avenues for income. Within the village no redevelopment work was undertaken. That is why construction within the village since then has been unplanned. The villagers suffer from a sense of neglect. This feeling gets further aggravated when they see planned housing colonies and neighbourhoods, receiving better amenities by the civic body, coming up on what was their land.

After the acquisition of agricultural land of the village, agriculture ceased to be the main economic activity and the habitation ceased to be a village. Even if some of the inhabitants purchased agricultural land on the fringe of Delhi, the livelihood system of the village could no longer be identified as depending on agriculture. At the same time, the integration with the city in terms of lifestyle and psyche was not complete till the beginning of the 1990s. Naturally, several of the villagers faced an existential and identity crises belonging neither to the city nor to a village in true sense of the term. The hiatus in physical, economic, social and psychological 'integration' with the metropolis also heightened the crisis of employment opportunities.

Commercialization of the village was clearly visible to anyone approaching the village from the North, i.e. facing R. K. Puram. The southern side of the village, facing JNU, was located on a steep mound, not suited for any kind of commercial activity. Barring that impossible side, the eastern, northern and western sides of the village, forming a crescent, had been put to commercial use. In fact, any one walking through the winding lanes of the village could clearly see that at least two layers of the village were converted into market or commercial space. The appearance of the market confirmed haphazard commercialization of residential space in the village. The shops in the market were assorted general stores, automobile repair workshops, furniture shops, building material, textile and garment, sweet shops and eating joints, etc. These shops had not been built in a planned manner. On the eastern side of the village, the ground floor of nearly all the houses had been converted into and rented out as commercial space.

The neglect manifested itself in several ways. There was, in the first place, a feeling of a basic disregard for the requirements of the village, compounded further by callousness in implementing what was sanctioned. Hence, even if the civic body had appointed staff for keeping the village clean, they did not work, and the enforcement staff of the MCD looked the other way. Consequently, cleaning was reported to be irregular, as the staff worked at their wish. The complaints of irregular water supply came from the entire village. Many houses, in the village, said some prominent elders, had been denied water connections because the main pipeline supplying municipal water to the village was only of 6-inch diameter, which was not sufficient to serve the increasing demands of the growing village population. Another villager pointed out that 75 per cent of the village residents had stomach problems because of the insufficient supply of potable water. One of the local inhabitants said, "Today we do not even have as much of water as we used to have milk in the olden days."

Though they had access to medical facilities in the capital, the villagers expected primary health care in the village. The neglect of civic amenities like parks in the village, dry and grassless in summer and waterlogged during winter and rainy seasons, created public health hazard. Munirkaites also expected a school in the village so that children did not have to travel far for education.

Alternative means of livelihood was the most critical question in the changed scenario. With affluent neighbourhoods coming up in the vicinity, it was easier for the lower middle class and the lower class providers of services to them. Many poor villagers served in them as sweepers, drivers, vegetable peddlers, etc. Some of them had started working as wage labour, while some others had started teashops. As government and DDA colonies sprung up, more avenues opened up. Those who could still maintain their cattle were in the dairy business. Some of them secured employment with the government and a couple of the villagers started transport business. A few worked as chauffeurs and drivers of heavy vehicles, i.e. buses and trucks. While the affluent and the middle class, those who had the space and those who could afford, capitalized on the space they had and turned rentier letting out residential or commercial space. Mid-1970s onwards, the outer fringe of the village began getting commercialized. As the benefits began pouring in, it became the trend.

Jawala Heri

Jawala Heri is situated in West Delhi. Located on the main road going through Paschim Vihar, a posh residential neighbourhood, the village is surrounded by densely inhabited residential colonies consisting of multi-storied flats and houses; so much so that the village is no longer visible from the main road. However, it is well-connected with the rest of the city both in terms of good roads and transport facility.

The total area of the village was 477 acres in 1971; it was reduced to 190 acres in 1981 (Census of India, 1971 and 1981). Obviously, the reduced area of the village between the two censuses shows the loss of 286 acres of land belonging to the village. The village was densely built with little open space left, except what was available as inverted open space, or *aangan* (courtyard). The only remaining small piece of land was at the rear of the village, used by some to keep their cattle. Sometimes there was a small brick and thatched structure for storing dung-cakes, which was also earmarked for construction of residential flats. A small unkempt ground, known as 'Dashahra Park' after the popular Hindu ten-day festival in the month of September-October, was used for Ramlila, for weddings and other social functions in the village.

Unfortunately, the census figures for the years 1951, 1961 and 1991 are not available for Jawala Heri. However, a population of 674 in 1971 is a sufficient indication that the population could not have been too large in the earlier years, neither did any dramatic demographic change took place within this small village between 1951 and 1971. Since the village was urbanized in the 1980s, the population figures are not available separately for the village for 1991. However, the demographic transition taking place in Jawala Heri is all too apparent and fascinating if we look at the census figures for 1971 and 1981. With 40 per cent less area in 1981, its population, both in terms of individuals (674 in 1971 and 1886 in 1981) and households (109 in 1971 and 348 in 1981), almost trebled in one decade. Simultaneously, the male-female ratio fell dramatically (379M: 295F in 1971 and 1149M: 348F in 1981). Obviously, Jawala Heri gained migrant male population, mostly wage-labour migrating to Delhi in search of employment, during the process of urbanization.

The most distinctive and interesting feature of this village is its transformation into a bazaar. Only a few houses in the core of the village had retained rural or semi-rural appearance, possibly because that kind of design is not conducive to commercial use of space. The process of change of structural design of the buildings in Jawala Heri has been rather fast. In commercializing the space available to them, the villagers seemed to have found the most convenient alternative to the loss of their traditional occupation and agrarian land. For many of them would have found it difficult, if not impossible, to immediately switch over to a new job or profession. Turning rentier was obviously the easiest thing to do. They either ploughed in the compensation they received in lieu of their agricultural land acquired by the government for developing urban neighbourhood, or arranged the finance through other sources. In this respect, Jawala Heri's case has been qualitatively different from the other two villages studied here. Commercialization of space has been much faster in Jawala Heri than in the other two cases. Obviously, Jawala Heri learned from the experience of villages preceding in urbanization.[12]

The villagers did not seem to grudge turning rentiers, as it gave them a regular source of income, despite the fact that it had robbed them of privacy and the peace of a residential neighbourhood during the day. The urban neighbourhoods in the vicinity helped the growth and development of commercial activity. Two kinds of commercial complexes are clearly visible in the village. One is a multistoried market-cum-office complex built on the outer fringe of the village facing Paschim Vihar as well as the row just behind these complexes, which have been built or are being built on similar lines. The other is a score of residential houses starting from the third area of the village and extending into its heart, where the ground floor have been transformed into a mini-market, while the upper floors are still used for residential purposes by the owners.

The main market-cum-office complexes built on the front side of Jawala Heri belong to the families of the siblings of Choudhary Jawala Singh Yadav. Although the family is splintered now, they continue to be economically dominant in the village. Thus, there are commercial complexes such as Kishan Chand Shopping Complex, Govardhan Complex, Ram Pal Sons, Murti Complex, and so on. The total number of shops in these commercial complexes range from twenty to six hundred. All sorts of items ranging from daily uses to building and construction material can be found in this market. All structures have been developed within the *lal dora* limit.

On an ideal pattern, the inner village area has lanes crossing in the core centres where there is also an old *peepal* tree. The proliferation of the market has not touched this area of the village because its narrow lanes make it unfit for commercial purposes. As a later addition to urbanization process, the villagers are happy to use the educational facilities offered by the new urban vicinity. Though a small school ran in the *chaupal* of the village and by 1981, it had one primary school, one middle/junior school, and one adult literacy centre, urbanization had

12 This obviously points to the integrational dimension of urbanization. Information flow, demonstration effect, exchange of experiences through village ties (villagers still speak of kin and clan ties across villages) and, of course, education, have made the villagers wiser over the years.

opened up new avenues for them. Similarly, aside from an MCD dispensary and a primary health centre existing there, Jawala Heri appeared satisfied about medical facilities offered by the metropolis too.

The decision to acquire the land owned by the villagers for residential purposes was taken by the DDA in 1961, which issued acquisition notices to the villagers received during 1962-8. The land acquired was developed by the DDA. As the acquisition began, the brick-kilns run by many of the villagers were closed and the land leveled. The compensation paid by the Government was Rs 1 per sq. yd. It started the familiar chain of reaction, in the form of appeal to the judiciary for upward revision of the compensation. In the year 1962, the Session's Court revised the compensation to Rs 1100 per *bigha*. Some of the villagers, not satisfied even with this revision, appealed to the High Court. The High Court revised this amount in the year 1964 to Rs 1700 per *bigha*. However, the maximum amount granted by the High Court did not exceed Rs 5 per square yard. However, in the process, the villagers spent a good part of this money on litigation.

Most of the villagers had smaller land holdings. Naturally, most of these small landowners received small amounts as compensation from the government. Worse, some of these villagers reported that they had still to receive the total compensation amount because of the delay in the court cases. Most of the villagers had spent or invested in some venture or the other 90 per cent of the compensation amount.

SOCIO-ECONOMIC CHANGES

The surrounding areas began to get inhabited around the 1970s. Large residential colonies with houses as well as multi-storied apartment complexes began to be constructed around Jawala Heri. Till 1971, the village remained a residential habitation, predominantly rural in morphology and life-style. However, by 1981, i.e. in just one decade, the face of the village had been transformed significantly. From a residential habitation it had turned into a market place. In the next decade, it was impossible to guess that behind the façade of multi-storied commercial complexes, huge billboards and neon signs, lay a sleepy village where it was still possible to find *dhoti*-clad, *hukkah*-smoking elders.

The villagers pointed out that since there was no market in the vicinity, which could cater to the daily requirements of the new upcoming colonies, the villagers saw an opportunity and the market developed. An owner of a commercial complex gave the information that real estate developers from nearby colonies began approaching the villagers, mainly the members of the dominant family of the village, for constructing shops. The members of the dominant family were their first and natural targets because they owned most of the land, or real estate in the village. The local residents availed of the emerging opportunities and gradually, but steadily, Jawala Heri began transforming from a sleepy rural hamlet engulfed by the rising tide of the expanding metropolitan ocean into a busy and thriving market place. Commercialization was initially restricted to the outer fringes, then gradually, as demands increased, the villagers used this new opportunity to construct shops on the ground floor of their houses.

The descendants of Choudhary Jawala Singh, who have remained the dominant family in the village, owned the largest chunk of landed property in Jawala Heri. Their property was divided amongst the siblings four or five generations later. Thus, the scions of the Jawala Singh family developed the two commercial complexes, which have become the nucleuses of Jawala Heri's business activity. As these two commercial complexes transformed the village into a bustling and busy trading centre, the demand for more commercial space in the area increased and other villagers naturally jumped at this opportunity. In most cases, the compensation money received from the DDA came in handy to effect these changes. It was a good and productive investment by any standard.

The owner of the Kishan Chand Shopping Complex in Jawala Heri, who is a scion of the Jawala Singh family, has constructed a shopping plaza on the first floor, which he claimed was unique not only in that area but in the entire city of Delhi. When he first came up with the idea, the people in the village scoffed at him. Nevertheless, the shopping plaza is a bustling market today. He even conceived the architectural design in which about 40 per cent area of the market had been left as open space and 'galleries' (lounge) had been provided after every two shops, making it a well planned market.

The emphasis in Jawala Heri was on letting out commercial space, mainly for retail trading and not for residential purposes. This gave them a steady income in rent as well as a lump sum as *pagadi*.[13] The *pagadi* in Jawala Heri ranged from Rs. 300,000 to as high as Rs. 2,000,000 at the time of the field work. In some cases, it reduced the tenants' burden on the monthly

---

13 *Pagadi*, literally turban, refers in real estate business parlance to the advance money collected from the tenant at the time of letting out the premises for commercial or residential purposes. This is mostly treated as premium, but in some cases, it is also treated as security.

rent, which ranged from Rs. 250 to Rs. 1,000, depending on the space. Shops in the front naturally fetched more money while those towards the back were let out at lower rates.

The owners of the shopping plaza took pride in traditional values. They had not allowed either a meat shop, or an alcohol shop in the market. The tenants too respected these conditions. The owners of the shopping plaza were happy that their relationship with the tenants was cordial, despite initial hiccups, when the retail trade in the area was going through teething problem. When the shopping complexes came up, for some time, the business was dull and the tenants found it difficult to pay rent. Each of the shopping plaza-owner claimed to have issued receipts for the rent received, indicating their fair intentions and fair deals.

The commercialization of space has had far reaching impact on the residents. The village elders have their own view of the impact of 'easy money' coming as rent. Nonetheless, availability of more cash changed the village a lot. It must be noted at the outset that to most of the villagers, the income from rent was not the primary income. As the village lost its agricultural land and its urbanization became inevitable, many of the residents gradually joined the urban workforce in various capacities. The income from the property thus became an additional income, adding to the families' cash flow.

Jawala Heri is a typical example of a commercial reincarnation of a sleepy village. A few bold initiatives by some members of the dominant family proved to be catalyst for the villagers, whose basic source of sustenance was taken away without any offer for viable and sustainable alternatives for livelihood. The so called compensation granted (not offered), like in case of other such urban villages, was insufficient and unjust, to put it mildly. In addition, litigation made things worse. The villagers adjusted to the changing situation by merging into the millions of metropolitan white and blue collar workers in the organized and unorganized sectors, but the opportunity to transform their living from rural to urban came only through commercialization.

The transformation from rural to urban, however, has not come without problems. Many of the commercial structures in the village being without proper civic authorization, increasing congestion has led to degradation of living environment in the area. For the villagers, the lure of lucre has made them ignore everything else. The problems Jawala Heri now faces is of parking, encroachment of public space, law and order and frequent breakdown of electric supply as unauthorized commercial use has affected the electricity transformers. The undercurrent of socio-psychological turmoil was visible at the individual, family and social levels, but neither this researcher, nor this study is competent to comment upon this phenomenon. It is nevertheless an important, but gray area of social science research.

CONCLUSION

This study of 'urban villages' of Delhi offers several policy conclusions. The three brief case studies of 'urban villages' 'urbanized' at different periods of time, while giving us a perspective and insight into the struggle for survival of these anachronistic 'urban villages' in Delhi, also give us an idea about what went wrong with the planning process. Also, this study is about a totally different move to urban transition from the rural. Naturally, all the activities connected with the basic source of livelihood, i.e. agriculture, cease to operate, or become economically unviable and are closed down. New activities do not start immediately for want of skills and capital; and when they do, they naturally become an appendage to the city. The habitation is not merely engulfed by urban surrounding; it is literally enclaved by and pushed behind urban fortification in the form of multi-storied concrete structures.

Looking at this process in terms of legal processes and administrative procedures, there was nothing wrong with the sequence of events. The land belonging to these villages was legally acquired, following all the administrative procedures of giving them due notice, under the Land Acquisition Act of 1894. The villagers, whose land was acquired, were paid compensation as per the procedure laid down in the Land Acquisition Act. Even complaints were admitted, where possible. The disputes over compensation were entertained by the judiciary and revised awards were accepted by the government.

The basic anomaly in the process surfaced in the way the land of the villages was taken away. It did not merely deprive the villagers of their basic source of livelihood; it also created a sense of directionlessness in the village economy. Despite grant of compensation, the rehabilitation of the village economy and economic and occupational rehabilitation of the villagers was not planned at all. The quantum of compensation immediately came under litigation. The result was that the capital, which could have become the source of restructuring the village economy, lay in abeyance. The urbanization that took away the basic source of the economy, and would support the village economy later, would take years to be completed. The autonomous regenerative capacity of the villages was thus killed.

It is not surprising that the 'urban villages' ceased to be their original self. For, any planning exercise for preventing physical and morphological degeneration was meaningless in the absence of rehabilitation of the village economy. It indeed is a simple planning logic that physical condition of a habitat can be supported through external resources and planning inputs, but in the long run only internal resources would sustain it. This point was completely missed in this context.

Even in the context of planning, it is difficult to surmise the thinking behind putting the so-called 'urban villages' under *lal dora*. For it literally excludes them from the process of urban planning. The protection given to the urban villages to carry out structural changes within the *lal dora* has not done them any good. The resultant chaos is visible in each of the villages. The fact that two of the villages in the sample were 'urbanized', an euphemism for losing their land, in the 1960s they are still neither urban nor rural habitats, which shows that despite some lip service towards their development and some cosmetic changes, these habitations have suffered due to the strange status accorded to them and their virtual exclusion from the process of urban planning.

Due to policy and planning anomalies the 'urban villages' were not given the necessary help to cope with the sudden change in their fortune caused by the acquisition of their agricultural land which was the mainstay of their economy and livelihood. The sudden loss of livelihood for the people, who did not have any other skill to start a new venture, or take up a job, was indeed a traumatic experience. They did cope with it and learnt through mistakes, which proved costly in some cases. The illiterate and unskilled small and marginal farmers and the landless labour were exposed to a vast urban expanse to hunt for a livelihood. Many of them joined the growing army of manual labour at construction sites.

The villages that were urbanized in the 1950s and 1960s took much longer to adjust to the changed situation. The villages urbanized later learnt from their experience. Moreover, by the 1970s and the 1980s the inhabitants of these villages became more aware of the existing and emerging opportunities. Since the villagers made use of educational opportunities available in the metropolis to educate their children, the next generation was better prepared to take on the challenges. This is supported by our data. The commercial use of space in the case of Jawala Heri was much faster than in the case of Munirka. Jawala Heri, of course, did not wait to see its cases settled. The moment residential neighbourhoods came up where the village used to have its farmland; it began offering its space for commercial uses. And, the spaces offered were grabbed like hot cakes. It is clear from the kind of *pagadi* being offered and demanded. This study also brings out the importance of human endeavour to succeed in the face of adversity.

The plight of 'urban villages' reveals the complete absence of participatory processes and transparency in urban planning. It is worthwhile to ask here whether the concept of *Eminent Domain* (requisition of land by the state for public purposes) cannot include participatory processes in a democratic context. In retrospect, even in the larger context of planning of the national capital, making the process participatory would have brought greater compliance and resulted in fewer aberrations to Delhi's Master Plan. The plight of the villages, of course, would certainly have been better had the entire process, beginning from the acquisition of land, been participatory. This would have saved time and resources as the legal disputes and court cases would have been far less. However, the biggest advantage of the planning process would have been that the resettlement of the village economy and of the villagers dispossessed of their land would have been painless and much faster. It was indeed an urgent requirement for the 'urban villages', but an obligation for the government.

REFERENCES

Banga, Indu, ed., *The City in Indian History*, Delhi: Manohar, 1994, rpt 2005.

Barker, D., 'A Conceptual Approach to the Description and Analysis of an Historical Urban System', in *Regional Studies*, 12 (1978), pp. 1-10.

Baxi, Upendra, 'The Travails of Land Use Planning: Compensation and Urbanization', in Indian Law Institute, ed., *Law and Urbanization in India*, Bombay: N. M. Tripathi Ltd., 1969.

Bose, Ashish, *India's Urbanization: 1901-2000*, New Delhi: Tata McGraw Hill, 1980.

Chandra, Umesh, 'Administrative Procedure Under the Land Acquisition Act', in Indian Law Institute, ed., *Law and Urbanization in India*, Bombay: N. M. Tripathi Ltd., 1969.

Childe, Gordon, *What happened in History*, 1964, rpt., Harmondsworth: Penguin Books, 1978.

Delhi Development Authority, *Work Studies relating to the Preparation of Mastar Plan for Delhi*, vol. 1, Delhi: Government of India Press, 1962.

Delhi Development Authority , *Master Plan for Delhi*, Delhi: Government of India Press, 1962.

Delhi Vikas Varta, *Delhi 2001*, A House Journal of DDA, vol. 2, no. 2, Special Issue. 1985.

Desai, P. B. and Pillai, S. Devadas, eds., *Slums and Urbanization*, Bombay: Popular Prakashan, 1990.

Eisenstadt, S.N and Shachar, A., *Society, Culture and Urbanization*, Newbury Park, Calif.: Sage Publications, 1987.

Howland, Marie, 'Delhi's Large-Scale Land Acquisition, Development, and Disposal Policy: An Appraisal', in *Urban rural Planning Thought,* XVIII (I), January, 1975, pp.23-54.

India, Government of, *Gazetteer of Rural Delhi*, New Delhi, 1987.

Jain, M.P., 'Administrative Procedure in Land Acquisition', in Indian Law Institute, ed., *Law and Urbanization in India*, Bombay: N. M. Tripathi Ltd., 1969.

Jha, Gangadhar 'Growing under Master Plan: A Study of Delhi', *NAGARLOK*, vol X, no. 3, July -Sept. 1978.

Mann, Peter H., *An approach to urban sociology*, London: Routledge and Kegan Paul, 1970.

Meadows, Paul, 'The City, Technology and History', in *Urbanism, urbanization and change: Comparative perspectives*, London: Addison Wesley, 1976.

Mehra, Ajay K., *The politics of urban redevelopment: A study of old Delhi*, New Delhi: Sage Publications India Pvt. Ltd., 1991.

Misra, S. C., 'Urban History in India', in Indu Banga, ed., *The City in Indian History*, Delhi: Manohar, 1991, pp. 1-7.

Mookherjee, Debnath, 'Density and Environment: An Exploratory Study of Rural-Urban Patterns', in Giriraj Gupta, ed., *Main currents in Indian sociology: Urban India*, New Delhi: Vikas, 1983, pp. 86-108.

Rai, P. Bhagwan Das and Shafi, Sayed S., 'The Planned Development of Delhi', in *City development plans and their implementation*, Papers and Proceedings of a Seminar, New Delhi: Centre for Urban Studies, Indian Institute Public Administration, 1977.

Sharma, C.L., Structural changes of villages on the periphery of a metropolis: A case study of Delhi, Unpublished Thesis, School of Planning and Architecture, New Delhi, 1981.

Sharma, R.C., ed., *India's urban land policy and development finance*, Delhi: Seema Publications, 1988.

Shukla, Vibhooti, *Urbanization and economic growth*, Bombay: OUP, 1996.

Sorokin, P. A. and Zimmerman, C. C., *Principles of rural-urban sociology*, New York, 1929.

Sundaram, K.V., *Urban and regional planning in India*, New Delhi: Vikas, 1977.

Tyagi, V. K., *Urban growth and urban villages: A case study of Delhi*, New Delhi: Kalyani Publishers, 1982.

Wirth, Louis, 'Urbanism as a Way of Life', in *American Journal of Sociology*, vol. 44, July 1938, pp. 3-24.

12

RESIDENTIAL PRACTICES, CREATION AND USE OF URBAN SPACE: UNAUTHORIZED COLONIES IN DELHI

VÉRONIQUE DUPONT

INTRODUCTION

The development of Delhi fits in a very interventionist context including the application of an urban Master Plan, regulatory measures specific to land use, ownership and acquisitions, and the implementation of various housing programmes. However, these measures did not prevent high speculation in land and proliferation of 'squatter settlements' and 'unauthorized colonies'. The public housing policies have failed to respond to the demands of large sections of the urban population, in particular the lower-middle classes and the poor who were relegated to the informal housing sector. In this chapter, we shall focus on the unauthorized colonies that have come up on agricultural land in the rural-urban fringe and shelter one fourth of the population of the Indian capital.

This study will allow us to examine several issues related to urban growth and urbanization problems in large developing metropolises:

- the modalities of creation and development of 'unauthorized colonies' in the urban periphery – that will illustrate a case of uncontrolled suburbanization;
- the interactions between the citizens' practices in the use of urban space and the measures of the public authorities;
- the housing and environment conditions in these estates and ensuing problems;
- the residential strategies of access to home ownership or affordable lodging on rent;

the population dynamics of these peripheral neighbourhoods including the migratory and intra-urban residential itineraries.

Some basic issues will be first examined at the level of the Delhi urban agglomeration, on the basis of secondary data provided by public agencies, as well as published reports and studies. This will be substantiated by a more detailed investigation of residential practices and trajectories at the micro level, with a case study of the Mayur Vihar zone in East Delhi. The latter is based on our own demographic surveys on population mobility and housing conditions, completed by qualitative observation and in-depth interviews.

It is necessary, at the outset, to clarify the concept of 'unauthorized colonies' in the context of a planned city and to distinguish this form of irregular settlement from the 'squatter settlements'.

Unauthorized colonies consist of illegal sub-divisions of land sold as plots to individual buyers by private owners or clandestine colonisers.

> The subdivision is illegal either because it violates zoning and/or subdivision regulations, or because the required permission for land subdivision has not been obtained. Land may be privately owned, under notification for expropriation, urban fringe agricultural land or common land of a village engulfed by city growth. The sale or transfer of land and hence ownership of the plot may have a legal or quasi-legal status, but because of the illegality of the subdivision, plot holders cannot get permission to build. In addition the area is not eligible for an extension of infrastructure services. (Banerjee 2002: 46)

Thus, they differ from *squatter settlements* where "land (public or private) is illegally occupied and building activity takes place regardless of, and/or in violation of, all development control regulations. Occupants have absolutely no legal rights over land or its development " (Banerjee 2002: 46).

Of course, while using the terms 'irregular' and 'illegal', and as warned by A. Gilbert (quoted by Smets and Hansen 1996: 95) one should realize that "illegality lies in the acts of the lawmaker" and that it "is dependent on the dominant economic, political, and social forces in society" (Gilbert 1990: 17-27).

While in general the squatter settlements shelter the poorest sections of the urban population in the most precarious housing conditions, the socio-economic status of the residents in Delhi's unauthorized colonies is fairly heterogeneous, as it will be shown below.

THE DEMOGRAPHIC AND URBAN PLANNING CONTEXT

The emergence and growth of unauthorized layouts in the fringes of developing metropolises is a widespread phenomenon, in India (Auclair 1998, Mussania 1997, Ramanchandra 1989, Schenk 1993, Banerjee 2000), as well as in other Third World countries (Durand-Lasserve 1986, Durand-Lasserve and Royston 2002, Dureau et al. 2000). Yet, in Delhi this process has taken place in a unique historical, demographic and urban political context which has contributed to its magnitude.

Historical Circumstances and Demographic Constraints

After Independence in 1947, the capital of the newly formed Indian Union had to face a massive transfer of population following the partition of India and Pakistan. Thus, immediately after 1947, Delhi with its 900,000 inhabitants, received 495,000 refugees from western Panjab and Sindh, whereas 329,000 Muslims left the capital for Pakistan.[1] The interim period between the two censuses, i.e. 1941-51, showed the highest demographic growth in the history of the capital: the population of the urban agglomeration increased from 0.7 million to 1.4 million, representing an annual growth rate of 7.5 per cent which has been unequalled since then.

Nevertheless, in the post-independence era, the population growth of Delhi has been remarkably rapid for an urban agglomeration of this size, oscillating between 4 per cent and 5 per cent per year, to reach 12.8 million inhabitants in 2001. During these last decades, migration continued to have a significant contribution to urban growth although it relatively slowed down in the eighties. Migrants with less than ten years of residence accounted for 62 per cent of the population of the National Capital Territory of Delhi in 1971, 60 per cent in 1981, and it declined to 50 per cent in 1991. In the five years preceding the 1991 census, about

1 Source of data: Ministry of Rehabilitation, Annual Report on Evacuation, Relief and Rehabilitation of Refugees, 1954-1955 (quoted in Datta 1986).

883,500 in-migrants settled in the Territory of Delhi, almost 90 per cent of whom settled in the Delhi urban agglomeration.[2]

The Urban Policy: Valuable Intentions and Adverse Effects

At the time of Independence, the capital was not prepared to face such demographic pressure. Because of the urgency of the situation, the central government undertook several urban development programmes from 1947 to 1957, but without co-ordination and planning (Milbert 1998). Thus, strong pressure on land and increasing demand for housing resulted in growing speculation in the private sector, while squatter settlements proliferated in the city, and unauthorized colonies in the urban fringes. By 1962, there were 110 unauthorized colonies, housing around 220,000 people, which accounted for 9 per cent of the city population (Gupta 1992: 37).

The need to formulate a master plan in order to orient and control the future growth of Delhi became evident. In 1957, the Delhi Development Authority (DDA) was established with the mandate to elaborate and execute the Master Plan. Due to Delhi's status as the national capital, this institution was placed under the control of the central government. In order to prevent land hoarding and speculation and to provide the DDA with the legal means to implement the plan, the bulk of agricultural land was notified for acquisition in 1959, and an urban land policy formulated in 1961: the 'scheme for large-scale acquisition, development and disposal of land'. Consequently, all lands (in the Territory of Delhi) which were meant to be urbanized according to the Plan were placed under the control of the DDA, thereby creating government monopoly both in land acquisition and supply (Billand 1990, Jain 1990, Datta 1995, Rishub, 2002). The first Master Plan of Delhi – and also the first of this kind in India – was promulgated in 1962 and is still in force.

The DDA further launched various housing programmes, including the construction of flats for sale to private households of different income groups and the allotment of serviced plots on a 99 year lease-hold basis to private households and co-operative group housing societies. On its internet website[3] the DDA claims to have 'generated' (directly or indirectly) more than a million dwelling units through these

[2] For a detailed analysis of the pattern of growth and the migration flows in Delhi, see Dupont 2000.

[3] www.ddadelhi.com

two modes since the inception of its housing activities in 1967-8. In the category of built apartments, approximately 276,000 dwellings units were constructed by the DDA from 1966-7 to 2000-01, which in 2001 housed nearly 10 per cent of families of the agglomeration.[4] Another scheme concerned the development and allotment of land for the resettlement of slum dwellers and squatters evicted from central areas of the city. This last policy which resorts to coercive measures including the demolition of slum and squatter settlements was pursued most actively during the 'Emergency' (1975-7) during which time about 152,300 families were forcibly evicted and sent to 'resettlement colonies', all located —at that time— on the urban outskirts.[5]

However, the restrictive land control measures of the Master Plan did not prevent the persistence of high speculation in land nor the multiplication of non conforming settlements and constructions (including squatter settlements and unauthorized colonies).[6] On the other hand, the public housing options were not able to fulfil the demand of large sections of the population.[7] If the extent of the unmet demand should be viewed in relation to the weight of the demographic constraints mentioned earlier, the housing deficit affected more particularly the lower-middle and working classes whose requirements were not satisfied and that were forced to resort to the informal housing sector.

Although the initial objective of the DDA's housing policy was to promote social equity through the allotment of a majority of plots and apartments to the low income groups and economically weaker sections, in the last analysis, the public sector housing schemes benefited much more the middle and upper income groups (Pugh 1990, Billand 1990, Gupta 1992, Milbert 1998). The major reason is that "the poorer people sell their housing rights for cash in order to meet the more pressing needs of food and other basic necessities" (Pugh 1990: 178). The target populations are often not touched, because the initial cost is too high,

---

4 For a detailed study of the DDA flats and the residential practices of its inhabitants, see Dupont 2003.

5 Source of data: Delhi Development Authority (see Jain 1990: 173).

6 The case of unauthorized colonies is detailed below. As for squatter settlements, their population was estimated to be approximately 3 million in 2000 – or nearly 25 per cent of Delhi's total population (source of data: Slum and Jhuggi Jhompri Wing, Municipal Corporation of Delhi). The numerous evictions of squatter settlements in 2000-2001 are however likely to have affected the population figure for 2001.

7 For instance, until 1981, the DDA was able to satisfy only 50 per cent of the demand for its built apartments (Billand 1990); in 1990, only 45 per cent of the demand was met (Misra et al. 1998). In 1999, the DDA acknowledged that there were some 48,000 applications for its apartments on the waiting list (DDA website).

the access to credit too difficult and, lastly, because the market price of the plots and apartments is much higher, inducing people to sell at a profit. The misuse of public sector housing schemes is a general tendency, also seen in other Indian cities and in other developing countries (Milbert 1986, Durand-Lasserve 1986).

To some extent, the proliferation of unplanned and illegal settlements can be seen as a perverse effect of the government policies for urban land and planning, and a consequence of the limitations and implementation failures of the Master Plan (Billand 1990; Gupta 1992). The Delhi land policy had excluded the private formal sector from the land delivery process. In such a context, the time lag between notification and actual acquisition of land, combined with the sluggishness and inadequacy of land development and housing programmes by the DDA, led clandestine colonisers to develop unauthorized colonies in the rural fringes to respond to the unmet demand for residential places. In addition, the adoption of high standards of development and construction by the Master Plan has favoured a model of elitist urbanism, at the expense of the housing needs of the mass of lower income groups (Milbert 1998, Rishub 2002). Thus, as stressed by R. C. Gupta: "Ironically, the Master Plan of Delhi, which was to control and direct the development of Delhi, saw the proliferation of unauthorised colonies at a pace faster than before" (Gupta 1992: 59).

Yet, from its inception, the Master Plan envisaged the development of Delhi within its regional framework, with the identification of a Metropolitan Area and subsequently a much larger National Capital Region, provided with a Planning Board since 1985. Planning policy laid emphasis on the promotion of peripheral towns and regional urban centres located beyond the metropolitan area through the strengthening of their economic base, in order to slow down the inflow of migrants in the capital by reorienting them towards other towns in the region (National Capital Region Planning Board 1988). One expected outcome was to ease the population pressure on Delhi and on its housing problems. Although the ring towns in the metropolitan area did grow at a much faster rate than the Delhi Urban Agglomeration,[8] the measures for developing them had in fact increased the attraction of the whole metropoli-

8 The differential of population growth between the ring towns as a whole (Gurgaon, Ghaziabad, Loni, Noida, Bahadurgarh and Faridabad-Ballabgarh) and the Delhi Urban Agglomeration proper reached a maximum during the 1971-81 decade (8.6 per cent per year as against 4.6 per cent), and it still was remarkable in the next two decades (6.5 per cent as against 3.9 per cent during the 1981-91 period, and 6.4 per cent as against 4.3 per cent in the 1991-2001 period).

tan area, including the capital and its hinterland. The spatial expansion of Delhi forms now a near-continuous urban spread encompassing the peripheral towns and the uncontrolled urbanization of the rural-urban fringe of the capital has continued unabated.

Emergence and Development of Unauthorized Colonies

The modalities by which unauthorized colonies in Delhi emerged and developed is well documented, therefore this section will attempt to provide a synthesis of published studies and reports, drawing in particular from A. Bose (1980), A. K. Jain (1990), C. Billand (1990), R. C. Gupta (1992), B. Banerjee (1994) and N. Rishub (2002).

In the post-independence period, the development of unauthorized colonies in Delhi is related to the massive influx of refugees into the capital, and thereafter to the shortage and inadequacy of housing options in the formal land and housing market. Initially, these settlements were set up around refugees' rehabilitation camps, taking advantage of existing infrastructure and of a lax government control over land on humanitarian grounds, while others were located along major access routes, for easier commuting to workplaces. Subsequent colonies emerged as extension of existing ones and around the nucleus of urban villages (Gupta 1992). More recently, the emergence of unauthorized estates has extended beyond the urbanized limits of Delhi, towards the rural hinterland, affecting the periphery of village settlements (Jain 1990). The proliferation of unauthorized colonies has contributed in a decisive way to the urbanization of the urban-rural fringes of the capital.

The foundation of unauthorized colonies has followed a more or less fixed pattern over time: the sale of agricultural land, after illegal subdivision, to individual households, either directly by the landlord or through a clandestine coloniser (Gupta 1992). The layouts are illegal because they do not conform to land-use zoning, sub-division and building regulations. Moreover, following the enforcement of the government policy of large-scale land acquisition, development and disposal, many colonies were located on land that was in various stages of compulsory public acquisition (Banerjee 1994: 1). Long delays between the notification of land and its actual acquisition by the DDA favoured transfers of notified land on power of the attorney (a procedure that allows a land owner to pass on the use rights of his property to someone without actually transferring its ownership). In order to ban such practices, the Delhi Lands

(Restrictions on Transfer) Act was enforced in June 1972. Yet, transfers of notified land continued through other arrangements such as gifting away the plot (Banerjee 1994: 12). Although unauthorized colonies show an urban morphology with a planned layout, they lack basic amenities, at least at the initial stages of their formation. The illegal status of agricultural land sub-division into a housing colony makes them ineligible for municipal services.[9]

Being aware of the illegality of the colony, and that municipal sanction for constructing a house cannot be obtained is, however, not a deterrent factor for many potential buyers who speculate on the future regularization of the settlement or who, in any case, cannot afford housing options in the formal market.

Illegality and Patronage

The development of unauthorized colonies in the periphery of Delhi represents at the same time a process of informal and uncontrolled suburbanization and the outcome of a very organized – though clandestine – system involving "a nexus of property agents, officials and politicians" (Jain 1990: 172). Furthermore, it is often associated with "a whole range of malpractices: municipal corruption, political nepotism and, above all, plain and simple swindling" (A. Bose 1980: 225). Land mafia,

---

[9] An evocative and detailed account of the formation of an unauthorized colony is given by A. Bose (1980: 226): "A typical illegal colonizer buys agricultural land from village on the outskirts of the city, does a superficial levelling of the land, places a row of bricks along the boundaries, demarcates the plots with chalklines, gets a simple blue print (very often not to scale) prepared for the colony, hires a tent, a table with a glass-top, half a dozen of chairs and puts up a signboard indicating the name of the colony. He then pitches his tent, puts in his tables and chairs, the blueprint under the glass-top of the table, and he is ready for business. He also hires a taxi to fetch customers. Sales are brisk, for the prices are fantastically low compared to the prevailing market rates in Delhi.

Clerks, school teachers, small traders and the like are all attracted – they dream of building their own house in Delhi and getting out of the clutches of landlords. When they buy the land, they are given receipts, the transaction is even registered and a stamp duty paid and the purchaser returns home greatly satisfied with the world. Perhaps it is his life-time's savings which he has invested in the land.

Very soon his trouble begin. He learns that the colony where he has bought land will get no water, sewerage connection or electricity – because the plan for the colony did not have the prior approval of the Municipal Corporation. Very often he learns that he cannot even build a house on his plot because area of Z Colony is in fact not a residential area."

land grabbing, corruption, the "shady nexus between land sharks, slumlords, property owners, government officials and politicians" (Kanungo 1999: 13) are regularly denounced by the press (see also T. Bose 1998). "The dynamics of patronage" seems to be inherent to the development of illegal settlements in Delhi like in other cities (Smets and Hansen 1996, Schenk 1993). The role of intermediary agents is crucial from the stage of formation of the colony and thereafter for its development: contacts with bureaucrats and politicians are needed to safeguard the settlement, to have access to civic amenities and lobby for its regularization (Banerjee 1994).

Regularization of Unauthorized Colonies

Although this chapter does not intend to present a thorough analysis of the government policies for unauthorized colonies and their regularization, some outlines need to be given at this point to better understand the process of development of these settlements, their population and social dynamics, and to highlight some significant issues at stake. For a detailed policy analysis and a presentation of the technical aspects and institutional framework of the regularization procedure, one can consult in particular the works of B. Banerjee (1994, 2002) and N. Rishub (2002) that will be primarily referred to in this section.

The lack of adequate infrastructure in unauthorized colonies and the pressure from politicians who are receptive to the demands of an important electorate, can create untenable or explosive situations for the town authorities. Therefore, government repeatedly introduced subsequent regularization procedures to legalise the unauthorized colonies. This attitude, combining *laisser-faire* and *a posteriori* regularization, does not exclude limited demolitions of offending structures. According to B. Banerjee (1994: 8): "It can be said that the public intervention in unauthorised colonies has followed a pragmatic approach, accepting the reality of the situation but at the same time not approving of its principle." It is recognized that the total demolition of the unauthorized colonies would entail a gross national waste, whereas regularization, by allowing for the provision of proper civic amenities, would contribute to maintain the conditions of hygiene and health in the city. Yet, for environmentalists, "regularisation has come to mean gaining legitimacy without substantially improving environmental conditions" (Rishub 2002: 72), and has provoked the opposition of some NGOs to the regularization process, as illustrated later in this chapter. Subsequent regularization and the absence of large-scale deterrent action has also been perceived as an indirect encouragement for the development of new unauthorized colonies, since prospective buyers hoped their settlement would obtain a regular status in the future, thereby guaranteeing the long-term economic profitability of their investments (Billand 1990, Rishub 2002).

When the first policy of regularization was initiated in 1961, it concerned around 110 colonies, and "was in response to political pressure exerted by plot holders under threat of losing their land through public acquisition" (Banerjee 1994: 15). A new regularization operation took place in 1969, for colonies that came in existence before February 1967; it covered 64 additional colonies. In 1977, government announced another regularization policy taking into consideration 612 settlements (Jain 1990: 172).

The regularization procedure is always subject to a cut-off date and to a series of conditions, including fitting the structures in a conforming layout plan and the payment of regularization and development charges by the residents. The entire process is a cumbersome and lengthy one, facing the resistance of the plots holders to comply with all the requirements. Thus,

> despite almost four decades of regularization operations, only five colonies, out of about 800, have been fully regularized in terms of layout, lease deeds, services and facilities and payment of regularization and development charges. [Yet,] the mere announcement of official policy or local government resolution to regularize settlements leads to immunity and lobbying for infrastructure provision. (...) Irrespective of whether a settlement is regularized or not, inclusion of the settlement in the 'list' is projected as a guarantee for regularization. (Banerjee 2002: 52-3)

A policy which aims at regularising unauthorized colonies that came into existence before 31 March 1993 is again on the agenda of the town planners with reference to a list of 1071 settlements identified by aerial survey. The implementation of this policy was delayed by judicial intervention, following a Public Interest Litigation filed in 1993 against the regularization move, on environmental grounds, by an NGO called 'Common Cause'. The Delhi High Court eventually ordered in 1998 that the regularization policy should be finalized and 'Common Cause' lost its case. Divergence between the Union Government (that is involved in the town and planning decisions affecting the national capital) and the Delhi Government over the conditions for regularization and the list of colonies to be taken into account further delayed the finalization of the procedure.[10] In particular, the Union government has ignored the demand of the Delhi government in 1998 for inclusion of settlements that appeared between 1993 and 31 December 1997. In February 2001, the Union Government submitted in the High Court the comprehensive guide lines for regularization, including more severe and restrictive provisions than in the previous policies.[11] For example, in addition to development charges at the cost of the residents, rates with penalties are also imputed, while certain categories of colonies are excluded from the regularization process.[12] Three and a half year later, the decision on the regularization of unauthorized colonies and its implementation were still pending matters.

How Many People Live in Unauthorized Colonies and Who are They?

In addition to nearly 800 unauthorized colonies that were declared for regularization in the 1960s and 1970s, another 1300 unauthorized colonies have come up in the following two decades (Government of National Capital Territory of Delhi 1996: 11).[13] In 1998, the population of these new settlements was roughly estimated at almost three millions by the NGO 'Common Cause', which would amount to one fourth of the total population of the capital city.

Beside the significant increase in numbers of unauthorized colonies, a twofold process of spatial expansion and densification has contributed to the growth of these settlements. Most of the existing colonies have increased their areas since their origin while, at the same time, sub-division of the plots, incremental construction and renting part of the houses raised the population density (Gupta 1992).

---

[10] The Union Government was led by the Bharatiya Janata Party and the Delhi government by the Congress party.

[11] Civil *Writ Petition No. 4771/93 – Common Cause (Regd) Society* Vs *Union of India and others.*

[12] See the above-mentioned CWP; and for a synthetic presentation of the official guidelines, see Rishub 2002: 69.

[13] This figure is quoted for the year 1995; it includes the list of 1071 colonies considered for regularization under the current proposed policy.

Initially, unauthorized colonies appealed to low and lower-middle income groups, households whose need to construct their homes so outweighed the lack and bad quality of the utilities and services provided, that they were willing to accept the minimum available (or even the deplorable conditions). Since some savings for initial investment in the plot is needed, the inhabitants of unauthorized colonies are better off than those residing in squatter settlements, but they are not well off enough to afford investment in the legal land market. The payment schedules proposed by the colonizers were also staggered to attract such potential buyers. Often, in order to make their investment profitable, the new house owners rent out one or several rooms, or one storey, in their habitation. Thus these settlements also supply a rental sector with relatively cheap lodgings, as compared to the rents in the formal housing market. According to sample surveys conducted by the DDA between 1981-6, unauthorized colonies (including those under regularization) provided accommodation mostly to low-income groups[14] (65 per cent) and to lower-middle income groups[15] (18 per cent). The same survey revealed that only 3 per cent families had piped water, 30 per cent depended upon public hydrant; sewage was available to 5 per cent of the families, while 60 per cent depended on septic tanks (Jain 1990: 172).

Nevertheless, the uncontrolled urbanization of the outskirts of Delhi is also, to a lesser extent, the effect of the residential strategies implemented by high-income groups. The construction of luxurious 'farm houses' in the southern rural-urban fringes of Delhi is a well-known case. As they are located within agricultural lands and were initially genuine farms, the civic authorities (the Municipal Corporation of Delhi and the DDA) continued to apply the rules governing farmlands to such zones, seeking to limit the built-up area in relation to the natural green and cultivated spaces. The agricultural nature of such lands is, however, often distorted. Luxurious, sprawling villas, surrounded by large parks and protected by high walls, have become the fashion instead, not to mention swimming pools which are filled even at times of water scarcity – as farmers do not have to pay for water and get subsidized power for tube-wells. Usually, 'farm house' owners are people from the top income bracket who have been able to build veritable havens of tranquillity and peace on the outskirts of one of the most polluted capitals of the world. When urban norms are flouted, the mushrooming of such estates in a specific area leads to the formation of unauthorized

---

[14] Households with Rs 500 to 1000 per month in 1981-6.

[15] Households with Rs 1000 to 2000 per month in 1981-6.

colonies of very high standing, benefiting moreover from a certain immunity owing to the efficient network with politicians and bureaucrats, maintained by the rich villa owners.[16]

Interestingly, the existence of 'rich' unauthorized colonies is recognized explicitly in the proposed policy of regularization that has introduced for the first time a distinction between 'affluent' and 'non affluent' colonies. Thus, in the guidelines for regularization of unauthorized colonies that the Union Government submitted in the High Court, section 1.8 reads as follows:

> In the case of unauthorized colonies on public lands, occupied by non-affluent sections, the cost of land as per notified rates of L&DO[17]/DDA together with a penalty of 10 per cent of the total land cost would be recovered. In cases where the unauthorized colonies on public land are inhabited by affluent sections, the cost of land at the current market value plus a penalty of 50 per cent on the same will be recovered. The affluent/non affluent colonies have been categorized on the basis of following parameters: (a) location of the colony, (b) average plot size, (c) quality of construction, and (c) standard of living of the average inhabitant of the colony based on indicators such as use of air-conditioners, cars, etc.[18]

It is important to underline that unauthorized colonies are far from constituting a homogenous category, they present a wide range of housing standards and different socio-economic statuses. Moreover, these settlements are subject to considerable physical transformations and socio-economic changes over time. At the initial stage, the unauthorized

---

16 For instance, A. Soni (2000: 76) denounced the process at work in the Mehrauli countryside: "Sainik Farms (South of Mehrauli-Badarpur Road), Ruchi Vihar (behind Vasant Kunj), Andheria Bagh (at the location of the ancient mango orchards of the same name, near Mehrauli), are arrogant complexes of palatial mansions with gardens, enclosed behind tall boundary walls. They are, from the point of view of civic authorities, none other than unauthorized colonies, built illegally on agricultural land. But somehow, this derogatory definition is never applied to them. Rather, they are regarded as 'farmhouses'. Their denizens are celebrities of the city's cocktail circuit, and have the means to arrange their own electricity, water, drainage and sewage disposal services. They often indulge in massive power theft with the connivance of law-enforcement agencies."

17 Land and Development Officer.

18 Civil Writ Petition No 4771/93 – *Common Cause (Regd) Society* Vs *Union of India and others*.

colonies are poorly equipped; their infrastructure and urban amenities improve gradually due to the concerted actions of the residents and their 'patrons'. Increase in land prices follows the process of consolidation of the colony, its infrastructure and commercial development, as well as regularization prospects, and eventually entails changes in the residents' socio-economic profile. As noted by C.J. Billand (1990: 2.26): "These trends in land markets are paralleled by similar trends in populations served. Increased trading activity in unauthorized colonies (...) resulting from rising prices forces low and in some cases middle-income groups out of these markets". The regularization of the colony further stimulates the trend toward its gentrification. Yet, there seems to be some reaction to this process, and when prices become unaffordable even for middle-class families, the process of plot subdivision and sale starts so that plots become smaller and more affordable (Mitra 1983, Banerjee 1994: 30, Rishub 2002: 72).

The subsequent case study of Mayur Vihar (East Delhi) provides a detailed illustration of the housing conditions in unauthorized colonies and the socio-economic characteristics of their residents, as well as their practices to cope with their illegal status.

MAYUR VIHAR IN EAST DELHI: A CASE STUDY

The zone selected for this case study,[19] Mayur Vihar – Trilokpuri, forms a widespread area located in the eastern periphery of Delhi – the Trans-

[19] This case study is part of a larger research programme on spatial mobility and residential practices of Delhi's population, and its effect on the dynamics of the metropolis (see Dupont 1997, Dupont and Prakash 1999). The programme was financed by the *Institut de Recherche pour le Développement* (ex-ORSTOM) with additional funding from the CNRS within the framework of *Action Concertée en Sciences Sociales* ORSTOM-CNRS and of *PIR-Villes*. In India, our programme was conducted with the collaboration and support of the *Centre de Sciences Humaines* of New Delhi (French Ministry of Foreign Affairs) and the Institute of Economic Growth (Delhi).

The methodology applied combined quantitative and qualitative approaches and different sources of information to integrate the following:

- an analysis of secondary data and information available on Delhi and its metropolitan area, including a press-review;
- a statistical survey of population samples from 7 zones in the metropolitan area, supplemented by in-depth interviews of sub-samples of individuals;
- the formation of a data base of background information on each zone studied, by the compilation of data and existing documents, direct observation and interviews (Sidhu 1995).

Yamuna sector. This zone is characterized by average to very high residential densities, and rapid population growth during the last 20 years (during the 1981-91 decade: 5 per cent to 13.8 per cent per year as against 3.9 per cent for the entire urban agglomeration within its 1991 boundaries). Various modes of urbanization are found which exemplify urban expansion in the peripheries of the capital and the outcome of the interactions between institutional and non-institutional actors. This allows us to better appraise the conditions of the unauthorized colonies as compared to other neighbouring settlements.[20]

The original villages of the zone are nowadays hemmed in by the new residential neighbourhoods that gradually developed from 1970-5:

- unauthorized (and *a posteriori* regularized) colonies;
- a large resettlement colony (Trilokpuri) set up during the emergency state (1975-77) to relocate the slum dwellers evicted from squatter settlements in the inner city;
- many blocks of flats of three to four storeys built by the Delhi Development Authority in the late 1970s and early 1980s for the middle-income and low-income groups (the 'DDA flats');
- many other blocks of flats built since 1985 by co-operative group housing societies;
- and, in the interstices of the urban fabric, slum pockets, or more precisely squatter settlement clusters with very precarious housing, sometimes just adjoining upper-class apartment blocks.

These different types of settlement correspond to very distinct segments of the housing stock in terms of housing standards and equipment; this variety also reflects directly the composition of the population that shows a juxtaposition of different socio-economic groups.

Mayur Vihar - Trilokpuri was one of the selected zones, located in the eastern periphery of Delhi. The statistical survey conducted in March 1995 in this zone covered a sample of 342 households, out of which 60 households in unauthorized colonies (or under regularization) corresponding to 282 individuals. In-depth interviews in this zone focused on the various factors influencing the choice of residence and the environmental conditions; most of them were conducted by Mriga Sidhu in 1996 (Sidhu 1996). The system of investigation was completed by new field visits in March 1997 in April 1999, in order to appraise the physical transformations at work in the studied areas.

20 This chapter does not intend, however, to present a systematic differential analysis of the various types of settlements and their socio-economic profile; for this purpose, see Dupont 2004.

Environmental and Housing Conditions

The unauthorized colonies were the first housing estates to emerge around the villages, according to the formation pattern common to this type of informal settlement (as described above). Like elsewhere in Delhi, since these housing estates came up in ignorance or disobedience of all urban planning norms, they are not recognized by the municipality and therefore do not have the benefit of its services (tarring of roads, drinking water connection, sewage disposal system, street cleaning and waste collection). It is therefore left to the residents to organise themselves in order to remedy the deficiencies: to install water hand-pumps, septic tanks, storm water drains, etc. Residents' committees were formed with elected representatives to lobby the concerned public authorities and ministries for provision of civic amenities. In that way most of the unauthorized colonies of Mayur Vihar have managed to obtain electricity supply for their houses, and in some sections also street lighting. In those blocks that were not electrified, the inhabitants tap the electricity illegally by hooking on wires to nearby poles. Through collective actions, the inhabitants try to have access to more urban services, the final objective being the status of an authorized colony for which they need to put pressure on the government officials.[21]

Due to political patronage and as part of the policies of regularization implemented by the Delhi Development Authority (see above), some unauthorized colonies in Mayur Vihar, or in some cases only certain sections of these colonies, have been recognized for regularization (in the sample households for this type of settlement, 21 per cent live in a regularized colony or block).[22] Since the regularization procedures are not systematic nor uniform, even within the same colony (which is due to criteria of eligibility, in particular the cut-off date), this entails an unequal access to urban services and basic amenities among the residents of the same neighbourhood. The colonies or sections still unauthorized are generally more recent than the regularized ones, and they undergo a continuous process of urbanization and consolidation.

The unauthorized colonies of Mayur Vihar cater mainly to lower to middle income groups. Thus, in the sample population living in this type

---

21 In some other unauthorized colonies, the residents have also resorted to public demonstrations.

22 However, for simplification purpose, in this section, and unless otherwise specified, the general term 'unauthorized colonies' will refer both to the unauthorized colonies without any official recognition and to those at various stages of the regularization procedure.

of settlement, 73 per cent of the employed declared a monthly income below 3000 rupees (in 1995), whereas in the DDA and co-operative group-housing societies apartments blocks, the corresponding proportion is only 13 per cent. The characteristics of the housing stock surveyed in 1995 reveal clearly not only the lack of comfort, but also the precariousness of many dwellings units in unauthorized colonies:

- 18 per cent of the structures were not fully consolidated,
- 66 per cent of households lived in a single room,
- 57 per cent had no separate room for the kitchen,
- 36 per cent had no bathroom,
- 18 per cent had no private toilets in their home nor shared toilets on the premises,
- 13 per cent had no access to drinking water in their home,
- and if only 3 per cent had no electricity, this is due to illegal connection when necessary.

For a general comparative perspective, it can be recalled here that, according to the 1991 Census, 45 per cent households in Delhi lived in single-room dwellings and 33 per cent had no access to toilets on their premises.[23]

Some sections of unauthorized colonies in Mayur Vihar are difficult to distinguish, in terms of housing as well as environmental conditions, from the adjoining squatter settlements. For example, there is no visible demarcation or space between the unauthorized colony of Shashi Garden and the squatter settlement of Jawarhar Mohalla. As a matter of fact, this squatter settlement benefited initially from a better provision of urban services (in particular, piped water and public toilets) as part of the 'environmental improvement of urban slum' and 'urban basic services' programmes implemented by the Municipal Corporation. Eventually, after repeated requests of the residents from the unauthorized colony, the Municipal Corporation extended the piped water connection from the squatter settlement to the unauthorized colony. Furthermore, those inhabitants of the unauthorized colony whose houses were not equipped

---

23 The census data pertaining to access to drinking water are not comparable with the results of our survey. According to the census, only 4 per cent of households did not have access to drinking water in 1991, the broad definition being: "If the household had access to drinking water supplied from a tap, hand pump or tube well situated within or outside the premises, it is considered as having access to safe drinking water". In our survey, 'having access to drinking water' meant 'from a tap, hand pump or tube well situated *within* the premises'.

with private toilet and septic tank made use of the public toilets located in the slum.

The characteristics of the dwelling for each type of settlement in the Mayur Vihar zone are given in Table 1. This shows the relative position of the unauthorized colonies. On the one hand, the housing conditions are considerably worse-off than in co-operative group housing societies apartments and DDA flats; on the other hand, they are clearly better-off on average than in squatter settlements, but not necessarily better than dwellings in urban villages and in resettlement colonies.

Table 1: Characteristics of the dwelling by type of settlement in Mayur Vihar (East Delhi)

Characteristics of the dwelling unit (d.u.)	TYPE OF SETTLEMENT						
	Resettlement Colony	DDA flats	Co-operative group housing societies	Urban villages	**Un-authorized or regularized colonies**	Squatter settlements	All types
No. of yrs since built	percentage distribution for each type of settlement						
< 5	1.5	–	28.2	2.2	**33.9**	–	10.2
5 – 9	7.5	–	71.8	11.1	**32.3**	4.8	18.7
10 – 19	91.0	100	-	11.1	**27.4**	85.7	59.4
> = 20	-	-	-	75.5	**6.5**	9.5	11.7
No. of living rooms	percentage distribution for each type of settlement						
1	35.3	-	-	37.2	**66.1**	78.3	35.7
2	50.4	-	17.9	30.3	**19.4**	13.0	29.8
3	7.5	85.7	41.1	11.6	**9.7**	8.7	21.9
> = 4	6.8	14.3	41.0	20.9	**4.8**	-	12.6
Status of occupancy	percentage distribution for each type of settlement						
owned	92.5	80.9	51.2	62.2	**58.3**	-	70.4
rented	6.8	16.7	48.8	26.7	**36.7**	-	20.5
other	0.7	2.4	-	6.7	**5.0**	100 (squatted)	9.1

Characteristics of the dwelling unit (d.u.)	TYPE OF SETTLEMENT						
	Resettle -ment Colony	DDA flats	Co-operative group housing societies	Urban villages	**Un-authorized or regularized colonies**	Squatter settle-ments	All types
% of d.u. with precarious or semi-precarious structure	9.0	0.0	0.0	11.6	**18.3**	91.3	13.8
% of d.u. without separate kitchen	78.9	0.0	0.0	46.5	**56.5**	96.0	53.2
% of d.u. without bathroom	80.4	0.0	0	32.6	**35.5**	96.0	48.2
% of d.u. without toilet	85.0	0.0	0.0	32.6	**20.2**	96.0	47.1
% of d.u. without drinking water	12.0	0.0	0.0	0.0	**13.3**	82.6	12.6
% of d.u. without electricity	0.0	0.0	0.0	0.0	**3. 3**	8.3	1.2
Total No. of d.u.	133	42	41	43	**60***	23	342
Row percentage	38.9	12.3	12.0	12.6	**17.5**	6.7	100.0

Note: Out of 60 dwellings, 47 are in unauthorized colonies or sections (=76 %), and 13 in regularized colonies or sections (= 21 %).
Source: ORSTOM-IEG household survey – 1995.

Residential Strategies and Mobility

Financial constraints of economically weaker sections of the population limit them in the housing options and the selection of the locality. Yet, an approach in terms of residential strategies seems relevant even for residents of irregular settlements, since "if the notion of strategies presupposes the availability of choices, the hold of strong constraints presupposes also to resort to specific strategies, aimed precisely at loosening these constraints" (Gautman 1990: 30).

For households who purchased a plot of land in an unauthorized colony (58 per cent of the households surveyed in this type of settlement in Mayur Vihar were owners), the first reason put forward was land price, which was much cheaper than in legal housing estates. The illegal status of the residential colony did not prevent the new plot holders building their own houses to get a feeling of residential stability and security. The new occupants were confident about the future regularization of their colony by the government, as this had happened several times for other such irregular settlements. To ensure immunity of their settlement, before a regularization operation is effectively announced, the residents use practical strategies like building places of worship[24] or showing electricity bills and even house tax receipts as an evidence of legitimate residence.[25] As a whole, investing in an unauthorized colony proves to be rational and safe in the long term. Often, house owners rent out one or several rooms to make their investment more profitable.

For tenants in unauthorized colonies (37 per cent of the sample households), the availability of a rental sector that was not saturated and most importantly offered cheaper options was the first pulling factor for choosing a peripheral residential location like Mayur Vihar. The co-operative housing societies' apartment blocks, which adjoin the unauthorized colonies and let almost half of their flats on rent (the highest proportion among the different types of habitation in Mayur Vihar, see Table 1), cater for much higher income groups. Yet, many tenants consider themselves transient and hoped to be later in a better economic position enabling them to settle in a better neighbourhood or, preferably, purchasing their own plot of land and build their own house.

---

24 The following example quoted by B. Banerjee concerns an unauthorized colony in the Mayur Vihar zone, Shashi Garden: "Inside information revealed that a major road was proposed to be constructed through the colony. Overnight the residents built a large temple within the proposed alignment, with near certainty that the government would not dare to touch religious sentiments by demolishing it, and instead realign the road" (Banerjee 1994: 19).

25 The Municipal Corporation of Delhi did collect house tax in some unauthorized colonies, and until 1983 the Delhi Electricity Supply Undertaking provided connections on demand irrespective of the legal status of the colony (Banerjee 1994: 12).

As found out through in-depth interviews, several residents complained about the unpleasant or even deplorable environmental conditions in their colony, heaped garbage in the streets and parks, pools of stagnant dirty water due to the lack of a draining system, and the inevitable proliferation of flies and mosquitoes.

Thus some inhabitants aspire to move to 'better' and 'more decent' localities, with a cleaner environment. If such a residential trajectory looks possible within the rental sector, access to property ownership for low-income households means resorting to buy a plot in another unauthorized colony, often further away on the outskirts, where cheap land is available. There, they will be able to build up gradually their house, at the pace of their savings, but they would probably have to renounce to their expectation in terms of infrastructure and environmental quality. The same type of outward residential mobility affects households which already own their house, but would need more space to accommodate their increased family. To afford a bigger plot and house, the only option would be to move away to another unauthorized colony in a more peripheral area.

Access to home ownership (despite the ambiguous status of the tenure) and cheap lodging on rent are the first two reasons reported most frequently by the residents of the Mayur Vihar unauthorized colonies to explain their last change of residence within the Delhi urban agglomeration and their present location: 55 per cent and 24 per cent respectively of the concerned persons in the sample.[26] It is however important to note that, in the choice of a specific locality among the affordable options, other factors also count, in particular better proximity to the workplace, or good facilities to commute to work as well as other places in the city, and the presence of relatives.

The 1995 survey on spatial mobility highlights the population dynamics of the unauthorized colonies. It is clearly based on migrant households,[27] who account for 92 per cent of the households surveyed (as compared to 83 per cent in the entire Mayur Vihar zone) and who represent the highest proportion among the different types of neighbouring settlements (Table 2). Among the migrants residing in unauthorized colonies, 44 per cent arrived directly from a town or village situated outside the capital (in whatever State), and 56 per cent resided previously

---

26 These proportions take into account the persons who were earlier living within the Delhi urban agglomeration; dependent members who moved with their family are excluded from these statistics (essentially the children).

27 By 'migrant household' we mean household whose head is a non native of Delhi.

in another locality (or several localities) within the Delhi urban agglomeration. Moreover, if we appraise the residential trajectories at the level of the households (migrants or not), the three fourths of them appear to have occupied another dwelling in Delhi before settling in the present one. The unauthorized colonies of Mayur Vihar prove to be mainly a place of resettlement within the urban agglomeration (as part of a strategy of access to home ownership or in a search of cheaper rents), rather than a place of initial reception for new migrants.

The initial formation and subsequent transformations of unauthorized colonies tend to generate a certain pattern of residential mobility, as suggested by the observations carried out in Mayur Vihar and other studies (Mitra 1983, Billand 1990, Banerjee 1994). At the first stage of their development, these settlements appeal to low or lower-middle income groups, in search of affordable land to build their house or cheap rental accommodations. At a second stage, the severe environment conditions and the lack of adequate urban services induces departures, in particular among tenant households who have improved their economic situation and thus can afford to live in a better developed residential area. Eventually, when the colony is officially recognized for regularization, the provision of civic amenities follows. Improved environment and living conditions, combined with legal status, provoke increase in property values and rents which tends to induce the displacement of low income families towards more affordable unauthorized colonies, and the arrival of richer ones.

Table 2: Migration status and place of last previous dwelling by type of settlement in Mayur-Vihar (East Delhi)

	TYPE OF SETTLEMENT						
	Re-settlement colony	DDA flats	Co-operative group housing societies	Urban villages	**Unauthorized or regularized colonies**	Squatter settlements	All types
	All usual residents						
MIGRATION STATUS	*Percentage distribution for each type of settlement*						
Migrant	39.0	47.8	52.2	34.8	**53.6**	44.4	43.5

Non migrant: - Same dwelling since birth	45.2	28.9	24.7	58.2	**30.7**	49.5	40.9
- Other previous dwelling in Delhi UA	15.8	23.2	23.0	7.0	**15.7**	6.1	15.7
Total	100.0	100.0	100.0	100.0	**100.0**	100.0	100.0
No. of valid cases	721	228	178	256	**280**	99	1762
Chi-Square test	Pearson Chi-Square: 101.42 df : 10 Significance : 0.000						
	Usual residents: household heads						
MIGRATION STATUS	*Percentage distribution for each type of settlement*						
Migrant	80.5	87.2	89.7	66.7	**91.9**	84.2	82.8
Non migrant: - Same dwelling since birth	0.0	0.0	0.0	31.1	**0.0**	0.0	4.2
- Other previous dwelling in Delhi UA	19.5	12.8	10.3	2.2	**8.1**	15.8	13.1
Total	100.0	100.0	100.0	100.0	**100.0**	100.0	100.0
No. of valid cases	133	39	41	45	**60**	19	337
Chi-Square test	Pearson Chi-Square: 103.162 df : 10 Significance : 0.000						
	TYPE OF SETTLEMENT						
	Re-settle-ment colony	DDA flats	Co-opera-tive group housing societies	Urban villages	**Unautho-rized or regula-rized colonies**	Squatter settle-ments	All types
	All usual residents						
PLACE OF LAST PREVIOUS DWELLING	*Percentage distribution for each type of settlement*						

Same dwelling since birth	45.2	28.9	24.9	58.2	**30.7**	49.5	40.9
In Delhi UA	39.9	53.5	67.8	19.1	**45.7**	22.2	41.4
Outside Delhi U.A.	14.8	17.5	7.3	22.7	**23.6**	28.3	17.7
Total	100.0	100.0	100.0	100.0	**100.0**	100.0	100.0
No. of valid cases	721	228	177	256	**280**	99	1761
Chi-Square test	Pearson Chi-Square: 158.261 df: 10 Significance : 0.000						
	Usual residents: household heads						
PLACE OF LAST PREVIOUS DWELLING	*Percentage distribution for each type of settlement*						
Same dwelling since birth	0.0	0.0	0.0	31.1	**0.0**	0.0	4.2
In Delhi UA	88.7	84.6	97.4	35.6	**74.2**	57.9	77.7
Outside Delhi U.A.	11.3	15.4	2.6	33.3	**25.8**	42.1	18.1
Total	100.0	100.0	100.0	100.0	**100.0**	100.0	100.0
No. of valid cases	133	39	41	45	**60**	19	337
Chi-Square test	Pearson Chi-Square: 129.024 df : 10 Significance : 0.000						
	TYPE OF SETTLEMENT						
	Re-settlement colony	DDA flats	Co-operative group housing societies	Urban villages	**Unauthorized or regularized colonies**	Squatter settlements	All types
	All migrants						
PLACE OF LAST PREVIOUS DWELLING	*Percentage distribution for each type of settlement*						
In Delhi U.A.	61.9	63.3	85.9	34.8	**56.3**	36.4	59.3
Outside Delhi U.A.	38.1	36.7	14.1	65.2	**43.7**	63.6	40.7

Total	100.0	100.0	100.0	100.0	**100.0**	100.0	100.0
No. of valid cases	281	109	92	89	**151**	44	766
Chi-Square test	Pearson Chi-Square: 60.65		df :5		Significance : 0.000		

Notes: The percentages appearing in **italic** have to be interpreted with special caution given the very small size of the sample in the category under consideration.
U.A.: urban agglomeration.
Source: ORSTOM-IEG Household Survey, 1995.

Anticipations about the regularization of unauthorized colonies combined with unavoidable land speculation (given the general context of insufficient housing supply by the public sector while the private sector has been excluded from the formal land delivery process) create the conditions for another type of residential mobility. This is the mobility enforced on the first occupants of some unauthorized colonies when they constitute an economically weaker group without any access to the political and administrative machinery. The case of Ashok Nagar, an unauthorized colony located at the fringe of the Mayur Vihar zone along the south-eastern border of the National Capital Territory of Delhi, provides a good illustration of this phenomenon. The presentation of this case draws from an article by Mukul (1996) that deserves to be summarized here for its exemplary value.

The creation of Ashok Nagar dates back to the early 1970s. The first buyers belonged to lower class families who built there their homes. Escalation in land prices in Delhi, coupled with the prime location of this settlement at the border of the new industrial town of Noida and near the main road leading to the capital centre within about 10 km., attracted covetous land developers and unscrupulous real estate agents. These people employed hooligans (*goondas*) to threaten the residents, destroy their hand-pumps and even to attack them physically. The welfare association founded by the residents proved to be ineffective against the economic power of property dealers who were moreover backed up by a nexus of local leaders, politicians, corrupt bureaucrats and conniving policemen. In this way about 500 families were forcibly displaced from their land and houses in the 1980s, and had to move to other places in Delhi, in rented accommodations. Most of them lost also the hope of buying again a house for their own. In spite of many protests and demonstrations organized by the residents' association, and many cases of property spoliation brought to the court of justice, most families have not yet received any compensation for their loss. After having been 'cleaned' from their first occupancy in this manner, some sections of the initial colony were sold to a co-operative group-housing society belonging to a much higher income group and who were better connected to the political and administrative machinery. Collected evidences suggest many irregularities (including at the level of the Delhi Development Authority) in the procedure of land acquisition for the co-operative group-housing society.

This example demonstrates the strong interests at stake in land matters of a capital like Delhi, as well as the role of land 'mafia'. The irregular or illegal status of so many colonies – considered by the planners as non-cities, and hence defined by default, negatively, as 'unauthorized' colonies – *de facto* pave the way for intermediary agents, patron-clients relations, political connivance, administrative corruption and distortion of rules.

CONCLUSION

The development pattern of Delhi highlights the magnitude of informal urbanization. Among irregular settlements, the unauthorized colonies founded on illegal land-division played a major role in the process of suburbanization of the capital. Despite regularization policies implemented in the 1960s and the 1970s, the unauthorized colonies that have emerged in the following decades provide today shelter to about one fourth of the population, mostly low and lower-middle income groups. The case study of Mayur Vihar, in East Delhi, reveals that the population dynamics of unauthorized colonies result mainly from intra-urban moves, motivated by the objective of accessing home ownership. Yet, the opportunities for cheap lodgings on rent attract also a significant numbers of settlers, including new migrants.

Although demographic growth and the resulting strong pressure on housing demand have undoubtedly contributed to the extent of the problem, the proliferation of unauthorized colonies in Delhi is also the consequence of a failure in town planning and housing policies, both at the conception and implementation levels. The persistent conflict about the regularization issue reveals again a failure in urban governance, if we adopt the UN-Habitat definition of urban governance as "a continuing process through which conflicting or diverse interests may be accommodated and co-operative action can be taken".[28] The case of Delhi's unauthorized colonies is indeed a complex situation involving various conflicting interests. It is not only a conflict between town planners – or civic authorities – and city dwellers indulging in 'illegal' residential practices, but also a conflict between two different sections of the civil society, opposing the environmentalist NGOs and the residents of unauthorized colonies and their associations.

In a broader perspective, this illustrates the opposition between the advocates of the 'green agenda' (who give priority to ecological issues in a long-term perspective) and the advocates of the 'brown agenda' who are more concerned with social justice and the immediate needs of the urban poor (McGranahan and Satterthwaite 2000). The blockage of the projected regularization policy for unauthorized colonies further points out the specificity of Delhi as the federal capital. This status exacerbates the complexity of the case as well as power games and conflicts among government agencies and different levels of power (Union government, State government and Municipal Corporation) that may be led by opposing parties. Lastly, in Delhi like in other Indian cities, the judiciary has emerged as a decisive actor in urban governance.

Since the public and private formal land and housing delivery systems cannot respond to the needs of large sections of the urban population, the government and planners should acknowledge the twofold role of unauthorized colonies in the making of the city:

- their direct contribution to land development and production of the housing stock,
- and the provision of an important rental sector for the working class, as both the public and the capitalist sectors are not able (or not willing) to respond to this demand.

The process of clandestine land division and informal housing activities is to be considered as a response to the persistent urban housing and planning crisis. This informal channel of access to land and housing may well constitute the most appropriate response for a large section of the urban population, given its socio-economic conditions, and the most realistic alternative from the planning point of view (Durand-Lasserve 1986, Durand-Lasserve and Royston, 2002). As recommended already in 1986 by Durand-Lasserve in the broader context of Third World cities,

---

[28] Referred to in the introduction of this volume and found at http://www.unhabitat.org/campaigns/governance/principles.asp.

the role of the town planners and urban governments should be more to facilitate the production of the city than to regulate it by imposing a rigid planning frame and strict (often inadequate) rules. Thus, the priority objective should be to induce a dynamics based on the existing forces (Durand-Lasserve 1986: 169) – without neglecting, however, the environmental issues. The case study of unauthorized colonies in Delhi confirms the relevance of this assessment.

REFERENCES

Auclair, Christine, *Ville à vendre. Voie libérale et privatisation du secteur de l'habitat à Chennai (Inde)*, Pondicherry: Institut Français de Pondichéry, 1998.

Banerjee, Banashree, *Policies, procedures and techniques for regularizing irregular settlements in Indian cities. The case of Delhi*, CASA, Urban Research Working Papers 34, Amsterdam: Universiteit Amsterdam, 1994.

Banerjee, Banashree, 'Security of tenure in Indian cities', in Alain Durand-Lasserve and Lauren Royston, eds., *Holding their Grounds. Secure Land tenure for the Urban Poor in Developing Countries*, London: Earthscan, 2002, pp. 37-58.

Billand, Charles J., *Delhi Case Study: Formal Serviced Land Development*, New Delhi: USAID, 1990.

Bose, Ashish, *India's urbanization 1901-2001*, Second revised edition, New Delhi: Tata McGraw Hill, 1980.

Bose, Tarun, 'Power Games in Unauthorized Colonies', Paper presented at the Seminar *Delhi Games. Use and Control of the Urban Space: Power Games and Actors Strategies*, mimeo, Delhi: Centre for the Study of Developing Societies, 3-4 April 1998.

Datta, V.N., 'Panjabi refugees and the urban development of Greater Delhi', in R.E. Frykenberg, ed., *Delhi through the ages. Essays in urban history, culture and society*, Delhi: Oxford University Press, 1986, pp. 442-460.

Datta, Abhikit, 'Sheltering the urban poor in Delhi: The experience of public provision, 1956-92', in *Urban India*, vol. XV, no. 2, July-December, 1995, pp. 95-107.

Dupont, Véronique, 'City history-Life histories: Changing equations. Migration surveys and biographical data collection in Delhi', *Contributions CSH 97/7*, New Delhi: Centre de Sciences Humaines, 1997.

Dupont, Véronique, 'Spatial and demographic growth of Delhi and the main migration flows', in Véronique Dupont, Emma Tarlo, Denis Vidal, eds., *Delhi. Urban Space and Human Destinies*, Delhi: Manohar – CSH, 2000, pp. 229-239.

Dupont, Véronique, 'Pratiques résidentielles dans le parc de logements publics d'une grande métropole indienne: L'exemple des DDA flats de Delhi', *autrepart*, no. 25, *Dynamiques résidentielles dans les villes du Sud: positions sociales en recomposition* (ed. Monique Bertrand), La Tour d'Aigues: Editions de L'Aube / IRD, 3/2003, pp. 21-36.

Dupont, Véronique, 'Socio-spatial differentiation and residential segregation in Delhi: a question of scale?', in *Geoforum*, vol. 35, issue 2, March 2004, pp. 157-175.

Dupont, Véronique et Prakash, Jay, 'Enquête Mobilités Spatiales dans l'Aire métropolitaine de Delhi ', in *Biographies d'enquête*, Paris: INED-PUF/Diffusion (Coll. Méthodes et savoirs), 1999, pp. 279-315.

Durand-Lasserve, Alain, *L'exclusion des pauvres dans les villes du Tiers Monde. Accès au sol et au logement*, Paris: L'Harmattan (Coll. Villes et Entreprises), 1986.

Durand-Lasserve, Alain and Royston, Lauren, eds., *Holding their Grounds. Secure land tenure for the urban poor in developing countries*, London: Earthscan, 2002.

Durand-Lasserve, Alain and Royston, Lauren, 'International trends and country contexts – from tenure regularization to tenure security', in Alain Durand-Lasserve and Lauren Royston, eds., *Holding their Grounds. Secure land tenure for the urban poor in developing countries*, London: Earthscan, 2002, pp. 1-34.

Dureau, Françoise, Dupont, Véronique, Lelièvre, Eva, Lévy, Jean-Pierre et Lulle, Thierry, eds., *Métropoles en mouvement. Une comparaison internationale*, Paris : Anthropos–IRD (Coll. Villes), 2000.

Gautman, Anne, 'Stratégies résidentielles, stratégies de recherche', in *Stratégies résidentielles* (Séminaire organisé par Catherine Bonvalet et Anne-Marie Fribourg, Paris, 1988), Paris: INED, Plan Construction et Architecte, MELTM, 1990, pp. 23-34.

Gilbert, Alan, 'The cost and benefits of illegality and irregularity in the supply of land', in Paul Barros and Jan van der Linden, eds., *The transformation of land supply systems in Third World Cities*, Aldershot: Avebury, 1990.

Gupta, R.C., *Land Assembly in the Indian Metropolis*, New Delhi: Uppal Publishing House, 1992.

Jain, A.K., *The Making of a Metropolis. Planning and growth of Delhi*, New Delhi: National Book Organization, 1990.

Kanungo, Anita, 'When laws is the father of crime', in *The Hindustan Times*, 24/10/1999, p. 13.

McGranahan, Gordon, and Satterthwaite, David, 'Environmental health or ecological sustainability? Reconciling the Brown and Green agendas in urban development ', in Cedric Pugh, ed., *Sustainable Cities in Developing Countries*, London: Earthscan, 2000, pp. 73-90.

Milbert, Isabelle, *L'urbanisme et l'habitat et Inde* (Thèse pour le doctorat d'Etat), Paris : Université de Droit, d'Economie et de Sciences Sociales de Paris (Paris II), 1986.

Milbert, Isabelle, *Politiques urbaines à Delhi,* Genève: IUED, 1998.

Misra, B., Singh, R.B. and Aupma, Malik, "Delhi Metropolis: housing and quality of life", in Misra, R.P. and Misra, Kamlesh, eds., *Millions Cities of India*, New Delhi: Sustainable Development Foundation, 1998, pp. 196-228.

Mitra, Banashree, *Substandard commercial residential subdivision in relation to housing options in Delhi*, Report no. 966, Rotterdam: Institute of Housing Studies, 1983.

Mukul, 'Building from above, displacing from below. Land development', in *Economic and Political Weekly*, vol. 31, no. 5, 1996 (February 3), pp. 259-261.

Mussania B.S., 'Impact of urbanization on fringe area development of metropolitan cities', in *Nagarlok*, New Delhi: The Indian Institute of Public Administration, vol. XXIX, no. 3, July-Sept. 1997, pp. 1-6.

National Capital Region Planning Board, *Regional Plan 2001, National Capital Region*, Delhi: Ministry of Urban Development, Government of India, 1988.

Pugh, Cedric, *Housing and urbanization. A study of India,* New Delhi: Sage, 1990.

Ramanchandra, R., *Urbanization and Urban Systems in India*, Delhi: Oxford University Press, 1989.

Rishub, Neelima, 'Policies for tenure Security in ·Delhi', in Alain Durand-Lasserve and Lauren Royston, eds., *Holding their Grounds. Secure Land tenure for the urban poor in developing countries,* London: Earthscan, 2002, pp. 59-74.

Schenk, Hans, The rurban fringe of Bangalore city, India, in *The Indian Geographical Journal*, vol. 68, no. 2, December 1993, pp. 1-9.

Sidhu, Mriga, 'Residential profile of the studied areas' (Survey on spatial mobility in the metropolitan area of Delhi, Working Paper no. 2), New Delhi: ORSTOM-IEG, 1995.

Sidhu, Mriga, 'In-depth interviews on environmental factors and residential practices. Type of settlement: Urban villages, Unauthorized colonies and regularized colonies', (Survey on spatial mobility in the metropolitan area of Delhi, Working paper no. 5, vol. I), New Delhi: ORSTOM-CSH, 1996.

Smets, Peer and Hansen, Evert, 'The dynamics of patronage in the development of illegal settlements', in *Urban India*, vol. XVI no. 1, January-June 1996, pp. 91-106.

Soni, Anita, 'Urban conquest of outer Delhi: beneficiaries, intermediaries and the victims. The case of the Mehrauli countryside', in Véronique Dupont, Emma Tarlo, Denis Vidal, eds., *Delhi. Urban Space and Human Destinies*, Delhi: Manohar–CSH, 2000, pp. 75-94.

Note on Contributors

Maren Bellwinkel-Schempp did her Ph.D. on the relationship of castes and classes in an urban-industrial setting. At present she is a senior research fellow of South Asia Institute of Heidelberg University, Department of Anthropology in Germany. Her fields of specialization are urban anthropology, labour migration and dalit religion and culture. She has recently completed a research project by the Volkswagen Foundation on 'Identity Construction of Scheduled Castes and the communal dimension in Kanpur'.

Véronique Dupont is a research fellow in economic-demography from the French Institute of Research for Development (IRD, Paris) and presently Director of the Centre de Sciences Humaines in New Delhi. She is also a member of the French Centre for Indian and South Asian Studies (CEIAS, Paris). After completing a doctoral thesis on urbanization and migraton in West Africa, her work has been focussed on India. She has carried out research on population mobility and the urbanization process in Gujarat and Delhi region. Her recent publications include *Delhi. Urban Space and Human Destinies*, edited with Emma Tarlo and Denis Vidal (Delhi: Manohar-CSH, 2000).

Martin Fuchs, Free University Berlin and South Asia Institute, University of Heidelberg, did his Ph.D. on Max Weber, Louis Dumont and the analysis of India's society. His main interests include theories of culture, interculturality and social praxis, the hermeneutics of cultural representation and translation, theories of modernity, social movements, conceptualisations of Indian society, Indian religions, the Dalit struggle for recognition, the development of citizenship rights and urban anthropology.

Evelin Hust has studied Political Science, Economics, and Classical Indology at the Universities of Freiburg, Brighton, and Heidelberg. Her dissertation was on political representation and empowerment of women in the Panchayati Raj in India. Evelin Hust has served as the representative of the South Asia Institute of the University of Heidelberg in Delhi from 2001-2004. She is currently working for the German Cultural Centre (Goethe-Institute). Her publications include: *Women's Political Representation and Empowerment in India: A Million Indiras Now?* Delhi: Manohar 2004.

Ravinder Kaur is a doctoral candidate engaged with the study of urban resettlement and identity making processes among the Partition migrants in Delhi city. She is currently pursuing her teaching and research interests at the Department of International Development Studies at Roskilde University Centre, Denmark and Danish Institute for International Studies, Copenhagen, Denmark.

Michael Köeberlein, Research Associate at the Department of Geography, South Asia Institute, University of Heidelberg, did research on 'Urban Solid Waste Management in India' for his Master thesis at the University of Bamberg, Germany and on 'Urban Livelihoods' for his Ph.D. dissertation at the University of Heidelberg. The dissertation is entitled *Living from Waste: A Case Study on the Livelihoods of the Actors Involved in Delhi's Informal Waste Recycling Economy.*

Michael Mann did his Ph.D. on an agrarian-cum-ecological study in north India during the first half of the nineteenth century. His current interests cover a variety of subjects like colonial state formation and problems of legitimate rule from the eighteenth to the twentieth centuries, problems of urbanization and migration in South Asia, early colonial forest management and environmental studies. Presently he works as an assistant professor at the FernUniversitaet in Hagen, Germany.

Ajay K. Mehra is Honorary Director of the Centre for Public Affairs, Noida, UP, India. A keen student of processes and institutions in Indian politics, Dr. Mehra is also a prolific writer, having authored and co-authored several books as also contributed articles to journals and edited collections. He currently teaches Indian politics at the Shaheed Bhagat Singh College (evening), University of Delhi, and is a regular contributor to the Indian media on issues of public affairs.

Joël Ruet holds a Ph.D. in industrial economics and is an alumni of Ecole des Mines, Paris. He has been heading the Department of Economics, Centre de Sciences Humaines, New Delhi, since 2000 (www.csh-delhi.com), and is an associate researcher with the CERNA, centre for industrial economics, Ecole des Mines, Paris.

Stéphanie Tawa Lama-Rewal, research fellow (political science) at the Centre d'Etudes de l'Inde et de l'Asie du Sud (Centre for the Study of India and South Asia), Paris. In 1999 she completed her Ph.D. thesis (Political Science) at the Institute of Political Studies, Aix-en-Provence (France): *Women's Representation on the Political Stage. A Comparative Study of West Bengal, Maharashtra and Nepal.* Her current research interests include the theories and practice of groups' representation in political assemblies, affirmative action policies, decentralization and local democracy.

Bhaskar Vira is University Lecturer in Environment and Development at the Department of Geography, and a Fellow of Fitzwilliam College, University of Cambridge. His research focuses on the political economy of environment and development issues, with specific interests in South Asia.

Shiraz Vira is trained in social and political science and anthropology, and works as an independent researcher. She has worked on rural development, forestry and pastoralism in India, as well as on environmental issues in urban India

Marie-Hélène Zérah holds a Ph.D. in urban studies from the Paris Institute of Urban Studies. Her latest publications include articles on urban services in India in international journals as well as a book on Delhi water supply (*Water. Unreliable Supply in Delhi.* Manohar, Delhi 2000). She is a research fellow at the Institute of Research for Development in Paris and her current research deals with issues of new forms of governance, production and regulation of urban services in large Indian cities.

